Essential French

Edited by

Shaina Malkin and Christine Boucher

 **LIVING LANGUAGE**®

Published in the United States by Living Language, an imprint of Random House, Inc.

www.livinglanguage.com

Editor: Shaina Malkin
Production Editor: Carolyn Roth
Production Manager: Tom Marshall
Interior Design: Sophie Chin
Illustrations: Sophie Chin

First Edition

ISBN: 978-0-307-97153-1

This book is available at special discounts for bulk purchases for sales promotions or premiums. Special editions, including personalized covers, excerpts of existing books, and corporate imprints, can be created in large quantities for special needs. For more information, write to Special Markets/ Premium Sales, 1745 Broadway, MD 3-1, New York, New York 10019 or e-mail specialmarkets@ randomhouse.com.

PRINTED IN THE UNITED STATES OF AMERICA

10

Acknowledgments

Thanks to the Living Language team: Amanda D'Acierno, Christopher Warnasch, Suzanne McQuade, Laura Riggio, Erin Quirk, Shaina Malkin, Amanda Munoz, Fabrizio La Rocca, Siobhan O'Hare, Sophie Chin, Sue Daulton, Alison Skrabek, Carolyn Roth, Ciara Robinson, Linda Schmidt, and Tom Marshall.

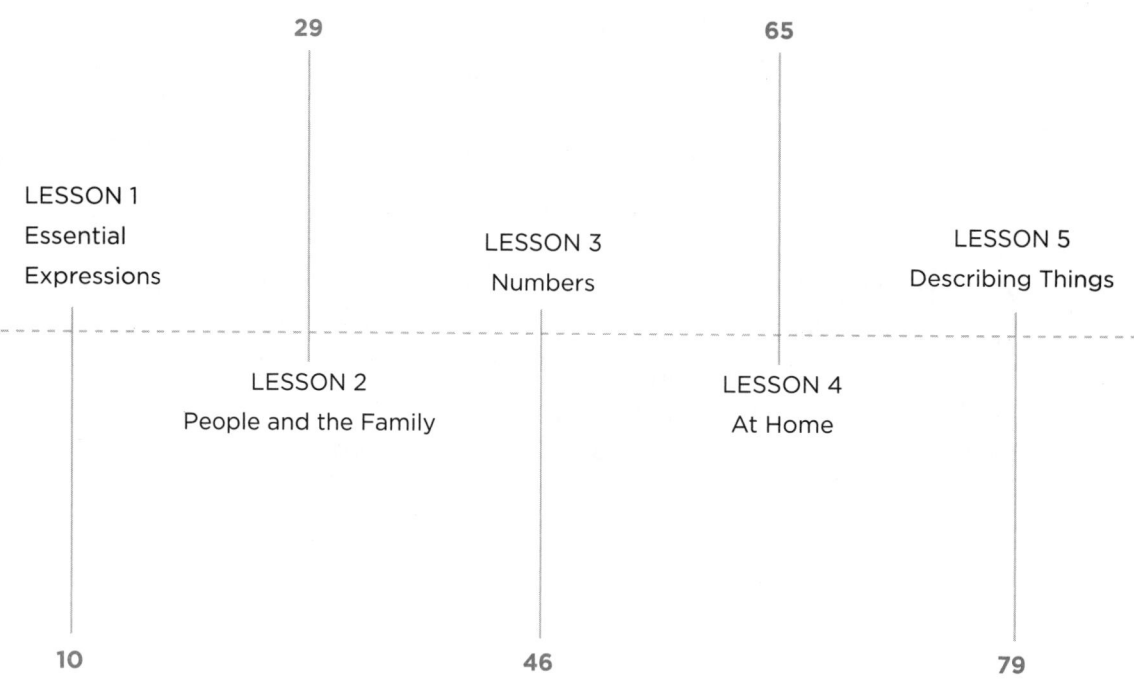
COURSE

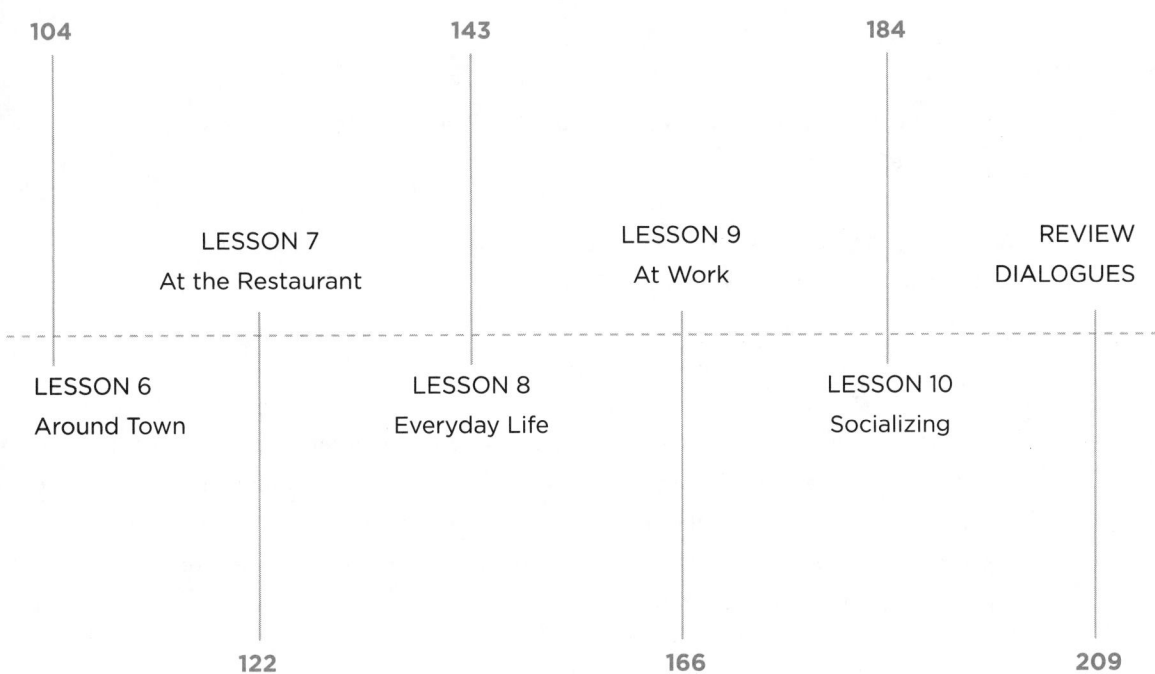

OUTLINE

How to Use This Course

Bonjour !

Welcome to *Living Language Essential French*! Ready to learn how to speak, read, and write French?

Before we begin, let's go over what you'll see in this course. It's very easy to use, but this section will help you get started.

PHONETICS

The first five lessons of this course contain phonetics (in other words, [bah-geht] in addition to **baguette**) to help you get started with French pronunciation. However, please keep in mind that phonetics are not exact—they are just a general approximation of sounds—and thus you should rely most on the audio, *not* the phonetics, to further your pronunciation skills.

For a guide to our phonetics system, see the Pronunciation Guide at the end of the course.

LESSONS

There are 10 lessons in this course. Each lesson is divided into three parts and has the following components:

- **Welcome** at the beginning outlining what you will cover in each of the three parts of the lesson.

PART 1

- **Vocabulary Builder 1** listing the key words and phrases for that lesson.

- **Vocabulary Practice 1** to practice what you learned in Vocabulary Builder 1.

- **Grammar Builder 1** to guide you through the structure of the French language (how to form sentences, questions, and so on).

PART 2

- **Vocabulary Builder 2** listing more key words and phrases.

- **Vocabulary Practice 2** to practice what you learned in Vocabulary Builder 2.

- **Grammar Builder 2** for more information on language structure.

- **Work Out 1** for a comprehensive practice of what you've learned so far.

PART 3

- **Bring It All Together** to put what you've learned in a conversational context through a dialogue, monologue, description, or other similar text.

- **Work Out 2** for another helpful practice exercise.

- **Drive It Home** to ingrain an important point of French structure for the long term.

- **Parting Words** outlining what you learned in the lesson.

TAKE IT FURTHER

- **Take It Further** sections scattered throughout the lesson to provide extra information about the new vocabulary you just saw, expand on some grammar points, or introduce additional words and phrases.

WORD RECALL

- **Word Recall** sections appear in between lessons. They review important vocabulary and grammar from previous lessons, including the one you just finished. These sections will reinforce what you've learned so far in the course, and help you retain the information for the long term.

QUIZZES

This course contains two quizzes: **Quiz 1** is halfway through the course (after Lesson 5), and **Quiz 2** appears after the last lesson (Lesson 10). The quizzes are self-graded so it's easy for you to test your progress and see if you should go back and review.

REVIEW DIALOGUES

There are five **Review Dialogues** at the end of the course, after Quiz 2. These everyday dialogues review what you learned in Lessons 1-10, introduce some new vocabulary and structures, and allow you to become more familiar with conversational French. Each dialogue is followed by comprehension questions that serve as the course's final review.

PROGRESS BAR

You will see a **Progress Bar** on almost every page that has course material. It indicates your current position in the course and lets you know how much progress you're making. Each line in the bar represents a lesson, with the final line representing the Review Dialogues.

AUDIO

Look for this symbol ⊙ to help guide you through the audio as you're reading the book. It will tell you which track to listen to for each section that has audio. When you see the symbol, select the indicated track and start listening! If you don't see the symbol, then there isn't any audio for that section. You'll also see ⊕, which will tell you where that track ends.

The audio can be used on its own—in other words, without the book—when you're on the go. Whether in your car or at the gym, you can listen to the audio to brush up on your pronunciation, review what you've learned in the book, or even use it as a standalone course.

PRONUNCIATION GUIDE, GRAMMAR SUMMARY, GLOSSARY

At the back of this book you will find a **Pronunciation Guide**, **Grammar Summary**, and **Glossary**. The Pronunciation Guide provides information on French pronunciation and the phonetics system used in this course. The Grammar Summary contains a helpful, brief overview of key points in the French grammar system. It is also includes a **Grammar Index**, which lists the principal grammar topics covered in this course and where to find them in the book. The Glossary (French-English and English-French) includes all of the essential words from the ten lessons, as well as additional key vocabulary.

FREE ONLINE TOOLS

Go to *www.livinglanguage.com/languagelab* to access your free online tools. The tools are organized around the lessons in this course, with audiovisual flashcards, and interactive games and quizzes. These tools will help you to review and practice the vocabulary and grammar that you've seen in the lessons, as well provide some extra words and phrases related to the lesson's topic.

Lesson 1: Essential Expressions

Leçon un : les expressions essentielles

luh-soh(n) uh(n): lay zehks-preh-syoh(n) eh-sah(n)-syehl

Bienvenue ! [bya(n)-vuh-new] *Welcome!* In this first lesson, you'll learn basic courtesy expressions and other useful words and phrases that will get you started speaking French. You will learn how to:

1 Greet someone and ask how they're doing
Address someone formally and informally

2 Introduce yourself
Respond when people ask *How are you?*

3 Use what you've learned when
meeting people for the first time

Remember to look for this symbol ⓘ to help guide you through the audio as you're reading the book. It will tell you which track to listen to for each section that has audio. When you see the symbol, select the indicated track and start listening! If you don't see the symbol, then there isn't any audio for that section. You'll also see ⓘ, which will tell you where that track ends. Finally, keep in mind that the audio can also be used on its own when you're on the go!

So, let's begin with some essential vocabulary. Ready?

1 Greet someone and ask how they're doing
Address someone formally and informally

Vocabulary Builder 1

You'll see phonetics in the first five lessons of *Essential French* to help you get started. For a guide to the phonetics system used here, see the Pronunciation Guide at the end of the course.

▶ 1B Vocabulary Builder 1 (CD 1, Track 2)

Hello.	**Bonjour.**	boh(n)-zhoor
Hi. (can also mean Bye.)	**Salut.**	sah-lew
Good-bye.	**Au revoir.**	oh ruh-vwahr
How are you? (familiar)	**Comment vas-tu ?***	koh-mah(n) vah-tew
How are you? (polite)	**Comment allez-vous ?**	koh-mah(n) tah-lay-voo
I'm fine.	**Ça va.**	sah vah
What's your name? (familiar)	**Comment t'appelles-tu ?**	koh-mah(n) tah-pehl-tew
What's your name? (polite)	**Comment vous appelez-vous ?**	koh-mah(n) voo zah-play-voo
ma'am, madam, Mrs., Ms.	**madame**	mah-dahm
sir, Mr.	**monsieur**	muh-syuh
miss	**mademoiselle**	mahd-mwah-zehl

* In writing, French usually adds a space before the punctuation marks ! ? : and ;. As a result, you will see **Comment vas-tu ?** and not **Comment vas-tu?**

✎ Vocabulary Practice 1

Now let's practice what you've learned!

Fill in the blanks with the correct French translations of the following English phrases. Always feel free to use a dictionary or the glossary if you need to.

Hello. _____

Hi./Bye. _____

Good-bye. _____

How are you? (familiar) _____

How are you? (polite) _____

I'm fine. _____

What's your name? (familiar) _____

What's your name? (polite) _____

ma'am, madam, Mrs., Ms. _____

sir, Mr. _____

miss _____

ANSWER KEY:
Bonjour. (*Hello.*); Salut. (*Hi./Bye.*); Au revoir. (*Good-bye.*); Comment vas-tu ? (*How are you?,* [*familiar*]); Comment allez-vous ? (*How are you?, polite*); Ça va. (*I'm fine.*); Comment t'appelles-tu ? (*What's your name?, familiar*); Comment vous appelez-vous ? (*What's your name?,* [*polite*]); madame (*ma'am, madam, Mrs., Ms.*); monsieur (*sir, Mr.*); mademoiselle (*miss*)

Grammar Builder 1

▶ 1C Grammar Builder 1 (CD 1, Track 3)

Okay, let's stop there. (Listen to the audio for a quick, audio-only review of the terms you just learned!)

Did you notice that there are two ways of asking how someone is or what someone's name is?

One is familiar (informal), used with friends, family, and children. Those are the questions with the word **tu** [tew], which is the familiar way of saying *you*:

Comment vas-tu ?
How are you?

Comment t'appelles-tu ?
What's your name?

The others use the polite (formal) form for *you*: **vous** [voo]. It is used with adults you don't know well, colleagues (particularly supervisors), and people in formal situations:

Comment allez-vous ?
How are you?

Comment vous appelez-vous ?
What's your name?

So, in French, **tu** and **vous** both mean *you*, but the first is familiar and the second is polite. When in doubt, use **vous** unless you're invited to use **tu**.

⏸

To summarize:

FAMILIAR (INFORMAL)	POLITE (FORMAL)
tu (*you*)	vous (*you*)
Comment vas-tu ? (*How are you?*)	Comment allez-vous ? (*How are you?*)
Comment t'appelles-tu ? (*What's your name?*)	Comment vous appelez-vous ? (*What's your name?*)

Take It Further

In these sections, we'll expand on what you've seen so far.

We might break down some of the new phrases or sentences that you've seen, look more closely at additional words that were introduced, or expand on some of the grammar points.

For example, let's break down **Comment vas-tu ?**, **Comment allez-vous ?**, and **Ça va** from Vocabulary Builder 1:

comment	koh-mah(n)	*how*
ça (before a vowel, ça changes to c')	sah	*it, that, this*
ça va	sah vah	*it goes*
tu vas	tew vah	*you go (familiar)*
vous allez	voo zah-lay	*you go (polite)*

As you can see, French often uses forms of *to go* in greetings, similar to *How's it going?* or *It's going fine* in English.

Comment allez-vous ?/Comment vas-tu ?
How are you? (literally, How are you going?)

Ça va.

I'm fine. (literally, It's going./It goes.)

You'll learn more about *to go* in Lesson 8. Are you wondering why the order of **tu vas** and **vous allez** is reversed in those questions? That's actually just one way of forming a question in French. You'll learn more in Lesson 6.

2 Introduce yourself
Respond when people ask *How are you?*

Vocabulary Builder 2

▶ 1D Vocabulary Builder 2 (CD 1, Track 4)

Good evening.	**Bonsoir.**	boh(n)-swahr
How's it going? (How are you?)	**Comment ça va ?***	koh-mah(n) sah vah
It's going well.	**Ça va bien.**	sah vah bya(n)
It's not going well. (It's going badly.)	**Ça va mal.**	sah vah mahl
Not bad.	**Pas mal.**	pah mahl
So-so. (literally, Like this, like that.)	**Comme ci, comme ça.**	kohm see, kohm sah
Super.	**Super.**	sew-pehr
Fantastic.	**Formidable.**	fohr-mee-dah-bluh
My name is … (literally, I am called …)	**Je m'appelle…**	zhuh mah-pehl

* In casual conversation, you will often just hear Ça va ? [sah vah]

Pleased to meet you./ Nice to meet you.	Enchanté. (said by a man)/ Enchantée. (said by a woman)	ah(n)-shah(n)-tay/ ah(n)-shah(n)-tay

✎ Vocabulary Practice 2

Just like in Vocabulary Practice 1, fill in the blanks with the correct French translations.

Good evening. _____

How's it going?/How are you? _____

It's going well. _____

It's not going well./It's going badly. _____

Not bad. _____

So-so. _____

Super. _____

Fantastic. _____

My name is .../I am called ... _____

Pleased to meet you./Nice to meet you. _____

ANSWER KEY:

Bonsoir. (*Good evening.*); Comment ça va? (*How's it going?/How are you?*); Ça va bien. (*It's going well.*); Ça va mal. (*It's not going well./It's going badly.*); Pas mal. (*Not bad.*); Comme ci, comme ça. (*So-so.*); Super. (*Super.*); Formidable. (*Fantastic.*); Je m'appelle... (*My name is .../I am called ...*); Enchanté./Enchantée. (*Pleased to meet you./Nice to meet you.*)

Grammar Builder 2

Let's pause there for a moment, and review some of what you've learned—
but this time, let's translate from French into English. How many of the following
words and phrases do you know without going back to review? Fill in as many of
the English translations as you can in the corresponding blank spaces.

Once you're done, you'll have a handy review sheet for the key phrases in
this lesson!

▶ 1E Grammar Builder 2 (CD 1, Track 5). Listen to the audio to practice your pronunciation
of the phrases below! The audio also includes some English translations, so try to fill in
the blanks below first before you listen.

Greetings

Bonjour.	
Salut.	
Bonsoir.	

Formal (vous)

Comment allez-vous ?	
Comment vous appelez-vous ?	

Informal (tu)

Comment vas-tu ?	
Comment t'appelles-tu ?	

Question and Answer

Comment ça va ?	
Ça va bien.	
Ça va mal.	

Pas mal.	
Comme ci, comme ça.	
Super.	
Formidable.	

And finally:

| Je m'appelle... | |
| Enchanté./Enchantée. | |

Take It Further

Now that you can introduce yourself with **je m'appelle**, let's look at how to introduce other people.

| tu t'appelles | tew tah-pehl | *you are called, your name is (familiar)* |
| vous vous appelez | voo voo zah-play | *you are called, your name is (polite)* |

Tu t'appelles Jean.
tew tah-pehl zhah(n)
Your name is Jean./You're called Jean.

Vous vous appelez Marie.
voo voo zah-play mah-ree
Your name is Marie./You're called Marie.

Notice the similarity to **Comment t'appelles-tu ?/Comment vous appelez-vous ?** (*What's your name?*)? They are, in fact, the same phrases, just re-ordered to form a question. Again, you'll learn more about forming questions in Lesson 6.

Finally, let's look at some of the new individual words you saw in Vocabulary Builder 2:

je (before a vowel, je changes to j')	zhuh	*I*
bien	bya(n)	*well, fine, good*
mal	mahl	*badly, bad, wrong*
pas	pah	*not*
comme	kohm	*like, as, how*
ci	see	*this, here*

Although **pas** can be used on its own to mean *not*, you will more often see the phrase **ne... pas** [nuh ... pah] used to mean *not* or to negate a sentence. You'll see an example of **ne... pas** in use at the end of this lesson.

✎ Work Out 1

Okay, let's put everything you've learned so far together in a short comprehension exercise. Fill in the blanks in the conversation below.

▶ 1F Work Out 1 (CD 1, Track 6). Listen to the audio to practice pronouncing the following phrases. The audio also includes the French translations, so try to complete the exercise here first before listening.

_____, **comment allez-vous ?**

Hello ma'am, how are you?

_____ **, merci.**

Not bad, thank you.

_____ **François.**

My name is François.

Je vous présente ma femme, Marguerite.

Let me introduce my wife, Marguerite.

_____ .

Pleased to meet you. *(said by a woman)*

_____ ?

What's your name? *(polite)*

_____ Madame Beaulieu.

My name is *Mrs. Beaulieu.*

Je vous présente mon mari, Monsieur Albert Beaulieu.

Let me introduce my husband, Mr. Albert Beaulieu.

_____ .

Ⓘ ***Pleased to meet you.*** *(said by a man)*

ANSWER KEY:
Bonjour madame; Pas mal; Je m'appelle; Enchantée; Comment vous appelez-vous; Je m'appelle; Enchanté

Take It Further

Notice some new vocabulary? Here are some of the new phrases that you saw:

merci	mehr-see	*thank you*
Je vous présente...	zhuh voo pray-zah(n)t	*Let me introduce ... (literally, I introduce to you ...) (polite)*
ma femme	mah fahm	*my wife*
mon mari	moh(n) mah-ree	*my husband*

You'll learn more about **mon** [moh(n)] and **ma** [mah], which both mean *my*, in Lesson 5.

---

3 Use what you've learned when meeting people for the first time

Bring It All Together

Now let's bring it all together and add a little bit more vocabulary and structure. Read and listen to the following short dialogue.

▶ 1G Bring It All Together (CD 1, Track 7)

A: *Hi, I'm Mark, what's your name?*
Salut, je suis Marc, comment t'appelles-tu ?
sah-lew, zhuh swee mahrk, koh-mah(n) tah-pehl-tew

B: *Hi, Mark, my name is Stephanie.*
Salut, Marc, je m'appelle Stéphanie.
sah-lew, mahrk, zhuh mah-pehl stay-fah-nee

A: *Nice to meet you. How's it going?*
Enchanté. Comment ça va ?
ah(n)-shah(n)-tay. koh-mah(n) sah vah

B: *Super!*
Super !
sew-pehr

A: *Let me introduce my father.*
Je te présente mon père.
zhuh tuh pray-zah(n)t moh(n) pehr

B: *Hello, sir. How are you?*
Bonjour monsieur. Comment allez-vous ?
boh(n)-zhoor, muh-syuh. koh-mah(n) tah-lay-voo

C: *I'm very well, thank you.*
Je vais très bien, merci.
zhuh veh treh bya(n), mehr-see

A: *Bye, Stephanie!*
Salut, Stéphanie !
sah-lew, stay-fah-nee

B: *Bye, Mark!*
Salut, Marc !
sah-lew, mahrk

Take It Further

1H Take It Further (CD 1, Track 8)

Okay, you already knew a lot of that vocabulary, but there were a few new words too.

Did you notice that you can introduce yourself by simply saying:

| je suis | zhuh swee | *I am* |

Say that again: je suis... je suis... je suis... Good!

And to introduce someone else, you can say:

| Je te présente... | zhuh tuh pray-zah(n)t | *Let me introduce ...* (if you're speaking to a friend or family member) |
| Je vous présente... | zhuh voo pray-zah(n)t | *Let me introduce ...* (if you're speaking more formally) |

(Remember je vous présente from Work Out 1? Now you know the familiar form: je te présente.)

Other helpful words and phrases from Bring It All Together include:

Je vais très bien.	zhuh veh treh bya(n)	*I'm very well.* (*literally, I go very well.*)
je vais	zhuh veh	*I go*
très	treh	*very*
père	pehr	*father*

You'll learn more family terms in the next lesson.

✎ Work Out 2

Now let's practice some of what you've learned.

▶ 1I Work Out 2 (CD 1, Track 9) for a different, audio-only exercise!

Can you find the French translations of the English phrases in the puzzle below?

1. *I am*

2. *Good evening*

3. *Hi*

4. *I'm fine*

5. *ma'am*

J	B	O	N	S	O	I	R
Ç	E	N	T	É	S	A	C
L	S	S	A	L	U	T	I
M	E	N	U	E	S	O	Ç
A	N	T	É	I	R	I	A
R	T	Ç	V	E	S	U	V
E	M	A	D	A	M	E	A
D	E	D	J	O	S	L	L

ANSWER KEY:

1. **Je suis** (*I am*); 2. **Bonsoir** (*Good evening*); 3. **Salut** (*Hi*); 4. **Ça va** (*I'm fine*); 5. **madame** (*ma'am*)

✎ Drive It Home

Let's do one more practice before the end of the lesson.

This exercise is designed to ingrain key information about French structure. Although it may seem repetitive, it is *very* important that you read through each question carefully, write out each response, and then read the whole question aloud. It will help you to retain the information beyond just this lesson and course.

A. First let's practice the familiar *you*. Fill in each blank with **tu**. Then, read each sentence aloud. Ready?

1. _____ vas *you go*

2. **Comment t'appelles-** _____ ? *What is your name?*

3. _____ **t'appelles Isabelle.** *Your name is Isabelle.*

4. **Comment vas-** _____ ? *How are you?*

B. Now let's practice the polite *you*. Fill in each blank with **vous**, and don't forget to read each sentence aloud.

1. **Comment allez-** _____ ? *How are you?*

2. _____ **allez** *you go*

3. **Comment** _____ **appelez-** _____ ? *What is your name?*

4. _____ **appelez Florian.** *Your name is Florian.*

ANSWER KEY:
A: all **tu**
B: all **vous** (there are two **vous** in 4)

Parting Words

Congratulations!

Félicitations !

fay-lee-see-tah-syoh(n)

You've finished the lesson! How did you do? You should now be able to:

☐ Greet someone and ask how they're doing (Still unsure? Go back to page 11)

☐ Address someone formally and informally (Still unsure? Go back to page 13)

☐ Introduce yourself (Still unsure? Go back to page 15)

☐ Respond when people ask *How are you?* (Still unsure? Go back to page 15)

☐ Use what you've learned when meeting people for the first time (Still unsure? Go back to page 21)

Take It Further

▶ 1K Take It Further (CD 1, Track 11)

Some other key phrases you might want to know are:

Comment ?*	koh-mah(n)	*Pardon?/* *What did you say?*
Répétez, s'il vous plaît.	ray-pay-tay, seel voo pleh	*Repeat (that), please.*
Parlez plus lentement, s'il vous plaît.	pahr-lay plew lah(n)t- mah(n), seel voo pleh	*Speak more slowly, please.*
Je ne comprends pas.**	zhuh nuh koh(m)-prah(n) pah	*I don't understand.*

* Remember that comment also means *how*.

** Notice the use of ne... pas here to mean *not*.

J'apprends le français.	zhah-prah(n) luh frah(n)-seh	*I'm learning French.*
Je parle un peu français.	zhuh pahrl uh(n) puh frah(n)-seh	*I speak a little French.*

Those few phrases are important for beginners of **français** [frah(n)-seh] (*French*) to know, so practice them a few times, **s'il vous plaît** [seel voo pleh] (*please*)!

In the next lesson, we'll learn how to talk about the family, but if you'd like to review Lesson 1 first, go right ahead! You can learn at your own pace.

Don't forget to go to ***www.livinglanguage.com/languagelab*** to access your free online tools for this lesson: flashcards, games, and quizzes.

Word Recall

You will see a Word Recall section in between lessons. Word Recalls review important vocabulary and grammar from any of the previous lessons, including the one you just finished. They reinforce what you've learned so far in the course, and help you remember the information for the long term.

Of course, since we're currently at the end of the first lesson, we'll only review key vocabulary and grammar from Lesson 1 here.

A. Match the French phrases on the left to the English translations on the right.

1. bonjour	a. *hi*
2. au revoir	b. *good-bye*
3. merci	c. *good evening*
4. s'il vous plaît	d. *hello*
5. enchanté	e. *please*
6. salut	f. *nice to meet you/pleased to meet you*
7. bonsoir	g. *thank you*

ANSWER KEY:
1. d; 2. b.; 3. g.; 4. e.; 5. f.; 6. a.; 7. c

Lesson 2: People and the Family

Leçon deux : les gens et la famille
luh-soh(n) duh: lay zhah(n) ay lah fah-meey

Bienvenue ! [bya(n)-vuh-new] *Welcome!* In this lesson, you'll learn how to talk about your family, and you'll learn some key vocabulary related to people in general. At the same time, you'll learn some of the basics of French grammar to get you speaking right away.

You will learn how to:

1 Talk about people
Use *a/an* in French

2 Talk about your family
Use *the* in French

3 Use what you've learned to tell someone about your family

But first, let's get started with some vocabulary. **Prête, madame ?**
[preht, mah-dahm] *Ready, ma'am?* **Prêt, monsieur ?** [preh, muh-syuh] *Ready, sir?*

Remember to look for these symbols, ▶ and ⏸, to help guide you through the audio as you're reading the book. If you don't see ▶, then there isn't any audio for that section.

1 Talk about people
Use *a/an* in French

Vocabulary Builder 1

▶ 2B Vocabulary Builder 1 (CD 1, Track 13)

a person	**une personne**	ewn pehr-sohn
a woman	**une femme***	ewn fahm
This is ...	**C'est...**	seh
This is a woman.	**C'est une femme.**	seh tewn fahm
a man	**un homme**	uh(n) nohm
This is a man.	**C'est un homme.**	seh tuh(n) nohm
a girl	**une fille****	ewn feey
This is a girl.	**C'est une fille.**	seh tewn feey
a boy	**un garçon**	uh(n) gahr-soh(n)
This is a boy.	**C'est un garçon.**	seh tuh(n) gahr-soh(n)
a child	**un enfant**	uh(n) nah(n)-fah(n)
This is a child.	**C'est un enfant.**	seh tuh(n) nah(n)-fah(n)

* As you saw in Lesson 1, **femme** can also mean *wife*.

⑪ ** **Fille** can also mean *daughter*, as you'll see in Vocabulary Builder 2.

✎ Vocabulary Practice 1

Time to practice! As always, fill in the blanks with the correct French translations.

This is ... _____

a person _____

a woman, a wife _____

a man _____

a girl, a daughter _____

a boy _____

a child _____

ANSWER KEY:
C'est... (*This is ...*); une personne (*a person*); une femme (*a woman, a wife*); un homme (*a man*); une fille (*a girl, a daughter*); un garçon (*a boy*); un enfant (*a child*)

Grammar Builder 1

▶ 2C Grammar Builder 1 (CD 1, Track 14)

Okay, let's stop there.

You learned how to say:

a person	une personne
a woman	une femme
a man	un homme
a girl	une fille
a boy	un garçon
a child	un enfant

Did you notice that there are two words for *a*, either **un** [uh(n)] or **une** [ewn]? That's because French nouns are all either masculine or feminine.

The feminine form of *a* (or *an*), also known as the "indefinite article," is **une**.

une femme	*a woman*
une fille	*a girl*

The masculine form of the indefinite article is **un**.

un homme	*a man*
un garçon	*a boy*

It's easy to remember the gender of nouns like *man*, *woman*, *girl*, or *boy*, but in French, all nouns have gender. Sometimes it's not logical; *a person* is **une personne**, and *a child* is **un enfant**.

And often it's downright impossible; cars, tables, houses, trees, rocks, and all other nouns have gender. It's best not to overthink it! Just memorize the gender of each new noun you learn.

So, to summarize:

FEMININE	MASCULINE
une (*a/an*)	un (*a/an*)
une femme (*a woman*)	un homme (*a man*)

Take It Further

Note that the word **enfant** (*child*) can actually be masculine **or** feminine. It's masculine (**un enfant**) if you're using it as a general term for *child* (as in, *a child would love that toy*), or if you're referring specifically to a male *child*. However, if you're referring specifically to a female *child*, then it's feminine: **une enfant**.

2 Talk about your family
Use *the* in French

Vocabulary Builder 2

2D Vocabulary Builder 2 (CD 1, Track 15)

This is a family.	**C'est une famille.**	seh tewn fah-meey
Here is ...	**Voilà...**	vwah-lah
Here's the father.	**Voilà le père.**	vwah-lah luh pehr
Here's the mother.	**Voilà la mère.**	vwah-lah lah mehr
Here's the son.	**Voilà le fils.**	vwah-lah luh fees
Here's the daughter.	**Voilà la fille.***	vwah-lah lah feey
Here's the brother.	**Voilà le frère.**	vwah-lah luh frehr
Here's the sister.	**Voilà la sœur.**	vwah-lah lah suhr

* Remember that fille can also mean *girl*.

✎ Vocabulary Practice 2

Just like in Vocabulary Practice 1, fill in blanks with the correct French translations.

Note that sometimes you will need to do a bit of deciphering to fill in these Vocabulary Practices—looking up words in a dictionary, breaking down a sentence on your own, and so on. This is meant to help you think more carefully and more in detail about the sentences that you're seeing, and to mimic situations where you won't always understand each word.

If you're confused, always feel free to look up a word in the dictionary or the glossary, or simply check the Answer Key.

Here is ... _____

a family _____

the father _____

the mother _____

the son _____

the daughter, the girl _____

the brother _____

the sister _____

ANSWER KEY:

Voilà... (*Here is ...*); une famille (*a family*); le père (*the father*); la mère (*the mother*); le fils (*the son*); la fille (*the daughter, the girl*); le frère (*the brother*); la sœur (*the sister*)

Grammar Builder 2

2E Grammar Builder 2 (CD 1, Track 16)

Let's pause again.

First you learned how to say *a* (or *an*) in French: **un** for masculine nouns, and **une** for feminine nouns.

Now you've just learned how to say *the*, also known as the "definite article." Again, gender is important. The masculine form is **le** [luh], and the feminine form is **la** [lah]. So far, you've learned a few feminine nouns:

FEMININE (LA)	
la famille	*the family*
la mère	*the mother*
la fille	*the daughter* or *the girl*

FEMININE (LA)	
la sœur	*the sister*
la personne	*the person*

And you've learned a few masculine nouns too:

MASCULINE (LE)	
le père	*the father*
le fils	*the son*
le garçon	*the boy*
le frère	*the brother*
l'homme	*the man*
l'enfant*	*the child*

* Remember that **enfant** (*child*) is masculine if you're using *child* in a general sense, or if you're talking about a male *child*. However, **enfant** is feminine if you're referring to a female *child*.

Notice in those last two words that **le** is shortened to just an **l'** before nouns that start with a vowel. The same thing happens to **la**.

So:

le (*the*) + **étudiant** (*male student*) = **l'étudiant** (*the male student*)

la (*the*) + **étudiante** (*female student*) = **l'étudiante** (*the female student*)

The same thing happens before many (but not all!) nouns that begin with **h**, such as **homme**, since **h** is silent in French.

(II)

Take It Further

In Vocabulary Builder 2, you saw the very useful word voilà.

Voilà means *here is* and *here are*, or *there is* and *there are*. Voilà can also be used on its own as an exclamation to mean *here it is!* and *here they are!*, or *there it is!* and *there they are!*.

A similar word is voici [vwah-see]. Voici can also be translated as *here is* and *here are*, and *here it is!* and *here they are!*.

So what's the difference between voici and voilà? Well, là [lah] on its own means *there*, while ci means *here*. So, technically, voici refers to something *here*, while voilà refers to something *there*. In other words, voici means *here is* and voilà means *there is*. However, in practice, voilà can also be used to mean *here is*, as you saw in this lesson.

✎ Work Out 1

Okay, let's put everything you've learned so far together in a short comprehension exercise.

▶ 2F Work Out 1 (CD 1, Track 17). Listen to the audio to practice your pronunciation of the phrases below. The audio also includes the English translations, so try to do the exercise below first before you listen.

Try to translate as much of the text below as you can, keeping in mind that est [eh] means *is*. You'll learn more about est in the next Take It Further.

C'est la famille Lacroix. Madame Lacroix est une femme. Monsieur Lacroix est un homme. Marc est un garçon. Sophie est une fille.

Madame Lacroix est la mère. Monsieur Lacroix est le père. Sophie est la fille. Marc est le fils.

_____

_____

_____

_____

_____

_____

_____

ANSWER KEY:
This is the Lacroix family. Mrs. Lacroix is a woman. Mr. Lacroix is a man. Marc is a boy. Sophie is a girl. Mrs. Lacroix is the mother. Mr. Lacroix is the father. Sophie is the daughter. Marc is the son.

3 Use what you've learned to tell someone about your family

Bring It All Together

Now let's bring it all together and add a little bit more vocabulary and structure. Read and listen to the following short monologue about Mark and his family.

▶ 2G Bring It All Together (CD 1, Track 18)

Hello!
Bonjour !
boh(n)-zhoor

I'm Marc.
Je suis Marc.
zhuh swee mahrk

I'm French.
Je suis français.
zhuh swee frah(n)-seh

I have a small family.
J'ai une petite famille.
zheh ewn puh-teet fah-meey

I have a father ...
J'ai un père...
zheh uh(n) pehr

He's a policeman.
Il est policier.
eel eh poh-lee-syay

And I have a mother ...
Et j'ai une mère...
ay zheh ewn mehr

She's a teacher.
Elle est professeure.
ehl eh proh-fay-suhr

And I have a sister.
Et j'ai une sœur.
ay zheh ewn suhr

She's a student.
Elle est étudiante.
ehl eh tay-tew-dyah(n)t

And me, too, I'm a student.
Et moi aussi, je suis étudiant.
ay mwah oh-see, zhuh swee ay-tew-dyah(n)

Take It Further

2H Take It Further (CD 1, Track 19)

Okay, you already knew a lot of that vocabulary, but there were a few new words, too.

You already know that **bonjour** [boh(n)-zhoor] means *hello* and **français** [frah(n)-seh] means *French* (both the language and the nationality!).

Did you remember that **je suis** [zhuh swee] means *I am*? You also learned two other forms:

| il est | eel eh | *he is* |
| elle est | ehl eh | *she is* |

You'll learn more about that useful verb (*to be*) later.

And speaking of useful verbs, you also saw Marc say **j'ai** [zheh], meaning *I have*, as in **j'ai une petite famille** [zheh ewn puh-teet fah-meey], or *I have a small family.* Repeat that: **j'ai... j'ai... j'ai...**

Finally, you saw Marc say:

un policier	uh(n) poh-lee-syay	a policeman
une professeure	ewn proh-fay-suhr	a (female) teacher
une étudiante	ewn ay-tew-dyah(n)t	a (female) student
un étudiant	uh(n) nay-tew-dyah(n)	a (male) student

(Remember étudiant/étudiante from earlier in the lesson?)

As an additional note, here is some more helpful vocabulary from Bring It All Together:

petit/petite	puh-tee/puh-teet	small, little, short
et	ay	and
aussi	oh-see	also, too
moi	mwah	me

Wondering why there are two different ways to say *small* in French (petit and petite)? You'll find out more in Lesson 5.

If you're also wondering why you don't use un (*a/an*) in il est policier (*he is a policeman*), it's actually due to a rule in French. In general, French doesn't use articles like *a/an* in front of professions. For example, as you can see in Bring It All Together, you also say elle est professeure, elle est étudiante, and je suis étudiant (you would **not** say elle est une professeure, etc.).

You'll learn more about professions in Lesson 9.

✎ Work Out 2

Now let's practice some of what you've learned.

▶ 21 Work Out 2 (CD 1, Track 20) for different, audio-only exercises!

A. **J'ai...** *I have* ... Fill in the blanks using **un** or **une**.

1. _____ **père.**

2. _____ **sœur.**

3. _____ **mère.**

4. _____ **fils.**

5. _____ **famille.**

B. **Je suis...** *I am* ... Match the professions to the correct English translations.

1. étudiante	a. *male student*
2. professeure	b. *policeman*
3. étudiant	c. *female teacher*
4. policier	d. *female student*

ANSWER KEY:

⏸ A: 1. un; 2. une; 3. une; 4. un; 5. une
B: 1. d; 2. c; 3. a; 4. b

✎ Drive It Home

Now let's do one final practice of the grammar you learned in this lesson. As we mentioned in Lesson 1, although this exercise may seem repetitive, it is **very** important that you complete each question carefully and then say it out loud. It will help you to retain the information for the long term.

A. Fill in the blanks with le (or l') and then read each French sentence aloud. Ready?

1. _____ homme est étudiant. (*The man is a student.*)

2. _____ frère est étudiant. (*The brother is a student.*)

3. _____ père est étudiant. (*The father is a student.*)

4. _____ fils est étudiant. (*The son is a student.*)

5. _____ garçon est étudiant. (*The boy is a student.*)

6. _____ mari est étudiant. (*The husband is a student.*)

B. Great. Now do the same thing, but this time with la (or l').

1. _____ fille est étudiante. (*The girl/daughter is a student.*)

2. _____ femme est étudiante. (*The woman/wife is a student.*)

3. _____ sœur est étudiante. (*The sister is a student.*)

4. _____ personne est étudiante. (*The person is a student.*)

5. _____ mère est étudiante. (*The mother is a student.*)

ANSWER KEY:
A: 1 is l' and the rest are le
B: all la

Parting Words

Congratulations!

Félicitations !

fay-lee-see-tah-syoh(n)

You've finished the lesson! How did you do? You should now be able to:

☐ Talk about people (Still unsure? Go back to page 30)

☐ Use *a/an* in French (Still unsure? Go back to page 31)

☐ Talk about your family (Still unsure? Go back to page 33)

☐ Use *the* in French (Still unsure? Go back to page 34)

☐ Use what you've learned to tell someone about your family
(Still unsure? Go back to page 37)

Take It Further

▶ 2K Take It Further (CD 1, Track 22)

You may of course want to extend the discussion a bit, and talk about:

an uncle	**un oncle**	uh(n) noh(n)k-luh
an aunt	**une tante**	ewn tah(n)t
a female cousin	**une cousine**	ewn koo-zeen
a male cousin	**un cousin**	uh(n) koo-za(n)

And what family reunion would be complete without:

a grandmother	**une grand-mère**	ewn grah(n)-mehr
a grandfather	**un grand-père**	uh(n) grah(n)-pehr

(Or, more generally, **un grand-parent** [uh(n) grah(n)-pah-rah(n)], *a grandparent*.)

If you're **un oncle** or **une tante**, that means you must have:

| *a nephew* | **un neveu** | uh(n) nuh-vuh |
| *a niece* | **une nièce** | ewn neeyehs |

Now, do you remember your survival phrases from Lesson 1? Here they are again:

Comment ?	koh-mah(n)	*Pardon?/ What did you say?*
Répétez, s'il vous plaît.	ray-pay-tay, seel voo pleh	*Repeat (that), please.*
Parlez plus lentement, s'il vous plaît.	pahr-lay plew lah(n)t-mah(n), seel voo pleh	*Speak more slowly, please.*
Je ne comprends pas.	zhuh nuh koh(m)-prah(n) pah	*I don't understand.*
J'apprends le français.	zhah-prah(n) luh frah(n)-seh	*I'm learning French.*
Je parle un peu français.	zhuh pahrl uh(n) puh frah(n)-seh	*I speak a little French.*

See that, you're learning more and more!

Don't forget to go to *www.livinglanguage.com/languagelab* to access your free online tools for this lesson: flashcards, games, and quizzes.

Word Recall

Let's review family vocabulary. Fill in the following family tree with the correct French word for each member of the family. Make sure to include **le** or **la** before each French word.

1.
_____
(Father)

2.
_____
(Mother)

3.
_____
(Sister)

you

4.
_____
(Brother)

ANSWER KEY:
1. **le père** (*the father*); 2. **la mère** (*the mother*); 3. **la sœur** (*the sister*); 4. **le frère** (*the brother*)

Lesson 3: Numbers

Leçon trois : les nombres
luh-soh(n) trwah: lay noh(m)-bruh

Déjà plus de français ? [day-zhah plews duh frah(n)-seh] *More French already?*
Mais, bien sûr ! [meh, bya(n) sewr] *But, of course!*

In this lesson, you'll learn how to:

1 Count from 1 to 22
Say *the men* and *the women*

2 Count from 22 to 1,000
Say *I am, you are,* etc.

3 Use what you've learned to describe a photograph

Allons-y ! [ah-loh(n)-zee] *Let's go!*

1 Count from 1 to 22
Say *the men* and *the women*

Vocabulary Builder 1

It helps to learn numbers in groups, so we'll count in sets of two or three. Note that *zero* in French is just **zéro** [zay-roh].

▶ 3B Vocabulary Builder 1 (CD 1, Track 24)

one, two, three	**un*, deux, trois**	uh(n), duh, trwah
four, five, six	**quatre, cinq, six**	kah-truh, sa(n)k, sees
seven, eight	**sept, huit**	seht, weet
nine, ten	**neuf, dix**	nuhf, dees
eleven, twelve, thirteen	**onze, douze, treize**	oh(n)z, dooz, trehz
fourteen, fifteen, sixteen	**quatorze, quinze, seize**	kah-tohrz, ka(n)z, sehz
seventeen, eighteen, nineteen	**dix-sept, dix-huit, dix-neuf**	dees-seht, dee-zweet, deez-nuhf
twenty, twenty-one, twenty-two	**vingt, vingt et un, vingt-deux**	va(n), va(n)-tay-uh(n), va(n)t-duh

* Un (*one*) is used when counting (*one, two, three, four ...*), or before a masculine noun. Before a feminine noun, however, you would use **une** (*one*). Remember that **un/une** also means *a* or *an*, so now you know that **un/une** can actually mean *a, an,* or *one*: **une personne** (*one person, a person*), **un homme** (*one man, a man*), and so on.

⏸

✎ Vocabulary Practice 1

Now let's practice the numbers you just learned. As always, fill in the blanks with the correct French translations.

zero _____   *twelve* _____

one _____   *thirteen* _____

two _____   *fourteen* _____

three _____   *fifteen* _____

four _____   *sixteen* _____

five _____   *seventeen* _____

six _____   *eighteen* _____

seven _____   *nineteen* _____

eight _____   *twenty* _____

nine _____   *twenty-one* _____

ten _____   *twenty-two* _____

eleven _____

ANSWER KEY:

zéro (*zero*); un/une (*one*); deux (*two*); trois (*three*); quatre (*four*); cinq (*five*); six (*six*); sept (*seven*); huit (*eight*); neuf (*nine*); dix (*ten*); onze (*eleven*); douze (*twelve*); treize (*thirteen*); quatorze (*fourteen*); quinze (*fifteen*); seize (*sixteen*); dix-sept (*seventeen*); dix-huit (*eighteen*); dix-neuf (*nineteen*); vingt (*twenty*); vingt et un (*twenty-one*); vingt-deux (*twenty-two*)

Grammar Builder 1

▶ 3C Grammar Builder 1 (CD 1, Track 25)

Now let's use some of those numbers to count things, which means using the plural form of nouns.

Plurals in French are usually written with an -s, but they sound just like the singular because the -s is (generally) silent. You can tell the difference (if you're unsure while listening to someone speak) because the plural noun comes with the plural form of *the*, which is les [lay], or a phrase like beaucoup de [boh-koo duh] (*a lot of, many*), or a number.

(In other words, it's easy to tell whether a noun is plural in writing because you can just look to see if it has an -s at the end of it. However, when listening to someone speak, you usually can't *hear* the difference, and that's where words like les, beaucoup de, and numbers can help let you know that the noun is plural.)

Here are some examples:

people *(literally, the people)*	les gens	lay zhah(n)
men and women *(literally, the men and the women)*	les hommes et les femmes	lay zohm ay lay fahm
one man and three boys	un homme et trois garçons	uh(n) nohm ay trwah gahr-soh(n)
two women and five girls	deux femmes et cinq filles	duh fahm ay sa(n)k feey
many families	beaucoup de familles	boh-koo duh fah-meey

So, even if a noun sounds the same in the singular and plural, if you hear it with a number, with **les**, or with **beaucoup de**, you know it's plural.

Okay, you just learned two key grammar points, so let's summarize.

1. The plural in French is usually formed by adding a silent -s to the end of a word. For example:

| **la femme** | lah fahm | *the woman* |
| **les femmes** | lay fahm | *the women* |

2. **Les** is the plural *the*. It can be used with both masculine and feminine plural nouns.

Take It Further

Note that French uses articles like **le**, **la**, and **les** a lot more than English does, so you don't always translate them. In fact, French nouns are almost always preceded by something, whether it's an article (**le**, **la**, **les**, **un**, **une**), a number, a phrase like **beaucoup de** (which, by the way, becomes **beaucoup d'** before a vowel), and so on. For example, French speakers would never just say *Books are inexpensive*. They would say *The books are inexpensive*. You'll see examples of this throughout the course.

2 Count from 22 to 1,000
Say *I am, you are,* etc.

Vocabulary Builder 2

▶ 3D Vocabulary Builder 2 (CD 1, Track 26)

Now let's add some more numbers.

The numbers **vingt-deux** [va(n)t-duh] (*twenty-two*) through **soixante-neuf** [swah-sah(n)t-nuhf] (*sixty-nine*) work a lot like in English. Just put the ones place (such as **deux**, *two*) after the tens place (such as **vingt**, *twenty*).

If the ones place is **un**, say the phrase **et un** [ay uh(n)] (*and one*), as in **trente et un** [trah(n)t ay uh(n)] (*thirty-one*). (Or literally, *thirty and one*.)

thirty, thirty-one, thirty-five	**trente, trente et un, trente-cinq**	trah(n)t, trah(n)t ay uh(n), trah(n)t-sa(n)k
forty, fifty, sixty-six	**quarante, cinquante, soixante-six**	kah-rah(n)t, sa(n)-kah(n)t, swah-sah(n)t-sees

Seventy through *ninety-nine* involve a little math:

seventy (*literally, sixty-ten*)	**soixante-dix**	swah-sah(n)t-dees
seventy-one (*literally, sixty and eleven*)	**soixante et onze**	swah-sah(n)t ay oh(n)z
eighty (*literally, four-twenties*)	**quatre-vingts**	kah-truh-va(n)
ninety (*literally, four-twenty-ten*)	**quatre-vingt-dix**	kah-truh-va(n)-dees

ninety-one (literally, four-twenty-eleven)	quatre-vingt-onze	kah-truh-va(n)-oh(n)z

Notice that the **et** (*and*) is dropped in **quatre-vingt-onze**, unlike in *seventy-one*: **soixante et onze**.

Here are more examples:

seventy, seventy-five, seventy-nine	soixante-dix, soixante-quinze, soixante-dix-neuf	swah-sah(n)t-dees, swah-sah(n)t-ka(n)z, swah-sah(n)t-deez-nuhf
eighty, eighty-five, ninety	quatre-vingts, quatre-vingt-cinq, quatre-vingt-dix*	kah-truh-va(n), kah-truh-va(n)-sa(n)k, kah-truh-va(n)-dees
one hundred, one thousand	cent, mille	sah(n), meel

* Note that **quatre-vingts** loses its final -s when it's followed by a number: **quatre-vingt-cinq, quatre-vingt-dix**.

✎ Vocabulary Practice 2

The higher numbers in French can be a bit confusing—there's even some math involved! However, the best thing to do is simply practice.

So with that in mind, fill in the blanks below with the correct French translations.

thirty _____   *fifty* _____

thirty-one _____   *sixty* _____

thirty-five _____   *seventy* _____

forty _____   *seventy-one* _____

seventy-five _____   *ninety-one* _____

eighty _____   *one hundred* _____

eighty-five _____   *one thousand* _____

ninety _____

ANSWER KEY:

trente (*thirty*); trente et un (*thirty-one*); trente-cinq (*thirty-five*); quarante (*forty*); cinquante (*fifty*); soixante (*sixty*); soixante-dix (*seventy*); soixante et onze (*seventy-one*); soixante-quinze (*seventy-five*); quatre-vingts (*eighty*); quatre-vingt-cinq (*eighty-five*); quatre-vingt-dix (*ninety*); quatre-vingt-onze (*ninety-one*); cent (*one hundred*); mille (*one thousand*)

Grammar Builder 2

▶ 3E Grammar Builder 2 (CD 1, Track 27)

Now let's look at pronouns (*I, you, he, she,* etc.) and être [eh-truh], or *to be*.

You've already seen a few forms, but let's look at the whole conjugation:

ÊTRE *(TO BE)*		
I am	**je suis**	zhuh swee
you are (familiar)	**tu es**	tew eh
he is, she is	**il est, elle est**	eel eh, ehl eh
we are	**nous sommes**	noo sohm
you are (polite/plural)	**vous êtes**	voo zeht
they are	**ils sont, elles sont**	eel soh(n), ehl soh(n)

Don't forget that in French there are two ways to say *you*. **Tu es** is the familiar *you are*, so you'd use it with your friends, family, or anyone you're close to. **Vous êtes** is more polite, **and** it is also used to refer to groups of people, as in *all of you are*.

Also note that there are two forms of *they are*:

Masculine/Mixed*	ils sont
Feminine	elles sont

* In other words, you would use it to refer to a group of men or to a mixed group of men and women.

Another common pronoun in French is on [oh(n)], which means *people in general*, but which also is **often** used to mean *we* (mainly in casual conversation). So, on est [oh(n) neh] can mean the same thing as nous sommes.

(Notice that on uses the same form as il and elle. You say il est, elle est, and on est.)

Take It Further

That was a good amount of information, so before continuing on, let's review.

Here are all of the French "subject pronouns" you just learned, with some additional detail provided. Subject pronouns are words like *I, you, he, she,* etc.

je (j')	zhuh	*I*
tu	tew	*you (familiar)*
il	eel	*he, it (masculine)*
elle	ehl	*she, it (feminine)*
on	oh(n)	*we (familiar), people in general, one*
nous	noo	*we*
vous	voo	*you (polite/plural)*
ils	eel	*they (masculine/mixed)*
elles	ehl	*they (feminine)*

Notice that **on** can also mean *one*, as in: *How does one get to the post office?*

In addition, it's important to reiterate that **vous** is the polite *you **and** the plural you* (familiar or polite). In other words, you would use **vous** to address your boss, but also a group of friends.

Furthermore, notice that **il** and **elle** can also mean *it*. So, **il est/elle est** can mean *he is/she is* or *it is*.

Il est petit.
eel eh puh-tee
It is little./He is little.

You would use **il** to mean *it* when referring to a masculine noun, and **elle** to mean *it* when referring to a feminine noun.

Also keep in mind that subject pronouns (**je, tu, il, elle,** etc.) ***replace*** nouns. For example, instead of **Marie**, you say **elle** (*she*). Consequently, you would use the same form of the verb for **Marie** that you would for **elle**:

Marie est étudiante. Elle est étudiante.
mah-ree eh tay-tew-dyah(n)t. ehl eh tay-tew-dyah(n)t.
Marie is a student. She is a student.

Here are a few more examples:

Paul et Marie sont étudiants. Ils sont étudiants.
pohl ay mah-ree soh(n) tay-tew-dyah(n). eel soh(n) tay-tew-dyah(n)
Paul and Marie are students. They are students.

Paul et moi sommes étudiants. Nous sommes étudiants.

pohl ay mwah sohm zay-tew-dyah(n). noo sohm zay-tew-dyah(n)

Paul and I are students (literally, Paul and me are students). We are students.

Le T-shirt est petit. Il est petit.

luh tee-shehrt eh puh-tee. eel eh puh-tee

The t-shirt is little. It is little.

✎ Work Out 1

Let's put everything you've learned so far together in a short comprehension exercise. Fill in the blanks in the sentences below.

▶ 3F Work Out 1 (CD 1, Track 28). Listen to the audio to practice pronouncing the following sentences! The audio also includes the French translations, so try to complete the exercise here first before listening.

1. **Amélie** _____ , **et Franck** _____

   _____ **amis.**

   *Amélie **is a girl**, and Franck **is a boy**. **They are** friends.*

2. **Êtes-vous américains ou français ?** _____ **suisses.**

   *Are you American or French? **We are** Swiss.*

3. _____ **?** _____ **ici.**

   *The (male) students? **They are** here.*

4. _____ **et** _____ **là-bas.**

   *The women and the men **are** over there.*

⏸ **ANSWER KEY:**

1. **est une fille, est un garçon, Ils sont;** 2. **Nous sommes/On est;** 3. **Les étudiants, Ils sont;** 4. **Les femmes, les hommes sont**

Take It Further

You saw some new vocabulary in that exercise:

ou	oo	*or*
l'ami/l'amie	lah-mee/lah-mee	*male friend/female friend*
américain/américaine (américains is simply the plural form of américain)	ah-may-ree-ka(n)/ ah-may-ree-kehn	*American*
suisse (suisses is simply the plural form of suisse)	swees	*Swiss*
ici	ee-see	*here*
là-bas	lah-bah	*over there*

Notice that *American* has two singular forms in French, but *Swiss* doesn't. You'll learn more in Lesson 5.

Finally, you learned earlier in this lesson that the pronoun ils is used for both masculine and mixed company. Well, masculine plural nouns work the same way. In other words, you would use les étudiants to refer to a group of male students or to a mixed group of male and female students. However, les étudiantes can only refer to a group of female students.

Similarly, you would use les amis to refer to a group of male friends or to a mixed group of male and female friends, while les amies can only refer to a group of female friends.

3 Use what you've learned to describe a photograph

🗨 Bring It All Together

Now let's bring it all together and add a little bit more vocabulary and structure.
Read and listen to the following dialogue between two friends looking at a photo.

▶ 3G Bring It All Together (CD 1, Track 29)

A: *It's a beautiful photo.*
C'est une belle photo.
seh tewn behl foh-toh

B: *There are six people.*
Il y a six personnes.
eel ee yah see pehr-sohn

A: *There are three men, two women, and a girl.*
Il y a trois hommes, deux femmes et une fille.
eel ee yah trwah zohm, duh fahm ay ewn feey

B: *Two men and one woman are standing.*
Deux hommes et une femme sont debout.
duh zohm ay ewn fahm soh(n) duh-boo

A: *And the others are sitting.*
Et les autres sont assis.
ay lay zoh-truh soh(n) tah-see

B: *There are also a lot of trees.*
Il y a aussi beaucoup d'arbres.
eel ee yah oh-see boh-koo dahr-bruh

Take It Further

Okay, you already knew a lot of that vocabulary, but there were a few new words, too.

Il y a...	eel ee yah	*There is .../There are ...*
beau/bel/belle	boh/behl/behl	*beautiful, handsome*
une photo	ewn foh-toh	*a photo*
un arbre	uh(n) nahr-bruh	*a tree*
autre	oh-truh	*other*
les autres	lay zoh-truh	*the others, the other ones*
debout	duh-boo	*standing*
assis/assise	ah-see/ah-seez	*sitting (down), seated*

Finally, as you saw in the dialogue, **c'est** can mean *it is* in addition to *this is*. It can also mean *that is*.

✎ Work Out 2

Now let's practice some of what you've learned.

▶ 3H Work Out 2 (CD 1, Track 30) for different, audio-only exercises! You'll also hear the helpful word **avec** [ah-vehk] (with).

⏸

Solve the math problems below to come up with the answers in French.

1. **deux + neuf =** _____

2. **sept - trois =** _____

3. **soixante et onze + deux =** _____

4. **vingt × deux =** _____

5. (vingt et un × deux) + quinze = _____

6. cinquante + cinquante = _____

ANSWER KEY:
1. onze; 2. quatre; 3. soixante-treize; 4. quarante; 5. cinquante-sept; 6. cent

✎ Drive It Home

A. Fill in the blanks with the appropriate form of être (*to be*). Then read each sentence aloud.

1. Vous _____ étudiant. (*You are a student.*)

2. Il _____ étudiant. (*He is a student.*)

3. Elles _____ étudiantes. (*They are students.*)

4. On _____ étudiants. (*We are students.*)

5. Tu _____ étudiant. (*You are a student.*)

6. Nous_____ étudiants. (*We are students.*)

7. Je_____ étudiant. (*I am a student.*)

8. Elle _____ étudiante. (*She is a student.*)

9. Ils _____ étudiants. (*They are students.*)

B. Good job! Now fill in the blanks with the appropriate subject pronoun (je, tu, il, etc.).

1. _____ sommes étudiants. (*We are students.*)

2. _____ est étudiante. (*She is a student.*)

3. _____ êtes étudiant. (*You are a student.*)

4. _____ sont étudiantes. (*They [feminine] are students.*)

5. _____ es étudiant. *(You are a student.)*

6. _____ suis étudiant. *(I am a student.)*

7. _____ est étudiants. *(We are students.)*

8. _____ est étudiant. *(He is a student.)*

9. _____ sont étudiants. *(They [masculine] are students.)*

ANSWER KEY:
A: 1. êtes; 2. est; 3. sont; 4. est; 5. es; 6. sommes; 7. suis; 8. est; 9. sont
B: 1. Nous; 2. Elle; 3. Vous; 4. Elles; 5. Tu; 6. Je; 7. On; 8. Il; 9. Ils

Parting Words

Congratulations!

Félicitations !

fay-lee-see-tah-syoh(n)

You've finished the lesson! How did you do? You should now be able to:

☐ Count from 1 to 22 (Still unsure? Go back to page 47)

☐ Say *the men* and *the women* (Still unsure? Go back to page 49)

☐ Count from 22 to 1,000 (Still unsure? Go back to page 51)

☐ Say *I am*, *you are*, etc. (Still unsure? Go back to page 53)

☐ Use what you've learned to describe a photograph (Still unsure? Go back to page 58)

Take It Further

(▶) 3J Take It Further (CD 1, Track 32)

In case you want to count a bit higher:

one hundred	cent	sah(n)
two hundred	deux cents	duh sah(n)

three hundred	**trois cents**	trwah sah(n)
one thousand	**mille**	meel
five thousand	**cinq mille**	sa(n) meel
eight thousand	**huit mille**	wee meel

A few other useful numbers are the "ordinals":

premier	pruh-myay	*first*
deuxième*	duh-zyehm	*second*
troisième	trwah-zyehm	*third*
quatrième	kah-tree-yehm	*fourth*
cinquième	sa(n)-kyehm	*fifth*
sixième	see-zyehm	*sixth*
septième	seh-tyehm	*seventh*
huitième	wee-tyehm	*eighth*
neuvième	nuh-vyehm	*ninth*
dixième	dee-zyehm	*tenth*

* Another common way of saying *second* is **second** [suh-goh(n)]. But **deuxième** means *second* in a series of three or more, while **second** means *second* or *last* in a pair.

And that wraps up Lesson 3! Feel free to go back and review, or go on for more French.

⏸

 Don't forget to go to ***www.livinglanguage.com/languagelab*** to access your free online tools for this lesson: flashcards, games, and quizzes.

Word Recall

Now let's review vocabulary and grammar from previous lessons.

A. Fill in the blanks using the following words:

suis	sont	appelle	fille	bonjour
est	parle	fils	mari	voilà

_____ ! Je m' _____

_____ Jennifer Mercier. Je _____

_____ américaine. Je _____

un peu français. Je vous présente mon _____, François Mercier.

Il _____ français. Et _____

_____ mes deux enfants: Sophie, ma _____ ,

et Vincent, mon _____ . Ils _____ étudiants.

Hello! My name is Jennifer Mercier. I am American. I speak a little French. Let me introduce my husband, François Mercier. He is French. And there are my two children: Sophie, my daughter, and Vincent, my son. They are students.

B. Translate the following phrases into French.

1. *ten women* _____

2. *one person* _____

3. *one female child* _____

4. *one male child* _____

5. *three brothers* _____

6. *the family* _____

7. *the families* _____

ANSWER KEY:
A: Bonjour; appelle; suis; parle; mari; est; voilà; fille; fils; sont
B: 1. dix femmes; 2. une personne; 3. une enfant; 4. un enfant; 5. trois frères; 6. la famille; 7. les familles

Lesson 4: At Home

Leçon quatre : à la maison

luh-soh(n) kah-truh: ah lah meh-zoh(n)

In this lesson, you'll learn how to:

1 Name common objects around the home

2 Talk about what you *have*
Say how old you are

3 Use what you've learned to talk about
your house and your family

As usual, let's get started with some vocabulary.

1 Name common objects around the home

Vocabulary Builder 1

Note that **dans** [dah(n)] means *in* or *into*.

▶ 4B Vocabulary Builder 1 (CD 1, Track 34)

I have a house.	J'ai une maison.*	zheh ewn meh-zoh(n)
My house has six rooms.	Ma maison a six pièces.	mah meh-zoh(n) ah see pyehs
There is a sofa in the living room.	Il y a un canapé dans le salon.	eel ee yah uh(n) kah-nah-pay dah(n) luh sah-loh(n)
There is also a TV and a computer.	Il y a aussi une télé** et un ordinateur.	eel ee yah oh-see ewn tay-lay ay uh(n) nohr-dee-nah-tuhr
There is a table in the dining room.	Il y a une table dans la salle à manger.	eel ee yah ewn tah-bluh dah(n) lah sahl ah mah(n)-zhay
There is a bed in the bedroom.	Il y a un lit dans la chambre (à coucher).	eel ee yah uh(n) lee dah(n) lah shah(m)-bruh (ah koo-shay)
There is a refrigerator in the kitchen.	Il y a un réfrigérateur dans la cuisine.	eel ee yah uh(n) ray-free-zhay-rah-tuhr dah(n) lah kwee-zeen
There is a shower in the bathroom.	Il y a une douche dans la salle de bains.	eel ee yah ewn doosh dah(n) lah sahl duh ba(n)

* Maison can mean both *house* and *home*.
** Télé is short for *télévision* [tay-lay-vee-zyoh(n)]. This is similar to *TV* versus *television* in English.

There are books in the library.	Il y a des livres dans la bibliothèque.	eel ee yah day lee-vruh dah(n) lah bee-blee-yoh-tehk
There is wine in the cellar.	Il y a du vin dans la cave.	eel ee yah dew va(n) dah(n) lah kahv
There are flowers in the garden.	Il y a des fleurs dans le jardin.	eel ee yah day fluhr dah(n) luh zhahr-da(n)
And there is a car in the garage.	Et il y a une voiture dans le garage.	ay eel ee yah ewn vwah-tewr dah(n) luh gah-rahzh

✎ Vocabulary Practice 1

Now let's practice what you've learned. As always, fill in the blanks with the correct French translations.

You'll have to do a bit of deciphering on your own for this exercise, but you should see patterns in the list that will help you.

a house, a home _____   *a shower* _____

a sofa _____   *a car* _____

a TV _____   *the living room* _____

a computer _____   *the dining room* _____

a table _____   *the bedroom* _____

a bed _____   *the kitchen* _____

a refrigerator _____   *the bathroom* _____

the library _____   *the garden* _____

the cellar _____   *the garage* _____

ANSWER KEY:
une maison (*a house, a home*); un canapé (*a sofa*); une télé[vision] (*a TV*); un ordinateur (*a computer*); une table (*a table*); un lit (*a bed*); un réfrigérateur (*a refrigerator*); une douche (*a shower*); une voiture (*a car*); le salon (*the living room*); la salle à manger (*the dining room*); la chambre à coucher (*the bedroom*); la cuisine (*the kitchen*); la salle de bains (*the bathroom*); la bibliothèque (*the library*); la cave (*the cellar*); le jardin (*the garden*); le garage (*the garage*)

Grammar Builder 1
▶ 4C Grammar Builder 1 (CD 1, Track 35)

Let's pause. You just learned a lot of useful vocabulary for talking about the home.

Did you notice *a room* can be called **une pièce** [ewn pyehs], or **une salle** [ewn sahl]? Also note that **bibliothèque** [bee-blee-yoh-tehk] means *library*. The word **librairie** [lee- breh-ree] exists in French, but it means *bookstore*. (Note that **librairie** is a feminine noun.)

Can you remember how to say *in*? You saw it in several sentences. It's **dans** [dah(n)]. With cities, *in* is à [ah]:

| à Paris | ah pah-ree | *in Paris* |
| à Montréal | ah moh(n)-ray-ahl | *in Montreal* |

And how about *also*? (Remember it from Lesson 2?) It's **aussi** [oh-see].

Finally, notice that the phrase **il y a** [eel ee yah] (which you were first introduced to in Lesson 3) means *there is* or *there are*.

So, you could say:

Il y a une belle fleur dans le jardin.	eel ee yah ewn behl fluhr dah(n) luh zhahr-da(n)	*There is a beautiful flower in the garden.*
Il y a six pièces dans ma maison aussi.	eel ee yah see pyehs dah(n) mah meh-zoh(n) oh-see	*There are six rooms in my home, too. (There are also six rooms in my home.)*

A good phrase to know with il y a is beaucoup de, which means *many* or *a lot of.* You learned it with the plurals (in Lesson 3).

Il y a beaucoup de musées à Paris.

eel ee yah boh-koo duh mew-zay ah pah-ree

There are a lot of museums in Paris.

Take It Further

You also saw the following new words in Vocabulary Builder 1 and Grammar Builder 1:

un musée	uh(n) mew-zay	*a museum*
un livre	uh(n) lee-vruh	*a book*
le vin	luh va(n)	*the wine*
une fleur	ewn fluhr	*a flower*
du	dew	*some, of the (masculine)*
des	day	*some, of the (plural)*

Like le, la, and les, du and des are used more often in French than in English, and they aren't always translated into English. In fact, while the use of a word like *some* is generally optional in English, it is usually required in French:

Il y a du vin dans la cave.

eel ee yah dew va(n) dah(n) lah kahv

There is wine in the cellar./There is some wine in the cellar.

Note that **des** is also used in French as the plural of **un/une**. For example, you would say **une fleur** (*a flower*) and **des fleurs** (*flowers*). There isn't really an equivalent to this in English since a plural of *a/an* doesn't exist. You'll learn more about other uses of **du** and **des** in Lesson 7.

2 Talk about what you *have*
Say how old you are

Vocabulary Builder 2
▶ 4D Vocabulary Builder 2 (CD 1, Track 36)

Jean and Marie have a big apartment.	Jean et Marie ont un grand* appartement.	zhah(n) ay mah-ree oh(n) tuh(n) grah(n) tah-pahr-tuh-mah(n)
The living room has a (grandfather) clock.	Le salon a une pendule.	luh sah-loh(n) ah ewn pah(n)-dewl
The library has a computer.	La bibliothèque a un ordinateur.	lah bee-blee-yoh-tehk ah uh(n) nohr-dee-nah-tuhr
The bathroom has a mirror.	La salle de bains a un miroir.	lah sahl duh ba(n) ah uh(n) mee-rwahr
The kitchen has a microwave (oven).	La cuisine a un micro-ondes.	lah kwee-zeen ah uh(n) mee-kroh-oh(n)d

* **Grand** [grah(n)] can mean *big* or *tall*. Like **petit** and **petite**, **grand** also has another form: **grande** [grah(n)d]. Again, you'll learn more in Lesson 5.

✎ Vocabulary Practice 2

Fill in the blanks with the correct French translations. Again, you may have to do a bit of deciphering on your own, but you should see patterns in the list that will help you.

an apartment _____   a mirror _____

a (grandfather) clock _____   a microwave (oven) _____

ANSWER KEY:

un appartement (*an apartment*); une pendule (*a grandfather clock*); un miroir (*a mirror*); un micro-ondes (*a microwave*)

Grammar Builder 2

▶ 4E Grammar Builder 2 (CD 1, Track 37)

Now let's take a closer look at the forms of avoir [ah-vwahr], *to have*.

AVOIR (*TO HAVE*)		
I have	j'ai	zheh
you have (familiar)	tu as	tew ah
he has, she has	il a, elle a	eel ah, ehl ah
we have	nous avons	noo zah-voh(n)
you have (polite/plural)	vous avez	voo zah-vay
they have (masculine, feminine)	ils ont, elles ont	eel zoh(n), ehl zoh(n)

Notice that in French you use avoir to give an age:

J'ai trente ans.

zheh trah(n)t ah(n)

I'm thirty years old. (literally, I have thirty years.)

It's also used in many other common expressions where English uses a form of *to be*:

j'ai chaud	zheh shoh	*I'm hot*
j'ai froid	zheh frwah	*I'm cold*
j'ai sommeil	zheh soh-mehy	*I'm sleepy*
j'ai peur	zheh puhr	*I'm afraid*
j'ai raison	zheh reh-zoh(n)	*I'm right*
j'ai tort	zheh tohr	*I'm wrong*

Take It Further

Remember that **on** uses the same form as **il** and **elle**. So for **avoir**, you would say **on a** (*we have, people in general have, one has*).

And remember that **il/elle** can also mean *it (masculine/feminine)*, so **il a/elle a** can mean *it has*.

✎ Work Out 1

Okay, let's put everything you've learned so far together in a short comprehension exercise. Form sentences by matching up the phrases that **best** go together.

▶ 4F Work Out 1 (CD 1, Track 38). Listen to the audio to practice pronouncing these and other phrases. The audio includes the completed sentences, so try to do the exercise here first before listening.

1. Il y a beaucoup de vin...	a. ... dans la chambre (à coucher).
2. Il y a une douche...	b. ... dans la cave.
3. Ils ont un canapé...	c. ... dans la salle de bains.
4. Elle a un grand lit...	d. ... dans le salon.

ANSWER KEY:

1. b (**Il y a beaucoup de vin dans la cave.** *There is a lot of wine in the cellar.*) 2. c (**Il y a une douche dans la salle de bains.** *There is a shower in the bathroom.*) 3. d (**Ils ont un canapé dans le salon.** *They have a sofa in the living room.*); 4. a (**Elle a un grand lit dans la chambre à coucher.** *She has a big bed in the bedroom.*)

3 Use what you've learned to talk about your house and your family

Bring It All Together

Now let's bring it all together and add a little bit more vocabulary and structure. Read and listen to the following monologue about Antoine's house and family.

▶ 4G Bring It All Together (CD 1, Track 39)

Hi! My name is Antoine.
Salut ! Je m'appelle Antoine.
sah-lew! zhuh mah-pehl ah(n)-twahn

I have a big family.
J'ai une grande famille.
zheh ewn grah(n)d fah-meey

And we have a big house.
Et nous avons une grande maison.
ay noo zah-voh(n) ewn grah(n)d meh-zoh(n)

My father has a new car.
Mon père a une nouvelle voiture.
moh(n) pehr ah ewn noo-vehl vwah-tewr

And my mother has a new computer.
Et ma mère a un nouvel ordinateur.
ay mah mehr ah uh(n) noo-vehl ohr-dee-nah-tuhr

My brother is thirteen years old.
Mon frère a treize ans.
moh(n) frehr ah trehz ah(n)

He has a lot of friends.
Il a beaucoup d'amis.
eel ah boh-koo dah-mee

My sister is eight.
Ma sœur a huit ans.
mah suhr ah wee tah(n)

She has a lot of video games.
Elle a beaucoup de jeux vidéo.
ehl ah boh-koo duh zhuh vee-day-oh

And me, I have a little dog.
Et moi, j'ai un petit chien.
ay mwah, zheh uh(n) puh-tee shya(n)

Ⅱ

Take It Further

Let's look at a few new words from Bring It All Together before we practice what you've learned:

nouveau/nouvel/ nouvelle	noo-voh/noo-vehl/noo- vehl	*new*

un jeu	uh(n) zhuh	*a game*
un jeu vidéo	uh(n) zhuh vee-day-oh	*a video game*
un chien	uh(n) shya(n)	*a dog*

You also saw **moi** [mwah] (*me*) again, which you first saw in Lesson 2.

✎ Work Out 2

▶ 4H Work Out 2 (CD 1, Track 40) for different, audio-only exercises!

Let's practice identifying the rooms of a house. Fill in the floor plan below with the correct French word for each room.

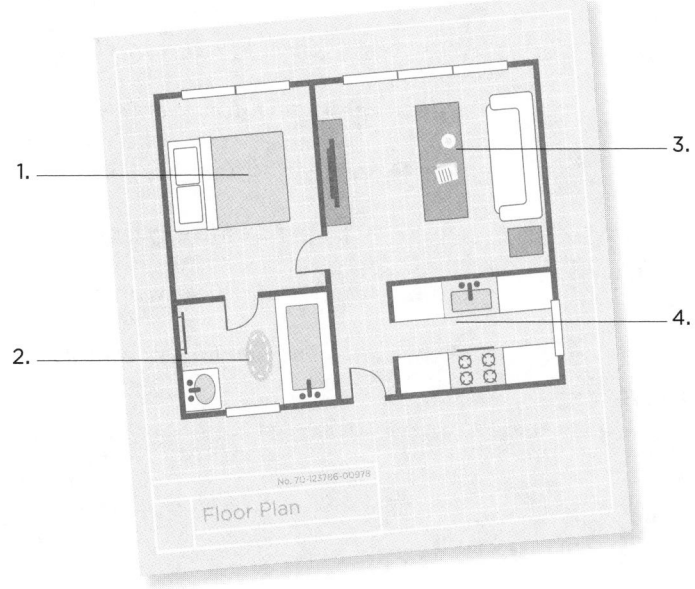

1. _____

2. _____

3. _____

4. _____

ANSWER KEY:

1. la chambre (à coucher) (*the bedroom*); 2 la salle de bains (*the bathroom*); 3. le salon (*the living room*); 4. la cuisine (*the kitchen*)

✎ Drive It Home

Fill in the blanks with the appropriate forms of avoir (*to have*) and don't forget to read each sentence aloud once you're done.

1. Ils _____ quinze ans. (*They're fifteen years old.*)

2. On _____ quinze ans. (*We are fifteen years old.*)

3. Vous _____ quinze ans. (*You are fifteen years old.*)

4. Elle _____ quinze ans. (*She is fifteen years old.*)

5. J' _____ quinze ans. (*I am fifteen years old.*)

6. Il _____ quinze ans. (*He is fifteen years old.*)

7. Tu _____ quinze ans. (*You are fifteen years old.*)

8. Nous _____ quinze ans. (*We are fifteen years old.*)

9. Elles _____ quinze ans. (*They are fifteen years old.*)

ANSWER KEY:

1. ont; 2. a; 3. avez; 4. a; 5. ai; 6. a; 7. as; 8. avons; 9. ont

Parting Words

▶ 4I Parting Words (CD 1, Track 41)

You've finished the lesson! How did you do? You should now be able to:

☐ Name common objects around the home (Still unsure? Go back to page 66)

☐ Talk about what you *have* (Still unsure? Go back to page 71)

☐ Say how old you are (Still unsure? Go back to page 71)

☐ Use what you've learned to talk about your house and your family
(Still unsure? Go back to page 73)

Now you know plenty of **vocabulaire** [voh-kah-bew-lehr]—that means **beaucoup de mots** [boh-koo duh moh] (*a lot of words*). And you can put them together in sentences, because you know **beaucoup de grammaire aussi** [boh-koo duh grah-mehr oh-see].

You're already speaking French!

If you're ready for Lesson 5, go right ahead. If you'd like to review, you can do that, too!

⏸

Don't forget to go to ***www.livinglanguage.com/languagelab*** to access your free online tools for this lesson: flashcards, games, and quizzes.

Word Recall

Now let's review vocabulary and expressions from previous lessons.
Choose the correct English translation for each of the following French
expressions.

1. Ça va mal.

   a. *It's going well.*
   b. *It's not going well.*
   c. *I'm fine.*
   d. *Not bad.*

2. J'ai peur.

   a. *I'm cold.*
   b. *I'm wrong.*
   c. *I'm afraid.*
   d. *I'm hot.*

3. Comment allez-vous ?

   a. *How are you? (polite)*
   b. *What's your name? (polite)*
   c. *How are you? (familiar)*
   d. *What's your name? (familiar)*

4. Il y a quarante livres.

   a. *He has fourteen books.*
   b. *He has forty books.*
   c. *There are fourteen books.*
   d. *There are forty books.*

5. Elle est étudiante.

   a. *They are students.*
   b. *She is a student.*
   c. *We are students.*
   d. *He is a student.*

6. Je ne comprends pas...

   a. *My name is ...*
   b. *I don't speak ...*
   c. *I don't understand ...*
   d. *It's going well ...*

ANSWER KEY:
1. b; 2. c; 3. a; 4. d; 5. b; 6. c

Lesson 5: Describing Things

Leçon cinq : les descriptions

luh-soh(n) sa(n)k: lay deh-skreep-syoh(n)

In this lesson, you'll learn how to:

1 Describe something or someone

2 Describe more than one person or thing
Say *my*, *your*, *his*, *her*, etc.

3 Use what you've learned to describe la Joconde
[lah zhoh-koh(n)d] (*the Mona Lisa*)

First, let's get started with a few simple descriptive adjectives.

1 Describe something or someone

Vocabulary Builder 1

You'll see two forms of each French adjective: masculine and feminine. We'll come back to how to use them in a moment. Ready?

▶ 5B Vocabulary Builder 1 (CD 1, Track 43)

*big**	**grand/grande**	grah(n)/grah(n)d
*small**	**petit/petite**	puh-tee/puh-teet
good	**bon/bonne**	boh(n)/bohn
bad	**mauvais/mauvaise**	moh-veh/moh-vehz
red	**rouge/rouge**	roozh/roozh
white	**blanc/blanche**	blah(n)/blah(n)sh
blue	**bleu/bleue**	bluh/bluh
new	**nouveau/nouvelle**	noo-voh/noo-vehl
old	**vieux/vieille**	vyuh/vyehy
handsome, beautiful	**beau/belle**	boh/behl
American	**américain/américaine**	ah-may-ree-ka(n)/ ah-may-ree-kehn
French	**français/française**	frah(n)-seh/frah(n)-sehz

* As you know, grand/grande can mean both big and tall, and petit/petite can mean *small, little,* or *short.*

✎ Vocabulary Practice 1

Now let's practice the adjectives you just learned. As always, fill in the blanks with the correct French translations.

Make sure to include both forms of each adjective.

big, tall _____

small, short, little _____

good _____

bad _____

red _____

white _____

blue _____

new _____

old _____

handsome, beautiful _____

American _____

French _____

ANSWER KEY:
grand/grande (*big, tall*); petit/petite (*small, short, little*); bon/bonne (*good*); mauvais/mauvaise (*bad*); rouge/rouge (*red*); blanc/blanche (*white*); bleu/bleue (*blue*); nouveau/nouvelle (*new*); vieux/vieille (*old*); beau/belle (*handsome, beautiful*); américain/américaine (*American*); français/française (*French*)

Grammar Builder 1

▶ 5C Grammar Builder 1 (CD 1, Track 44)

Okay, let's stop there.

Adjectives in French have to agree with the noun they describe. That means that you have to use a masculine singular adjective with a masculine singular noun, as in:

MASCULINE SINGULAR		
un homme français	uh(n) nohm frah(n)-seh	*a French man*

And a feminine singular adjective with a feminine singular noun, as in:

FEMININE SINGULAR		
une femme française	ewn fahm frah(n)-sehz	*a French woman*

You usually add an **-e** to the masculine to get the feminine (**français** + **-e** = **française**).

In pronunciation, that usually means that a consonant ending that's silent in the masculine, like the **-s** in **français** [frah(n)-seh] or the **-d** in **grand** [grah(n)], will be pronounced in the feminine:

française	frah-sehz
grande	grah(n)d

If an adjective already ends in **-e** in the masculine singular, like **rouge** (or **suisse**, remember?), the feminine is the same.

In some cases, you double the final consonant and add an **-e** (**bon/bonne**), and in other cases there are irregulars, like:

vieux/vieille	old
blanc/blanche	white
nouveau/nouvelle	new

Take It Further

Beau (*beautiful, handsome*) is obviously another example of an adjective with an irregular form in the feminine: **belle**. You may have also noticed that a third form of *beautiful* was introduced in Lesson 3: **bel** [behl]. Furthermore, you saw *new* written as **nouvel** [noo-vehl] in Lesson 4.

Nouvel and **bel** are special forms of the adjective. They're used with masculine nouns that begin with a vowel or silent **h** (see the Pronunciation Guide for more information on the "silent **h**").

un nouvel ami	a new friend
un bel homme	a handsome man

Same goes for *old*, which uses **vieil** [vyehy] with those types of masculine nouns.

Apart from *beautiful*, *new*, and *old*, most adjectives don't have special forms for nouns like that. They just use their regular masculine singular forms.

2 Describe more than one person or thing
Say *my, your, his, her,* etc.

Vocabulary Builder 2

▶ 5D Vocabulary Builder 2 (CD 2, Track 1)

an athletic boy	**un garçon sportif**	uh(n) gahr-soh(n) spohr-teef
an athletic girl	**une fille sportive**	ewn feey spohr-teev
a happy boy	**un garçon heureux**	uh(n) gahr-soh(n) uh-ruh
a happy girl	**une fille heureuse**	ewn feey uh-ruhz
my old grandfather	**mon vieux grand-père**	moh(n) vyuh grah(n)-pehr
my dear mother	**ma chère* mère**	mah shehr mehr
my charming children	**mes charmants enfants**	may shahr-mah(n) zah(n)-fah(n)
an amusing game	**un jeu amusant**	uh(n) zhuh ah-mew-zah(n)
a beautiful house	**une belle maison**	ewn behl meh-zoh(n)
a red car	**une voiture rouge**	ewn vwah-tewr roozh
a new sofa	**un nouveau canapé**	uh(n) noo-voh kah-nah-pay
a good library	**une bonne bibliothèque**	ewn bohn bee-blee-yoh-tehk

Ⅱ * The masculine form of **chère** is **cher**. **Cher/chère** can also mean *expensive.*

✎ Vocabulary Practice 2

Fill in the blanks with the correct French translations. Try to include **both** the masculine and feminine forms of each adjective.

(Hint: the masculine singular forms of *amusing* and *charming* are amusant and charmant. Those adjectives form the feminine singular normally, so you should be able to fill in the feminine forms based on what you learned in Grammar Builder 1.)

athletic _____   *charming* _____

happy _____   *amusing* _____

dear, expensive _____

ANSWER KEY:
sportif/sportive (*athletic*); heureux/heureuse (*happy*); cher/chère (*dear, expensive*); charmant/charmante (*charming*); amusant/amusante (*amusing*)

Grammar Builder 2
▶ 5E Grammar Builder 2 (CD 2, Track 2)

You probably noticed that most French adjectives come **after** the noun they describe, but a few common ones come **before** it, like:*

grand/grande	grah(n)/grah(n)d	*big*
petit/petite	puh-tee/puh-teet	*small*
bon/bonne	boh(n)/bohn	*good*
mauvais/mauvaise	moh-veh/moh-vehz	*bad*
beau/belle	boh/behl	*beautiful*
vieux/vieille	vyuh/vyehy	*old*
nouveau/nouvelle	noo-voh/noo-vehl	*new*

* Note that the adjective charmant/charmante [shahr-mah(n)/shahr-mah(n)t] (*charming*) can come before **or** after a noun. You'll learn more if you bought *Complete French* and are continuing on to *Intermediate French*.

Adjectives also have to agree in number (with the noun), but the good news is, the pronunciation is just about always the same in the plural as it is in the singular. In writing, there's usually an -s added. So:

MASCULINE		
le garçon sportif	luh gahr-soh(n) spohr-teef	*the athletic boy*
les garçons sportifs	lay gahr-soh(n) spohr-teef	*the athletic boys*

In the feminine, we have:

FEMININE		
la fille sportive	lah feey spohr-teev	*the athletic girl*
les filles sportives	lay feey spohr-teev	*the athletic girls*

(Note that French adjectives—and nouns!—that already end in -s in the masculine singular, don't change in the masculine plural: **le garçon français** and **les garçons français**.)

You probably also noticed the possessive **mon/ma** (*my*). Now let's look at some other possessives, which agree in gender and number with the *possession* (not the person who's speaking or who has the item).

mon/ma	moh(n)/mah	*my*
ton/ta	toh(n)/tah	*your (familiar)*
son/sa	soh(n)/sah	*his, her, or its*

For plural possessions (*my cars* instead of *my car*), use:

mes	may	*my*
tes	tay	*your (familiar)*
ses	say	*his, her, or its*

Let's see some examples:

my father and my mother	mon père et ma mère	moh(n) pehr ay mah mehr
your brother and your sister	ton frère et ta sœur	toh(n) frehr ay tah suhr
his/her bike	son vélo	soh(n) vay-loh
his/her car	sa voiture	sah vwah-tewr
my notebooks	mes cahiers	may kah-yay
your friends	tes amis	tay zah-mee
his/her things	ses choses	say shohz

(Note that **mes**, **tes**, and **ses** can be used with both masculine plural nouns—such as **cahiers** and **amis**—and feminine plural nouns—such as **choses**.)

Did you notice the pronunciation of **tes amis**? The **-s** (in **tes**) is usually silent: **tes** [tay]. But if the next word begins with a vowel sound, that **-s** is pronounced: **tes amis** [tay zah-mee]. This happens a lot in French, and not just with **-s**:

mes amis	may zah-mee	my friends
ses amis	say zah-mee	his/her friends
mon ami	moh(n) nah-mee	my friend
ton ami	toh(n) nah-mee	your friend

And so on.

(Don't forget to listen to the audio for a clearer understanding of this pronunciation! Also check out the Pronunciation Guide at the end of the book for more information on why the **-s** and **-n** sounds are pronounced with the following word.)

Finally, we have:

notre	noh-truh	*our*
votre	voh-truh	*your (plural/polite)*
leur	luhr	*their*

These forms are used for both masculine and feminine singular possessions:

notre maison	noh-truh meh-zoh(n)	*our house*
votre voiture	voh-truh vwah-tewr	*your car*
leur ami	luhr ah-mee	*their friend*

For plural possessions, use:

nos	noh	*our*
vos	voh	*your (plural/polite)*
leurs	luhr	*their*

Here are some examples:

our father and our mother	**notre père et notre mère**	noh-truh pehr ay noh-truh mehr
our parents	**nos parents**	noh pah-rah(n)
your brother and your sister	**votre frère et votre sœur**	voh-truh frehr ay voh-truh suhr
your friends	**vos amis**	voh zah-mee
their car and their bike	**leur voiture et leur vélo**	luhr vwah-tewr ay luhr vay-loh
their things	**leurs choses**	luhr shohz

It is also important to mention that **mon** (*my*), **ton** (*your*), and **son** (*his/her*) are not just used with masculine singular nouns. They are also used with feminine singular nouns that begin with a vowel or silent **h** (don't forget to go to the

Pronunciation Guide at the end of the book for more information on the "silent **h**"). For example:

| my female friend | mon amie | moh(n) nah-mee |

You would not say **ma amie**.

And note that you can also talk about possessions by using the word **de** [duh] (*of, from, for*):

C'est le frère de Marie.
seh luh frehr duh mah-ree
This is Marie's brother. (literally, This is the brother of Marie.)

Voilà le livre de Paul.
vwah-lah luh lee-vruh duh pohl
Here is Paul's book.

Take It Further

So, just to clarify, because this is important, French possessive adjectives agree with the ***possession***. For example, a French possessive adjective would agree with the word *car* in *his car*, and ***not*** with the person who is speaking or who owns the car. So you would use the feminine **sa** in **sa voiture** (*his/her car*) because **voiture** (*car*) is a feminine noun; it doesn't matter whether a man or a woman owns the car. This is different from English, where the possessive sometimes depends on who has the possession: *his car* or *her car*.

And you would use **ses** if there is more than one car: **ses voitures** (*his/her cars*). **Ses** is used with both masculine and feminine nouns. Again, this is different from English, where the possessive adjective doesn't change between singular and plural: *his car, his cars.*

Lesson 5: Describing Things   89

Now let's quickly review some of the new words you saw in Grammar Builder 2:

un vélo	uh(n) vay-loh	*a bike*
un cahier	uh(n) kah-yay	*a notebook*
une chose	ewn shohz	*a thing*
un parent	uh(n) pah-rah(n)	*a parent, a relative*

✎ Work Out 1

Translate the following sentences using the words that you've learned plus the new words from the word bank below:

nice, kind	**gentil/gentille**	zhah(n)-tee/zhah(n)-teey
generous	**généreux/généreuse**	zhay-nay-ruh/ zhay-nay-ruhz
Canadian	**canadien/canadienne**	kah-nah-dya(n)/ kah-nah-dyehn
a company, a firm	**une firme**	ewn feerm
a boss	**un patron/une patronne**	uh(n) pah-troh(n)/ ewn pah-trohn
a colleague	**un collègue/une collègue**	uh(n) koh-lehg/ ewn koh-lehg
a flag	**un drapeau**	uh(n) drah-poh

▶ 5F Work Out 1 (CD 2, Track 3). Listen to the audio to practice pronouncing the sentences below! Of course, the audio also includes the French translations, so try to complete the exercise here first before listening.

1. *I am French. (masculine)* _____

2. *I am French. (feminine)* _____

3. *My flag is blue, white, and red.* _____

_____

4. *You are American. (familiar, feminine)* _____

5. *Your flag is red, white, and blue. (familiar)* _____

_____

6. *He is Canadian.* _____

7. *His flag is white and red.* _____

8. *My company is good and generous.* _____

_____

9. *My (male) boss is nice.* _____

10. *My (male) colleagues are athletic.* _____

ANSWER KEY:
1. Je suis français. 2. Je suis française. 3. Mon drapeau est bleu, blanc et rouge. 4. Tu es américaine.
5. Ton drapeau est rouge, blanc et bleu. 6. Il est canadien. 7. Son drapeau est blanc et rouge.
8. Ma firme est bonne et généreuse. 9. Mon patron est gentil. 10. Mes collègues sont sportifs.

3 Use what you've learned to describe **la Joconde** [lah zhoh-koh(n)d] (*the Mona Lisa*)

Bring It All Together

Now let's bring it all together and add a little bit more vocabulary and structure. Read and listen to the following dialogue between two friends looking at the Mona Lisa.

5G Bring It All Together (CD 2, Track 4)

Lesson 5: Describing Things   91

A: *I'm admiring an old painting.*
J'admire un vieux tableau.
zhah-dmeer uh(n) vyuh tah-bloh

B: *It's the Mona Lisa.*
C'est la Joconde.
seh lah zhoh-koh(n)d

A: *She is beautiful.*
Elle est belle.
ehl eh behl

B: *Her smile is mysterious.*
Son sourire est mystérieux.
soh(n) soo-reer eh mee-stay-ryuh

A: *Her hair is black.*
Ses cheveux sont noirs.
say shuh-vuh soh(n) nwahr

B: *Her skin is very white.*
Sa peau est très blanche.
sah poh eh treh blah(n)sh

A: *What are your favorite paintings?*
Quels sont tes tableaux préférés ?
kehl soh(n) tay tah-bloh pray-fay-ray

B: *Paintings are expensive.*
Les tableaux sont chers.
lay tah-bloh soh(n) shehr

(II)

Take It Further

Let's look at some of the new words you saw in Bring It All Together, starting with:

quel/quelle (*singular*), quels/quelles (*plural*)	kehl	*what, which*

You'll learn more about **quel** and its different forms in the next lesson. And did you remember **très** [treh] from Lesson 1? It means *very*.

Here are some other new words that you saw:

J'admire...	zhahd-meer	*I admire .../ I'm admiring ...*
un tableau	uh(n) tah-bloh	*a painting*
un sourire	uh(n) soo-reer	*a smile*
mystérieux/ mystérieuse	mee-stay-ryuh/ mee-stay-ryuhz	*mysterious*
préféré/préférée	pray-fay-ray/pray-fay-ray	*favorite*
noir/noire	nwahr/nwahr	*black*
un cheveu	uh(n) shuh-vuh	*a hair (single strand)*
les cheveux	lay shuh-vuh	*hair*
la peau	lah poh	*the skin*

Unlike most French nouns, the plural of **tableau** ends in **-x**, not **-s**. Similarly, the plural of **cheveu** is **cheveux**. Many words that end in **-eau** and **-eu**, and some words that end in **-ou**, add **-x** in the plural instead of **-s**.

For example:

SINGULAR		PLURAL	
le gâteau luh gah-toh	*the cake*	**les gâteaux** lay gah-toh	*the cakes*
le jeu luh zhuh	*the game*	**les jeux** lay zhuh	*the games*
le bijou luh bee-zhoo	*the jewel*	**les bijoux** lay bee-zhoo	*the jewels, the jewelry*

The good news is that, like the -s plural ending, the -x plural ending is normally silent when speaking.

✎ Work Out 2

▶ 5H Work Out 2 (CD 2, Track 5) for different, audio-only exercises! Do the exercise here first before doing the audio exercises.

Match the English adjectives to their correct French translations:

1. *nice*	a. **grand**
2. *red*	b. **heureux**
3. *big*	c. **riche**
4. *happy*	d. **gentil**
5. *small*	e. **bon**
6. *good*	f. **intelligent**
7. *intelligent*	g. **rouge**
8. *rich*	h. **petit**

Okay, you hadn't been introduced to **riche** [reesh] or **intelligent** [a(n)-teh-lee-zhah(n)] yet, but they were pretty easy to figure out, weren't they? Fortunately,

French has many words that are very similar to English, like **la table**, **le restaurant**, **l'animal**, **l'université**, etc. So you already know a lot of French vocabulary just by knowing English! Just be careful though; there are "false" similar words too, like **la librairie** (*the bookstore*) and **le collège** (*the secondary school, the junior high school, the middle school*).

ANSWER KEY:
1. d; 2. g; 3. a; 4. b; 5. h; 6. e; 7. f; 8. c

✎ Drive It Home

A. Rewrite the following French sentences by putting the adjectives in the feminine. Don't forget to read each sentence aloud once you're done. Ready?

1. **Je suis français.** (*I am French.*) _____

2. **Je suis américain.** (*I am American.*) _____

3. **Je suis grand.** (*I am big.*) _____

4. **Je suis petit.** (*I am small.*) _____

5. **Je suis mauvais.** (*I am bad.*) _____

6. **Je suis amusant.** (*I am amusing.*) _____

7. **Je suis beau.** (*I am handsome.*) _____

8. **Je suis vieux.** (*I am old.*) _____

B. Now fill in the blanks with either **mon**, **ma**, or **mes**.

1. _____ **cuisine est nouvelle.** (*My kitchen is new.*)

2. _____ **amie est heureuse.** (*My friend is happy.*)

3. _____ **frère est intelligent.** (*My brother is intelligent.*)

4. _____ parents sont gentils. (*My parents/relatives are nice.*)

5. _____ drapeau est bleu, blanc et rouge. (*My flag is blue, white, and red.*)

6. _____ tableaux sont chers. (*My paintings are expensive.*)

7. _____ voiture est noire. (*My car is black.*)

8. _____ femme est charmante. (*My wife is charming.*)

ANSWER KEY:
A. 1. Je suis française. 2. Je suis américaine. 3. Je suis grande. 4. Je suis petite. 5. Je suis mauvaise. 6. Je suis amusante. 7. Je suis belle. 8. Je suis vieille.
B. 1. Ma; 2. Mon; 3. Mon; 4. Mes; 5. Mon; 6. Mes; 7. Ma; 8. Ma

Parting Words

Congratulations!

Félicitations !

fay-lee-see-tah-syoh(n)

You've finished the lesson! You've learned the basic vocabulary and grammar you need to describe things.

How did you do? You should now be able to:

☐ Describe something or someone (Still unsure? Go back to page 82)

☐ Describe more than one person or thing (Still unsure? Go back to page 86)

☐ Say *my, your, his, her,* etc. (Still unsure? Go back to page 86)

☐ Use what you've learned to describe la Joconde (Don't know what la Joconde is? Go back to page 91)

Take It Further

▶ 5J Take It Further (CD 2, Track 7)

Here are some other descriptive terms you can use, in both their masculine and feminine forms:

chaud/chaude	shoh/shohd	*hot*
froid/froide	frwah/frwahd	*cold*
laid/laide	leh/lehd	*ugly*
long/longue	loh(n)/loh(n)g	*long*
court/courte	koor/koort	*short*
fort/forte	fohr/fohrt	*strong*
doux/douce	doo/doos	*sweet, soft*
haut/haute	oh/oht	*high*
bas/basse	bah/bahs	*low*
délicieux/délicieuse	day-lee-syuh/ day-lee-syuhz	*delicious*

A few others have the same forms for both genders:

facile	fah-seel	*easy*
difficile	dee-fee-seel	*difficult*
malade	mah-lahd	*sick*
jeune	zhuhn	*young*
triste	treest	*sad*
pauvre	poh-vruh	*poor*
sale	sahl	*dirty*
propre	proh-pruh	*clean*

| agréable | ah-gray-ah-bluh | *pleasant, enjoyable* |
| calme | kahlm | *quiet* |

Don't forget to go to *www.livinglanguage.com/languagelab* to access your free online tools for this lesson: flashcards, games, and quizzes.

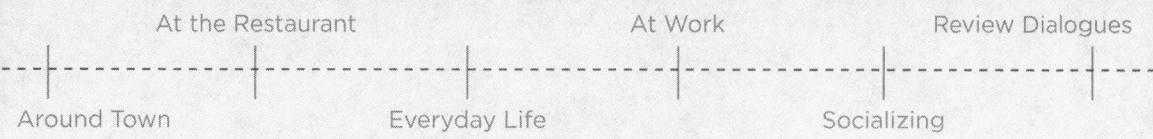

Word Recall

For this Word Recall, let's focus on grammar and review one of the most important verbs in French.

Fill in the following table with all of the forms of *avoir* (*to have*):

I have	
you have (familiar)	
he has, it has (masculine)	
she has, it has (feminine)	
we have, one has, people in general have	
we have	
you have (polite/plural)	
they have (masculine)	
they have (feminine)	

ANSWER KEY:
j'ai; tu as; il a; elle a; on a; nous avons; vous avez; ils ont; elles ont

Quiz 1

Petit Test 1
puh-tee tehst uh(n)

You've made it halfway through the course! Congratulations!

Now let's see how you've done so far. In this section you'll find a short quiz testing what you learned in Lessons 1-5. After you've answered all of the questions, score your quiz and see how you did! If you find that you need to go back and review, please do so before continuing on to Lesson 6.

You'll get a second quiz after Lesson 10, followed by a final review with five dialogues and comprehension questions.

Let's get started!

A. Match the following English words to the correct French translations:

1. **la maison**	a. *the kitchen*
2. **la chambre (à coucher)**	b. *the house/home*
3. **la salle de bains**	c. *the room*
4. **la cuisine**	d. *the bedroom*
5. **la pièce**	e. *the bathroom*

B. Translate the following English expressions into French.

1. *What is your name? (polite)*

   _____

2. *Pleased to meet you. (said by a woman)*

   _____

3. *How's it going?*

   _____

4. *Repeat (that), please. (polite)*

   _____

5. *I am twenty-two years old.*

   _____

C. Fill in the blanks with le, la, les, or l':

1. _____ personne

2. _____ garçon

3. _____ enfant

4. _____ sœurs

5. _____ homme

D. Fill in the table with the correct forms of être (*to be*):

I am	1.
you are (familiar)	2.
she is, it is (feminine)	3.
you are (polite/plural)	4.
they are (masculine)	5.

ANSWER KEY:

A: 1. b; 2. d; 3. e; 4. a; 5. c
B: 1. Comment vous appelez-vous ? 2. Enchantée. 3. Comment ça va ?/Ça va ? 4. Répétez, s'il vous plaît.
5. J'ai vingt-deux ans.
C: 1. la; 2. le; 3. l'; 4. les; 5. l'
D: 1. je suis; 2. tu es; 3. elle est; 4. vous êtes; 5. ils sont

How Did You Do?

Give yourself a point for every correct answer, then use the following key to determine whether or not you're ready to move on:

0-7 points: It's probably best to go back and study the lessons again to make sure you understood everything completely. Take your time; it's not a race! Make sure you spend time reviewing the vocabulary and reading through each Grammar Builder section carefully.

8-16 points: If the questions you missed were in sections A or B, you may want to review the vocabulary from previous lessons; if you missed answers mostly in sections C or D, check the Grammar Builder sections to make sure you have your grammar basics down.

17-20 points: Feel free to move on to Lesson 6! You're doing a great job.

 **Points**

Lesson 6: Around Town

Leçon six : en ville

In this lesson, you'll learn how to:

1 Ask questions

2 Ask for directions
Understand directions

3 Use what you've learned to get around Paris

Let's get started with some basic question words. Ready? On y va ! (*Let's go!*)

1 Ask questions

Vocabulary Builder 1

Remember that, from this point on, there won't be any more phonetics. However, just continue listening to the audio to learn and practice pronunciation and you'll do great! Don't be afraid to listen to each track as many times as you need to.

▶ 6B Vocabulary Builder 1 (CD 2, Track 9)

Where?	Où ?
Where is the Eiffel Tower, please?	Où est la Tour Eiffel, s'il vous plaît ?
Where is Sacré Cœur?	Où se trouve le Sacré-Cœur ?
Which? (What?)	Quel/Quelle ?
Which is the subway station for the Arc de Triomphe?	Quelle est la station de métro pour l'Arc de Triomphe ?
Which is the bus stop for the Louvre museum?	Quel est l'arrêt de bus pour le musée du Louvre ?
How?	Comment ?
How does one get to the post office? (literally, How does one go to the post office?)	Comment va-t-on à la poste ?*
Who?	Qui ?
Who is the guide?	Qui est le guide ?
What... ?	Qu'est-ce que... ?
What do you want to do?	Qu'est-ce que vous voulez faire ?

* Remember that the pronoun on means *one, people in general*, and *we*. To review pronouns, see Lesson 3.

✎ Vocabulary Practice 1

Let's practice! As always, fill in the blanks with the correct French translations.

Don't forget to put a space in between the French word and the quotation mark. If a word has two forms, make sure to include both of them.

Where? _____   *How?* _____

Which?/What? _____   *Who?* _____

_____   *What?* _____

ANSWER KEY:

Où ? (*Where?*); Quel/Quelle ? (*Which?/What?*); Comment ? (*How?*); Qui ? (*Who?*); Qu'est-ce que...? (*What?*)

Grammar Builder 1

▷ 6C Grammar Builder 1 (CD 2, Track 10)

Okay, you've just learned a few useful question words:

où	where
quel/quelle	which (what)
comment	how
qui	who
qu'est-ce que	what

Notice that you can ask *where* things are in two ways:

1. *By using the verb* être, *as in:*

où est... ?

where is ... ?

où sont... ?
where are ... ?

2. *Or you can say* où se trouve... ? *which asks specifically where something is located.*

   To ask *what*, start a sentence with qu'est-ce que... A useful question to know is qu'est-ce que c'est ? (*what is this?*)

   The question word quel (*which*) is like the adjectives that you've learned; it actually agrees with the noun it's asking about (quel homme–*which man*, quelle maison–*which house*).

   Finally, since we're talking about questions, let's go over asking "yes-no questions."

   We'll use the sentence vous êtes de Paris (*you're from Paris*) as a starting point. You can ask *are you from Paris?* in three different ways.

1. *Switch the order of the subject (such as* vous*) and verb (such as* êtes*):*

   Êtes-vous de Paris ?
   Are you from Paris?

   (This is often called "inversion.")

2. *Begin the question with* Est-ce que... ? *(no direct translation)*

   Est-ce que vous êtes de Paris ?
   Are you from Paris?

3. *Simply use question intonation.*

Vous êtes de Paris ?
Are you from Paris? (literally, You are from Paris?)

To answer *yes*, say:

Oui, je suis de Paris.
Yes, I'm from Paris.

To answer *no*, put ne (or n' before a vowel or silent h) and pas around the verb:

Non, je ne suis pas de Paris.
No, I'm not from Paris.

Take It Further

If you use "inversion" to ask a question, then there is an additional rule you should know about. If the verb ends with a vowel, and the pronoun is il, elle, or on, then -t- needs to be inserted in between the verb and the pronoun:

Elle a le livre. A-t-elle le livre ?
She has the book. Does she have the book?

Comment va-t-on à la poste ?
How does one get to the post office?

Notice in that last example that the question word comment (*how*) is followed by inversion. Many question words are often followed by est-ce que, inversion, or sometimes just a verb, as you've seen.

Also, although qu'est-ce que... ? does mean *what?*, it's important to mention that it can't be used on its own. It must be followed by something: Qu'est-ce que vous voulez faire ? (*What do you want to do?*) If you want to simply ask *What?*, you should instead say:

Quoi ?
What?

Note that vous voulez (*you want*) is a form of the verb vouloir (*to want*). You'll learn more about this useful verb in Lesson 10. Faire (*to do, to make*) is another common and important verb. You'll learn about it in Lesson 8.

Finally, remember that à means *in*. You were introduced to it in Lesson 4. As you can see, à also means *to* or *at*. Also, pour means *for* or *to*.

2 Ask for directions
Understand directions

Vocabulary Builder 2
6D Vocabulary Builder 2 (CD 2, Track 11)

Is the post office far from here?	Est-ce que la poste est loin d'ici ?
No, it's not far.	Non, ce n'est pas loin.
It's very close. (It's very near.)	C'est tout près.
Is the train station close to here? (Is the train station near here/nearby?)	Est-ce que la gare est près d'ici ?
No, it's farther.	Non, c'est plus loin.
Is this the Île de la Cité?	Est-ce que c'est l'Île de la Cité ?

No, you have to cross the bridge.	Non, il faut traverser le pont.
Is this the way to Beaubourg? (literally, Is this the direction of Beaubourg?)	Est-ce que c'est la direction de Beaubourg ?
Yes, go straight ahead.	Oui, allez tout droit.
Turn right. (literally, Turn to the right.)	Tournez à droite.
Turn left. (literally, Turn to the left.)	Tournez à gauche.

✎ Vocabulary Practice 2

Fill in the blanks with the correct French translations. As always, feel free to use your dictionary or the glossary for help.

yes _____

no _____

It's not far. _____

It's very close./It's very near. _____

It's farther. _____

Is this the way to … ?/Is this the direction of … ? _____

Turn right. _____

Turn left. _____

ANSWER KEY:
oui (*yes*); non (*no*); Ce n'est pas loin. (*It's not far.*); C'est tout près. (*It's very close./It's very near.*); C'est plus loin. (*It's farther.*); Est-ce que c'est la direction de… ? (*Is this the way to … ?/Is this the direction of … ?*); Tournez à droite. (*Turn right.*); Tournez à gauche. (*Turn left.*)

Grammar Builder 2

6E Grammar Builder 2 (CD 2, Track 12)

You've just seen examples of questions and answers, and you've also learned some more vocabulary.

VOCABULARY FOR ASKING DIRECTIONS	
loin	*far*
près	*close (near)*
tout près	*very close (very near)*
plus loin	*farther*
ici	*here*
là	*there*
droite	*right*
gauche	*left*

You learned some vocabulary for getting around town:

VOCABULARY FOR AROUND TOWN	
la station de métro	*the metro station (the subway station)*
l'arrêt *(masc.)* de bus	*the bus stop*
la poste	*the post office*
le musée	*the museum*
la gare	*the train station*
le pont	*the bridge*

You also saw the very useful expression il faut, which means *you have to* or *it's necessary to* (or *you need to/you must*), as in:

Il faut traverser le pont.
You have to cross the bridge.

Allez tout droit means *go straight ahead,* and you probably recognized that tournez means *turn.*

Take It Further

There's one more new word to mention:

traverser	to cross, to go across

And speaking of allez tout droit, allez comes from vous allez (*you go*), which you first saw in Lesson 1. You actually already know several forms of *to go:*

je vais	*I go*
tu vas	*you go (familiar)*
ça va	*it goes*
vous allez	*you go (polite/plural)*

Plus, you saw Allons-y (*Let's go*) in Lesson 3, and On y va (*Let's go*) and Comment va-t-on... (*How do we go/get to ...*) earlier in this lesson.

You'll learn all of the forms of *to go* in Lesson 8, but as you can see, you've already gotten a pretty good head start!

Work Out 1

Okay, let's put everything you've learned so far together in a short comprehension exercise. Fill in the blanks in the conversation below.

▶ 6F Work Out 1 (CD 2, Track 13). Listen to the audio to practice pronouncing the sentences below! The audio also includes the French translations, so try to complete the exercise here first before listening.

Pardon, madame, quelle est la direction pour la Cathédrale de Notre-Dame ?

Excuse me, ma'am, which way is Notre Dame Cathedral?

(literally, Excuse me, ma'am, which is the way for the Cathedral of Notre Dame?)

C'est la première rue après _____.

*It's the first street after **the bridge**.*

Est-ce que la place de la Concorde est _____ ?

*Is the Place de la Concorde **far**?*

_____ la Seine.

***Yes, you need to cross** the Seine.*

_____ pour la Tour Eiffel ?

***Which is the bus stop** for the Eiffel Tower?*

C'est l'arrêt du Champ-de-Mars.

It's the Champ-de-Mars stop.

_____ pour l'Arc de Triomphe ?

***Which is the subway station** for the Arc de Triomphe?*

C'est la station Charles-de-Gaulle(-Étoile).

It is the Charles-de-Gaulle(-Étoile) station.

_____ ?

Where is the train station?

_____ est tout droit.

***The train station** is straight ahead.*

Take It Further

Notice the new words pardon, après, and rue? Instead of looking at them right away, we're going to see more examples of those words in the next section, and then we'll go over each individual word.

As for première (*first*), you already know it! It's just the feminine form of the ordinal number premier (*first*), which you learned in Lesson 3. The rest of the ordinal numbers have the same form in the masculine and the feminine, except for second (*second*), which becomes seconde in the feminine.

Finally, as you have probably already figured out, while l'arrêt de bus means *bus stop*, the masculine noun arrêt on its own just means *stop*. Also:

la station	station
le métro	*subway, metro*
le bus	*bus*

3 Use what you've learned to get around Paris

ᴿ Bring It All Together

Now let's bring it all together and add a little bit more vocabulary and structure. Read and listen to the following dialogue of a tourist asking for directions in Paris.

▶ 6G Bring It All Together (CD 2, Track 14)

A: *Pardon me, sir, I'm lost. Where's the Champs-Elysées theater?*
Pardon, monsieur, je suis perdue. Où se trouve le théâtre des Champs-Élysées ?

B: *It's the third street on the right (literally, to the right).*
And it's after the avenue Montaigne.
C'est la troisième rue à droite. Et c'est après l'avenue Montaigne.

A: *Is the Café de la Gare far from here?*
Est-ce que le Café de la Gare est loin d'ici ?

B: *No, it's very near.*
Non, c'est tout près.

A: *Which is the subway station for Sacré Cœur?*
Quelle est la station de métro pour le Sacré-Cœur ?

B: *It's Montmartre.*
C'est Montmartre.

A: *Thank you.*
Merci.

B: *You're welcome.*
De rien.

⏸

Take It Further

▶ 6H Take It Further (CD 2, Track 15)

You already knew a lot of that vocabulary, but there were a few new words, too.

perdu/perdue	lost
je suis perdu/je suis perdue	I'm lost
le théâtre	the theater
la rue	the street
l'avenue (*fem.*)	the avenue
le café	the café (the coffee shop, the coffee)
la troisième rue	the third street
la première rue	the first street
la deuxième rue (la seconde rue)	the second street
après	after
avant	before

You also saw some polite expressions that are useful when asking directions:

pardon	pardon (excuse me, pardon me)
merci	thank you
de rien	you're welcome, it's nothing

✎ Work Out 2

Now let's practice some of what you've learned.

▶ 6I Work Out 2 (CD 2, Track 16) for different, audio-only exercises!

Can you find the French translations of the following English phrases in the puzzle below?

1. *near*

2. *here*

3. *there*

4. *thank you*

5. *left*

6. *street*

R	É	S	U	N	I	V	E
O	P	R	È	S	M	U	D
U	R	E	S	A	E	L	O
T	O	O	Y	H	R	È	S
I	C	P	C	Ê	C	R	U
È	H	U	I	C	I	S	T
N	A	G	E	L	U	L	À
G	O	T	R	U	E	D	T

ANSWER KEY:
1. près (*near*); 2. ici (*here*); 3. là (*there*); 4. merci (*thank you*); 5. gauche (*left*); 6. rue (*street*)

✎ Drive It Home

A. Rewrite these yes/no questions using est-ce que. Remember to read each sentence aloud once you're done.

1. **Parlez-vous français ?** (*Do you speak French?*)

_____

2. **La gare est loin d'ici ?** (*Is the train station far from here?*)

_____

3. **Le pont est tout près ?** *(Is the bridge very close?)*

_____

4. **Le théâtre est à droite ?** *(Is the theater to the right?)*

_____

5. **Es-tu américain ?** *(Are you American?)*

_____

6. **Êtes-vous perdue ?** *(Are you lost?)*

_____

7. **C'est la station Charles de Gaulle-Étoile ?** *(Is this the Charles de Gaulle-Étoile*

station?) _____

B. Remember how to negate sentences? You first saw how in Lesson 1, and then
   again here in Grammar Builder 1. Let's practice: negate the following sentences by
   filling in the blanks with ne... pas or n'... pas.

1. **Je** _____ **suis** _____ **perdu.** *(I'm not lost.)*

2. **L'avenue** _____ **est** _____ **loin.** *(The avenue isn't far.)*

3. **Nous** _____ **sommes** _____ **américains.**

   (We aren't American.)

4. **Tu** _____ **parles** _____ **français.**

   (You don't speak French.)

5. **Vous** _____ **êtes** _____ **près de la Tour Eiffel.**

   (You're not close to the Eiffel Tower.)

6. **Je** _____ **comprends** _____ **.** *(I don't understand.)*

7. La gare _____ est _____ loin d'ici.

(The train station isn't far from here.)

8. Je _____ ai _____ froid. *(I'm not cold.)*

ANSWER KEY:
A: 1. Est-ce que vous parlez français ? 2. Est-ce que la gare est loin d'ici ? 3. Est-ce que le pont est tout près ? 4. Est-ce que le théâtre est à droite ? 5. Est-ce que tu es américain ? 6. Est-ce que vous êtes perdue ? 7. Est-ce que c'est la station Charles de Gaulle-Étoile ?
B: 1. ne... pas; 2. n'... pas; 3. ne... pas; 4. ne... pas; 5. n'... pas; 6. ne... pas; 7. n'... pas; 8. n'... pas

Parting Words

Congratulations!
Félicitations !

You've finished the lesson! You've learned the basic vocabulary you need to ask for directions around une ville (*a city*).

How did you do? You should now be able to:

☐ Ask questions (Still unsure? Go back to page 106)

☐ Ask for directions (Still unsure? Go back to page 109)

☐ Understand directions (Still unsure? Go back to page 109)

☐ Use what you've learned to get around Paris (Still unsure? Go back to page 114)

Take It Further

▶ 6K Take It Further (CD 2, Track 18)

You may of course want to extend your vocabulary a bit. Some other useful vocabulary to know is:

un magasin	a store
une école	a school
un hôpital	a hospital
un cinéma*	a movie theater
un boulevard	a boulevard
un supermarché	a supermarket
un restaurant	a restaurant
une boulangerie	a bakery
une pâtisserie	a pastry shop
une pharmacie	a pharmacy (a drugstore)

* Le cinéma can also mean *the movies,* as in *I like going to the movies.*

⏸

Don't forget to go to *www.livinglanguage.com/languagelab* to access your free online tools for this lesson: flashcards, games, and quizzes.

Word Recall

Now let's review vocabulary from previous lessons.
Using the word bank below, translate the following English words. Some French words may not be used.

un lit	une télé
un canapé	un réfrigérateur
un livre	une voiture
une table	une douche
un jardin	un ordinateur

1. *a refrigerator* _____

2. *a TV* _____

3. *a garden* _____

4. *a shower* _____

5. *a book* _____

6. *a bed* _____

7. *a computer* _____

8. *a table* _____

ANSWER KEY:
1. un réfrigérateur; 2. une télé; 3. un jardin; 4. une douche; 5. un livre; 6. un lit; 7. un ordinateur; 8. une table

Lesson 7: At the Restaurant

Leçon sept : au restaurant

In this lesson, you'll learn how to:

1 Order at a restaurant
Name different types of food
Say *this* and *that*

2 Make a polite request

3 Use what you've learned to talk to a
waiter at a French restaurant

So, bon appétit ! Ready for some vocabulary?

1 Order at a restaurant
Name different types of food
Say *this* and *that*

Vocabulary Builder 1

▶ 7B Vocabulary Builder 1 (CD 2, Track 20)

this restaurant	ce restaurant
this table	cette table
a fork, a knife, and a spoon	une fourchette, un couteau et une cuillère
the plate and the napkin	l'assiette (*fem.*) et la serviette
the menu	la carte, le menu
this menu	cette carte, ce menu
The wine list, please. (*literally, The menu/card of the wines, please.*)	La carte des vins, s'il vous plaît.
a dish	un plat
This dish is delicious.	Ce plat est délicieux.
the appetizer	le hors-d'œuvre*
I'd like ... (I would like ...)	Je voudrais...
I'd like some soup.	Je voudrais de la soupe.
I'd like a drink.	Je voudrais une boisson.
I'd like a salad.	Je voudrais une salade.
some bread and some butter	du pain et du beurre
the salt and the pepper	le sel et le poivre

* Another common French word for *appetizer* is l'entrée (*fem.*). You'll see it on a lot of French menus. Just remember that it actually means *appetizer* and not *entrée*! Also note that you will usually see hors-d'œuvre in the plural: les hors-d'œuvre (*appetizers*).

the meat and the fish	la viande et le poisson
Chicken, beef, or pork? (literally, The chicken, the beef, or the pork?)	Le poulet, le bœuf ou le porc ?
some cheese and a dessert	du fromage et un dessert
some coffee and some tea	du café et du thé
With some sugar and some milk? (With sugar and milk?)	Avec du sucre et du lait ?

✎ Vocabulary Practice 1

Now let's practice some of the food and restaurant terms you just learned. As always, fill in the blanks with the correct French translations.

If the definite article is l', make sure to write down the gender as well.

a fork _____

a knife _____

a spoon _____

the plate _____

the napkin _____

the menu _____

the wine list _____

a dish _____

the appetizer _____

I'd like .../I would like ... _____

a drink _____

a salad _____

the salt _____

the pepper _____

the meat _____

the fish _____

the chicken _____

the beef _____

the pork _____

ANSWER KEY:

une fourchette (*a fork*); un couteau (*a knife*); une cuillère (*a spoon*); l'assiette (*fem.*) (*the plate*); la serviette (*the napkin*); la carte/le menu (*the menu*); la carte des vins (*the wine list*); un plat (*a dish*); le hors-d'œuvre/l'entrée (*fem.*) (*the appetizer*); Je voudrais... (*I'd like .../I would like ...*); une boisson (*a drink*); une salade (*a salad*); le sel (*the salt*); le poivre (*the pepper*); la viande (*the meat*); le poisson (*the fish*); le poulet (*the chicken*); le bœuf (*the beef*); le porc (*the pork*)

Grammar Builder 1

▶ 7C Grammar Builder 1 (CD 2, Track 21)

Okay, let's stop there. You've learned a lot of useful vocabulary for food and other items associated with a restaurant or with eating.

And you also learned how to say *this*. Again, gender is important. *This* is ce for masculine nouns so:

le restaurant (*the restaurant*) → ce restaurant (*this restaurant*)

This is cette for feminine nouns, so:

la table (*the table*) → cette table (*this table*)

With masculine nouns beginning with a silent h or a vowel, ce becomes cet: cet œuf (*this egg*). In the plural (*these*), it's ces: ces fromages (*these cheeses*). (Note that ces can be used with both masculine and feminine nouns.)

You also saw the very common preposition de (*of*) used in a few different ways. You can say, for example:

le goût + de + la soupe → le goût de la soupe (*the taste of the soup*)

If de is followed by le, you use du instead:

le goût + de + le plat → le goût du plat (*the taste of the dish*)

(Note that if le or la is followed by a noun beginning with a vowel or silent h, use de l' instead of du or de la: le goût de l'œuf, *the taste of the egg*.)

And when de is followed by les, you say des:

la carte + de + les vins → la carte des vins (*the wine list*, or literally, *the list or card of wines*)

The same constructions (de la, du, de l', des) can be used to mean *some*:*

du pain	some bread
de la salade	some salad
du thé	some tea
de la viande	some meat
des légumes (*masc.*)	some vegetables

* Keep in mind that des is also the plural of un/une in French. In other words, des can mean *some*, *of the*, or the plural of *a/an*.

du lait	some milk
du vin	some wine
des vins (masc.)	some wines

And so on.

Finally, you learned avec (with), so we can add its opposite sans (without):

du café avec du sucre
some coffee with some sugar

du thé sans lait
some tea without milk

So, to summarize:

	FEMININE	MASCULINE	MASCULINE BEFORE A VOWEL OR SILENT H
this	cette	ce	cet
these	ces	ces	ces

	FEMININE	MASCULINE	MASCULINE/ FEMININE BEFORE A VOWEL OR SILENT H
of the, some	de la	du	de l'
of the, some (plural)	des	des	des

Also remember that while *some* is often optional in English, it is usually required in French. For example, you could say either *coffee with sugar* or *some coffee with some sugar* in English, but you have to say du café avec du sucre in French.

Take It Further

Ce, cette, and cet actually mean both *this* and *that*. Similarly, ces means both *these* and *those*.

If you want to emphasize that you mean *that* and not *this*, or vice versa, you can use two words that you're already familiar with: -ci (*here*) and -là (*there*). Just add them after the noun. For example, you could say:

| cette table-ci | *this table (here)* |
| cette table-là | *that table (there)* |

You could also say:

| ces tables-ci | *these tables (here)* |
| ces tables-là | *those tables (there)* |

You may have noticed the word au in the title of this lesson: au restaurant (*at the restaurant*). You just learned that de + le forms du (*of the, some*). Well, it's a similar situation with the word à, which as you know means *to, at,* or *in.* In other words:

à + le = au

à + la = à la

à + l' = à l'

à + les = aux

So au restaurant is actually à + le restaurant (*at the restaurant*).

Je voudrais (*I would like*), as you can imagine, is a very useful phrase to know whenever you need something. The phrase is actually a "conditional" form of the verb **vouloir** (*to want*). You'll learn more about the conditional if you bought *Complete French* and choose to continue on after this book.

Finally, if you're a little confused about all of the different words for *this, that,* and *of the*, don't worry. You'll have a chance to practice them in Work Out 2 and Drive It Home.

2 Make a polite request

Vocabulary Builder 2

▶ 7D Vocabulary Builder 2 (CD 2, Track 22)

I'd like a table for two, please.	**Je voudrais une table pour deux, s'il vous plaît.**
Give me the menu, please.	**Donnez-moi le menu (la carte), s'il vous plaît.**
Have you chosen?	**Vous avez choisi ?**
To start?	**Pour commencer ?**
Bring me some bread, please.	**Apportez-moi du pain, s'il vous plaît.**
Give me these appetizers, please.	**Donnez-moi ces hors-d'œuvre, s'il vous plaît.**
Bring me this drink, please.	**Apportez-moi cette boisson, s'il vous plaît.**
And for dessert?	**Et pour le dessert ?**

Show me these pastries, please.	Montrez-moi ces pâtisseries, s'il vous plaît.
Give me a coffee with cream, please.	Donnez-moi un café-crème, s'il vous plaît.
Bring me the check, please.	Apportez-moi l'addition, s'il vous plaît.

✎ Vocabulary Practice 2

Fill in the blanks with the correct French translations. If the article is l', make sure to include the gender as well. (Hint: the French words for *pastry* and *check* are feminine.)

a table for two _____

the pastry _____

a coffee with cream _____

the check _____

ANSWER KEY:
une table pour deux (*a table for two*); la pâtisserie (*the pastry*); un café-crème (*a coffee with cream*); l'addition (*fem.*) (*the check*)

Grammar Builder 2

▶ 7E Grammar Builder 2 (CD 2, Track 23)

Let's pause there for a moment.

You've already seen the polite request je voudrais (*I'd like*), which of course is often used with s'il vous plaît (*please*). You could also simply say je veux (*I want*). (Although that isn't as polite.)

Other ways to ask for things are to say:

| apportez-moi | *bring me* |
| donnez-moi | *give me* |

Notice that these command forms end in -ez. Another example of this was:

| montrez-moi | *show me* |

Take It Further

You now know two forms of the verb vouloir (to want):

| je veux | *I want* |
| vous voulez | *you want (polite/plural)* |

Plus a conditional form: je voudrais (*I would like*). You'll learn more (non-conditional) forms of the verb in Lesson 10, but you're already off to a great start!

You were also introduced to the past tense of the verb choisir (*to choose*) in the phrase:

Vous avez choisi ?
Have you chosen?

Vous avez, as you know, means *you have*. However, it is also used in French to form the past tense, as it is in English (***Have you** chosen?*). You'll learn more about the past tense if you bought *Complete French* and are continuing on to *Intermediate French*.

As an additional note, you learned in Lesson 6 that une pâtisserie meant *a pastry shop*. However, as you saw in this lesson, it can also mean *a pastry*.

✎ Work Out 1

Okay, let's put everything you've learned so far together in a short comprehension exercise. Fill in the appropriate polite requests in the conversation below.

▶ 7F Work Out 1 (CD 2, Track 24). Listen to the audio to practice pronouncing the sentences below! The audio also includes the French translations, so try to complete the exercise here first before listening.

Mademoiselle, _____. Quelles sont les spécialités du jour ?

Les crudités, qu'est-ce que c'est ?

*Miss, **bring me the menu, please**. What are the specialties of the day? What are crudités? (literally, Crudités, what is that?)*

Des légumes crus, surtout des radis.

Raw vegetables, mostly radishes.

_____.

Bring me the fish, please.

Et pour le dessert, monsieur ?

And for dessert, sir?

_____ les fromages, les pâtisseries et les fruits, _____.

_____. Avec du sucre et du lait.

***Show me** the cheeses, pastries, and fruit, **please. Give me a coffee, please**. With some sugar and some milk.*

And at the end of the meal:

_____.

Bring me the check, please.

ANSWER KEY:
apportez-moi la carte/le menu, s'il vous plaît; Apportez-moi le poisson, s'il vous plaît; Montrez-moi; s'il vous plaît; Donnez-moi un café, s'il vous plaît; Apportez-moi l'addition, s'il vous plaît

Take It Further

Notice some new words? Let's review:

surtout	*mostly, above all, especially*
la spécialité	*the specialty*
le jour	*the day*
les crudités (*fem.*)	*the crudités – a French appetizer of raw, mixed vegetables*
cru/crue	*raw*
le radis	*the radish*
le fruit	*the fruit*

Remember qu'est-ce que c'est ? from the previous lesson? It means *what is it/this/that?* or *what are they/these/those?*. It can be a very helpful expression to know if you're in a store or at a restaurant and you're unsure of what something is. Just indicate the item or phrase on the menu and politely say: Qu'est-ce que c'est ?

3 Use what you've learned to talk to a waiter at a French restaurant

🗨 Bring It All Together

Now let's bring it all together and add a little bit more vocabulary and structure. Read and listen to the following dialogue at a restaurant, as two customers reserve a table, order, and get the check.

▶ 7G Bring It All Together (CD 2, Track 25)

A: *I'd like to reserve a table, please.*
Je voudrais réserver une table, s'il vous plaît.

B: *Bring me the menu, please.*
Apportez-moi le menu, s'il vous plaît.

C: *To start, madam, some appetizers?*
Pour commencer, madame, des hors-d'œuvre ?

B: *Give me some homemade pâté.*
Donnez-moi du pâté maison.

A: *And a bottle of red wine, too.*
Et une bouteille de vin rouge, aussi.

B: *I'd like this onion soup.*
Je voudrais cette soupe à l'oignon.

A: *Bring me this duck à l'orange.*
Apportez-moi ce canard à l'orange.

C: *And for dessert?*
Et pour le dessert ?

A: *Some Crêpes Suzette.*
Des crêpes Suzette.

B: *Give me the check, please.*
Donnez-moi l'addition, s'il vous plaît.

Ⅱ

Take It Further

You already knew a lot of that vocabulary, but there were a few new words, too:

réserver	*to reserve*
le pâté	*the pâté* – a spreadable purée of meat
une bouteille	*a bottle*
la soupe à l'oignon	*the onion soup*
l'oignon (*masc.*)	*the onion*
le canard à l'orange	*the duck à l'orange, the duck with orange sauce*
le canard	*the duck*
l'orange (*fem.*)	*the orange*
la crêpe Suzette	*the Crêpe Suzette* – a crêpe with sugar, orange, and liqueur
la crêpe	*the crêpe* – a tissue-thin pancake

Finally, you already knew that la maison meant *house* or *home*, but now you know that maison can also be used as an adjective to mean *homemade*.

✎ Work Out 2

▶ 7H Work Out 2 (CD 2, Track 26) for different, audio-only exercises! You'll practice talking about food and dishes like **une quiche lorraine,** which is a type of quiche made with bacon.

In this lesson, you learned how to combine de and à with the definite articles (le, la, l', les). Now let's practice what you learned by filling in the blanks below.

1. de + le = _____   5. à + le = _____

2. de + la = _____   6. à + la = _____

3. de + l' = _____   7. à + l' = _____

4. de + les = _____   8. à + les = _____

⏸

ANSWER KEY:
1. du; 2. de la; 3. de l'; 4. des; 5. au; 6. à la; 7. à l'; 8. aux

✎ Drive It Home

A. Fill in the blanks with du or de la. Don't forget to read each sentence aloud once you're done. Ready?

1. Je voudrais _____ lait, s'il vous plaît.

   (I'd like some milk, please.)

2. Je voudrais _____ sucre, s'il vous plaît.

   (I'd like some sugar, please.)

3. Je voudrais _____ poulet, s'il vous plaît.

   (I'd like some chicken, please.)

4. Je voudrais _____ soupe, s'il vous plaît.

   (I'd like some soup, please.)

5. Je voudrais _____ thé, s'il vous plaît.

   (I'd like some tea, please.)

6. Je voudrais _____ sel, s'il vous plaît.

   (I'd like some salt, please.)

7. Je voudrais _____ café, s'il vous plaît.

   (I'd like some coffee, please.)

8. Je voudrais _____ salade, s'il vous plaît.

   (I'd like some salad, please.)

B. Now fill in the blanks with ce or cette. Ready?

1. Apportez-moi _____ pâtisserie, s'il vous plaît.

   (Bring me this/that pastry, please.)

2. Apportez-moi _____ pain, s'il vous plaît.

   (Bring me this/that bread, please.)

3. Apportez-moi _____ soupe, s'il vous plaît.

   (Bring me this/that soup, please.)

4. Apportez-moi _____ spécialité, s'il vous plaît.

   (Bring me this/that specialty, please.)

5. Apportez-moi _____ fromage, s'il vous plaît.

   (Bring me this/that cheese, please.)

6. **Apportez-moi** _____ **viande, s'il vous plaît.**

(Bring me this/that meat, please.)

7. **Apportez-moi** _____ **vin, s'il vous plaît.**

(Bring me this/that wine, please.)

8. **Apportez-moi** _____ **dessert, s'il vous plaît.**

(Bring me this/that dessert, please.)

ANSWER KEY:
A: 1. du; 2. du; 3. du; 4. de la; 5. du; 6. du; 7. du; 8. de la
B: 1. cette; 2. ce; 3. cette; 4. cette; 5. ce; 6. cette; 7. ce; 8. ce

Parting Words

Congratulations!
Félicitations !

You've finished the lesson! How did you do? You should now be able to:

☐ Order at a restaurant (Still unsure? Go back to page 123)

☐ Name different types of food (Still unsure? Go back to page 123)

☐ Say *this* and *that* (Still unsure? Go back to page 125)

☐ Make a polite request (Still unsure? Go back to page 130)

☐ Use what you've learned to talk to a waiter at a French restaurant (Still unsure? Go back to page 134)

Take It Further

7J Take It Further (CD 2, Track 28)

You may of course want to extend your vocabulary a bit. Here are some other well-known **hors-d'œuvre**:

les sardines *(fem.)* sauce tomate	*the sardines in tomato sauce*
le melon	*the melon*

Some other *dishes*, or **plats**, are:

le consommé aux vermicelles	*the noodle soup*
la bisque de homard	*the lobster bisque*
la côte de porc	*the pork chop*
le carré d'agneau rôti	*the roast rack of lamb*
la truite au bleu	*the trout cooked in wine (and vinegar)*
le rôti de bœuf	*the roast beef*

Side dishes include:

le riz	*the rice*

And **des légumes** (*some vegetables*) like:

les haricots *(masc.)* verts	*the green beans*
les pommes *(fem.)* de terre	*the potatoes*

(Another popular side dish is **les frites** [*fem.*], or *the French fries.*)

Red, white and *rosé wines* are:

le vin rouge	*the red wine*
le vin blanc	*the white wine*
le (vin) rosé*	*the rosé wine*

* When talking about *rosé wine*, the word vin is often dropped.

For dessert, you might want to try:

la pêche Melba	*the peaches with ice cream*
la salade de fruits	*the fruit salad*
la mousse au chocolat	*the chocolate mousse*
la crème caramel	*the creamy dessert made with caramel*

And remember, if you just order un café (in France), you'll get a black coffee. If you want cream in your coffee, order un café-crème.

Bon appétit !

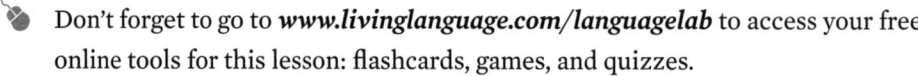

Don't forget to go to ***www.livinglanguage.com/languagelab*** to access your free online tools for this lesson: flashcards, games, and quizzes.

At the Restaurant

At Work

Review Dialogues

Around Town

Everyday Life

Socializing

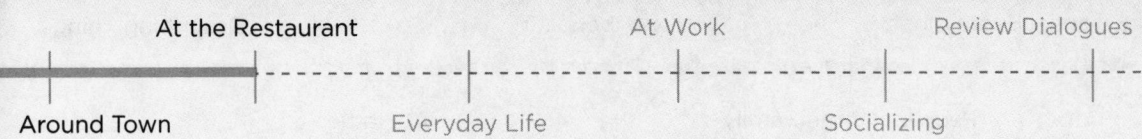

Word Recall

Now let's review vocabulary from previous lessons.

A. First, let's practice family vocabulary. Fill in the following family tree with the correct French word for each member of the family. Make sure to include **le**, **la**, or **l'** before each French word.

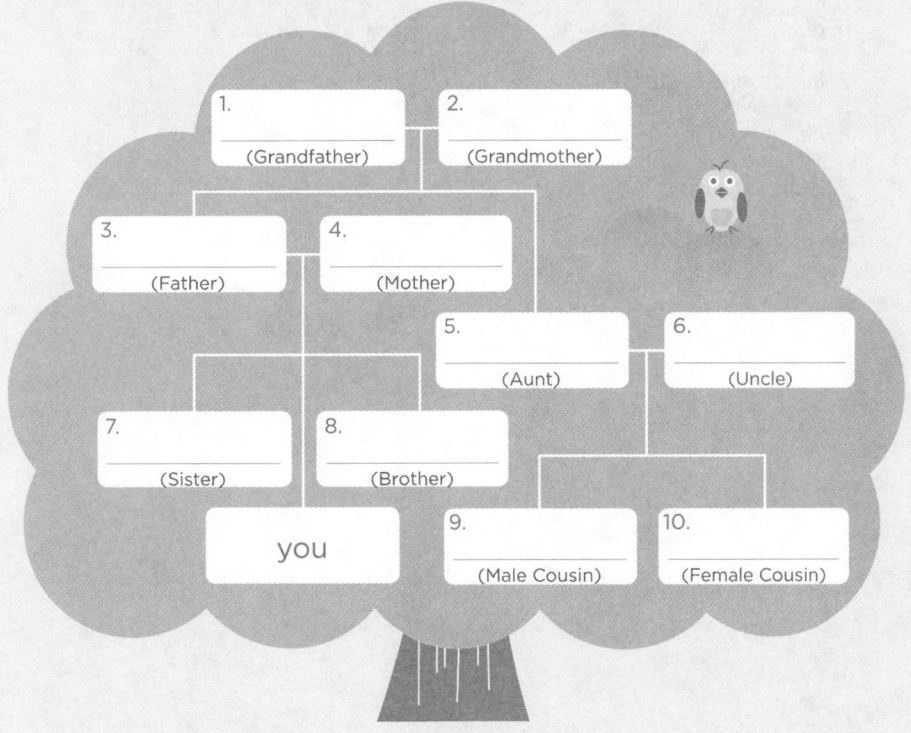

1. _____ (Grandfather)

2. _____ (Grandmother)

3. _____ (Father)

4. _____ (Mother)

5. _____ (Aunt)

6. _____ (Uncle)

7. _____ (Sister)

8. _____ (Brother)

you

9. _____ (Male Cousin)

10. _____ (Female Cousin)

B. Now match the English adjectives on the left to the correct French translations on the right:

1. *big*	a. mauvais/mauvaise
2. *small*	b. nouveau/nouvelle
3. *good*	c. amusant/amusante
4. *bad*	d. petit/petite
5. *new*	e. cher/chère
6. *old*	f. beau/belle
7. *handsome, beautiful*	g. bon/bonne
8. *happy*	h. vieux/vieille
9. *dear, expensive*	i. grand/grande
10. *amusing*	j. heureux/heureuse

Lesson 8: Everyday Life

Leçon huit : la vie quotidienne

In this lesson, you'll learn some common verbs so you can talk about everyday life. You'll learn how to:

1 Talk about different actions in the present
Talk about doing something *yourself*

2 Say what you *do*, where you *go*, and what you *take*

3 Use what you've learned to describe what you do every day

First, let's get started with typical activities of your daily routine.

1 Talk about different actions in the present
Talk about doing something *yourself*

Vocabulary Builder 1

▶ 8B Vocabulary Builder 1 (CD 2, Track 30)

I get up.	Je me lève.
I wash up.	Je me lave.
I have my breakfast. (literally, I take my breakfast.)	Je prends mon petit déjeuner.
I get dressed.	Je m'habille.
I go to the office.	Je vais au bureau.
I go to school. (literally, I go to the school.)	Je vais à l'école.
I work a lot.	Je travaille beaucoup.
I have lunch.	Je déjeune.
I go home.	Je rentre à la maison.
I watch television.	Je regarde la télé.
I read a book.	Je lis un livre.
I go to bed.	Je me couche.

✎ Vocabulary Practice 1

Now let's practice what you just learned. As always, fill in the blanks with the correct French translations.

I wash up _____

I have my breakfast _____

I get dressed _____

I go to the office _____

I go to school _____

I go home _____

I watch television _____

I read a book _____

I go to bed _____

ANSWER KEY:

Je me lave (*I wash up*); Je prends mon petit déjeuner (*I have my breakfast*); Je m'habille (*I get dressed*); Je vais au bureau (*I go to the office*); Je vais à l'école (*I go to school*); Je rentre à la maison (*I go home*); Je regarde la télé (*I watch television*); Je lis un livre (*I read a book*); Je me couche (*I go to bed*)

Grammar Builder 1

8C Grammar Builder 1 (CD 2, Track 31)

Verbs are an important part of any language, and they're also usually difficult to master. We're not going to go into a lot of detail about French verbs in this program, but you'll learn enough of the basics so that you can get started using them.

Verbs in French are conjugated, which means that they change forms slightly depending on the subject. The basic form of a verb is its infinitive, which is just like the *to* form in English (*to speak, to work, to have*, etc.).

French infinitives have a few different endings, but the most common is -er, pronounced [ay]. So, for example:

travailler	to work
déjeuner	to have lunch
rentrer	to go home*

* So does **Je rentre à la maison** mean *I go home to the home*? Well, **rentrer** can also be translated as *to return, to come back (in)*, or *to go in*. As a result, sometimes the phrase **à la maison** is added for clarification.

And so on.

To conjugate these verbs in the **je** (*I*) form, the -er ending is replaced by just -e, which is silent, and gives you:

je travaille	zhuh trah-vahy	I work
je déjeune	zhuh day-zhuhn	I have lunch
je rentre	zhuh rah(n)-truh	I go home

(Note the phonetics provided, but don't forget to listen to the audio to get a better sense of the pronunciation!)

Try that now with **regarder** (*to watch*). Can you think of the **je** form?

It's **je regarde** (*I watch*).

If you know the **je** form of an -er ending verb like these, you automatically know the **tu** (*you, familiar*), **il** or **elle** (*he or she*), and **ils** or **elles** (*they*) forms. They're spelled differently, but they're all pronounced just like the **je** forms.

| tu regardes | tew ruh-gahrd | you watch (*familiar*) |
| il rentre | eel rah(n)-truh | he goes home |

| elle travaille | ehl trah-vahy | *she works* |
| ils travaillent | eel trah-vahy | *they work (masc.)* |

In spelling, the **tu** form ends in -es, the **il** and **elle** forms end in -e, just like the **je** form, and the **ils** and **elles** forms end in -ent, which is completely silent. But they're all pronounced the same:

TRAVAILLER *(TO WORK)*		
je travaille	zhuh trah-vahy	*I work*
tu travailles	tew trah-vahy	*you work (familiar)*
il travaille	eel trah-vahy	*he works*
elle travaille	ehl trah-vahy	*she works*
ils travaillent	eel trah-vahy	*they work (masc.)*
elles travaillent	ehl trah-vahy	*they work (fem.)*

The missing forms are the **nous** (*we*) and **vous** (*you, polite or plural*) forms. For **nous**, add -ons, pronounced [oh(n)]. And for **vous**, add -ez, which is pronounced [ay], just like the *to* infinitive form. So:

TRAVAILLER *(TO WORK)*		
nous travaillons	noo trah vah-yoh(n)	*we work*
vous travaillez	voo trah-vah-yay	*you work (polite/plural)*

Now, let's do the whole thing with another common verb, **parler** (*to speak*). Ready?

PARLER *(TO SPEAK)*	
je parle	*I speak*
tu parles	*you speak (familiar)*
il parle*	*he speaks*
elle parle	*she speaks*

* Remember that on (*we, one, people in general*) uses the same form as il and elle. So: on parle, on travaille, etc.

PARLER *(TO SPEAK)*	
nous parlons	*we speak*
vous parlez	*you speak (polite/plural)*
ils parlent	*they speak (masc.)*
elles parlent	*they speak (fem.)*

And that is how to conjugate a verb in French!

You may have noticed that some of the verbs in the examples you saw in Vocabulary Builder 1 have a little me (or m') before them:

je me lève	*I get up*
je me lave	*I wash up*
je m'habille	*I get dressed*
je me couche	*I go to bed*

These are, in technical terms, called "reflexive verbs," and French has a lot of them. All that means is that they're conjugated with an extra pronoun, in this case, me (or m' before a silent h or vowel), which can be thought of as meaning *myself.*

So, je me lève (literally) means something like *I lift myself out of bed.* And:

je me lave	*I wash myself*
je m'habille	*I dress myself*
je me couche	*I put myself in bed*

In the infinitive, the pronoun is se (or s' before a silent h or vowel), so se laver means *to wash oneself.* That pronoun is also used with *he, she,* and *they,* so:

il se couche	*he goes to bed (literally, he puts himself in bed)*
elle s'habille	*she gets dressed (literally, she dresses herself)*

And so on (ils se lavent, elles se lèvent, etc.).

(Note that se is used with the pronoun on as well: on se couche.)

With tu, use te (or t'):

| tu te lèves | you get up (literally, you lift yourself out of bed) |

Nous and vous are easy; just use the same pronoun twice.

| nous nous lavons | we wash up (literally, we wash ourselves) |
| vous vous habillez | you get dressed (literally, you dress yourself/yourselves) |

Finally, even though most French verbs end in -er in the infinitive form and are conjugated like parler (to speak) or travailler (to work), there are some verbs that end in -ir, like finir (to finish), some that end in -re like prendre (to take), and plenty of irregulars, like être (to be) and avoir (to have), which you've already learned.

You could spend a lot of time on French verbs, but in this program we're just going to cover enough of the basics to get you started.

Ⅱ

Take It Further

You've actually seen a reflexive verb before: je m'appelle, tu t'appelles, and vous vous appelez are all forms of the reflexive verb s'appeler (to be called). Here is its full conjugation:

S'APPELER (TO BE CALLED)	
je m'appelle	I am called
tu t'appelles	you are called (familiar)

S'APPELER *(TO BE CALLED)*	
il s'appelle	*he is called*
elle s'appelle	*she is called*
nous nous appelons	*we are called*
vous vous appelez	*you are called (polite/plural)*
ils s'appellent	*they are called (masc.)*
elles s'appellent	*they are called (fem.)*

Notice that s'appeler is an -er verb, but it actually conjugates slightly irregularly: it doubles the l in every form except for nous and vous. Otherwise, it is formed like any other -er verb.

Another reflexive verb that's slightly irregular is se lever *(to get up)*:

SE LEVER *(TO GET UP)*	
je me lève	*I get up*
tu te lèves	*you get up (familiar)*
il se lève	*he gets up*
elle se lève	*she gets up*
nous nous levons	*we get up*
vous vous levez	*you get up (polite/plural)*
ils se lèvent	*they get up (masc.)*
elles se lèvent	*they get up (fem.)*

Notice that the first e changes to an è in every form except for nous and vous.

Fortunately, s'habiller *(to get dressed)*, se coucher *(to go to bed)*, and se laver *(to wash oneself, to wash up)* conjugate just like any other -er verb, plus the extra pronoun.

You also saw examples of these verbs in Vocabulary Builder 1:

| lire | to read |
| prendre | to take, to have |

Je lis is the je form of lire, and je prends is the je form of prendre. As was noted in Grammar Builder 1, prendre is an -re verb, but it's actually an irregular -re verb. You'll learn its full conjugation in Grammar Builder 2.

Lire is also an -re verb and it's also irregular. Its full conjugation is as follows:

LIRE *(TO READ)*	
je lis	*I read*
tu lis	*you read (familiar)*
il lit	*he reads*
elle lit	*she reads*
nous lisons	*we read*
vous lisez	*you read (polite/plural)*
ils lisent	*they read (masc.)*
elles lisent	*they read (fem.)*

2 Say what you *do*, where you *go*, and what you *take*

Vocabulary Builder 2
▶ 8D Vocabulary Builder 2 (CD 2, Track 32)

I do the house cleaning.	Je fais le ménage.
You do the cooking.	Tu fais la cuisine.
He does the shopping.	Il fait les courses.

She consults the doctor.	Elle consulte le médecin.
We have fun.	Nous nous amusons.
You go to the movies. (You go to the movie theater.)	Vous allez au cinéma.
They go to the theater.	Ils vont au théâtre.
Pierre and Louis go to the soccer stadium.	Pierre et Louis vont au stade de foot.
I take a vacation.	Je prends des vacances.*
We take the train.	Nous prenons le train.

* Although singular in English, *vacation* is always plural in French: les vacances (*the vacation*), des vacances (*a vacation*), etc. It's a feminine plural noun.

✎ Vocabulary Practice 2

Fill in the blanks with the correct French translations. As always, feel free to use a dictionary or the glossary if you need to.

the doctor _____

the movies, the movie theater _____

the theater _____

the soccer stadium _____

a vacation _____

the train _____

ANSWER KEY:

le médecin (*the doctor*); le cinéma (*the movies, the movie theater*); le théâtre (*the theater*); le stade de foot (*the soccer stadium*); des vacances (*a vacation*); le train (*the train*)

Grammar Builder 2

▶ 8E Grammar Builder 2 (CD 2, Track 33)

Let's pause.

You've seen two important irregular verbs in that list: faire (*to do*) and aller (*to go*).

The full conjugation of faire is:

FAIRE *(TO DO)*	
je fais	*I do*
tu fais	*you do (familiar)*
il fait	*he does*
elle fait	*she does*
nous faisons	*we do*
vous faites	*you do (polite/plural)*
ils font	*they do (masc.)*
elles font	*they do (fem.)*

Aller (*to go*) is also irregular. Its forms are:

ALLER *(TO GO)*	
je vais	*I go*
tu vas	*you go (familiar)*
il va*	*he goes*
elle va	*she goes*
nous allons	*we go*
vous allez	*you go (polite/plural)*
ils vont	*they go (masc.)*
elles vont	*they go (fem.)*

* Remember ça va? Since ça and il/elle can both mean *it*, ça uses the same form as il/elle: va.

You also saw prendre (*to take*), whose forms are:

PRENDRE (*TO TAKE*)	
je prends	*I take*
tu prends	*you take (familiar)*
il prend	*he takes*
elle prend	*she takes*
nous prenons	*we take*
vous prenez	*you take (polite/plural)*
ils prennent	*they take (masc.)*
elles prennent	*they take (fem.)*

These three verbs are good irregular verbs to know, since they come up very often in French. Practice them by reading and listening to their forms and repeating them until you're comfortable.

Also, go back over the examples you saw in Vocabulary Builder 2 and change the subjects. For example, instead of saying nous prenons le train (*we take the train*), say:

je prends le train
I take the train

or

elles prennent le train
they take the train

Take It Further

Just one additional verb to mention:

consulter	to consult

Consulter is a regular **-er** verb, so it follows the same pattern as other **-er** verbs: **je consulte, tu consultes**, etc.

You also saw the phrase **nous nous amusons** (*we have fun*) in Vocabulary Builder 2. As you can probably guess, it's the **nous** form of a reflexive verb. You'll learn more about it later on in the lesson.

✎ Work Out 1

Let's practice what you've learned. Translate the following text as best you can, using the word bank below to help you.

rester	to stay
puis	then
parfois	sometimes
ensemble	together
le week-end	the weekend, over the weekend, on the weekend
le travail	work
un taxi	a taxi

▶ 8F Work Out 1 (CD 2, Track 34). Listen to the audio to practice pronouncing the following sentences! The audio also includes the English translations, so try to translate the text below first before listening.

Michel et Julie se lèvent, et puis ils se lavent. Ils vont au bureau. Michel prend le bus, et Julie prend le métro. Après le travail, ils rentrent à la maison. Michel et Julie font les courses. Ils vont au supermarché. Ils prennent un taxi.

Le week-end, ils restent à la maison. Julie fait la cuisine et Michel fait le ménage. Puis ils regardent la télé ensemble. Parfois, ils vont au cinéma.

ANSWER KEY:

Michel and Julie get up, and then they wash up/wash themselves. They go to the office. Michel takes the bus, and Julie takes the subway/metro. After work, they go home. Michel and Julie do the shopping (go shopping). They go to the supermarket. They take a taxi.

Over/On the weekend, they stay at home. Julie does the cooking and Michel does the house cleaning. Then they watch television/TV together. Sometimes, they go to the movies/the movie theater.

Take It Further

Good job! Isn't it amazing how much you already know? You can already translate two full paragraphs about everyday life!

3 Use what you've learned to describe what you do every day

Bring It All Together

Now let's bring it all together and add a little bit more vocabulary and structure. Read and listen to the following monologue describing the activities of friends and family.

▶ 8G Bring It All Together (CD 2, Track 35)

Robert gets up.
Robert se lève.

You go to school.
Tu vas à l'école.

Henri has fun at recess.
Henri s'amuse à la récréation.

I go home.
Je rentre à la maison.

Marlène does her homework.
Marlène fait ses devoirs.

We watch TV.
Nous regardons la télé.

Paul goes to bed.
Paul se couche.

Rémy visits the museum.
Rémy visite le musée.

Odile buys clothes at the store.
Odile achète des vêtements au magasin.

You buy stamps at the post office.
Tu achètes des timbres à la poste.

You wait in line.
Tu fais la queue.

Take It Further

8H Take It Further (CD 2, Track 36)

Okay, you already knew a lot of that vocabulary, but there were a few new words, too:

acheter*	to buy
visiter	to visit (a place)
s'amuser (reflexive verb)	to have fun

* Note that acheter conjugates like se lever, minus the extra reflexive pronoun of course. You'll learn more if you bought *Complete French* and are continuing on after this course. Also, remember nous nous amusons? Now you know the infinitive form: s'amuser. It's a regular -er reflexive verb.

Other words that will come in handy in everyday life are:

la récréation (la récré)	recess
les devoirs (*masc.*)	homework
les vêtements (*masc.*)	clothes
le magasin	store
les timbres (*masc.*)	stamps

The expression **faire la queue** means *to wait in line.* (Or literally, *to do the line.*)

✎ Work Out 2

▶ 8I Work Out 2 (CD 3, Track 1) for different, audio-only exercises!

Let's practice conjugating irregular verbs. If you feel unclear about any of the verbs you saw in Grammar Builder 2, you may want to first go back and review.

Fill in the crossword with the correct French conjugations based on the pronoun and infinitive provided. For example, if you saw [**tu, faire**], you would write **fais** in the crossword.

ACROSS

1 je, faire

3 elle, prendre

5 nous, aller

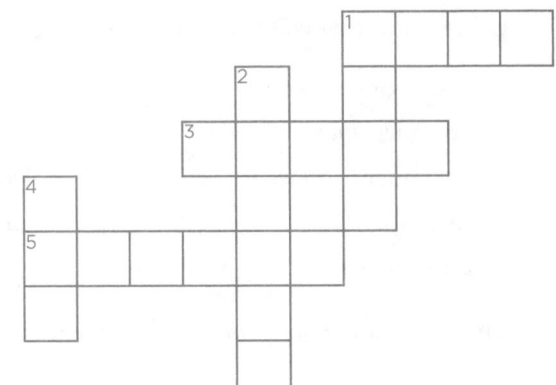

DOWN

1 elles, faire

2 vous, prendre

4 tu, aller

ANSWER KEY:

Across: 1. fais; 3. prend; 5. allons Down: 1. font; 2. prenez; 4. vas

✎ Drive It Home

A. Fill in the blanks with the correct form of the verb regarder (*to watch*), and then read each sentence aloud.

1. Je _____ la télé. (*I watch TV.*)

2. Tu _____ la télé. (*You watch TV.*)

3. Il _____ la télé. (*He watches TV.*)

4. Elle _____ la télé. (*She watches TV.*)

5. Nous _____ la télé. (*We watch TV.*)

6. Vous _____ la télé. (*You watch TV.*)

7. Ils _____ la télé. (*They watch TV.*)

8. Elles _____ la télé. (*They watch TV.*)

B. Great! Now complete the following sentences with the appropriate reflexive pronoun.

1. Je _____ amuse. (*I have fun.*)

2. Tu _____ amuses. (*You have fun.*)

3. Il _____ amuse. (*He has fun.*)

4. Elle _____ amuse. (*She has fun.*)

5. Nous _____ amusons. (*We have fun.*)

6. Vous _____ amusez. (*You have fun.*)

7. Ils _____ amusent. (*They have fun.*)

8. Elles _____ amusent. (*They have fun.*)

ANSWER KEY:
A: 1. regarde; 2. regardes; 3. regarde; 4. regarde; 5. regardons; 6. regardez; 7. regardent; 8. regardent
B: 1. m'; 2. t'; 3. s'; 4. s'; 5. nous; 6. vous; 7. s'; 8. s'

Parting Words

Congratulations!
Félicitations !

You've finished the lesson! You've learned the basic vocabulary you need to describe a few aspects of your everyday life. You've also learned a lot about using verbs in French.

How did you do? You should now be able to:

☐ Talk about different actions in the present (Still unsure? Go back to page 145)

☐ Talk about doing something *yourself* (Still unsure? Go back to page 148)

☐ Say what you *do*, where you *go*, and what you *take*
(Still unsure? Go back to page 153)

☐ Use what you've learned to describe what you do every day
(Still unsure? Go back to page 157)

Take It Further
▶ 8K Take It Further (CD 3, Track 3)

Some other -er verbs that may come in handy are:

étudier	to study
penser	to think
manger	to eat
payer	to pay
aimer	to love, to like
arriver	to arrive (to get somewhere, to reach)
entrer	to enter, to come in
célébrer	to celebrate
chercher	to look for
écouter	to listen (to)
voyager	to travel
commencer	to begin (to start)
téléphoner	to phone (to call, to make a phone call)
demander	to ask
détester	to hate
donner	to give
fermer	to close
habiter	to live
inviter	to invite

jouer	to play
chanter	to sing
montrer	to show
porter	to carry, to wear
présenter	to introduce
décider	to decide
trouver	to find
terminer	to finish

They all follow the same pattern as the regular -er verbs you've learned in this lesson (with some exceptions, such as manger and payer, that you'll learn more about if you bought *Complete French* and choose to continue past this book).

Don't forget that to say that you *don't* do something, just use ne (n') and pas around the verb:

je ne chante pas	I don't sing
ils ne voyagent pas beaucoup	they don't travel a lot
nous n'habitons pas ici	we don't live here

If you want to review this lesson to really master the basics of French verbs, go right ahead!

Don't forget to go to *www.livinglanguage.com/languagelab* to access your free online tools for this lesson: flashcards, games, and quizzes.

Word Recall

Now let's review vocabulary from previous lessons. Ready?

A. Translate the following numbers into French:

1. *eight* _____

2. *thirty-one* _____

3. *fifty-seven* _____

4. *ninety* _____

5. *ninety-two* _____

6. *one hundred* _____

7. *sixty* _____

8. *seventy-one* _____

9. *one thousand* _____

10. *thirteen* _____

B. Fill in the table below by placing each of the following words in the appropriate box, and then translating it into English. Each box will have four words once completed.

le poulet, le vin, les pommes de terre, le porc, le poivre, le thé, le riz, le beurre, le sucre, le bœuf, le lait, le canard, les haricots verts, le café, les frites, le sel

Hot/Cold Drinks	
Meats	
Side Dishes	
Condiments/Seasonings	

ANSWER KEY:
A: 1. huit; 2. trente et un; 3. cinquante-sept; 4. quatre-vingt-dix; 5. quatre-vingt-douze; 6. cent; 7. soixante; 8. soixante et onze; 9. mille; 10. treize

B: Hot/Cold Drinks: le vin, le thé, le lait, le café (*the wine, the tea, the milk, the coffee*)

Meats: le poulet, le porc, le bœuf, le canard (*the chicken, the pork, the beef, the duck*)

Side Dishes: les pommes de terre, le riz, les haricots verts, les frites (*the potatoes, the rice, the green beans, the French fries*)

Condiments/Seasonings: le poivre, le beurre, le sucre, le sel (*the pepper, the butter, the sugar, the salt*)

Word Recall   165

Lesson 9: At Work

Leçon neuf : au travail

In this lesson, you'll learn vocabulary related to your work life. You'll learn how to:

1 Talk about different professions

2 Say the days of the week
Tell time

3 Use what you've learned to discuss professions and schedules

And we'll go over negation with ne... pas again. Ready?

1 Talk about different professions

Vocabulary Builder 1

▶ 9B Vocabulary Builder 1 (CD 3, Track 5)

The doctor practices medicine.	Le médecin pratique la médecine.
The artist paints paintings.	L'artiste peint des tableaux.
A lawyer is speaking with a client.	Une avocate parle avec un client.
The actor plays roles.	L'acteur joue des rôles.
A cook cooks (prepares) dishes.	Un cuisinier prépare des plats.
The singer sings songs.	La chanteuse chante des chansons.
The writer writes books.	L'écrivain écrit des livres.
The soccer player plays matches.	Le footballeur joue des matches.
The manager organizes a meeting.	La gérante organise une réunion.

✎ Vocabulary Practice 1

Now let's practice what you just learned.

Make sure to include the appropriate definite article (le, la, l', les) before the French word for *medicine*. (Hint: the French words for *role* and *match* are masculine and the French word for *song* is feminine.)

medicine _____

a role _____

a song _____

a (sports) match _____

a meeting _____

ANSWER KEY:
la médecine (*medicine*); un rôle (*a role*); une chanson (*a song*); un match (*a [sports] match*); une réunion (*a meeting*)

Grammar Builder 1

▶ 9C Grammar Builder 1 (CD 3, Track 6)

You probably noticed that the names of professions have different forms for different genders. Sometimes just the article changes, as in:

| un artiste/une artiste | *an artist (male/female)* |

Sometimes an -e is added to the masculine to form the feminine, as in:

le professeur/la professeure*	*the teacher (male/female)*
le gérant/la gérante	*the manager (male/female)*
un avocat/une avocate	*a lawyer (male/female)*

* As you've probably guessed, professeur/professeure can also mean *professor*. Also note that, in casual conversation, professeur/professeure is often shortened to just prof. Furthermore, le professeur is sometimes used to refer to a *female teacher/professor* since the word la professeure is relatively new.

There are also a few common patterns of changes to word endings:

le chanteur/la chanteuse	*the singer (male/female)*
un acteur/une actrice	*an actor/actress*
le cuisinier/la cuisinière	*the cook (male/female)*

A few professions don't change at all:

| le médecin | *the male/female doctor* |
| un écrivain* | *a male/female writer* |

⏸ * Although occasionally you do see une écrivaine for *a female writer*.

Take It Further

Other professions and roles mentioned in Vocabulary Builder 1 include:

| le client/la cliente | the client (male/female) |
| le footballeur/la footballeuse | the soccer player (male/female) |

Notice that footballeur/footballeuse follows the same pattern as chanteur/chanteuse.

You also saw some new verbs related to professions:

pratiquer	to practice, to play
peindre	to paint
préparer	to prepare, to make, to cook
écrire	to write
organiser	to organize

Another good verb to know when talking about professions is:

| enseigner | to teach |

And to review, you first saw these verbs at the end of Lesson 8 and then again in Vocabulary Builder 1:

| jouer | to play, to perform, to act |
| chanter | to sing |

2 Say the days of the week
Tell time

Vocabulary Builder 2

Notice that the days of the week are not capitalized in French. The same is true for the months of the year, as you'll see later on in this lesson.

▶ 9D Vocabulary Builder 2 (CD 3, Track 7)

Monday, Tuesday, Wednesday	lundi, mardi, mercredi
Thursday, Friday	jeudi, vendredi
Saturday, Sunday	samedi, dimanche
What time is it? *(literally, What hour is it?)*	Quelle heure est-il ?*
It's 1:00.	Il est une heure.
It's half past two.	Il est deux heures et demie.
It's a quarter after four.	Il est quatre heures et quart.
It's a quarter to seven.	Il est sept heures moins le quart.
It's noon.	Il est midi.
It's midnight.	Il est minuit.

* Note that the word heure (*hour*) is feminine: quelle heure, une heure.

✎ Vocabulary Practice 2

Fill in the blanks with the correct French translations. Remember that the days of the week are not capitalized in French.

Monday _____

Tuesday _____

Wednesday _____

Thursday _____

Friday _____

Saturday _____

Sunday _____

What time is it? _____

It's noon. _____

It's midnight. _____

ANSWER KEY:
lundi (*Monday*); mardi (*Tuesday*); mercredi (*Wednesday*); jeudi (*Thursday*); vendredi (*Friday*); samedi (*Saturday*); dimanche (*Sunday*); Quelle heure est-il ? (*What time is it?*); Il est midi. (*It's noon.*); Il est minuit. (*It's midnight.*)

Grammar Builder 2

▶ 9E Grammar Builder 2 (CD 3, Track 8)

Notice that to answer the question quelle heure est-il ? (*what time is it?*) you just say:

il est (*it is*) + number + heure/heures (*hour/hours*)

So, il est cinq heures means *it's 5:00* (or literally, *it's five hours*).

(Note that you would write une heure for 1:00 but cinq heure**s** for 5:00, since the phrases literally mean *one hour* and *five hours* respectively.)

Also:

... et demie	*half past ...*
... et quart	*a quarter past ...* or *a quarter after ...*

| ... moins le quart | a quarter to ... |

So:

Il est huit heures et demie.	It's half past eight.
Il est onze heures et quart.	It's a quarter past eleven./ It's a quarter after eleven.
Il est neuf heures moins le quart.	It's a quarter to nine.

It's important to note that most people in France use the 24-hour clock, so you'll see:

| Il est quinze heures. | It's 3:00 p.m. (literally, It's 15:00.) |
| Il est dix-huit heures. | It's 6:00 p.m. (literally, It's 18:00.) |

Take It Further

In addition to et demie, et quart, and moins le quart, you can also just say the appropriate number after heure/heures:

huit heures trente	8:30
deux heures trente-huit	2:38
onze heures cinq	11:05

Notice that, in French, you don't express the zero with minutes less than ten, as you do in English. In other words, you literally say *eleven five* in French instead of *eleven oh five* for 11:05.

It's important to mention that when you use the 24-hour clock after noon, you actually should **not** use the phrases et quart, et demie, or moins le quart. You should use numbers only. For example, you cannot say quatorze heures moins le quart (*a quarter to 2 p.m.*). Instead, you would have to say **treize heures quarante-cinq** (*1:45 p.m.*).

Not familiar with the 24-hour clock? It simply means that the hours in a day start at 0 and go up to 23. So:

0:00	*12 a.m.*
1:00	*1 a.m.*
2:00	*2 a.m.*
11:00	*11 a.m.*
12:00	*12 p.m.*
13:00	*1 p.m.*
14:00	*2 p.m.*
23:00	*11 p.m.*

There are no words for *a.m.* or *p.m.* in French; the 24-hour clock is used instead, or phrases like *in the morning* or *in the evening*. You'll learn more in the next Take It Further.

Also note that, in French, you will normally see the time written as shown on the left:

1h	1:00
8h30	8:30
15h45	15:45
0h15	0:15

The **h**, of course, stands for **heure(s)**.

✎ Work Out 1

Okay, let's put everything you've learned so far together in a short comprehension exercise.

Below is a description of someone's day. Fill in the appropriate times in French. Make sure to write each time out in full.

▶ 9F Work Out 1 (CD 3, Track 9). Listen to the audio to practice pronouncing the sentences below! The audio also includes the French translations, so try to complete the exercise here first before listening.

Aujourd'hui c'est lundi, et la gérante va au travail.
It's Monday today, and the (female) manager goes to work.

Elle arrive à la gare à _____.
*She arrives at the train station at **8:10**.*

Elle prend le train à _____.
*She takes the train at **a quarter past eight**.*

Elle arrive au bureau à _____ **du matin.**
*She arrives at the office at **9:00** in the morning.*

Elle boit du café et lit ses emails. Elle parle avec ses collègues.
She drinks some coffee and reads her emails. She speaks with her colleagues.

Ils vont à une réunion à _____.
*They go to a meeting at **10:30**.*

Ils déjeunent ensemble à _____.

*They have lunch together at **13:00 (1:00 p.m.)**.*

ANSWER KEY:

huit heures dix; huit heures et quart; neuf heures; dix heures trente (dix heures et demie); treize heures

Take It Further

Now you know how to tell time! Pretty easy, n'est-ce pas [nehs pah] (*isn't it*)?

Some new words you saw in the exercise include:

aujourd'hui	*today*
le matin	*the morning*
boire	*to drink*
l'email (*masc.*), le mail/mèl, le courriel, le courrier électronique	*the email*

Also, notice that the exercise used the phrase neuf heures du matin (*9:00 in the morning*). You know that France often uses the 24-hour clock, so why do you need to specify du matin (*in the morning*, or literally, *of the morning*) after neuf heures, since *9:00 p.m.* would be vingt et une heures (21:00)?

Well, the 24-hour clock isn't always used, especially in casual conversation, so you will often hear phrases like du matin, de l'après-midi (*in the afternoon*), and du soir (*in the evening, at night*) added after the time to clarify.

3 Use what you've learned to discuss professions and schedules

💬 Bring It All Together

Now let's bring it all together and add a little bit more vocabulary and structure. Read and listen to the following monologue and pay careful attention to how the times and days of the week are being used.

▶ 9G Bring It All Together (CD 3, Track 10)

The actress performs Sunday at 8:00.
L'actrice joue dimanche à huit heures.

The (male) teacher teaches on Mondays.
Le professeur enseigne le lundi.

The (male) singer sings Saturday at 10:00.
Le chanteur chante samedi à dix heures.

The (female) lawyer doesn't sing.
L'avocate ne chante pas.

The salesman never arrives before 9:00.
Le vendeur n'arrive jamais avant neuf heures.

The (female) director always works on the weekend.
La directrice travaille toujours le week-end.
Ⅱ

Take It Further

9H Take It Further (CD 3, Track 11)

You just saw a few examples of times and days being used in sentences. To say that something happens *at* a particular time, use the preposition à:

J'arrive à huit heures et demie.
I arrive at half past eight.

To say that something happens *on* a particular day, just say that day, as in:

Nous arrivons lundi.
We're arriving on Monday.

To say that something happens in general, use le:

Vous allez à l'école le lundi et le mercredi.
You go to school Mondays and Wednesdays.

Finally, don't forget that you can negate a verb by putting ne (n') and pas around it:

je ne voyage pas	I don't travel
elle n'étudie pas	she doesn't study

If you use jamais instead of pas (in other words, if you use ne... jamais), that means *never*:

elle n'étudie jamais
she never studies

The opposite is *toujours*:

elle étudie toujours
she always studies

You also saw two new professions:

| le directeur/la directrice | *the director, the manager (male/female)* |
| le vendeur/la vendeuse | *the salesman/the saleswoman* |

Notice that the endings used in the two professions above (-eur/-rice, -eur/
-euse) correspond with some of the endings you saw in Grammar Builder 1.

Finally, you also got a good chance to review the verb *arriver* (*to arrive, to get
somewhere*), which you first saw at the end of Lesson 8.

✎ Work Out 2

 9I Work Out 2 (CD 3, Track 12) for different, audio-only exercises!

Let's practice professions. Match each profession to the correct French translation.

1. *female doctor*	a. avocat
2. *male lawyer*	b. vendeur
3. *male teacher*	c. médecin
4. *actor*	d. professeur
5. *saleswoman*	e. cuisinier
6. *writer*	f. vendeuse
7. *male cook*	g. acteur
8. *salesman*	h. écrivain

✎ Drive It Home

Now let's practice telling time. Fill in the blanks with heure or heures, and then read each sentence aloud.

1. Il est une _____ vingt. *(It's 1:20.)*

2. Il est trois _____ et quart. *(It's a quarter past three.)*

3. Il est vingt et une _____ quinze. *(It's 9:15 p.m.)*

4. Il est une _____ du matin. *(It's 1:00 in the morning.)*

5. Il est six _____ et demie du soir. *(It's half past six in the evening.)*

6. Il est vingt-trois _____ quarante. *(It's 11:40 p.m.)*

7. Il est quatorze _____ trente. *(It's 2:30 p.m.)*

8. Il est dix _____ cinquante-cinq. *(It's 10:55.)*

ANSWER KEY:
1 and 4 are heure and the rest are heures.

Parting Words

Félicitations !

You've finished the lesson! How did you do? You should now be able to:

☐ Talk about different professions (Still unsure? Go back to page 168)

☐ Say the days of the week (Still unsure? Go back to page 170)

☐ Tell time (Still unsure? Go back to page 171)

☐ Use what you've learned to discuss professions and schedules
(Still unsure? Go back to page 176)

Take It Further

▶ 9K Take It Further (CD 3, Track 14)

Now that you've learned *the days of the week*, or les jours de la semaine, you might want to know les mois de l'année (*the months of the year*). They're easy to understand:

MONTHS OF THE YEAR	
janvier	*January*
février	*February*
mars	*March*
avril	*April*
mai	*May*
juin	*June*
juillet	*July*
août	*August*
septembre	*September*
octobre	*October*
novembre	*November*
décembre	*December*

To say that something is *in* a particular month, say en (*in, to, into*), as in:

Mon anniversaire est en novembre.
My birthday is in November.

Seasons might come in handy, too:

au printemps*	in (the) spring
en été	in (the) summer
en automne	in (the) fall (in autumn)
en hiver	in (the) winter

* As you can see, you use en with all of the seasons except printemps, where you have to use au. Also note that all of the seasons are masculine nouns.

So you could say:

Il fait froid en hiver.	It's cold in winter.
Il fait chaud en été.	It's hot in summer.
Il pleut au printemps.	It rains in the spring.
Il fait du vent en automne.	It's windy in fall.
(or Il y a du vent en automne.)	

As you can see, the verb faire, which means *to do* and also *to make*, is often used in place of *to be* when talking about the weather in French:

Il fait froid.	It's cold.
Il fait chaud.	It's hot.
Il fait du vent.	It's windy.

Quel temps fait-il aujourd'hui ?
What is the weather today? (literally, What weather does it make today?)

Note that temps, pronounced [tah(m)], means both *weather* and *time*.

Don't forget to go to *www.livinglanguage.com/languagelab* to access your free online tools for this lesson: flashcards, games, and quizzes.

Word Recall

Now let's review vocabulary and grammar from previous lessons.

A. First, let's practice directions. Fill in the blanks with the phrases *Turn right., Turn left.,* or *Go straight ahead.* in French.

1. _____

2. _____

3. _____

B. Now let's describe someone's day. Fill in the blanks with the correct **il** form of the following verbs:

rentrer	aller
se coucher	prendre
regarder	

1. Il _____ son petit déjeuner à six heures et demie.

   (He has his breakfast at half past six.)

2. Il _____ au travail à sept heures.

   (He goes to work at 7:00.)

3. Il _____ à six heures moins le quart.

   (He goes home at a quarter to six.)

4. Il _____ la télé à vingt heures.

   (He watches TV at 8 p.m.)

5. Il _____ à vingt-trois heures.

   (He goes to bed at 11 p.m.)

ANSWER KEY:
A: 1. Allez tout droit. 2. Tournez à gauche. 3. Tournez à droite.
B: 1. prend; 2. va; 3. rentre; 4. regarde; 5. se couche

Lesson 10: Socializing

Leçon dix : la vie sociale

In this lesson, we'll talk about all the things that you like to do for fun.
You'll learn how to:

1 Talk about entertainment activities and sports
Make a suggestion
Say whether you like or dislike something
Say when you *finish* something and what you *choose* to do

2 Talk about what you *want* and what you *can* do

3 Use what you've learned to talk about
likes, dislikes, and going out

Commençons ! *Let's begin!*

1 Talk about entertainment activities and sports
Make a suggestion
Say whether you like or dislike something
Say when you *finish* something and what you *choose* to do

Vocabulary Builder 1

10B Vocabulary Builder 1 (CD 3, Track 16)

Let's go to the movies.	Allons au cinéma.
The film starts at 10 p.m. and finishes at midnight.	Le film commence à vingt-deux heures et finit à minuit.
Who's choosing the film?	Qui choisit le film ?
I have theatre tickets.	J'ai des places de théâtre.
We're going to a party tonight.	On va à une soirée ce soir.*
Let's go dance!	Allons danser !
I love this (night)club!	J'adore cette boîte (de nuit) !
We're having dinner at a friend's house.	Nous dînons chez un ami.
I like soccer.	J'aime le football.**
Do you like swimming?	Aimes-tu la natation ?
I prefer tennis.	Je préfère le tennis.
I don't like horseback riding.	Je n'aime pas l'équitation.

* Ce soir literally means *this evening* but it is also commonly used to mean *tonight*.

** Note that football (*soccer*) is often shortened to just foot in French, as you saw earlier in this course with stade de foot (*soccer stadium*).

✎ Vocabulary Practice 1

Now let's practice what you just learned. As always, fill in the blanks with the correct French translations, and feel free to use a dictionary or the glossary if you need to.

Make sure to include the appropriate definite article (la, le, l') before each sport.
If the definite article is l', remember to write down the gender as well.

(Hint: the French word for *ticket* is feminine.)

the film _____

a ticket _____

a party _____

this evening, tonight _____

a (night)club _____

soccer _____

swimming _____

tennis _____

horseback riding _____

ANSWER KEY:
le film (*the film*); une place (*a ticket*); une soirée (*a party*); ce soir (*this evening, tonight*); une boîte
(de nuit) (*a [night]club*); le foot(ball) (*soccer*); la natation (*swimming*); le tennis (*tennis*); l'équitation
(*f.*) (*horseback riding*)

Grammar Builder 1
▶ 10C Grammar Builder 1 (CD 3, Track 17)

There are a few things worth mentioning.

You can make a suggestion with the -ons form of a verb, so:

Allons... !	Let's go ... !
Sortons... !	Let's go out ... !

You also saw quite a few ways of expressing what you like or dislike:

| j'aime | I like |
| je n'aime pas | I don't like |

You can ask what someone else likes with:

| aimes-tu... ? | do you like ... ? |
| est-ce que tu aimes... ? | do you like ... ? |

Of course, you can be more polite by asking:

| aimez-vous... ? | do you like ... ? |
| est-ce que vous aimez... ? | do you like ... ? |

If you really *love* something, you can say j'adore, and je préfère means *I prefer*.

You also saw two examples of verbs that end in -ir in the infinitive: finir (*to finish*) and choisir (*to choose*). The conjugation of -ir verbs is a bit different from -er verbs. The singular forms *sound* the same (note the phonetics):

FINIR *(TO FINISH)* **AND** CHOISIR *(TO CHOOSE)*		
je finis	zhuh fee-nee	I finish
je choisis	zhuh shwah-zee	I choose
tu finis	tew fee-nee	you finish (familiar)
tu choisis	tew shwah-zee	you choose (familiar)
il ou elle finit	eel/ehl fee-nee	he or she finishes
il ou elle choisit	eel/ehl shwah-zee	he or she chooses

But in spelling, the je and tu forms end in -is, and the il/elle form ends in -it.

In the plural, these verbs take the same endings as -er verbs—that's -ons, -ez, and the silent -ent—but -iss is inserted first. So you have:

FINIR *(TO FINISH)* **AND** CHOISIR *(TO CHOOSE)*	
nous finissons	*we finish*
nous choisissons	*we choose*
vous finissez	*you finish (polite/plural)*
vous choisissez	*you choose (polite/plural)*
ils ou elles finissent	*they finish (masc. or fem.)*
ils ou elles choisissent	*they choose (masc. or fem.)*

Take It Further

You also saw two new -er verbs in Vocabulary Builder 1:

danser	*to dance*
dîner	*to dine, to have dinner*

And let's look at the infinitive forms of the verbs discussed in Grammar Builder 1:

sortir	*to go out, to leave*
aimer	*to like, to love*
adorer	*to love, to adore*
préférer	*to prefer*

Note that **sortir** is an irregular **-ir** verb, so it is not formed in the same way as **finir** and **choisir**. Fortunately, it's still pretty straightforward:

SORTIR *(TO GO OUT, TO LEAVE)*	
je sors	*I go out*
tu sors	*you go out (familiar)*
il sort	*he goes out*
elle sort	*she goes out*
nous sortons	*we go out*
vous sortez	*you go out (polite/plural)*
ils sortent	*they go out (masc.)*
elles sortent	*they go out (fem.)*

The verb **partir** (*to leave, to go away*) is conjugated in the same way.

Also, if you're going to talk about *going out, dining,* and *dancing,* then it's helpful to know the phrase **en ville**. You saw **en ville** used in Lesson 6 to mean *around town*. **La ville** means *the town* or *the city,* and **en** means *in/to/into,* so the phrase literally means *in/to/into town,* or *in/to/into the city,* but it can also be translated as *around town,* depending on the context.

Allons en ville !
Let's go into town!

Nous dînons en ville.
We're having dinner in the city.

Finally, you saw the new word **chez** in Vocabulary Builder 1. You'll learn more about **chez** later on in the lesson.

2 Talk about what you *want* and what you *can* do

Vocabulary Builder 2

▶ 10D Vocabulary Builder 2 (CD 3, Track 18)

I want ...	Je veux...
I want to go to the movies.	Je veux aller au cinéma.
Do you want to go to a party with me?	Veux-tu aller à une soirée avec moi ?
I like to go out to clubs. (I like to go out clubbing.)	J'aime sortir en boîte.
We want to go to the park.	Nous voulons aller au parc.
He wants to go to a (female) friend's house.	Il veut aller chez une amie.
The girls want to play soccer.	Les filles veulent jouer au foot.
I don't want to play tennis.	Je ne veux pas jouer au tennis.
We can go horseback riding. (literally, We can do horseback riding.)	Nous pouvons faire de l'équitation.
I can go swimming. (literally, I can do swimming.)	Je peux faire de la natation.
You can choose the restaurant.	Tu peux choisir le restaurant.

✎ Vocabulary Practice 2

Fill in the blanks with the correct French translations. Don't forget to use a dictionary or the glossary if you need to.

to go out to clubs, to go out clubbing _____

to go to the park _____

to play soccer _____

to play tennis _____

to go horseback riding _____

to go swimming _____

ANSWER KEY:

sortir en boîte (*to go out to clubs, to go out clubbing*); aller au parc (*to go to the park*); jouer au foot (*to play soccer*); jouer au tennis (*to play tennis*); faire de l'équitation (*to go horseback riding*); faire de la natation (*to go swimming*)

Grammar Builder 2

▶ 10E Grammar Builder 2 (CD 3, Track 19)

You've just seen some examples of the verbs vouloir (*to want*) and pouvoir (*can, to be able*). Both of these verbs can be used with another verb in the infinitive, so:

je veux rester	I want to stay
je peux rester	I can stay (I am able to stay)

These verbs are irregular, but a lot of the forms are pronounced in the same way (note the phonetics below). The conjugation of vouloir is:

VOULOIR (TO WANT)		
je veux	zhuh vuh	I want
tu veux	tew vuh	you want (familiar)
il veut	eel vuh	he wants
elle veut	ehl vuh	she wants
nous voulons	noo voo-loh(n)	we want
vous voulez	voo voo-lay	you want (polite/plural)
ils veulent	eel vuhl	they want (masc.)
elles veulent	ehl vuhl	they want (fem.)

The conjugation of **pouvoir** is:

POUVOIR (CAN, TO BE ABLE TO)		
je peux	zhuh puh	I can
tu peux	tew puh	you can (familiar)
il peut	eel puh	he can
elle peut	ehl puh	she can
nous pouvons	noo poo-voh(n)	we can
vous pouvez	voo poo-vay	you can (polite/plural)
ils peuvent	eel puhv	they can (masc.)
elles peuvent	ehl puhv	they can (fem.)

Notice that you can also use the verbs **aimer**, **adorer**, and **préférer** with other infinitives, just like **vouloir** and **pouvoir**. So, you can say:

J'aime aller au cinéma.	I like to go to the movies.
J'adore aller au cinéma.	I love to go to the movies.
Je préfère aller au cinéma.	I prefer to go to the movies.
Je veux aller au cinéma.	I want to go to the movies.
Je peux aller au cinéma.	I can go to the movies. (I am able to go to the movies.)

Finally, notice that **chez** is used to mean *at someone's house* or *place*, so:

chez mes amis	at my friends' house
chez Marc	at Marc's house
chez moi	at my place (at home, at my home)

✎ Work Out 1

Let's practice! Try to translate the following paragraph using what you've learned so far. The only phrase you haven't seen yet is:

tous les + day of the week in the plural

For example: **tous les lundis** (*every Monday*), **tous les mercredis** (*every Wednesday*), etc.

▶ 10F Work Out 1 (CD 3, Track 20). Listen to the audio to practice pronouncing the following paragraph. The audio also includes the English translation, so try to translate the paragraph below first before listening.

Voici Camille. Camille est sportive. Elle aime jouer au tennis. Elle n'aime pas le cinéma. Jean préfère aller au théâtre. Jean va en ville tous les samedis. Jean va chez un ami. Ils adorent sortir en boîte.

_____

_____

_____

_____

_____

⑪

ANSWER KEY:
Here is Camille. Camille is athletic. She likes to play tennis. She doesn't like the movies/movie theater. Jean prefers to go to the theater. Jean goes to town (into town, to/into the city) every Saturday. Jean goes to a (male) friend's house. They love to go out to clubs/to go out clubbing.

3 Use what you've learned to talk about likes, dislikes, and going out

🔊 Bring It All Together

Now let's bring it all together and add a little bit more vocabulary and structure. Read and listen to the following dialogue between two new friends.

▶ 10G Bring It All Together (CD 3, Track 21)

A: *Hi, I'm Léon. I am athletic. And you?*
Salut, je suis Léon. Je suis sportif. Et toi ?

B: *No, I prefer the theater. I like movies and museums, too.*
Non, moi je préfère le théâtre. J'aime aussi le cinéma et les musées.

A: *Me too, I like museums!*
Moi aussi, j'aime les musées !

B: *Do you want to come with me?*
Veux-tu venir avec moi ?

A: *Okay.*
D'accord.

B: *After, there's a party at my friend's house. All my friends are coming.*
Après, il y a une fête chez mon ami. Tous mes amis viennent.

A: *Perfect. Let's go!*
Parfait. Allons-y !

⏸

Take It Further

▶ 10H Take It Further (CD 3, Track 22)

You saw one more common verb. That's the (irregular) verb **venir** (to come). The forms are:*

VENIR *(TO COME)*	
je viens	I come
tu viens	you come (familiar)
il vient	he comes
elle vient	she comes
nous venons	we come
vous venez	you come (polite/plural)
ils viennent	they come (masc.)
elles viennent	they come (fem.)

* Note that the verbs **revenir** (to come back, to return) and **devenir** (to become) are conjugated like **venir**.

You can say, for example:

Je veux venir avec toi.
I want to come with you.

Notice that you use the pronoun **toi** (*you, familiar*) after **avec** (*with*). You could also say:

avec moi	with me
avec lui	with him
avec elle	with her

avec nous	with us
avec vous	with you (polite/plural)
avec eux	with them (masc.)
avec elles	with them (fem.)

These are good phrases to know when you're making plans:

Tu veux venir au cinéma avec nous ce soir ?	Do you want to come to the movies with us tonight?
Non, je ne veux pas aller à la soirée avec eux.	No, I don't want to go to the party with them.

Note that moi, toi, lui, etc. can also be used for emphasis, as in:

Non, moi je préfère le théâtre.
No, I prefer the theater.

This literally means *No, me I prefer the theater*, emphasizing that *I* prefer the theater, unlike *you*. Sometimes this type of emphasis is used in English as well, mainly in casual conversation: *You like playing sports, but me, I like the theater.*

You also saw the following new words:

la fête	the party, the festival, the holiday
parfait/parfaite	perfect
d'accord	okay, all right (literally, of agreement)

And remember that **tous les samedis** means *every Saturday* and **tous mes amis** means *all my friends*? Well, **tous** is actually the masculine plural form of **tout**, which means *all* or *every*. Here are all of the forms of **tout**:

masculine singular	tout
feminine singular	toute
masculine plural	tous
feminine plural	toutes

✎ Work Out 2

▶ 10I Work Out 2 (CD 3, Track 23) for different, audio-only exercises!

Let's do some basic practice of the important verb **venir**. Fill in the following table:

I come	
you come (familiar)	
he comes	
she comes	
we come	
you come (polite/plural)	
they come (masc.)	
they come (fem.)	

ANSWER KEY:
je viens; tu viens; il vient; elle vient; nous venons (on vient); vous venez; ils viennent; elles viennent

✎ Drive It Home

A. Let's practice making suggestions. Conjugate each verb in parentheses in the **nous** form.

1. _____ (aller) au cinéma !

   (Let's go to the movies/the movie theater!)

2. _____ (sortir) ce soir ! *(Let's go out tonight!)*

3. _____ (faire) de l'équitation ! *(Let's go horseback riding!)*

4. _____ (jouer) au tennis ! *(Let's play tennis!)*

5. _____ (regarder) le télé ! *(Let's watch television!)*

6. _____ (prendre) le métro ! *(Let's take the subway!)*

B. Now fill in the blanks with the correct form of the verb choisir *(to choose)*.

1. Je _____ le film. *(I choose the film.)*

2. Tu _____ le film. *(You choose the film.)*

3. Il _____ le film. *(He chooses the film.)*

4. Elle _____ le film. *(She chooses the film.)*

5. Nous _____ le film. *(We choose the film.)*

6. Vous _____ le film. *(You choose the film.)*

7. Ils _____ le film. *(They choose the film.)*

8. Elles _____ le film. *(They choose the film.)*

C. Fill in the blanks with the correct form of the verb vouloir (*to want*).

1. Je _____ sortir en boîte ce soir.

   (*I want to go out clubbing tonight.*)

2. _____-tu sortir en boîte ce soir ?

   (*Do you want to go out clubbing tonight?*)

3. Il _____ sortir en boîte ce soir.

   (*He wants to go out clubbing tonight.*)

4. Elle ne _____ pas sortir en boîte ce soir.

   (*She doesn't want to go out clubbing tonight.*)

5. Nous _____ sortir en boîte ce soir.

   (*We want to go out clubbing tonight.*)

6. _____-vous sortir en boîte ce soir ?

   (*Do you want to go out clubbing tonight?*)

7. Ils ne _____ pas sortir en boîte ce soir ?

   (*They don't want to go out clubbing tonight?*)

8. Est-ce qu'elles _____ sortir en boîte ce soir ?

   (*Do they want to go out clubbing tonight?*)

ANSWER KEY:
A: 1. Allons; 2. Sortons; 3. Faisons; 4. Jouons; 5. Regardons; 6. Prenons
B: 1. choisis; 2. choisis; 3. choisit; 4. choisit; 5. choisissons; 6. choisissez; 7. choisissent; 8. choisissent
C: 1. veux; 2. Veux; 3. veut; 4. veut; 5. voulons; 6. Voulez; 7. veulent; 8. veulent

Parting Words

You've learned the basic vocabulary you need to talk about some recreational activities. You should now be able to:

☐ Talk about entertainment activities and **les sports** (*masc.*) (*sports*) (Still unsure? Go back to page 185)

☐ Make a suggestion (Still unsure? Go back to page 186)

☐ Say whether you like or dislike something (Still unsure? Go back to page 187)

☐ Say when you *finish* something and what you *choose* to do (Still unsure? Go back to page 187)

☐ Talk about what you *want* and what you *can* do (Still unsure? Go back to page 191)

☐ Use what you've learned to talk about likes, dislikes, and going out (Still unsure? Go back to page 194)

Don't forget to go to *www.livinglanguage.com/languagelab* to access your free online tools for this lesson: flashcards, games, and quizzes.

Take It Further

▶ 10K Take It Further (CD 3, Track 25)

You may want to extend your vocabulary with some more popular activities:

le ski	*skiing*
l'alpinisme *(masc.)*	*climbing*
l'haltérophilie *(fem.)*	*weight lifting*
la course à pied	*running*
le patin à glace	*ice skating*
la voile	*sailing*
les jeux *(masc.)* électroniques	*electronic games*
la danse	*dancing*
la cuisine	*cooking*
la moto	*motorcycling*
prendre un verre avec des amis	*having a drink with friends* *(to have a drink with friends)*

À votre santé ! *To your health!*

⏸

And that brings us to the end of our last lesson! You can now test and practice what you've learned with the final Word Recall and self-graded quiz, followed by five conversational dialogues that will bring together the French you've seen so far.

Keep in mind that if you want to go back and review anything in the lessons at any time, you should always feel free to do so. Move at your own pace.

Bonne chance ! *Good luck!*

Word Recall

Now let's review vocabulary and grammar from previous lessons.

A. Remember how to tell time in French? Let's practice. Fill in the blanks below with the time indicated on each clock. Make sure to write each time out in full in French, and start with *It is ...* (but in French, of course!). Don't worry about the 24-hour clock.

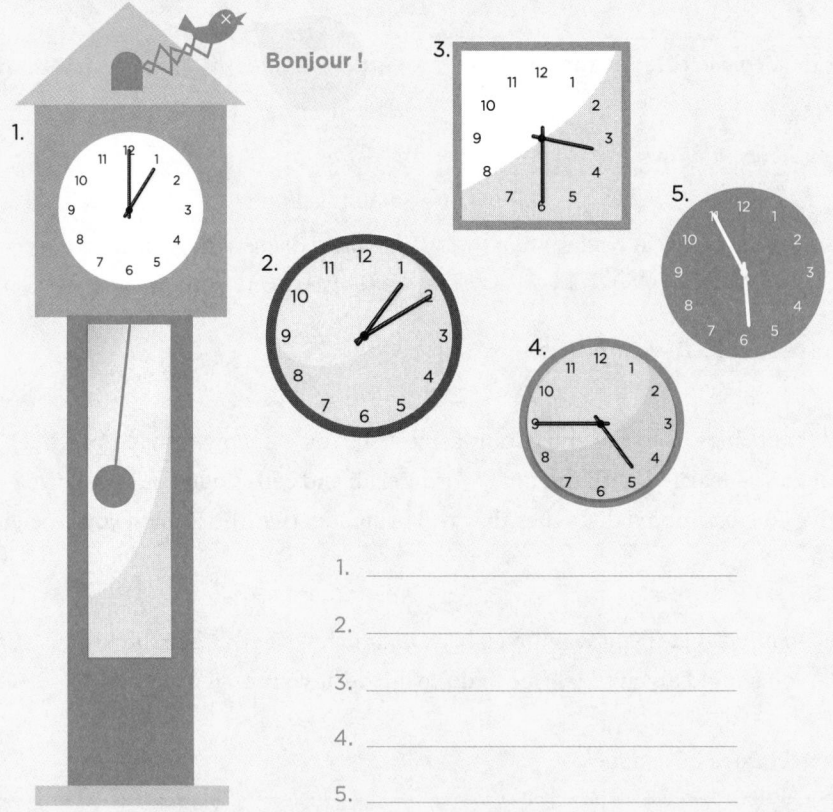

1. _____

2. _____

3. _____

4. _____

5. _____

B. Now let's practice verbs. Match each French verb to its correct English translation:

1. commencer	a. *to want*
2. parler	b. *to show*
3. manger	c. *to start, to begin*
4. habiter	d. *to ask*
5. demander	e. *to understand*
6. vouloir	f. *to think*
7. donner	g. *to give*
8. écouter	h. *to sing*
9. penser	i. *to listen*
10. chanter	j. *to speak*
11. comprendre	k. *to live*
12. montrer	l. *to eat*

ANSWER KEY:
A: 1. Il est une heure. 2. Il est une heure dix. 3. Il est trois heures trente./Il est trois heures et demie. 4. Il est quatre heures quarante-cinq./Il est cinq heures moins le quart. 5. Il est cinq heures cinquante-cinq./Il est six heures moins cinq.
B: 1. c; 2. j; 3. l; 4. k; 5. d; 6. a; 7. g; 8. i; 9. f; 10. h; 11. e; 12. b

Word Recall

Quiz 2

Petit Test 2

You've completed all ten lessons! Bravo ! (*Well done!*)

Now let's review! In this section you'll find a final quiz testing what you learned in Lessons 1-10. Once you've completed it, score yourself to see how well you've done. If you find that you need to go back and review, please do so before continuing on to the Review Dialogues and comprehension questions.

A. Match the French expressions on the left to the correct English translations on the right.

1. Ça va.	a. *Good-bye.*
2. Enchanté.	b. *Hi.*
3. Bonsoir.	c. *Pleased to meet you.*
4. Salut.	d. *Good evening.*
5. Au revoir.	e. *I'm fine.*

B. Rewrite the following times using numbers instead of words. For example, you might write 0h30, 2h25, 18h12, etc.

1. **Il est cinq heures quarante-sept.** _____

2. **Il est vingt-deux heures trente.** _____

3. **Il est minuit et quart.** _____

4. **Il est trois heures moins le quart.** _____

5. **Il est dix-huit heures cinquante-trois.** _____

C. Fill in the blanks with the appropriate French adjective in the correct form.

1. **Ce plat n'est pas bon ; ce plat est** _____ .
   (This dish isn't good; it's bad.)

2. **Ma maison est** _____ **; il y a vingt-cinq pièces.**
   (My house is big; there are 25 rooms.)

3. **Mon grand-père a quatre-vingt-dix-huit ans. Il est** _____ .
   (My grandfather is 98 years old. He is old.)

4. **Elle fait de la natation et de l'équitation, et elle joue au tennis. Elle est**

   _____ !

   (She goes swimming and horseback riding, and she plays tennis. She's athletic!)

5. **Le drapeau américain est** _____ **, blanc et** _____ .
   (The American flag is red, white, and blue.)

D. Conjugate the verbs in parentheses in the correct form and then translate each sentence into English.

1. Nous _____ (*venir*) à la soirée.

2. Vous _____ (*fait*) le ménage.

3. Ils _____ (*prendre*) le bus.

4. Elles _____ (*aller*) au restaurant.

5. Je _____ (*pouvoir*) aller à Paris.

E. Conjugate the following reflexive verbs in the correct form and then translate each sentence into English.

1. Vous _____ (*s'appeler*) Christine.

2. Elle _____ (*se laver*) à sept heures.

3. Je _____ (*s'habiller*) à huit heures.

4. Tu _____ (*s'appeler*) Jean.

5. Nous _____ (*se coucher*) à vingt-deux heures.

F. Rewrite the following sentences in the plural based on the English translations provided.

1. **Tu es américaine.** *(You are American.)*

   _____

   (You [plural] are American.)

2. **Cette chanteuse est petite !** *(That singer is short!)*

   _____

   (Those singers are short!)

3. **Ma nièce n'a pas son vélo.** *(My niece doesn't have her bike.)*

   _____

   (My nieces don't have their bikes.)

4. **Tu as une place de théâtre.** *(You have a theater ticket.)*

   _____

   (You [plural] have theater tickets.)

5. **La vieille femme a un livre.** *(The old woman has a book.)*

   _____

   (The old women have a lot of books.)

How Did You Do?

Give yourself a point for every correct answer, then use the following key to determine whether or not you're ready to move on:

0-11 points: It's probably best to go back and study the lessons again. Take as much time as you need to. Review the vocabulary lists and carefully read through each Grammar Builder section.

12-24 points: If the questions you missed were in sections A, B, or C, you may want to review the vocabulary again; if you missed answers mostly in sections D, E, or F, check the Grammar Builder sections to make sure you have your conjugations and other grammar basics down.

25-30 points: Feel free to move on to the Review Dialogues! Great job!

 Points

Review Dialogues
Bienvenue ! *Welcome!*

Here's your chance to practice everything you've mastered in ten lessons of *Living Language Essential French* with these five everyday dialogues. Each dialogue is followed by comprehension questions.

To practice your pronunciation, don't forget to listen to the audio! As always, look for ⏵ and ⏸. You'll hear the dialogue in French first, then in French and English. Next, for practice, you'll do some role play by taking part in the conversation yourself!

Have fun!

Dialogue 1
TALKING ABOUT THE FAMILY

First, try to read (and listen to!) the whole dialogue in French. Then read and listen to the French and English together. How much did you understand? Next, take part in the role play exercise in the audio and answer the comprehension questions here in the book.

Note that there will be words and phrases in these dialogues that you haven't seen yet. This is because we want to give you the feel of a real French conversation. As a result, feel free to use your dictionary or the glossary if you're unclear about anything you see.

▶ French Only – 12A Dialogue 1 French (CD 3, Track 27); French and English – 12B Dialogue 1 French and English (CD 3, Track 28); Role Play Exercise – 12C Dialogue 1 Exercise (CD 3, Track 29)

Corinne :   J'ai une petite famille. Et toi, Jean-Louis ?
              I have a small family. How about you, Jean-Louis?
              (And you, Jean-Louis?)

Jean-Louis : Moi, j'ai une grande famille.
              Me, I have a big family.

Corinne :   Vous êtes combien ?
              How many are you?

Jean-Louis : Il y a sept personnes dans ma famille.
              There are seven people in my family. (not including Jean-Louis)

Corinne :   Combien de frères as-tu ?
              How many brothers do you have?

Jean-Louis : J'ai deux frères.
              I have two brothers.

Corinne :   Et combien de sœurs ?
              And how many sisters?

Jean-Louis : J'ai trois sœurs. Avec moi, ça fait six enfants. Avec maman et
              papa, ça fait huit personnes en tout.
              *I have three sisters. With me, that's six children. With Mom and
              Dad, that's eight people in all.*

Corinne :   Oui, en effet, c'est une grande famille.
              Yes, really, that is a big family.

Jean-Louis : Et dans ta famille, il y a combien de personnes ?
              And in your family, how many people are there?

Corinne :   Il y a quatre personnes : papa, maman, et moi. Je n'ai pas de
              frères ou de sœurs. Je suis fille unique.
              *There are four people: Dad, Mom, and me. I don't have any brothers
              or sisters. I'm an only child.*

Jean-Louis :   **Mais qui est la quatrième personne ?**
            But who's the fourth person?

Corinne :   **C'est ma grand-mère. Elle habite chez nous.**
            That's my grandmother. She lives with us. (She lives at our house.)

Jean-Louis :   **Que fait ton père ?**
            What does your father do?

Corinne :   **Il est musicien. Et ton père ?**
            He's a musician. And your father?

Jean-Louis :   **Mon père et ma mère sont profs.**
            My father and my mother are professors.

Corinne :   **Ma mère est prof aussi, à l'université.**
            My mother is also a professor, at the university.

Jean-Louis :   **Quelle coïncidence !**
            What a coincidence!

✎ Dialogue 1 Practice

Now let's check your comprehension of the dialogue and review what you learned in Lessons 1-10 with the following exercises. Ready?

A. You saw a few new words for members of the family in the dialogue. What are they?

1. _____ *(Mom)*

2. _____ *(Dad)*

3. _____ *(only child, female)*

And now let's review the other family vocabulary you saw. Don't forget to translate the definite articles!

4. _____ (the mother)

5. _____ (the father)

6. _____ (the brother)

7. _____ (the sister)

8. _____ (the children)

9. _____ (the grandmother)

10. _____ (the family)

B. In the dialogue, you saw the phrase avec moi (with me). Rewrite that phrase to match each of the English phrases below.

1. *with you (familiar)* _____

2. *with her* _____

3. *with them (masc.)* _____

4. *with us* _____

5. *with him* _____

C. You also saw a few new question words in the dialogue. Fill in the table below with the new question words:

how many	1.
what	2.

Now let's review the question words you learned earlier in the course. Fill in the table below with the correct French translations. If the question word has a masculine and feminine form, make sure to include both of them.

where	3.
which, what	4.
how	5.
who	6.
what	7.

ANSWER KEY:

A: 1. **maman**; 2. **papa**; 3. **fille unique**; 4. **la mère**; 5. **le père**; 6. **le frère**; 7. **la sœur**; 8. **les enfants**; 9. **la grand-mère**; 10. **la famille**

B: 1. **avec toi**; 2. **avec elle**; 3. **avec eux**; 4. **avec nous**; 5. **avec lui**

C: 1. **combien (de)**; 2. **que**; 3. **où**; 4. **quel/quelle**; 5. **comment**; 6. **qui**; 7. **qu'est-ce que**

🔊 Dialogue 2
THE NEW HOUSE

As with Dialogue 1, first read and listen to the whole dialogue in French. Then read and listen to the French and English together. How much did you understand? Next, do the role play in the audio as well as the comprehension exercises here in the book.

▶ French Only – 13A Dialogue 2 French (CD 3, Track 30); French and English – 13B Dialogue 2 French and English (CD 3, Track 31); Role Play Exercise – 13C Dialogue 2 Exercise (CD 3, Track 32)

Thierry :	**Salut, Naomi, bienvenue dans ma nouvelle maison !**
	Hi, Naomi, welcome (in)to my new house!
Naomi :	**Combien de pièces y a-t-il ?**
	How many rooms are there?

Thierry : Il y a neuf pièces. Veux-tu faire un tour de la maison ?

There are nine rooms. Do you want to take a tour of the house?

Naomi : Avec plaisir.

With pleasure.

Thierry : Voilà le salon, avec un canapé confortable, une vieille pendule et une grande télé.

Here's the living room, with a comfortable sofa, an old (grandfather) clock, and a large TV.

Naomi : Et ensuite...

And then ...

Thierry : Maintenant nous entrons dans la salle à manger, avec sa belle table et son lustre.

Now we enter (into) the dining room, with its beautiful table and its chandelier.

Naomi : C'est très joli. Et où est la cuisine ?

It's very nice. And where is the kitchen?

Thierry : La cuisine ? C'est tout droit. Entrons. Il y a un grand réfrigérateur et un micro-ondes.

The kitchen? It's straight ahead. Let's go in. (literally, Let's enter.)
There is a large refrigerator and a microwave (oven).

Naomi : Et par ici, qu'est-ce que c'est ?

And what is this way? (literally, And this way, what is this?)

Thierry : Voici la bibliothèque, ma pièce préférée. Il y a beaucoup de beaux livres, non ?

Here's the library, my favorite room. There are a lot of beautiful books, no?

Naomi : Oui. Quelle collection !

Yes. What a collection!

Thierry : Et maintenant, voyons les chambres. Il y en a trois.

And now, let's see the bedrooms. There are three of them.

Naomi : Chaque enfant a sa propre chambre ?

Each child has his or her own bedroom?

Thierry :	Oui, et ils ont chacun un ordinateur !
	Yes, and they each have a computer!
Naomi :	Thierry, où sont les toilettes ?
	Thierry, where is the toilet?
Thierry :	À côté de ma chambre. Et la salle de bains aussi.
	Next to my bedroom. And the bathroom, too.*
Naomi :	Merci. Tu m'excuses un moment ?
	Thank you. Will you excuse me a moment?
Thierry :	Bien sûr.
	Of course.

⑪ * Note that, in France, the toilet and the bathroom (where you shower/take a bath and wash your hands) are typically separate rooms.

✎ Dialogue 2 Practice

In that dialogue, you saw a lot of vocabulary—both familiar and new—relating to rooms and objects in a house.

A. First, let's review the rooms in a house. Match the following French words to the correct English translations.

1. *the room*	a. la chambre (à coucher)
2. *the toilet*	b. la pièce
3. *the living room*	c. la salle à manger
4. *the kitchen*	d. la bibliothèque
5. *the bedroom*	e. la salle de bains
6. *the dining room*	f. les toilettes (fem.)
7. *the library*	g. la cuisine
8. *the bathroom*	h. le salon

B. Now let's review the objects in a house. Match the following French words to the correct English translations.

1. *the sofa*	a. le micro-ondes
2. *the chandelier*	b. la pendule
3. *the computer*	c. le canapé
4. *the microwave (oven)*	d. la télé
5. *the TV*	e. la table
6. *the refrigerator*	f. le lustre
7. *the grandfather clock*	g. le réfrigérateur
8. *the table*	h. l'ordinateur (masc.)
9. *the book*	i. le livre

ANSWER KEY:
A: 1. b; 2. f; 3. h; 4. g; 5. a; 6. c; 7. d; 8. e
B: 1. c; 2. f; 3. h; 4. a; 5. d; 6. g; 7. b; 8. e; 9. i

Dialogue 3
GETTING AROUND TOWN

Remember, feel free to use your dictionary or the glossary to look up any words you don't know.

French Only – 14A Dialogue 3 French (CD 3, Track 33); French and English – 14B Dialogue 3 French and English (CD 3, Track 34); Role Play Exercise – 14C Dialogue 3 Exercise (CD 3, Track 35)

Colette :	**Vous êtes perdu ?**
	Are you lost?

Omar : Oui, mademoiselle. Où est la pharmacie, s'il vous plaît ?
Yes, miss. Where's the drugstore, please?

Colette : La pharmacie ? Il faut traverser le pont.
The drugstore? You have to cross the bridge.

Omar : C'est près d'ici ?
Is it near here?

Colette : Non, c'est assez loin. Après le pont, il faut prendre la première rue à droite et descendre jusqu'au boulevard...
No, it's quite far. After the bridge, you have to take the first street on the right and go down until the boulevard ...

Omar : Oui, et au boulevard ?
Yes, and at the boulevard?

Colette : Vous traversez le boulevard et vous montez jusqu'au parc.
You cross the boulevard and you go up to the park.

Omar : C'est tout ?
Is that all?

Colette : Non, vous traversez le parc et vous arrivez devant une grande statue...
No, you cross the park and you arrive in front of a big statue ...

Omar : Une grande statue, oui... Et puis ?
A big statue, yes ... And then?

Colette : Vous passez à gauche de la statue, et la pharmacie est dans la quatrième rue à gauche.
You go (pass) to the left of the statue, and the drugstore is on (literally, in) the fourth street to the left.

Omar : Ah, enfin ! C'est bien compliqué. Merci, mademoiselle.
Oh, finally! It sure is complicated. Thank you, miss.

Colette : Je vous en prie, monsieur.
You're welcome, sir.

Omar : Mais j'ai aussi une lettre à mettre à la poste. Où est la poste, s'il vous plaît ?
But I also have a letter to mail. Where's the post office, please?

Colette :	La poste? C'est tout près d'ici.
	The post office? It's very close to here.
Omar :	Super ! Dans quelle direction ?
	Great! In which direction?
Colette :	Vous allez tout droit. Elle est devant vous.
	You go straight ahead. It's in front of you.
Omar :	Alors, ça, c'est moins compliqué !
	Now, that's less complicated! (literally, Well, that, that's less complicated!)

✎ Dialogue 3 Practice

You saw a variety of verbs in that dialogue, so for this practice section, let's review verbs.

A. Each phrase below is from the dialogue and contains one verb. Identify the verb and then write its infinitive form in the blank space provided, followed by the English translation. (There may be several English translations for a verb; just write down one.)

For example, if the phrase was il fait froid, you would write down faire (*to do*).

1. vous êtes perdu _____

2. où est la pharmacie _____

3. prendre la première rue à droite _____

4. vous traversez le parc _____

5. vous arrivez devant une grande statue _____

6. j'ai aussi une lettre _____

7. vous allez tout droit_____

B. Now conjugate each of those infinitives in the tu form. For example, if the verb was faire, you would write tu fais.

1. _____

2. _____

3. _____

4. _____

5. _____

6. _____

7. _____

ANSWER KEY:
A: 1. être (*to be*); 2. être (*to be*); 3. prendre (*to take*); 4. traverser (*to cross, to go across*); 5. arriver (*to arrive, to get somewhere, to reach*); 6. avoir (*to have*); 7. aller (*to go*)
B: 1. tu es; 2. tu es; 3. tu prends; 4. tu traverses; 5. tu arrives; 6. tu as; 7. tu vas

🎧 Dialogue 4
AT A RESTAURANT

How are you doing so far? Ready to try another dialogue? (Hint: le serveur means *the waiter.*)

▶ French Only – 15A Dialogue 4 French (CD 3, Track 36); French and English – 15B Dialogue 4 French and English (CD 3, Track 37); Role Play Exercise – 15C Dialogue 4 Exercise (CD 3, Track 38)

Élodie :	Monsieur, apportez-moi le menu, s'il vous plaît.
	Sir, bring me the menu, please.
Le serveur :	Voilà, madame.
	Here it is, madam.
Élodie :	Quelle est la soupe du jour ?
	What's the soup of the day?
Le serveur :	C'est la bisque de homard, madame.
	It's lobster bisque, madam.
Élodie :	Et quels sont les hors-d'œuvre ?
	And what are the appetizers?
Le serveur :	Nous avons des crudités ou du pâté maison.
	We have crudités or homemade pâté.
Élodie :	Hmm, vous avez aussi de la soupe à l'oignon ?
	Hmm, do you also have onion soup?
Le serveur :	Oui, madame, et elle est excellente !
	Yes, madam, and it is excellent!
Élodie :	Alors, donnez-moi une soupe à l'oignon.
	Then, give me an onion soup.
Le serveur :	Et comme plat principal, madame ?
	And as a main dish, madam?
Élodie :	Donnez-moi une côte de bœuf avec des pommes de terre.
	Give me a beef rib (bone-in ribeye) with potatoes.
Le serveur :	Et comme boisson ?
	And as a drink?
Élodie :	Du vin rouge, s'il vous plaît.
	Some red wine, please.
Le serveur :	Et pour le dessert, madame ?
	And for dessert, madam?
Élodie :	Une mousse au chocolat et un café-crème.
	A chocolate mousse and a coffee with cream.

Le serveur :	Voilà.
	Here it is.
Élodie :	Merci, monsieur. Apportez-moi l'addition, s'il vous plaît.
	Thank you, sir. Bring me the check, please.

Ⅱ

✎ Dialogue 4 Practice

A. Vrai (*true*) or faux (*false*)? Next to each sentence, write down V for vrai or F for faux.

1. **Les hors-d'œuvre : Élodie choisit les crudités.** _____

2. **Le plat principal : Élodie mange de la viande.** _____

3. **La boisson : Élodie veut du vin.** _____

4. **Le dessert : Élodie n'aime pas le dessert.** _____

B. Below are some of the vocabulary words you saw in the dialogue. Next to each one, write **un** or **une** and then translate the phrase into English.

1. _____ soupe _____

2. _____ addition _____

3. _____ pomme de terre _____

4. _____ plat _____

5. _____ café-crème _____

6. _____ mousse au chocolate _____

7. _____ menu _____

8. _____ côte de bœuf _____

ANSWER KEY:

A: 1. F (No, she chooses onion soup, not crudités, as an appetizer); 2. V (Yes, she is eating meat for her main course); 3. V (Yes, she does want wine as her drink); 4. F (No, she does like dessert; she has a chocolate mousse and coffee with cream for dessert)

B: 1. une soupe (*one/a soup*); 2. une addition (*one/a check*); 3. une pomme de terre (*one/a potato*); 4. un plat (*one/a dish*); 5. un café-crème (*one/a coffee with cream*); 6. une mousse au chocolat (*one/a chocolate mousse*); 7. un menu (*one/a menu*); 8. une côte de bœuf (*one/a beef rib, one/a bone-in ribeye*)

⌘ Dialogue 5
GOING TO THE MOVIES

Last one! You're almost done with *Essential French*, so let's talk about something fun: the movies. Enjoy!

▶ French Only – 16A Dialogue 5 French (CD 3, Track 39); French and English – 16B Dialogue 5 French and English (CD 3, Track 40); Role Play Exercise – 16C Dialogue 5 Exercise (CD 3, Track 41)

Joël :	**Allô, Liliane ?**
	Hello, Liliane?
Liliane :	**Oui, qui est à l'appareil ?**
	Yes, who is calling?
Joël :	**C'est Joël. Veux-tu venir au cinéma avec moi samedi soir ?**
	It's Joël. Do you want to come to the movies with me Saturday night?
Liliane :	**Oui, d'accord. Qu'est-ce qu'on donne ?**
	Yes, okay. What are they showing?
Joël :	**Le dernier film de Hugh Grant.**
	Hugh Grant's last (latest) film.
Liliane :	**Est-ce que c'est en version originale* ?**
	Is it in the original version?

Joël :	Oui, bien sûr, et il y a des sous-titres.
	Yes, of course, and there are subtitles.
Liliane :	Parfait. Je n'aime pas les films doublés.
	Perfect. I don't like dubbed movies.
Joël :	J'aime les comédies romantiques.
	I like romantic comedies.
Liliane :	Moi aussi. Et j'aime beaucoup Hugh Grant.
	Me too. And I like Hugh Grant a lot.
Joël :	J'aime aussi les films d'action et les films policiers.
	I also like action films and crime dramas.
Liliane :	Moi, je n'aime pas les films policiers.
	Me, I don't like crime dramas.
Joël :	Même pas avec Robert de Niro ?
	Not even with Robert de Niro?
Liliane :	Ah, si Robert de Niro joue dans le film, c'est différent. Et ce week-end, on va dîner ensemble avant le film ?
	Oh, if Robert de Niro is acting in the film, that's different. And this weekend, we'll have dinner together before the film?
Joël :	Oui. Il y a un nouveau restaurant vietnamien dans le coin.
	Yes. There's a new Vietnamese restaurant in the neighborhood.
Liliane :	Super. J'adore la nourriture vietnamienne.
	Super. I love Vietnamese food.

* In French, la version originale (*original version*)—commonly abbreviated v.o.—of a movie means that the film is in its original language and hasn't been dubbed into French (although it usually has French subtitles). On the other hand, v.f. (or la version française) means that the movie has been dubbed into French.

✎ Dialogue 5 Practice

A. Let's review adjectives, starting with the ones you saw in the dialogue. Fill in the table below with the masculine and feminine singular form of each adjective. If the adjective has two different masculine forms, make sure to include both of them.

MASCULINE SINGULAR	FEMININE SINGULAR	ENGLISH
1.		*original*
2.		*new*
3.		*Vietnamese*

Now let's review some of the other adjectives that you know. Fill in the table below.

MASCULINE SINGULAR	FEMININE SINGULAR	ENGLISH
4.		*beautiful, handsome*
5.		*old*
6.		*happy*
7.		*dear, expensive*

B. Translate the following phrases into English.

1. la comédie romantique _____

2. le film doublé _____

3. le film d'action _____

4. le film policier _____

5. les sous-titres _____

ANSWER KEY:
A: 1. original, originale; 2. nouveau/nouvel, nouvelle; 3. vietnamien, vietnamienne;
4. beau/bel, belle; 5. vieux/vieil, vieille; 6. heureux, heureuse; 7. cher, chère
B: 1. *the romantic comedy*; 2. *the dubbed movie/film*; 3. *the action movie/film*; 4. *the crime drama*;
5. *the subtitles*

You've come to the end of *Living Language Essential French*! Congratulations! We hope you've enjoyed your experience. If you bought *Complete French*, you can now continue on to *Intermediate French*. And of course, feel free to go back and review at any time if you need to.

For more information on other Living Language French courses and supplementary materials, visit www.livinglanguage.com.

Pronunciation Guide

Consonants

Note that the letter h can act as either a vowel or a consonant. See the end of the Pronunciation Guide for more information.

FRENCH	APPROXIMATE SOUND	PHONETIC SYMBOL	EXAMPLES
b, d, f, k, m, n, p, t, v, z	same as in English	same as in English	
ç	*s*	[s]	**français** [frah(n)-seh] (*French*)
c before a, o, u	*k*	[k]	**cave** [kahv] (*cellar*)
c before e, i, y	*s*	[s]	**cinéma** [see-nay-mah] (*movie theater*)
ch	*sh* sometimes *k*	[sh], [k]	**chaud** [shoh] (*hot*) **psychologie** [psee-koh-loh-zhee] (*psychology*)
g before a, o, u	*g* in *game*	[g]	**gâteau** [gah-toh] (*cake*)
g before e, i, y	*s* in *measure*	[zh]	**âge** [ahzh] (*age*)
gn	*ni* in *onion*	[ny]	**agneau** [ah-nyoh] (*lamb*)
j	*s* in *measure*	[zh]	**jeu** [zhuh] (*game*)
l	*l*	[l]	**lent** [lah(n)] (*slow*)
l when it's at the end of the word and follows i	*y* in *yes*	[y]	**fauteuil** [foh-tuhy] (*armchair*)
ll	*ll* in *ill*	[l]	**elle** [ehl] (*she*)

FRENCH	APPROXIMATE SOUND	PHONETIC SYMBOL	EXAMPLES
ll between i and e	y in *yes*	[y]	fille [feey] (*girl, daughter*)
qu, final q	k	[k]	qui [kee] (*who*), cinq [sa(n)k] (*five*)
r	pronounced in the back of the mouth, like a light gargling sound	[r]	Paris [pah-ree] (*Paris*)
s between vowels	z in *zebra*	[z]	maison [meh-zoh(n)] (*house*)
s at the beginning of a word or before/after a consonant	s	[s]	salle [sahl] (*hall, room*), course [koors] (*errand*)
ss	s	[s]	tasse [tahs] (*cup*)
th	t	[t]	thé [tay] (*tea*)
w	v	[v]	wagon-lit [vah-goh(n)-lee] (*sleeping car*)
x usually before a vowel	x in *exact*	[gz]	exact [ehg-zahkt] (*exact*)
x before a consonant or final e	x in *exterior*	[ks]	extérieur [ehks-tay-ree-uhr] (*outside*)

Keep in mind that most final consonants are silent in French, as with the -s in Paris [pah-ree] (*Paris*). However, there are five letters that are often (but not always) pronounced when final: c, f, l, q, and r.

French speakers also pronounce some final consonants when the next word begins with a vowel or silent h (see the end of the Pronunciation Guide for more information on the "silent h"). This is known as liaison [lyeh-zoh(n)] (*link*).

For example, the -s in nous [noo] (*we*) normally isn't pronounced. However, if it's followed by a word that begins with a vowel, such as allons [ah-loh(n)], then you do pronounce it: nous allons [noo zah-loh(n)] (*we go*). Notice that, in liaison, the s is pronounced *z* and it is "linked" to the following word: [zah-loh(n)].

Here's another example of liaison: un grand arbre [uh(n) grah(n) tahr-bruh] (*a big tree*). Normally, the -d in grand [grah(n)] is not pronounced, but, in liaison, it is pronounced *t* and linked to the following word.

Vowels

FRENCH	APPROXIMATE SOUND	PHONETIC SYMBOL	EXAMPLES
a, à, â	*a* in *father*	[ah]	laver [lah-vay] (*to wash*), à [ah] (*in, to, at*)
é, er, ez (end of a word), et	*ay* in *lay*	[ay]	été [ay-tay] (*summer*), aller [ah-lay] (*to go*), ballet [bah-lay] (*ballet*)
è, ê, ei, ai, aî	*e* in *bed*, with relaxed lips	[eh]	père [pehr] (*father*), forêt [foh-reh] (*forest*), faire [fehr] (*to do*)

FRENCH	APPROXIMATE SOUND	PHONETIC SYMBOL	EXAMPLES
e without an accent (and not combined with another vowel or r, z, t)	*a* in *above,* or *e* in *bed* with relaxed lips, or silent	[uh] or [eh] or n/a	le [luh] (*the*), belle [behl] (*beautiful*), danse [dah(n)s] (*dance*)
eu, œu followed by a consonant sound	*u* in *fur* with lips very rounded and loose	[uh]	cœur [kuhr] (*heart*)
eu, œu not followed by any sound	*u* in *fur* with lips very rounded and tight	[uh]	feu [fuh] (*fire*)
eille, ey	*ey* in *hey*	[ehy]	bouteille [boo-tehy] (*bottle*)
euille, œil	*a* in *above* + *y* in *yesterday*	[uhy]	œil [uhy] (*eye*)
i	*ee* in *beet*	[ee]	ici [ee-see] (*here*)
i plus vowel	*ee* in *beet* + *y* in *yesterday*	[y]	violon [vyoh-loh(n)] (*violin*)
o, au, eau, ô	*o* in *both*	[oh]	mot [moh] (*word*), eau [oh] (*water*), hôtel [oh-tehl] (*hotel*)
oi	*wa* in *watt*	[wah]	moi [mwah] (*me*)
ou	*oo* in *boot*	[oo]	vous [voo] (*you*)
ou before a vowel	*w* in *week*	[w]	ouest [wehst] (*west*), oui [wee] (*yes*)
oy	*wa* in *watt* + *y* in *yesterday*	[wah-y]	foyer [fwah-yay] (*home*)

FRENCH	APPROXIMATE SOUND	PHONETIC SYMBOL	EXAMPLES
u	keep your lips rounded as you pronounce *ee* in *beet*	[ew]	**tu** [tew] (*you*)
ui	*wee* in *week*	[wee]	**lui** [lwee] (*he, him, her*)

Nasal Vowels

FRENCH	APPROXIMATE SOUND	PHONETIC SYMBOL	EXAMPLES
an/en or am/em	*a* in *balm,* pronounced through both the mouth and the nose	[ah(n)] or [ah(m)]	**France** [frah(n)s] (*France*), **entrer** [ah(n)-tray] (*to enter*), **emmener** [ah(m)-muh-nay] (*to take along*)
in/yn/ain/ein or im/ym/aim/eim	*a* in *mad,* pronounced through both the mouth and the nose	[a(n)] or [a(m)]	**vin** [va(n)] (*wine*), **vain** [va(n)] (*vain*), **sympa** [sa(m)-pah] (*cool, nice, good*), **faim** [fa(m)] (*hunger*)
ien	*ee* in *beet* + *y* in *yesterday* + nasal *a* in *mad*	[ya(n)]	**rien** [rya(n)] (*nothing*)
oin	*w* + nasal *a* in *mad*	[wa(n)]	**loin** [lwa(n)] (*far*)

FRENCH	APPROXIMATE SOUND	PHONETIC SYMBOL	EXAMPLES
on or om	*o* in *song*, pronounced through both the mouth and the nose	[oh(n)] or [oh(m)]	bon [boh(n)] (*good*), tomber [toh(m)-bay] (*to fall*)
ion	*ee* in *beet* + *y* in *yesterday* + nasal *o* in *song*	[yoh(n)]	station [stah-syoh(n)] (*station*)
un or um	*u* in *lung*, pronounced through both the mouth and the nose	[uh(n)] or [uh(m)]	un [uh(n)] (*one, a/an*), parfum [pahr-fuh(m)] (*perfume*)

The Letter H

In French, the letter h is not pronounced. For example, huit (*eight*) would be pronounced [weet].

However, there are actually two different types of h in French: the silent or mute h and the aspirated h. While you wouldn't pronounce either one, they behave differently.

The silent h acts like a vowel. For example, words like le, la, se, de, and so on become "contracted" (l', s', d', etc.) before a silent h:

l'homme (le + homme)	*the man*
s'habiller (se + habiller)	*to get dressed*

Also, you usually use liaison with a silent h. For instance, les hommes would be pronounced [lay zohm].

However, the aspirated h acts like a consonant. Words like le, la, se, de, etc. do **not** become l', s', d', and so on before an aspirated h:

| le homard | *the lobster* |
| se hâter | *to rush* |

Also, you do not use liaison with an aspirated h: les homards would be pronounced [lay oh-mahr].

Most h are silent, not aspirated. Still, there are many words that begin with an aspirated h. Unfortunately, there isn't an easy way to tell which are which. Just start by learning the common ones, and then continue memorizing others that you come across.

Apart from homme and habiller, here are some other examples of common words that begin with a silent h: habiter (*to live*), heure (*hour*), heureux/heureuse (*happy*), hier (*yesterday*), hôpital (*hospital*), horaire (*schedule*), and huile (*oil*). Apart from homard and hâter, here are some other examples of common words that begin with an aspirated h: huit (*eight*), héros (*hero*), haine (*hatred*), hasard (*chance*), hâte (*haste*), haut (*high*), honte (*shame*), and hors (*outside*).

Grammar Summary

Here is a brief snapshot of French grammar from this course. Keep in mind that there are exceptions to many grammar rules.

1. NUMBERS

CARDINAL		ORDINAL	
un/une	one	premier/première	first
deux	two	deuxième, second/seconde	second
trois	three	troisième	third
quatre	four	quatrième	fourth
cinq	five	cinquième	fifth
six	six	sixième	sixth
sept	seven	septième	seventh
huit	eight	huitième	eighth
neuf	nine	neuvième	ninth
dix	ten	dixième	tenth

2. ARTICLES

	DEFINITE		INDEFINITE	
	Singular	Plural	Singular	Plural
Masculine	le	les	un	des
Feminine	la	les	une	des

Note that l' is used instead of le and la before words beginning with a vowel or silent h.

3. CONTRACTIONS

de + le = du (*some/of the, masculine*)

de + les = des (*some/of the, plural*)

à + le = au (*to/at/in the, masculine*)

à + les = aux (*to/at/in the, plural*)

There is no contraction with la or l'.

4. PLURALS

Most nouns add -s to form the plural. However, nouns ending in -eau or -eu, and some nouns ending in -ou, add -x instead of -s to form the plural.

5. ADJECTIVES

Adjectives agree with the nouns they modify in gender and number; that is, they are masculine if the noun is masculine, plural if the noun is plural, etc.

a. The feminine of an adjective is normally formed by adding -e to the masculine singular.

b. If the masculine singular already ends in -e, the adjective has the same form in the feminine.

c. Some adjectives double the final consonant of the masculine singular form and then add -e to form the feminine.

d. The plural of adjectives is usually formed by adding -s to the masculine or feminine singular form.

6. POSSESSIVE ADJECTIVES

Possessive adjectives agree in gender and number with the possession.

BEFORE SINGULAR NOUNS		BEFORE PLURAL NOUNS	
Masculine	Feminine	Masculine and Feminine	
mon	ma	mes	*my*
ton	ta	tes	*your (familiar)*
son	sa	ses	*his, her, its*
notre	notre	nos	*our*
votre	votre	vos	*your (polite/plural)*
leur	leur	leurs	*their*

Before feminine singular nouns beginning with a vowel or silent **h**, use **mon, ton,** and **son.**

7. PRONOUNS

	SUBJECT	STRESSED	REFLEXIVE
1st singular	je/j'	moi	me/m'
2nd singular	tu	toi	te/t'
3rd masculine singular	il	lui	se/s'
3rd feminine singular	elle	elle	se/s'
1st plural	nous	nous	nous
2nd plural	vous	vous	vous
3rd masculine plural	ils	eux	se / s'
3rd feminine plural	elles	elles	se / s'

On is an indefinite subject pronoun that means *we, one,* or *people/you/they in general.*

Stressed pronouns are generally used after prepositions (**avec moi**, etc.) or for emphasis (**moi, j'ai vingt ans**).

8. QUESTION WORDS

où	*where*
qu'est-ce que	*what*
quel/quelle, quels/quelles	*which, what*
qui	*who*
comment	*how*

9. DEMONSTRATIVE ADJECTIVES

Masculine Singular	ce	*this, that*
Masculine Singular (before a vowel or silent **h**)	cet	*this, that*
Feminine Singular	cette	*this, that*
Masculine Plural	ces	*these, those*
Feminine Plural	ces	*these, those*

When it is necessary to distinguish between *this* and *that*, **-ci** and **-là** are added to the noun: **Donnez-moi ce livre-ci.** (*Give me this book.*)

10. NEGATION

A sentence is made negative by placing **ne** before the verb and **pas** after it. When placed before a vowel or silent **h**, **ne** becomes **n'**.

11. VERBS

There are three types of French verbs:

TYPE	EXAMPLE
verbs ending in -er	parler (*to speak*)
verbs ending in -ir	finir (*to finish*)
verbs ending in -re	vendre (*to sell*)

For regular verbs, the present tense is formed by taking the -er, -ir, or -re off the infinitive and adding the following endings:

PRONOUN	-ER VERB ENDING	-IR VERB ENDING	-RE VERB ENDING
je	-e	-is	-s
tu	-es	-is	-s
il/elle*	-e	-it	- (no ending added)
nous	-ons	-issons	-ons
vous	-ez	-issez	-ez
ils/elles	-ent	-issent	-ent

* Remember that on (*we, one, people in general*) has the same verb form as il and elle.

The verbs **aller** (*to go*), **venir** (*to come*), and **prendre** (*to take*) are examples of irregular verbs. Although they end in -er, -ir, and -re respectively, they are not formed as shown above.

12. ÊTRE AND AVOIR

ÊTRE (TO BE)	
je suis	I am
tu es	you are (familiar)
il est	he is
elle est	she is
nous sommes	we are
vous êtes	you are (polite/plural)
ils sont	they are (masculine)
elles sont	they are (feminine)

AVOIR (TO HAVE)	
j'ai	I have
tu as	you have (familiar)
il a	he has
elle a	she has
nous avons	we have
vous avez	you have (polite/plural)
ils ont	they have (masculine)
elles ont	they have (feminine)

13. GRAMMAR INDEX

Here is a list of the principal grammar topics in this course and where to find them in the book.

LOCATION	GRAMMAR TOPICS
Lesson 1 Grammar Builder 1	Informal vs. formal *you* (**tu** and **vous**)
Lesson 1 Grammar Builder 2	Review of greetings and introductions
Lesson 2 Grammar Builder 1	Gender (masculine and feminine) and indefinite articles (**un** and **une**)
Lesson 2 Grammar Builder 2	Definite articles (**le, la, l'**)
Lesson 3 Grammar Builder 1	Plurals (**les** and **beaucoup de**)
Lesson 3 Grammar Builder 2	Subject pronouns (*I, you,* etc.) and **être** (*to be*)
Lesson 4 Grammar Builder 1	Vocabulary for talking about the home, the word *in*, and **il y a** (*there is/there are*)
Lesson 4 Grammar Builder 2	**Avoir** (*to have*)
Lesson 5 Grammar Builder 1	Masculine and feminine forms of adjectives
Lesson 5 Grammar Builder 2	Using adjectives with nouns, plural forms of adjectives, and possessives (*my*, etc.)
Lesson 6 Grammar Builder 1	Question words (*who, what,* etc.), yes/no questions, and negating a verb (*not*)
Lesson 6 Grammar Builder 2	Vocabulary for asking directions and getting around town, and the expression **il faut** (*you have to, it's necessary to*)
Lesson 7 Grammar Builder 1	*This* and *these*, and using **de** (*of*) with the definite articles to create *of the* and *some*
Lesson 7 Grammar Builder 2	Polite requests and other ways to ask for things
Lesson 8 Grammar Builder 1	Verbs ending in **-er** and reflexive verbs (*myself*, etc.)

LOCATION	GRAMMAR TOPICS
Lesson 8 Grammar Builder 2	Faire (*to do*), aller (*to go*), and prendre (*to take*)
Lesson 9 Grammar Builder 1	Professions
Lesson 9 Grammar Builder 2	Telling time and the 24-hour clock
Lesson 10 Grammar Builder 1	Making suggestions, expressing likes and dislikes, and verbs ending in -ir
Lesson 10 Grammar Builder 2	Vouloir (*to want*), pouvoir (*can, to be able*), following a verb with an infinitive, and chez (*at someone's house/place*)

Essential French

Glossary

Note that the following abbreviations will be used in this glossary:
(m.) = masculine, (f.) = feminine, (sg.) = singular, (pl.) = plural,
(fml.) = formal/polite, (infml.) = informal/familiar. If a word has two
grammatical genders, (m./f.) or (f./m.) is used.

French-English

A

à *in, at, to*
  à la / à l' / au / aux (f./m. or f. before a vowel or
  silent h/m./pl.): *in/at/to the*
  à côté de *next to*
  À votre santé ! *To your health!*
  à plein temps *full-time*
  à temps partiel *part-time*
acheter *to buy*
acteur / actrice (m./f.) *actor/actress*
action (f.) *action*
  film (m.) d'action *action film*
addition (f.) *check, bill*
admirer *to admire*
adolescent / adolescente (m./f.) *teenager,
  adolescent*
adorer *to love, to adore*
adulte (m./f.) *adult*
aéroport (m.) *airport*
affaires (f. pl.) *business, belongings*
  homme / femme (m./f.)
    d'affaires *businessman / businesswoman*
âge (m.) *age*
agneau (m.) *lamb*
agréable *pleasant, enjoyable*
aigre *sour*
aimer *to love, to like*
aller *to go*
  aller visiter *to go sightseeing*
  Allons-y. *Let's go.*
  On y va. *Let's go.* (infml.)
  Comment allez-vous ? *How are you?* (pl./fml.)
  Comment vas-tu ? *How are you?* (infml.)
  Je vais très bien. *I'm very well.*

Allô. *Hello. (only on the phone)*
alors... *well ..., so ..., then ...*
alpinisme (m.) *climbing*
américain / américaine (m./f.) *American*
ami / amie (m./f.) *friend*
amical / amicale (m./f.) *friendly*
amusant / amusante (m./f.) *amusing, funny*
an (m.) *year*
animal (m.) *animal*
année (f.) *year*
anniversaire (m.) *birthday, anniversary*
août *August*
appareil (m.) *device, telephone*
  Qui est à l'appareil ? *Who is it?/Who's
    calling?*
  appareil (m.) photo *camera*
appartement (m.) *apartment*
apporter *to bring*
apprendre *to learn*
  J'apprends le français. *I'm learning French.*
après *after, afterwards*
après-midi (m./f.) *afternoon*
arbre (m.) *tree*
Arc (m.) de Triomphe *Arc de Triomphe (Arch of
  Triumph)*
architecte (m./f.) *architect*
armoire (f.) *wardrobe, cabinet*
  armoire à pharmacie *medicine cabinet*
arrêt (m.) *stop*
  arrêt de bus *bus stop*
arriver *to arrive, to get somewhere, to reach*
art (m.) *art*
artiste (m./f.) *artist*
assez *quite, enough*
assiette (f.) *plate*
assis / assise (m./f.) *sitting (down), seated*
assistant / assistante (m./f.) *assistant*
au *to/at/in the* (m.)

Au revoir. *Good-bye.*
auberge (f.) *inn*
  auberge de jeunesse *youth hostel*
aujourd'hui *today*
aussi *also, too*
autobus (m.) *bus*
autocar (m.) *bus*
automne (m.) *fall, autumn*
  en automne *in (the) fall, in autumn*
autre *other*
  un / une autre (m./f.) *another*
aux *to/at/in the* (pl.)
avant *before*
avec *with*
  Avec plaisir. *With pleasure.*
avenue (f.) *avenue*
avion (m.) *airplane*
avocat / avocate (m./f.) *lawyer*
avoir *to have*
  avoir chaud *to be hot/warm*
  avoir froid *to be cold*
  avoir faim *to be hungry*
  avoir soif *to be thirsty*
  avoir raison *to be right*
  avoir tort *to be wrong*
  avoir honte *to be ashamed*
  avoir peur *to be afraid*
  avoir sommeil *to be sleepy*
  avoir hâte *to look forward to (can't wait)*
avril *April*

B

bague (f.) *ring*
baguette (f.) *baguette (French bread), chopstick*
baignoire (f.) *bathtub*
balai (m.) *broom*
balle (f.) *ball (small – tennis, etc.)*
ballet (m.) *ballet*
ballon (m.) *ball (large – basketball, etc.)*
banane (f.) *banana*
bandage (m.) *bandage*
banlieue (f.) *suburbs*
  de banlieue *suburban*
banque (f.) *bank*
banquier / banquière (m./f.) *banker*
bar (m.) *counter, bar*

bas / basse (m./f.) *low*
baseball (m.) *baseball*
basket (m./f.) *sneaker, tennis shoe*
basket(-ball) (m.) *basketball*
bâtiment (m.) *building*
beau / bel / belle (m./m. before vowel or silent h/f.)
  beautiful, handsome, nice
  Il fait beau. *It's beautiful (outside).*
Beaubourg *Beaubourg (area in Paris and another name for the Pompidou Center)*
beaucoup de *a lot of, many*
beau-fils (m.) *stepson, son-in-law*
beau-père (m.) *father-in-law, stepfather*
bébé (m.) *baby*
belle-fille (f.) *stepdaughter, daughter-in-law*
belle-mère (f.) *mother-in-law, stepmother*
beurre (m.) *butter*
bibliothèque (f.) *library, bookshelf*
bien *well, good, fine, really, very*
  Ça va bien. *It's going well.*
  très bien *very good, very well*
  Bien sûr. *Of course.*
Bienvenue. *Welcome.*
bière (f.) *beer*
bijou (m.) *jewel*
  bijoux (m. pl.) *jewelry*
billard (m.) *pool, billiards*
biologie (f.) *biology*
bisque (f.) *bisque (creamy soup)*
  bisque de homard *lobster bisque*
blanc / blanche (m./f.) *white*
bleu / bleue (m./f.) *blue*
bœuf (m.) *beef*
boire *to drink*
bois (m.) *wood*
  en bois *wooden*
boisson (f.) *drink*
  boisson gazeuse *soft drink*
boîte (f.) *club, nightclub, box*
  boîte de nuit *nightclub*
  sortir en boîte *to go out to clubs, to go out clubbing*
  boîte de conserve *can*
  boîte en carton *carton*
bon / bonne (m./f.) *good*
  très bon / bonne (m./f.) *very good*
  Bon appétit. *Bon appetit.*
  Bonne chance. *Good luck.*

Bonjour. *Hello.*
Bonsoir. *Good evening.*
bouche (f.) *mouth*
boucherie (f.) *butcher shop*
boucle (f.) d'oreille *earring*
boulangerie (f.) *bakery*
boulevard (m.) *boulevard*
boulot (m.) *job*
bouteille (f.) *bottle*
bracelet (m.) *bracelet*
bras (m.) *arm*
Bravo. *Well done.*
brochure (f.) *brochure*
brouillard (m.) *fog*
brun / brune (m./f.) *brown*
bulletin (m.) scolaire *report card*
bureau (m.) *office, desk*
　bureau de poste *post office*
bus (m.) *bus*

C

c'est *this is, that is, it is*
　C'est nuageux. *It's cloudy.*
　C'est tout ? *Is that all?*
　Qu'est-ce que c'est ? *What is this/that?*
ça / c' *this, that, it*
　(Comment) ça va ? *How's it going?/How are you?*
　Ça va. *I'm fine./It's going fine.*
　Ça va bien. *It's going well.*
　Ça va mal. *It's not going well./It's going badly.*
　Ça fait... *That makes .../That is ...*
câble (m.) *cable*
café (m.) *café, coffee shop, coffee*
　café-crème (m.) *coffee with cream*
cafetière (f.) *coffeemaker*
cahier (m.) *notebook*
caleçon (m.) *underpants*
calme *quiet, calm*
camper *to go camping*
canadien / canadienne (m./f.) *Canadian*
canapé (m.) *sofa, couch*
canard (m.) *duck*
　canard à l'orange *duck à l'orange, duck with orange sauce*
caramel (m.) *caramel*
carotte (f.) *carrot*

carré (m.) *square, rack (of meat)*
　carré d'agneau *rack of lamb*
carte (f.) *menu, card, map*
　carte des vins *wine list*
　cartes (f. pl.) à jouer *playing cards*
cave (f.) *cellar*
CD-ROM (m.) *CD-ROM*
ce / cet / cette (m./m. before a vowel or silent h/f.) *this, that*
ceinture (f.) *belt*
célèbre *famous*
célébrer *to celebrate*
cent *hundred*
centre (m.) d'informations *information center*
cerveau (m.) *brain*
ces *these, those*
cette / ce / cet (f./m./m. before a vowel or silent h) *this, that*
chacun / chacune (m./f.) *each, each one*
chaîne (f.) hi-fi *sound system*
chaise (f.) *chair*
chambre (f.) (à coucher) *bedroom*
champ (m.) *field*
champion / championne (m./f.) *champion*
changer de chaîne *to change channels*
chanson (f.) *song*
chanter *to sing*
chanteur / chanteuse (m./f.) *singer*
chapeau (m.) *hat*
chaque *each, every*
charmant / charmante (m./f.) *charming*
charpentier (m.) *carpenter*
chaud / chaude (m./f.) *hot, warm*
　Il fait chaud. *It's hot./It's warm.*
　avoir chaud *to be hot/warm*
chauffeur (m.) de taxi *taxi driver*
chaussette (f.) *sock*
chaussure (f.) *shoe*
　chaussure (f.) de basket *sneaker, tennis shoe*
chemise (f.) *shirt*
chemisier (m.) *blouse*
cher / chère (m./f.) *dear, expensive*
chercher *to look for*
cheveux (m. pl.) *hair*
　cheveu (m.) *hair (single strand)*
cheville (f.) *ankle*
chez *at someone's house/place*
chien (m.) *dog*

chimie (f.) *chemistry*
chocolat (m.) *chocolate*
choisir *to choose*
chômage (m.) *unemployment*
  au chômage *unemployed*
chose (f.) *thing*
ci *this, here*
ciel (m.) *sky*
cil (m.) *eyelash*
cinéma (m.) *movie theater, the movies*
cinq *five*
cinquante *fifty*
cinquième *fifth*
circuit (m.) en bus *bus tour*
circulation (f.) *traffic*
cirque (m.) *circus*
clavier (m.) *keyboard*
client / cliente (m./f.) *client*
club (m.) *club (organization)*
cochon (m.) *pig*
cœur (m.) *heart*
coin (m.) *neighborhood, corner*
coïncidence (f.) *coincidence*
  Quelle coïncidence ! *What a coincidence!*
collection (f.) *collection*
collège (m.) *secondary school, junior high school, middle school*
collègue / collègue (m./f.) *colleague*
collier (m.) *necklace*
colline (f.) *hill*
combien *how many, how much*
comédie (f.) *comedy*
  comédie romantique *romantic comedy*
comme *like, as, how*
  Comme ci, comme ça. *So-so.*
commencer *to start, to begin*
comment *how*
  Comment ? *Pardon?/What did you say?/How?*
  (Comment) ça va ? *How's it going?/How are you?*
  Comment allez-vous ? *How are you?* (pl./fml.)
  Comment vas-tu ? *How are you?* (infml.)
  Comment vous appelez-vous ? *What's your name?* (pl./fml.)
  Comment t'appelles-tu ?
    What's your name? (infml.)
compliqué / compliquée (m./f.) *complicated*
comprendre *to understand*

Je ne comprends pas. *I don't understand.*
comptoir (m.) *counter*
concert (m.) *concert*
concombre (m.) *cucumber*
confortable *comfortable*
connaître *to know, to be familiar with*
consommé (m.) *consommé (clear soup made from stock)*
  consommé aux vermicelles *noodle soup (vermicelli pasta consommé)*
consulter *to consult*
copain / copine (m./f.) *boyfriend/girlfriend*
costume (m.) *suit*
côte (f.) *chop, rib, coast*
  côte de porc *pork chop*
côté (m.) *side*
  à côté de *next to (at the side of)*
coton (m.) *cotton*
cou (m.) *neck*
coude (m.) *elbow*
couloir (m.) *hall*
courriel (m.) *email*
courrier (m.) électronique *email*
cours (m.) *course, class*
course (f.) *errand, run, race*
  course à pied *running*
court / courte (m./f.) *short*
cousin / cousine (m./f.) *cousin*
couteau (m.) *knife*
crème (f.) *cream, creamy dessert*
  crème à raser *shaving cream*
  crème caramel *creamy dessert made with caramel*
crêpe (f.) *crêpe (tissue-thin pancake)*
  crêpe Suzette *Crêpe Suzette (crêpe with sugar, orange, and liqueur)*
crevettes (f. pl.) *shrimp*
cru / crue (m./f.) *raw*
crudités (f. pl.) *crudités (French appetizer of raw, mixed vegetables)*
cuillère (f.) *spoon*
cuir (m.) *leather*
cuisine (f.) *kitchen, cooking*
  faire la cuisine *to do the cooking*
  évier (m.) de la cuisine *kitchen sink*
cuisiner *to cook*
cuisinier / cuisinière (m./f.) *cook*
cuisinière (f.) *stove*

D

D'accord. *Okay./All right.*
dans *in, into*
danse (f.) *dancing, dance*
danser *to dance*
de / d' *of, for, from*
   de la / de l' / du / des (f./m. or f. before a vowel or silent h/m./pl.) *of the, some*
   d'ici *from here*
   De rien. *You're welcome./It's nothing.*
debout *standing (up)*
décembre *December*
décider *to decide*
degré (m.) *degree*
déjà *already*
déjeuner *to have lunch*
déjeuner (m.) *lunch*
délicieux / délicieuse (m./f.) *delicious*
demain *tomorrow*
demander *to ask*
demi / demie (m./f.) *half*
   ... et demie *half past ...*
dent (f.) *tooth*
dentiste (m.) *dentist*
déodorant (m.) *deodorant*
dernier / dernière (m./f.) *last, final, latest, recent*
des *some* (pl.), *of the* (pl.), *plural of un / une*
descendre *to go down, to come down, to descend*
description (f.) *description*
désert (m.) *desert*
dessert (m.) *dessert*
détester *to hate, to detest*
deux *two*
deuxième *second*
devant *in front (of), ahead*
devenir *to become*
devoirs (m. pl.) *homework*
différent / différente (m./f.) *different*
difficile *difficult*
dimanche *Sunday*
dîner *to dine, to have dinner*
dîner (m.) *dinner*
diplôme (m.) *diploma*
   diplôme universitaire *college degree*
directeur / directrice (m./f.) *director, manager*
direction (f.) *direction, way*

divorcer *to get a divorce*
dix *ten*
dix-huit *eighteen*
dixième *tenth*
dix-neuf *nineteen*
dix-sept *seventeen*
docteur (m.) *doctor*
document (m.) *document*
documentaire (m.) *documentary*
doigt (m.) *finger*
   doigt de pied *toe*
donner *to give, to show*
doublé / doublée (m./f.) *dubbed*
douche (f.) *shower*
   gel (m.) douche *shower gel*
doux / douce (m./f.) *sweet, soft, gentle*
douze *twelve*
drame (m.) *drama*
drapeau (m.) *flag*
droit *straight*
   tout droit *straight ahead*
droite (f.) *right (opposite of left)*
du / de l' / de la / des (m./m. or f. before a vowel or silent h/f./pl.) *some, of the*

E

eau (f.) *water*
   eau de Cologne *cologne*
   eau de Javel *bleach*
écharpe (f.) *scarf (winter)*
éclair (m.) *lightning*
école (f.) *school*
écouter *to listen (to)*
écran (m.) *monitor, screen*
écrire *to write*
écrivain (m.) (sometimes: écrivaine, f.) *writer*
effrayant / effrayante (m./f.) *scary*
église (f.) *church*
électricien (m.) *electrician*
elle *she, it* (f.), *her*
elles *they* (f.), *it* (f. pl.), *them* (f.)
email (m.) *email*
émission (f.) *television program*
emmener *to take along*
emploi (m.) *employment, job*
   emploi régulier *steady job*
   sans emploi *unemployed*

employé / employée (m./f.) *employee*
en *in, into, to, some, of it, of them*
  en effet *really, indeed*
Enchanté. / Enchantée. (m./f.) *Pleased to meet you./Nice to meet you.*
enfant (m./f.) *child*
enfin *finally*
enseignant / enseignante (m./f.) *teacher*
enseigner *to teach*
ensemble *together*
ensuite *then, next*
entraîneur (m.) *coach*
entrée (f.) *appetizer, entrance*
entrer *to enter, to come in*
envoyer *to send, to throw*
  envoyer en pièce jointe *to attach a file*
  envoyer un fichier *to send a file*
  envoyer un mail / mél / email / courriel / courrier électronique *to send an email*
épaule (f.) *shoulder*
épouser (quelqu'un) *to marry (someone)*
équipe (f.) *team*
équitation (f.) *horseback riding*
  faire de l'équitation *to go horseback riding*
escaliers (m. pl.) *stairs*
essentiel / essentielle (m./f.) *essential*
est (m.) *east*
estomac (m.) *stomach, abdomen*
et *and*
étagère (f.) *shelf, bookshelf*
étang (m.) *pond*
été (m.) *summer*
  en été *in (the) summer*
étoile (f.) *star*
être *to be*
étudiant / étudiante (m./f.) *student*
étudier *to study*
eux *them*
évier (m.) *sink*
  évier (m.) de la cuisine *kitchen sink*
exact / exacte (m./f.) *exact, correct*
examen (m.) *test*
  rater (un examen) *to fail (a test)*
  réussir à (un examen) *to pass (a test)*
excellent / excellente (m./f.) *excellent*
excuser *to excuse*
expression (f.) *expression*
extérieur (m.) *outside, exterior*

F

facile *easy*
faible *weak*
faim (f.) *hunger*
  avoir faim *to be hungry*
faire *to do, to make*
  faire la cuisine *to do the cooking*
  faire la lessive *to do the laundry*
  faire la vaisselle *to do the dishes*
  faire le ménage *to do the house cleaning*
  faire les courses *to do the shopping, to go shopping*
  faire un tour *to take/do a tour*
  faire de la marche *to go hiking*
  faire du sport *to play a sport*
  faire match nul *to tie (in a game/match)*
  faire de l'équitation *to go horseback riding*
  faire de la natation *to go swimming*
  faire la queue *to wait in line*
  faire suivre *to forward*
  Ça fait... *That makes .../That is ...*
  Il fait beau. *It's beautiful (outside).*
  Il fait chaud. *It's hot./It's warm.*
  Il fait froid. *It's cold.*
  Il fait (du) soleil. *It's sunny.*
  Il fait du vent. *It's windy.*
falloir *to be necessary*
  il faut *it's necessary to, you have/need to, you must*
famille (f.) *family*
fauteuil (m.) *armchair*
faux / fausse (m./f.) *false, wrong*
Félicitations. *Congratulations.*
femme (f.) *woman, wife*
  femme d'affaires *businesswoman*
fenêtre (f.) *window*
fer (m.) à repasser *iron*
fermer *to close*
  fermer un fichier *to close a file*
fermier / fermière (m./f.) *farmer*
fête (f.) *party, festival, holiday*
feu (m.) *fire*
février *February*
fiancé / fiancée (m./f.) *fiancé/fiancée*
fichier (m.) *file*
fille (f.) *girl, daughter*
  fille unique *only child* (f.)

film (m.) *movie, film*
  film d'action *action film*
  film policier *crime drama/film, detective drama/film*
fils (m.) *son*
  fils unique *only child* (m.)
finir *to finish*
firme (f.) *company, firm*
fleur (f.) *flower*
fois (f.) *time*
  une fois *once (one time)*
foot(ball) (m.) *soccer*
football (m.) américain *(American) football*
footballeur / footballeuse (m./f.) *soccer player*
forêt (f.) *forest*
Formidable. *Fantastic.*
fort / forte (m./f.) *strong*
foulard (m.) *scarf (fashion)*
four (m.) *oven*
fourchette (f.) *fork*
foyer (m.) *home*
français (m.) *French language*
français / française (m./f.) *French*
frère (m.) *brother*
frites (f. pl.) *French fries*
froid / froide (m./f.) *cold*
  Il fait froid. *It's cold.*
  avoir froid *to be cold*
fromage (m.) *cheese*
front (m.) *forehead*
fruit (m.) *fruit*

G

gagner *to win, to earn*
galerie (f.) *gallery*
gant (m.) *glove*
garage (m.) *garage*
garçon (m.) *boy*
gare (f.) *train station*
gâteau (m.) *cake*
gauche (f.) *left*
gel (m.) douche *shower gel*
généreux / généreuse (m./f.) *generous*
genou (m.) *knee*
gens (m. pl.) *people*
gentil / gentille (m./f.) *nice, kind*
gérant / gérante (m./f.) *manager*

goût (m.) *taste*
grammaire (f.) *grammar*
grand / grande (m./f.) *big, large, tall*
  grand magasin (m.) *department store*
grand-mère (f.) *grandmother*
grand-parent (m.) *grandparent*
grand-père (m.) *grandfather*
grêle (f.) *hail*
  Il grêle. *It's hailing.*
gros / grosse (m./f.) *fat*
groupe (m.) de musique *band*
guide (m.) *guide*
gymnastique (f.) *gym (physical education), gymnastics*

H

habiter *to live*
haine (f.) *hatred*
haltérophilie (f.) *weight lifting*
haricot (m.) *bean*
  haricot vert *green bean*
hasard (m.) *chance*
hâte (f.) *haste*
  avoir hâte *to look forward to (can't wait)*
hâter *to hasten*
  se hâter *to rush*
haut / haute (m./f.) *high*
hériter *to inherit*
héros / héroïne (m./f.) *hero / heroine*
heure (f.) *hour*
  Quelle heure est-il ? *What time is it?*
heureux / heureuse (m./f.) *happy*
hier *yesterday*
histoire (f.) *history, story*
hiver (m.) *winter*
  en hiver *in (the) winter*
hockey (m.) *hockey*
homard (m.) *lobster*
homme (m.) *man*
  homme d'affaires *businessman*
honte (f.) *shame*
  avoir honte *to be ashamed*
hôpital (m.) *hospital*
horaire (m.) *schedule*
hors *outside (of)*
hors-d'œuvre (m.) *appetizer*
hôtel (m.) *hotel*

huile (f.) *oil*
huit *eight*
huitième *eighth*

I

ici *here*
  d'ici *from here*
  par ici *this way*
idée (f.) *idea*
il *he, it* (m.)
  Il fait beau. *It's beautiful (outside).*
  Il fait chaud. *It's hot./It's warm.*
  Il fait froid. *It's cold.*
  Il fait (du) soleil. *It's sunny.*
  Il fait du vent. *It's windy.*
  Il grêle. *It's hailing.*
  Il neige. *It's snowing.*
  Il pleut. *It's raining./It rains.*
  il faut *it's necessary to, you have/need to, you
    must*
il y a *there is/are*
  Il y a du vent. *It's windy.*
Île (f.) de la Cité *Île de la Cité (City Island)*
ils *they* (m./mixed), *it* (m. pl.)
immeuble (m.) *apartment building*
imprimante (f.) *printer*
ingénieur (m.) *engineer*
intelligent / intelligente (m./f.) *intelligent*
intéressant / intéressante (m./f.) *interesting*
Internet (m.) *internet*
intersection (f.) *intersection*
inviter *to invite*

J

jamais *never*
jambe (f.) *leg*
janvier *January*
jardin (m.) *garden*
jaune *yellow*
je / j' *I*
  Je m'appelle... *My name is .../I am called ...*
  Je ne comprends pas. *I don't understand.*
  Je vais très bien. *I'm very well.*
  Je veux... *I want ...*
  Je voudrais... *I would like ...*
  Je te présente... / Je vous présente...

  Let me introduce ... (infml./pl., fml.)
  Je vous en prie. *You're welcome.* (fml.)
jean (m.) *jeans*
jeu (m.) *game*
  jeu électronique *electronic game*
  jeu vidéo *video game*
jeudi *Thursday*
jeune *young*
Joconde (f.) *Mona Lisa*
joli / jolie (m./f.) *nice, pretty*
joue (f.) *cheek*
jouer *to play, to perform, to act*
  cartes (f. pl.) à jouer *playing cards*
joueur / joueuse (m./f.) *player
  (games, sports, etc.)*
jour (m.) *day*
journaliste (m./f.) *journalist*
journée (f.) *day*
juillet *July*
juin *June*
jupe (f.) *skirt*
jus (m.) *juice*
jusqu'à *to, until, up to, up until*

L

là *there*
la / l' / le / les (f./m. or f. before a vowel or silent
  h/m./pl.) *the*
là-bas *over there, there*
lac (m.) *lake*
laid / laide (m./f.) *ugly*
lait (m.) *milk*
laitue (f.) *lettuce*
lampadaire (m.) *streetlight*
lampe (f.) *lamp*
langue (f.) *language, tongue*
lave-linge (m.) *washing machine*
laver *to wash*
  se laver *to wash up, to wash oneself*
lave-vaisselle (m.) *dishwasher*
le / l' / la / les (m./m. or f. before a vowel or silent
  h/f./pl.) *the*
leçon (f.) *lesson*
lecteur (m.) *player (CDs, DVDs, etc.), drive
  (computer)*
  lecteur de CD *CD player*
  lecteur de DVD *DVD player*

lecteur de CD-ROM *CD-ROM drive*
légume (m.) *vegetable*
lent / lente (m./f.) *slow*
lentement *slowly*
les *the* (pl.)
lessive (f.) *laundry detergent*
lettre (f.) *letter*
leur / leurs (m. or f./pl.) *their*
liaison (f.) *link*
librairie (f.) *bookstore*
liquide (m.) vaisselle *dishwashing detergent*
lire *to read*
lit (m.) *bed*
littérature (f.) *literature*
livre (m.) *book*
  livre scolaire *textbook*
loin *far*
  loin d'ici *far from here*
  plus loin *farther*
long / longue (m./f.) *long*
Louvre (m.) *Louvre*
lui *him*
lundi *Monday*
lune (f.) *moon*
lunettes (f. pl.) *eyeglasses*
  lunettes de soleil *sunglasses*
lustre (m.) *chandelier*

M

ma / mon / mes (f./m./pl.) *my*
machine (f.) à laver *washing machine*
madame *ma'am, Mrs., Ms., madam*
mademoiselle *miss*
magasin (m.) *store*
  grand magasin *department store*
  magasin d'électronique *electronics store*
  magasin de chaussures *shoe store*
  magasin de vêtements *clothing store*
magazine (m.) *magazine*
mai *May*
mail (m.) *email*
maillot (m.) de bain *bathing suit, bathing trunks*
maillot (m.) de corps *undershirt*
main (f.) *hand*
maintenant *now*
maire (m.) *mayor*
mairie (f.) *city hall, municipal building*

mais *but*
maison *homemade*
maison (f.) *house, home*
mal *badly, bad, wrong*
  Ça va mal. *It's going badly./It's not going well.*
malade *sick*
maman *Mom, Mommy*
manger *to eat*
manteau (m.) *coat*
marché (m.) *market*
mardi *Tuesday*
mare (f.) *pond*
mari (m.) *husband*
marron *brown*
mars *March*
match (m.) *match, game*
mathématiques (f.) *math*
maths (f.) *math*
matin (m.) *morning*
matinée (f.) *morning*
mauvais / mauvaise (m./f.) *bad*
me / m' (reflexive pronoun): *myself*
  Je m'appelle... *My name is .../I am called ...*
médecin (m.) *doctor*
médecine (f.) *medicine*
mél (m.) *email*
melon (m.) *melon*
même *same, even*
mémoire (f.) *memory*
ménage (m.) *house cleaning*
menton (m.) *chin*
menu (m.) *menu*
mer (f.) *sea*
merci *thank you*
mercredi *Wednesday*
mère (f.) *mother*
mes / mon / ma (pl./m./f.) *my*
message (m.) instantané *instant message*
métro (m.) *subway, metro*
mettre *to put*
  mettre à la poste *to mail, to put in the mail*
micro-ondes (m.) *microwave (oven)*
midi (m.) *noon*
miel (m.) *honey*
mille *thousand*
mince *thin*
minuit (m.) *midnight*
miroir (m.) *mirror*

mixer (m.) *blender*
modem (m.) *modem*
moi *me*
moins *less, minus*
   ... moins le quart *quarter to ...*
mois (m.) *month*
moment (m.) *moment*
mon / ma / mes (m./f./pl.) *my*
monsieur *sir, Mr.*
montagne (f.) *mountain*
monter *to go up, to come up, to rise*
montre (f.) *watch*
montrer *to show*
monument (m.) *monument*
moquette (f.) *carpet*
mosquée (f.) *mosque*
mot (m.) *word*
moto (f.) *motorcycling, motorcycle*
mousse (f.) *mousse*
mur (m.) *wall*
muscle (m.) *muscle*
musée (m.) *museum*
musicien / musicienne (m./f.) *musician*
musique (f.) *music*
mystérieux / mystérieuse (m./f.) *mysterious*

N

natation (f.) *swimming*
   faire de la natation *to go swimming*
ne / n'... pas *not*
   n'est-ce pas ? *isn't it?, isn't that so?, right?*
neige (f.) *snow*
neiger *to snow*
   Il neige. *It's snowing.*
neuf *nine*
neuvième *ninth*
neveu (m.) *nephew*
nez (m.) *nose*
nièce (f.) *niece*
noir / noire (m./f.) *black*
nom (m.) *name*
nombre (m.) *number*
non *no*
nord (m.) *north*
note (f.) *grade, note*
notre / nos (m. or f./pl.) *our*
nourriture (f.) *food*

nous *we, us*
nous (reflexive pronoun): *ourselves*
nouveau / nouvel / nouvelle (m./m. before a
   vowel or silent h/f.) *new*
nouvelles (f. pl.) *news (the news)*
novembre *November*
nuage (m.) *cloud*
nuageux / nuageuse (m./f.) *cloudy*
   C'est nuageux. *It's cloudy.*
nuit (f.) *night*

O

occupé / occupée (m./f.) *busy*
océan (m.) *ocean*
octobre *October*
œil (m.) (yeux, pl.) *eye (eyes)*
œuf (m.) *egg*
oignon (m.) *onion*
on *we (infml.), people in general, one (pronoun)*
   On y va. *Let's go. (infml.)*
oncle (m.) *uncle*
onze *eleven*
opéra (m.) *opera*
orage (m.) *storm*
orange (f.) *orange*
ordinateur (m.) *computer*
oreille (f.) *ear*
organiser *to organize*
   organiser une fête *to have a party*
original / originale (m./f.) *original*
orteil (m.) *toe*
os (m.) *bone*
ou *or*
où *where*
   Où se trouve... ? / Où est... ? *Where is ... ?*
   Où sont les toilettes ? *Where is the restroom?*
ouest (m.) *west*
oui *yes*
ouragan (m.) *hurricane*
ouvrier (m.) en bâtiment *construction worker*
ouvrir *to open*
   ouvrir un fichier *to open a file*

P

page (f.) web *webpage*
pain (m.) *bread*

pansement (m.) *bandage*
pantalon (m.) *pants*
papa *Dad, Daddy*
papier (m.) hygiénique *toilet paper*
parapluie (m.) *umbrella*
parc (m.) *park*
Pardon. *Pardon (me)./Excuse me.*
parent (m.) *relative, parent*
parfait / parfaite (m./f.) *perfect*
parfois *sometimes*
parfum (m.) *perfume, flavor*
Paris *Paris*
parler *to speak, to talk*
  Parlez plus lentement, s'il vous plaît. *Speak more slowly, please.*
  Je parle un peu français. *I speak a little French.*
partie (f.) *party*
partir *to leave, to go away*
pas *not*
  Pas mal. *Not bad.*
passeport (m.) *passport*
passer *to pass, to go (past)*
passionnant / passionnante (m./f.) *exciting*
pâté (m.) *pâté (spreadable purée of meat)*
patin (m.) *skating, skate*
  patin à glace *ice skating, ice skate*
pâtisserie (f.) *pastry shop, pastry*
patron / patronne (m./f.) *boss*
pauvre *poor, impoverished*
payer *to pay*
peau (f.) *skin*
pêche (f.) *peach*
  pêche Melba *peaches with ice cream*
peindre *to paint*
pendule (f.) *grandfather clock*
penser *to think*
perdre *to lose*
perdu / perdue (m./f.) *lost*
  Je suis perdu / perdue. *I'm lost.*
père (m.) *father*
personne (f.) *person*
personnel (m.) *staff*
petit / petite (m./f.) *small, little, short*
  petit ami / petite amie (m./f.) *boyfriend/ girlfriend*
  petit déjeuner (m.) *breakfast*
  prendre le petit déjeuner *to have breakfast*

peu amical / peu amicale (m./f.) *unfriendly*
pharmacie (f.) *pharmacy, drugstore*
photo (f.) *photo*
  Pourriez-vous nous prendre en photo, s'il vous plaît ? *Can you take our picture (photo), please?*
pièce (f.) *room, play (theater), piece*
  pièce jointe *attachment*
pied (m.) *foot*
placard (m.) *cupboard, closet*
place (f.) *place, seat, ticket, room*
plafond (m.) *ceiling*
plage (f.) *beach*
plaisir (m.) *pleasure*
  Avec plaisir. *With pleasure.*
plan (m.) *map*
planche (f.) à repasser *ironing board*
plante (f.) *plant*
plastique (m.) *plastic*
  en plastique *made of plastic*
plat (m.) *dish*
plat principal *main dish/course*
pleuvoir *to rain*
  Il pleut. *It's raining./It rains.*
plombier (m.) *plumber*
pluie (f.) *rain*
plus *more*
  plus loin *farther*
poignet (m.) *wrist*
poire (f.) *pear*
poisson (m.) *fish*
poitrine (f.) *chest*
poivre (m.) *pepper (condiment)*
poivron (m.) *pepper (vegetable)*
policier / femme policier (m./f.) *policeman/woman*
policier / policière (m./f.) *police, detective (adjective)*
  film (m.) policier *detective drama/film, crime drama/film*
pomme (f.) *apple*
  pomme de terre *potato*
pont (m.) *bridge*
porc (m.) *pork, pig*
porte (f.) *door*
porter *to carry, to wear*
poste (f.) *post office, mail*
  bureau (m.) de poste *post office*

mettre à la poste *to mail, to put in the mail*
poudre (f.) *powder*
poulet (m.) *chicken*
poumon (m.) *lung*
pour *for, to*
pouvoir *can, to be able*
pratiquer *to practice*
préféré / préférée (m./f.) *favorite*
préférer *to prefer*
premier / première (m./f.) *first*
prendre *to take, to have (food/drink)*
  prendre un bain *to take a bath*
  prendre une douche *to take a shower*
  prendre un verre *to have a drink*
  prendre le petit déjeuner *to have breakfast*
  prendre une chambre *to check in*
  prendre une photo *to take a picture (photo)*
  Pourriez-vous nous prendre en photo, s'il vous plaît ? *Can you take our picture (photo) please?*
préparer *to prepare, to make, to cook*
près *close, near*
  tout près *very close, very near*
  près d'ici *nearby, near here, close to here*
présenter *to introduce, to show, to present*
  Je te présente… / Je vous présente… *Let me introduce …* (infml./pl., fml.)
prêt / prête (m./f.) *ready*
prier *to beg*
  Je vous en prie. *You're welcome.* (fml.)
printemps (m.) *spring*
  au printemps *in (the) spring*
prof (m./f.) *professor, teacher* (infml.)
professeur / professeure (m./f.) *professor, teacher*
progrès (m.) *progress*
propre *clean, own*
puis *then*
pyjama (m.) *pajamas*

Q

qu'est-ce que *what*
  Qu'est-ce que c'est ? *What is this/that?*
quarante *forty*
quart (m.) *quarter*
  … et quart *quarter after/past …*
  … moins le quart *quarter to …*

quartier (m.) *neighborhood*
quatorze *fourteen*
quatre *four*
quatre-vingt-dix *ninety*
quatre-vingts *eighty*
quatrième *fourth*
que *what, that, which, whom*
quel / quelle (m./f.) *which, what*
  Quel temps fait-il aujourd'hui ? *What is the weather today?*
  Quelle heure est-il ? *What time is it?*
queue (f.) *line, tail*
  faire la queue *to wait in line*
qui *who, that*
  Qui est à l'appareil ? *Who is it?/Who's calling?*
quiche (f.) *quiche*
  quiche lorraine *type of quiche made with bacon*
quinze *fifteen*
quoi *what*
quotidien / quotidienne (m./f.) *everyday, daily*

R

radis (m.) *radish*
raisin (m.) *grape(s)*
rasoir (m.) *razor*
rater (un examen) *to fail (a test)*
réception (f.) *reception desk*
récré(ation) (f.) *recess*
réfrigérateur (m.) *refrigerator*
regarder *to watch*
régler sa note *to check out*
rencontrer (une personne/quelqu'un) *to meet (a person/someone)*
rendez-vous (m.) *meeting, appointment*
rentrer *to go home, to return, to come back (in), to go in*
répéter *to repeat*
  Répétez, s'il vous plaît. *Repeat (that), please.*
répondre *to reply*
réservation (f.) *reservation*
réserver *to reserve*
restaurant (m.) *restaurant*
rester *to stay*
retraite (f.) *retirement*
  à la retraite *retired*

réunion (f.) *meeting, reunion*
réussir à (un examen) *to succeed, to pass (a test)*
revenir *to come back, to return*
réverbère (m.) *lamppost*
revue (f.) *magazine*
riche *rich*
rideau (m.) *curtain*
rien *nothing, anything*
 De rien. *You're welcome./It's nothing.*
rivière (f.) *river*
riz (m.) *rice*
robe (f.) *dress*
rocher (m.) *rock*
rôle (m.) *role, part (in a play, movie, etc.)*
romantique *romantic*
rôti (m.) *roast, joint (of meat)*
rôti / rôtie (m./f.) *roast(ed)*
rouge *red*
rue (f.) *street*
rural / rurale (m./f.) *rural*

S

s'amuser *to have fun, to have a good time*
s'appeler *to be called*
 Comment vous appelez-vous ? *What's your name?* (pl./fml.)
 Comment t'appelles-tu ? *What's your name?* (infml.)
 Je m'appelle... *My name is ... /I am called ...*
s'ennuyer *to be bored*
s'habiller *to get dressed, to dress oneself*
s'il te plaît / s'il vous plaît *please* (infml./pl., fml.)
sa / son / ses (f./m./pl.) *his, her, its*
sable (m.) *sand*
Sacré-Cœur (m.) *Sacré Cœur (Sacred Heart)*
salade (f.) *salad*
 salade de fruits *fruit salad*
saladier (m.) *bowl*
salaire (m.) *salary*
sale *dirty*
salle (f.) *room, hall*
 salle à manger *dining room*
 salle de bains *bathroom, washroom*
 salle de classe *classroom*
 salle de réunion *meeting room*
salon (m.) *living room*
Salut. *Hi./Bye.*

samedi *Saturday*
sang (m.) *blood*
sans *without*
santé (f.) *health*
 À votre santé ! *To your health!*
 en bonne santé *healthy*
sardines (f. pl.) *sardines*
 sardines sauce tomate *sardines in tomato sauce*
sauce (f.) *sauce*
sauvegarder un document *to save a document*
savoir *to know*
savon (m.) *soap*
sculpture (f.) *sculpture*
se / s' (reflexive pronoun): *himself, herself, itself, themselves, oneself*
 s'amuser *to have fun, to have a good time*
 s'appeler *to be called*
 s'ennuyer *to be bored*
 s'habiller *to get dressed, to dress oneself*
 se coucher *to go to bed*
 se hâter *to rush*
 se laver *to wash up, to wash oneself*
 se lever *to get up*
 se raser *to shave*
 se trouver *to find oneself (somewhere), to be situated*
sèche-linge (m.) *dryer*
second / seconde (m./f.) *second*
secrétaire (m./f.) *secretary*
seize *sixteen*
sel (m.) *salt*
semaine (f.) *week*
sept *seven*
septembre *September*
septième *seventh*
serveur / serveuse (m./f.) *waiter/waitress, server*
serviette (f.) *napkin, towel, briefcase*
 serviette de bain *bath towel*
ses / son / sa (pl./m./f.) *his, her, its*
shampooing (m.) *shampoo*
si *if, yes (negative)*
site (m.) **web** *website*
six *six*
sixième *sixth*
ski (m.) *skiing*
social / sociale (m./f.) *social*

société (f.) *company*
sœur (f.) *sister*
soie (f.) *silk*
soif (f.) *thirst*
  avoir soif *to be thirsty*
soir (m.) *evening, night*
  ce soir *tonight, this evening*
soirée (f.) *party, evening*
soixante *sixty*
soixante-dix *seventy*
sol (m.) *floor*
sole (f.) *sole (fish)*
  sole meunière *sole covered in flour and sau-téed in butter*
soleil (m.) *sun*
  Il fait (du) soleil. *It's sunny.*
son / sa / ses (m./f./pl.) *his, her, its*
sortir *to leave, to go out*
  sortir en boîte *to go out to clubs, to go out clubbing*
soupe (f.) *soup*
  soupe à l'oignon *onion soup*
sourcil (m.) *eyebrow*
sourire (m.) *smile*
souris (f.) *mouse*
sous-titre (m.) *subtitle*
sous-vêtements (m. pl.) *underwear*
spécialité (f.) *specialty*
sportif / sportive (m./f.) *athletic*
sports (m. pl.) *sports*
stade (m.) *stadium*
  stade de foot *soccer stadium*
station (f.) *station*
  station de métro *subway station, metro sta-tion*
statue (f.) *statue*
sucre (m.) *sugar*
sud (m.) *south*
suisse *Swiss*
sujet (m.) *subject*
Super. *Super./Great.*
supermarché (m.) *supermarket*
supprimer *to delete*
surtout *mostly, above all, especially*
sympa *cool, nice, good*
  très sympa *very cool/nice/good*
synagogue (f.) *synagogue*

T

ta / ton / tes (f./m./pl.) *your* (infml.)
table (f.) *table*
  table pour deux *table for two*
tableau (m.) *painting*
taille (f.) *size*
talc (m.) *powder*
talentueux / talentueuse (m./f.) *talented*
tante (f.) *aunt*
tasse (f.) *cup*
taxi (m.) *taxi, cab*
te / t' (reflexive pronoun) *yourself* (infml.)
télé(vision) (f.) *television, TV*
télécopieur (m.) *fax machine*
téléphone (m.) *telephone*
téléphoner *to phone, to call, to make a phone call*
température (f.) *temperature*
temple (m.) *temple*
temps (m.) *weather, time*
  Quel temps fait-il aujourd'hui ? *What is the weather today?*
tendon (m.) *tendon*
tennis (m.) *tennis*
terminer *to finish, to end*
terre (f.) *land*
tes / ton / ta (pl./m./f.) *your* (infml.)
tête (f.) *head*
thé (m.) *tea*
théâtre (m.) *theater*
théière (f.) *teakettle, teapot*
timbre (m.) *stamp*
tiroir (m.) *drawer*
toi *you* (infml.)
toilettes (f. pl.) *toilet, restroom*
  Où sont les toilettes ? *Where is the restroom?*
tomate (f.) *tomato*
tomber *to fall*
ton / ta / tes (m./f./pl.) *your* (infml.)
tonnerre (m.) *thunder*
toujours *always, still*
tour (f.) *tower*
  Tour Eiffel *Eiffel Tower*
tour (m.) *tour, turn*
touriste (m./f.) *tourist*
tourner *to turn*
tout / toute (m./f.) *all, every*
  C'est tout ? *Is that all?*

train (m.) *train*
travail (m.) *work*
travailler *to work*
traverser *to cross, to go across*
treize *thirteen*
trente *thirty*
très *very*
  très bien *very good, very well*
  très bon / bonne *very good*
triste *sad*
trois *three*
troisième *third*
trottoir (m.) *sidewalk*
trouver *to find*
  se trouver *to find oneself (somewhere), to be situated*
  Où se trouve... ? *Where is ... ?*
truite (f.) *trout*
  truite au bleu *trout cooked in wine and vinegar*
T-shirt (m.) *T-shirt*
tu *you* (infml.)

U

un / une (m./f.) (plural of un / une is des) *a, an, one*
  un peu *a little*
université (f.) *university, college*
urbain / urbaine (m./f.) *urban*
usine (f.) *factory*

V

vacances (f. pl.) *vacation*
vain / vaine (m./f.) *vain*
vélo (m.) *bike*
vendeur / vendeuse (m./f.) *salesman/woman*
vendre *to sell*
vendredi *Friday*
venir *to come*
vent (m.) *wind*
  Il fait du vent. / Il y a du vent. *It's windy.*
vermicelle (m.) *vermicelli pasta*
  consommé (m.) aux vermicelles *noodle soup (vermicelli pasta consommé)*
verre (m.) *glass*
  prendre un verre *to have a drink*

version (f.) *version*
  version française (v.f.) *French version of a film (dubbed into French)*
  version originale (v.o.) *original version of a film (not dubbed into French)*
veste (f.) *jacket*
vêtements (m. pl.) *clothes, clothing*
vétérinaire (m.) *veterinarian*
viande (f.) *meat*
vie (f.) *life*
vietnamien / vietnamienne (m./f.) *Vietnamese*
vieux / vieil / vieille (m./m. before a vowel or silent h/f.) *old*
village (m.) *village*
ville (f.) *town, city*
vin (m.) *wine*
  vin rouge / blanc / rosé *red/white/rosé wine*
vingt *twenty*
violet / violette (m./f.) *purple*
violon (m.) *violin*
visage (m.) *face*
visite (f.) guidée *guided tour*
visiter *to visit (a place)*
vocabulaire (m.) *vocabulary*
voici *here is/are, here it is/they are*
voilà *there is/are, here is/are, there it is/they are, here it is/they are*
voile (f.) *sailing*
voir *to see*
voiture (f.) *car*
votre / vos (m. or f./pl.) *your* (pl./fml.)
vouloir *to want*
  Je veux... *I want ...*
  Je voudrais... *I would like ...*
vous *you* (pl./fml.)
vous (reflexive pronoun) *yourself* (fml.), *yourselves*
voyager *to travel*
vrai / vraie (m./f.) *true, real*

W

wagon (m.) *car (on a train)*
  wagon-lit (m.) *sleeping/sleeper car*
week-end (m.) *weekend*

Y

yeux (m. pl.) (œil, *sg.*) *eyes (eye)*

Z

zéro *zero*

English-French

A

a, an *un / une* (m./f.) (plural of *un / une* is des)
  a little *un peu*
  a lot of *beaucoup de*
abdomen *estomac* (m.)
able (to be) *pouvoir*
above all *surtout*
act (to) *jouer*
action *action* (f.)
  action film *film* (m.) *d'action*
actor/actress *acteur / actrice* (m./f.)
admire (to) *admirer*
adolescent *adolescent / adolescente* (m./f.)
adore (to) *adorer*
adult *adulte* (m./f.)
afraid (to be) *avoir peur*
after *après*
afternoon *après-midi* (m./f.)
afterwards *après*
age *âge* (m.)
ahead *devant*
airplane *avion* (m.)
airport *aéroport* (m.)
all *tout / toute* (m./f.)
  All right. *D'accord.*
  Is that all? *C'est tout ?*
already *déjà*
also *aussi*
always *toujours*
American *américain / américaine* (m./f.)
amusing *amusant / amusante* (m./f.)
and *et*
animal *animal* (m.)
ankle *cheville* (f.)
anniversary *anniversaire* (m.)
another *un / une autre* (m./f.)

anything *rien*
apartment *appartement* (m.)
  apartment building *immeuble* (m.)
appetizer *entrée* (f.), *hors-d'œuvre* (m.)
apple *pomme* (f.)
appointment *rendez-vous* (m.)
April *avril*
Arc de Triomphe (Arch of Triumph) *Arc* (m.)
  de Triomphe
architect *architecte* (m./f.)
arm *bras* (m.)
armchair *fauteuil* (m.)
arrive (to) *arriver*
art *art* (m.)
artist *artiste* (m./f.)
as *comme*
ashamed (to be) *avoir honte*
ask (to) *demander*
assistant *assistant / assistante* (m./f.)
at *à*
  at the *au / à la / à l' / aux* (m./f./m. or f. before a
    vowel or silent h/pl.)
  at someone's house/place *chez*
athletic *sportif / sportive* (m./f.)
attach a file (to) *envoyer en pièce jointe*
attachment *pièce* (f.) *jointe*
August *août*
aunt *tante* (f.)
autumn *automne* (m.)
  in autumn *en automne*
avenue *avenue* (f.)

B

baby *bébé* (m.)
bad *mauvais / mauvaise* (m./f.), *mal*
badly *mal*
  It's going badly./It's not going well. *Ça va
    mal.*
baguette (French bread) *baguette* (f.)
bakery *boulangerie* (f.)
ball (large – basketball, etc.) *ballon* (m.)
ball (small – tennis, etc.) *balle* (f.)
ballet *ballet* (m.)
banana *banane* (f.)
band *groupe* (m.) *de musique*
bandage *bandage* (m.), *pansement* (m.)
bank *banque* (f.)

banker *banquier / banquière* (m./f.)
baseball *baseball* (m.)
basketball *basket(-ball)* (m.)
bath towel *serviette* (f.) *de bain*
bathing suit *maillot* (m.) *de bain*
bathing trunks *maillot* (m.) *de bain*
bathroom *salle* (f.) *de bains*
bathtub *baignoire* (f.)
be (to) *être*
　be able (to) *pouvoir*
　be afraid (to) *avoir peur*
　be ashamed (to) *avoir honte*
　be bored (to) *s'ennuyer*
　be cold (to) *avoir froid*
　be hot/warm (to) *avoir chaud*
　be hungry (to) *avoir faim*
　be thirsty (to) *avoir soif*
　be sleepy (to) *avoir sommeil*
　be right (to) *avoir raison*
　be wrong (to) *avoir tort*
　be familiar with (to) *connaître*
　be situated (to) *se trouver*
　be called (to) *s'appeler*
　be necessary (to) *falloir*
beach *plage* (f.)
bean *haricot* (m.)
　green bean *haricot vert*
Beaubourg (area in Paris and another name
　for the Pompidou Center) *Beaubourg*
beautiful *beau / bel / belle* (m./m. before vowel or
　silent h/f.)
　It's beautiful (outside). *Il fait beau.*
become (to) *devenir*
bed *lit* (m.)
bedroom *chambre* (f.) *(à coucher)*
beef *bœuf* (m.)
beer *bière* (f.)
before *avant*
beg (to) *prier*
begin (to) *commencer*
belongings *affaires* (f. pl.)
belt *ceinture* (f.)
big *grand / grande* (m./f.)
bike *vélo* (m.)
bill (restaurant, café, etc.) *addition* (f.)
billiards *billard* (m.)
biology *biologie* (f.)
birthday *anniversaire* (m.)

bisque (creamy soup) *bisque* (f.)
　lobster bisque *bisque de homard*
black *noir / noire* (m./f.)
bleach *eau* (f.) *de Javel*
blender *mixer* (m.)
blood *sang* (m.)
blouse *chemisier* (m.)
blue *bleu / bleue* (m./f.)
Bon appetit. *Bon appétit.*
bone *os* (m.)
book *livre* (m.)
bookshelf *étagère* (f.), *bibliothèque* (f.)
bookstore *librairie* (f.)
bored (to be) *s'ennuyer*
boss *patron / patronne* (m./f.)
bottle *bouteille* (f.)
boulevard *boulevard* (m.)
bowl *saladier* (m.)
box *boîte* (f.)
boy *garçon* (m.)
boyfriend *copain* (m.), *petit ami* (m.)
bracelet *bracelet* (m.)
brain *cerveau* (m.)
bread *pain* (m.)
breakfast *petit déjeuner* (m.)
　have breakfast (to) *prendre le petit déjeuner*
bridge *pont* (m.)
briefcase *serviette* (f.)
bring (to) *apporter*
brochure *brochure* (f.)
broom *balai* (m.)
brother *frère* (m.)
brown *marron, brun / brune* (m./f.)
building *bâtiment* (m.)
bus *bus* (m.), *autobus* (m.), *autocar* (m.)
　bus stop *arrêt* (m.) *de bus*
　bus tour *circuit* (m.) *en bus*
business *affaires* (f. pl.)
businessman/woman *homme / femme
　d'affaires* (m./f.)
busy *occupé / occupée* (m./f.)
but *mais*
butcher shop *boucherie* (f.)
butter *beurre* (m.)
buy (to) *acheter*
Bye. *Salut.*

C

cab *taxi* (m.)

cabinet *armoire* (f.)

  medicine cabinet *armoire à pharmacie*

cable *câble* (m.)

café *café* (m.)

cake *gâteau* (m.)

call (to) *téléphoner*

called (to be) *s'appeler*

calm *calme*

camera *appareil* (m.) *photo*

can (container) *boîte* (f.) *de conserve*

can (verb) *pouvoir*

Canadian *canadien / canadienne* (m./f.)

car *voiture* (f.), *wagon (on a train)* (m.)

caramel *caramel* (m.)

card *carte* (f.)

  playing cards *cartes* (f. pl.) *à jouer*

carpenter *charpentier* (m.)

carpet *moquette* (f.)

carrot *carotte* (f.)

carry (to) *porter*

carton *boîte* (f.) *en carton*

CD player *lecteur* (m.) *de CD*

CD-ROM *CD-ROM* (m.)

  CD-ROM drive *lecteur* (m.) *de CD-ROM*

ceiling *plafond* (m.)

celebrate (to) *célébrer*

cellar *cave* (f.)

chair *chaise* (f.)

champion *champion / championne* (m./f.)

chance *hasard* (m.)

chandelier *lustre* (m.)

change channels (to) *changer de chaîne*

charming *charmant / charmante* (m./f.)

check (restaurant, café, etc.) *addition* (f.)

check in (to) *prendre une chambre*

check out (to) *régler sa note*

cheek *joue* (f.)

cheese *fromage* (m.)

chemistry *chimie* (f.)

chest *poitrine* (f.)

chicken *poulet* (m.)

child *enfant* (m./f.)

chin *menton* (m.)

chocolate *chocolat* (m.)

choose (to) *choisir*

chop *côte* (f.)

  pork chop *côte de porc*

chopstick *baguette* (f.)

church *église* (f.)

circus *cirque* (m.)

city *ville* (f.)

  city hall *mairie* (f.)

class *cours* (m.)

classroom *salle* (f.) *de classe*

clean *propre*

client *client / cliente* (m./f.)

climbing *alpinisme* (m.)

close *près*

  very close *tout près*

  close to here *près d'ici*

close (to) *fermer*

  close a file (to) *fermer un fichier*

closet *placard* (m.)

clothing/clothes *vêtements* (m. pl.)

  clothing store *magasin* (m.) *de vêtements*

cloud *nuage* (m.)

cloudy *nuageux / nuageuse* (m./f.)

  It's cloudy. *C'est nuageux.*

club *boîte* (f.)

  nightclub *boîte de nuit*

  go out to clubs (to), go out clubbing
    (to) *sortir en boîte*

club (organization) *club* (m.)

coach *entraîneur* (m.)

coast *côte* (f.)

coat *manteau* (m.)

coffee *café* (m.)

  coffee with cream *café-crème* (m.)

  coffee shop *café* (m.)

coffeemaker *cafetière* (f.)

coincidence *coïncidence* (f.)

  What a coincidence! *Quelle coïncidence !*

cold *froid / froide* (m./f.)

  It's cold. *Il fait froid.*

  be cold (to) *avoir froid*

colleague *collègue / collègue* (m./f.)

collection *collection* (f.)

college *université* (f.)

  college degree *diplôme* (m.) *universitaire*

cologne *eau* (f.) *de Cologne*

come (to) *venir*

  come back (to) *revenir*

  come back (in) (to) *rentrer*

come in (to) *entrer*
come up (to) *monter*
come down (to) *descendre*
comedy *comédie* (f.)
  romantic comedy *comédie romantique*
comfortable *confortable*
company *société* (f.), *firme* (f.)
complicated *compliqué / compliquée* (m./f.)
computer *ordinateur* (m.)
concert *concert* (m.)
Congratulations. *Félicitations.*
consommé (clear soup made from
  stock) *consommé* (m.)
  vermicelli pasta consommé (noodle
    soup) *consommé aux vermicelles*
construction worker *ouvrier* (m.) *en bâtiment*
consult (to) *consulter*
cook *cuisinier / cuisinière* (m./f.)
cook (to) *cuisiner, préparer*
cooking *cuisine* (f.)
cool (good) *sympa*
corner *coin* (m.)
correct *exact / exacte* (m./f.)
cotton *coton* (m.)
couch *canapé* (m.)
counter *bar* (m.), *comptoir* (m.)
course *cours* (m.)
cousin *cousin / cousine* (m./f.)
cream, creamy dessert *crème* (f.)
  creamy dessert made with caramel *crème
    caramel*
crêpe (tissue-thin pancake) *crêpe* (f.)
  Crêpe Suzette *(crêpe with sugar, orange, and
    liqueur) crêpe Suzette*
crime drama/film *film* (m.) *policier*
cross (to) *traverser*
crudités (French appetizer of raw, mixed
  vegetables) *crudités* (f. pl.)
cucumber *concombre* (m.)
cup *tasse* (f.)
cupboard *placard* (m.)
curtain *rideau* (m.)

D

Dad/Daddy *papa*
daily *quotidien / quotidienne* (m./f.)
dance/dancing *danse* (f.)

dance (to) *danser*
daughter *fille* (f.)
daughter-in-law *belle-fille* (f.)
day *jour* (m.), *journée* (f.)
dear *cher / chère* (m./f.)
December *décembre*
decide (to) *décider*
degree *degré* (m.)
degree (college) *diplôme* (m.) *universitaire*
delete (to) *supprimer*
delicious *délicieux / délicieuse* (m./f.)
dentist *dentiste* (m.)
deodorant *déodorant* (m.)
department store *grand magasin* (m.)
descend (to) *descendre*
description *description* (f.)
desert *désert* (m.)
desk *bureau* (m.)
dessert *dessert* (m.)
detective (adjective) *policier / policière* (m./f.)
  detective drama/film *film* (m.) *policier*
detest (to) *détester*
device *appareil* (m.)
different *différent / différente* (m./f.)
difficult *difficile*
dine (to) *dîner*
dining room *salle* (f.) *à manger*
dinner *dîner* (m.)
  have dinner (to) *dîner*
diploma *diplôme* (m.)
direction *direction* (f.)
director *directeur / directrice* (m./f.)
dirty *sale*
dish *plat* (m.)
dishwasher *lave-vaisselle* (m.)
dishwashing detergent *liquide* (m.) *vaisselle*
do (to) *faire*
  do a tour (to) *faire un tour*
  do the cooking (to) *faire la cuisine*
  do the dishes (to) *faire la vaisselle*
  do the house cleaning (to) *faire le ménage*
  do the laundry (to) *faire la lessive*
  do the shopping (to) *faire les courses*
doctor *médecin* (m.), *docteur* (m.)
document *document* (m.)
documentary *documentaire* (m.)
dog *chien* (m.)
door *porte* (f.)

drama *drame* (m.)
drawer *tiroir* (m.)
dress *robe* (f.)
dress oneself (to) *s'habiller*
drink *boisson* (f.)
drink (to) *boire*
drive (computer) *lecteur* (m.)
  CD-ROM drive *lecteur de CD-ROM*
drugstore *pharmacie* (f.)
dryer *sèche-linge* (m.)
dubbed *doublé / doublée* (m./f.)
duck *canard* (m.)
  duck à l'orange, duck with orange
    sauce *canard à l'orange*
DVD player *lecteur* (m.) *de DVD*

E

each *chaque, chacun / chacune* (m./f.)
each one *chacun / chacune* (m./f.)
ear *oreille* (f.)
earn (to) *gagner*
earring *boucle* (f.) *d'oreille*
east *est* (m.)
easy *facile*
eat (to) *manger*
egg *œuf* (m.)
Eiffel Tower *Tour* (f.) *Eiffel*
eight *huit*
eighteen *dix-huit*
eighth *huitième*
eighty *quatre-vingts*
elbow *coude* (m.)
electrician *électricien* (m.)
electronic game *jeu* (m.) *électronique*
electronics store *magasin* (m.) *d'électronique*
eleven *onze*
email *mail* (m.), *mél* (m.), *email* (m.), *courriel* (m.),
  courrier (m.) *électronique*
employee *employé / employée* (m./f.)
employment *emploi* (m.)
end (to) *terminer*
engineer *ingénieur* (m.)
enjoyable *agréable*
enough *assez*
enter (to) *entrer*
entrance *entrée* (f.)
errand *course* (f.)

especially *surtout*
essential *essentiel / essentielle* (m./f.)
even *même*
evening *soir* (m.), *soirée* (f.)
  this evening *ce soir*
every *tout / toute* (m./f.), *chaque*
everyday *quotidien / quotidienne* (m./f.)
exact *exact / exacte* (m./f.)
excellent *excellent / excellente* (m./f.)
exciting *passionnant / passionnante* (m./f.)
excuse (to) *excuser*
  Excuse me. *Pardon.*
expensive *cher / chère* (m./f.)
expression *expression* (f.)
exterior *extérieur* (m.)
eye (eyes) *œil* (m.) (*yeux, pl.*)
eyebrow *sourcil* (m.)
eyeglasses *lunettes* (f. pl.)
eyelash *cil* (m.)

F

face *visage* (m.)
factory *usine* (f.)
fail (a test) (to) *rater (un examen)*
fall (season) *automne* (m.)
  in (the) fall *en automne*
fall (to) *tomber*
false *faux / fausse* (m./f.)
familiar with (to be) *connaître*
family *famille* (f.)
famous *célèbre*
Fantastic. *Formidable.*
far *loin*
  far from here *loin d'ici*
  farther *plus loin*
farmer *fermier / fermière* (m./f.)
fat *gros / grosse* (m./f.)
father *père* (m.)
  father-in-law *beau-père* (m.)
favorite *préféré / préférée* (m./f.)
fax machine *télécopieur* (m.)
February *février*
festival *fête* (f.)
fiancé/fiancée *fiancé / fiancée* (m./f.)
field *champ* (m.)
fifteen *quinze*
fifth *cinquième*

fifty *cinquante*
file *fichier* (m.)
film *film* (m.)
  action film *film d'action*
  crime/detective film, crime/detective
    drama *film policier*
  original version of a film (not dubbed into
    French) *version* (f.) *originale (v.o.)*
  French version of a film (dubbed into
    French) *version* (f.) *française (v.f.)*
final *dernier / dernière* (m./f.)
finally *enfin*
find (to) *trouver*
find oneself (somewhere) (to) *se trouver*
fine *bien*
finger *doigt* (m.)
finish (to) *finir, terminer*
fire *feu* (m.)
firm (company) *firme* (f.)
first *premier / première* (m./f.)
fish *poisson* (m.)
five *cinq*
flag *drapeau* (m.)
flavor *parfum* (m.)
floor *sol* (m.)
flower *fleur* (f.)
fog *brouillard* (m.)
food *nourriture* (f.)
foot *pied* (m.)
(American) football *football* (m.) *américain*
for *pour, de / d'*
forehead *front* (m.)
forest *forêt* (f.)
fork *fourchette* (f.)
forty *quarante*
forward (to) *faire suivre*
four *quatre*
fourteen *quatorze*
fourth *quatrième*
French *français / française* (m./f.)
  French language *français* (m.)
  French version of a film (dubbed into
    French) *version* (f.) *française (v.f.)*
  French fries *frites* (f. pl.)
Friday *vendredi*
friend *ami / amie* (m./f.)
friendly *amical / amicale* (m./f.)
from *de / d'*

from here *d'ici*
fruit *fruit* (m.)
  fruit salad *salade* (f.) *de fruits*
full-time *à plein temps*
funny *amusant / amusante* (m./f.)

G

gallery *galerie* (f.)
game *jeu* (m.), *match* (m.)
garage *garage* (m.)
garden *jardin* (m.)
generous *généreux / généreuse* (m./f.)
gentle *doux / douce* (m./f.)
get a divorce (to) *divorcer*
get dressed (to) *s'habiller*
get somewhere (to) *arriver*
get up (to) *se lever*
girl *fille* (f.)
girlfriend *copine* (f.), *petite amie* (f.)
give (to) *donner*
glass *verre* (m.)
glove *gant* (m.)
go (to) *aller*
  Let's go. *Allons-y. / On y va.*
  go across (to) *traverser*
  go away (to) *partir*
  go down (to) *descendre*
  go horseback riding (to) *faire de l'équitation*
  go swimming (to) *faire de la natation*
  go camping (to) *camper*
  go hiking (to) *faire de la marche, de la randonée*
  go home (to) *rentrer*
  go in (to) *rentrer*
  go out (to) *partir*
  go out clubbing (to), go out to clubs
    (to) *sortir en boîte*
  go (past) (to) *passer*
  go shopping (to) *faire les courses*
  go sightseeing (to) *aller visiter*
  go to bed (to) *se coucher*
  go up (to) *monter*
good *bon / bonne* (m./f.), *bien, sympa*
  very good *très bien, très bon / bonne,*
    très sympa
  Good luck. *Bonne chance.*
  Good evening. *Bonsoir.*
  Good-bye. *Au revoir.*

grade note *(score)* (f.)
grammar *grammaire* (f.)
grandfather *grand-père* (m.)
  grandfather clock *pendule* (f.)
grandmother *grand-mère* (f.)
grandparent *grand-parent* (m.)
grape(s) *raisin* (m.)
Great. Super.
green *vert / verte* (m./f.)
  green bean *haricot* (m.) *vert*
guide *guide* (m.)
guided tour *visite* (f.) *guidée*
gym (physical education) *gymnastique* (f.)
gymnastics *gymnastique* (f.)

H

hail *grêle* (f.)
  It's hailing. *Il grêle.*
hair *cheveux* (m. pl.)
  hair (single strand) *cheveu* (m.)
half *demi / demie* (m./f.)
  half past ... *... et demie*
hall *couloir* (m.), *salle* (f.)
hand *main* (f.)
handsome *beau / bel / belle* (m./m. before vowel or silent h/f.)
happy *heureux / heureuse* (m./f.)
haste *hâte* (f.)
hasten (to) *hâter*
hat *chapeau* (m.)
hate (to) *détester*
hatred *haine* (f.)
have (to) *avoir*
  have (food/drink) (to) *prendre*
  have a drink (to) *prendre un verre*
  have breakfast (to) *prendre le petit déjeuner*
  have lunch (to) *déjeuner*
  have dinner (to) *dîner*
  have a good time (to), have fun (to) *s'amuser*
  have a party (to) *organiser une fête*
he *il*
head *tête* (f.)
health *santé* (f.)
  To your health! *À votre santé !*
  healthy *en bonne santé*
heart *cœur* (m.)

Hello. *Bonjour.*
  Hello. (on the phone) *Allô.*
her *son / sa / ses* (m./f./pl.), *elle*
here *ici, ci*
  from here *d'ici*
  here is/are, here it is/they are *voici, voilà*
hero/heroine *héros / héroïne* (m./f.)
herself (reflexive pronoun) *se / s'*
Hi. *Salut.*
high *haut / haute* (m./f.)
hill *colline* (f.)
him *lui*
himself (reflexive pronoun) *se / s'*
his *son / sa / ses* (m./f./pl.)
history *histoire* (f.)
hockey *hockey* (m.)
holiday *fête* (f.)
home *maison* (f.), *foyer* (m.)
homemade *maison*
homework *devoirs* (m. pl.)
honey *miel* (m.)
horseback riding *équitation* (f.)
  go horseback riding (to) *faire de l'équitation*
hospital *hôpital* (m.)
hot *chaud / chaude* (m./f.)
  It's hot./It's warm. *Il fait chaud.*
  be hot/warm (to) *avoir chaud*
hotel *hôtel* (m.)
hour *heure* (f.)
house cleaning *ménage* (m.)
house *maison* (f.)
  at someone's house/place *chez*
how *comment, comme*
  how many, how much *combien*
  How? (Pardon?/What did you say?) *Comment ?*
  How's it going?/How are you? *(Comment) ça va ?*
  How are you? *Comment vas-tu ?* (infml.) / *Comment allez-vous ?* (pl./fml.)
hundred *cent*
hunger *faim* (f.)
  be hungry (to) *avoir faim*
hurricane *ouragan* (m.)
husband *mari* (m.)

I

I *je / j'*
  I am called … (My name is …) *Je m'appelle…*
  I don't understand. *Je ne comprends pas.*
  I'm fine. *Ça va.*
  I'm very well. *Je vais très bien.*
  I want … *Je veux…*
  I would like … *Je voudrais…*
ice skate/skating *patin* (m.) *à glace*
idea *idée* (f.)
if *si*
Île de la Cité (City Island) *Île* (f.) *de la Cité*
impoverished *pauvre*
in *à, dans, en*
  in the *au / à la / à l' / aux* (m./f./m. or f. before a vowel or silent h/pl.)
  in front (of) *devant*
indeed *en effet*
information center *centre* (m.) *d'informations*
inherit (to) *hériter*
inn *auberge* (f.)
instant message *message* (m.) *instantané*
intelligent *intelligent / intelligente* (m./f.)
interesting *intéressant / intéressante* (m./f.)
internet *Internet* (m.)
intersection *intersection* (f.)
into *dans, en*
introduce (to) *présenter*
  Let me introduce … *Je te présente…* (infml.) / *Je vous présente…* (pl./fml.)
invite (to) *inviter*
iron *fer* (m.) *à repasser*
ironing board *planche* (f.) *à repasser*
Is that all? *C'est tout ?*
isn't it?/isn't that so? *n'est-ce pas ?*
it *ça / c', il / elle / ils / elles* (m./f./m. pl./f. pl.)
  It rains. *Il pleut.*
it is *c'est*
  isn't it? *n'est-ce pas ?*
  it's necessary to *il faut*
  It's going well. *Ça va bien.*
  It's not going well./It's going badly. *Ça va mal.*
  It's beautiful (outside). *Il fait beau.*
  It's hot./It's warm. *Il fait chaud.*
  It's cold. *Il fait froid.*
  It's sunny. *Il fait (du) soleil.*
  It's windy. *Il fait du vent. / Il y a du vent.*
  It's hailing. *Il grêle.*
  It's snowing. *Il neige.*
  It's raining. *Il pleut.*
its *son / sa / ses* (m./f./pl.)
itself (reflexive pronoun) *se / s'*

J

jacket *veste* (f.)
January *janvier*
jeans *jean* (m.)
jewel *bijou* (m.)
  jewelry *bijoux* (m. pl.)
job *boulot* (m.), *emploi* (m.)
joint (of meat) *rôti* (m.)
journalist *journaliste* (m./f.)
juice *jus* (m.)
July *juillet*
June *juin*
junior high school *collège* (m.)

K

keyboard *clavier* (m.)
kind *gentil / gentille* (m./f.)
kitchen *cuisine* (f.)
  kitchen sink *évier* (m.) *de la cuisine*
knee *genou* (m.)
knife *couteau* (m.)
know (to) *savoir, connaître*

L

lake *lac* (m.)
lamb *agneau* (m.)
lamp *lampe* (f.)
lamppost *réverbère* (m.)
land *terre* (f.)
language *langue* (f.)
large *grand / grande* (m./f.)
last *dernier / dernière* (m./f.)
latest *dernier / dernière* (m./f.)
laundry detergent *lessive* (f.)
lawyer *avocat / avocate* (m./f.)
learn (to) *apprendre*
  I'm learning French. *J'apprends le français.*
leather *cuir* (m.)

leave (to) *partir, sortir*
left *gauche* (f.)
leg *jambe* (f.)
less *moins*
lesson *leçon* (f.)
Let me introduce ... *Je te présente...* (infml.) / *Je vous présente...*(pl./fml.)
Let's go. *Allons-y. / On y va.* (infml.)
letter *lettre* (f.)
lettuce *laitue* (f.)
library *bibliothèque* (f.)
life *vie* (f.)
lightning *éclair* (m.)
like *comme*
like (to) *aimer*
line *queue* (f.)
　wait in line (to) *faire la queue*
link *liaison* (f.)
listen (to) (to) *écouter*
literature *littérature* (f.)
little *petit / petite* (m./f.)
　a little *un peu*
live (to) *habiter*
living room *salon* (m.)
lobster *homard* (m.)
　lobster bisque *bisque* (f.) *de homard*
long *long / longue* (m./f.)
look for (to) *chercher*
look forward to (to) (can't wait) *avoir hâte*
lose (to) *perdre*
lost *perdu / perdue* (m./f.)
　I'm lost. *Je suis perdu / perdue.*
Louvre *Louvre* (m.)
love (to) *aimer, adorer*
low *bas / basse* (m./f.)
lunch *déjeuner* (m.)
　have lunch (to) *déjeuner*
lung *poumon* (m.)

M

ma'am/madam *madame*
magazine *magazine* (m.), *revue* (f.)
mail *poste* (f.)
mail (to) *mettre à la poste*
main course/dish *plat* (m.) *principal*
make (to) *faire, préparer*
　make a phone call (to) *téléphoner*

　That makes ... *Ça fait...*
man *homme* (m.)
manager *gérant / gérante* (m./f.), *directeur / directrice* (m./f.)
many *beaucoup de*
map *carte* (f.), *plan* (m.)
March *mars*
market *marché* (m.)
marry (someone) (to) *épouser (quelqu'un)*
match (in sports) *match* (m.)
math *maths* (f.), *mathématiques* (f.)
May *mai*
mayor *maire* (m.)
me *moi*
meat *viande* (f.)
medicine *médecine* (f.)
　medicine cabinet *armoire* (f.) *à pharmacie*
meet (a person/someone) (to) *rencontrer (une personne/quelqu'un)*
meeting *rendez-vous* (m.), *réunion* (f.)
　meeting room *salle* (f.) *de réunion*
melon *melon* (m.)
memory *mémoire* (f.)
menu *menu* (m.), *carte* (f.)
metro *métro* (m.)
　metro station *station* (f.) *de métro*
microwave (oven) *micro-ondes* (m.)
middle school *collège* (m.)
midnight *minuit* (m.)
milk *lait* (m.)
minus *moins*
mirror *miroir* (m.)
miss *mademoiselle*
modem *modem* (m.)
Mom/Mommy *maman*
moment *moment* (m.)
Mona Lisa *Joconde* (f.)
Monday *lundi*
monitor *écran* (m.)
month *mois* (m.)
monument *monument* (m.)
moon *lune* (f.)
more *plus*
morning *matin* (m.), *matinée* (f.)
mosque *mosquée* (f.)
mostly *surtout*
mother *mère* (f.)
　mother-in-law *belle-mère* (f.)

motorcycle/motorcycling *moto* (f.)

mountain *montagne* (f.)

mouse *souris* (f.)

mousse *mousse* (f.)

mouth *bouche* (f.)

movie *film* (m.)

   movie theater, the movies *cinéma* (m.)

Mr. *monsieur*

Mrs. *madame*

Ms. *madame*

municipal building *mairie* (f.)

muscle *muscle* (m.)

museum *musée* (m.)

music *musique* (f.)

musician *musicien / musicienne* (m./f.)

my *mon / ma / mes* (m./f./pl.)

   My name is … *Je m'appelle…*

myself (reflexive pronoun) *me / m'*

mysterious *mystérieux / mystérieuse* (m./f.)

N

name *nom* (m.)

napkin *serviette* (f.)

near *près*

   very near *tout près*

   nearby, near here *près d'ici*

necessary (to be) *falloir*

neck *cou* (m.)

necklace *collier* (m.)

neighborhood *quartier* (m.), *coin* (m.)

nephew *neveu* (m.)

never *jamais*

new *nouveau / nouvel / nouvelle* (m./m. before a vowel or silent h/f.)

news (the news) *nouvelles* (f. pl.)

next *ensuite*

   next to *à côté de*

nice *gentil / gentille* (m./f.), *sympa, joli / jolie* (m./f.), *beau / bel / belle* (m./m. before vowel or silent h/f.)

   Nice to meet you. *Enchanté. / Enchantée.* (m./f.)

niece *nièce* (f.)

night *nuit* (f.), *soir* (m.)

nightclub *boîte de nuit* (f.)

   go out to clubs (to), go out clubbing (to) *sortir en boîte*

nine *neuf*

nineteen *dix-neuf*

ninety *quatre-vingt-dix*

ninth *neuvième*

no *non*

noodle soup (vermicelli pasta consommé) *consommé* (m.) *aux vermicelles*

noon *midi* (m.)

north *nord* (m.)

nose *nez* (m.)

not *ne / n'… pas, pas*

   Not bad. *Pas mal.*

note *note* (f.)

notebook *cahier* (m.)

nothing *rien*

   It's nothing. *De rien.*

November *novembre*

now *maintenant*

number *nombre* (m.)

O

ocean *océan* (m.)

October *octobre*

of *de / d'*

   of it, of them *en*

   of the *du / de la / de l' / des* (m./f./m. or f. before a vowel or silent h/pl.)

   Of course. *Bien sûr.*

office *bureau* (m.)

oil *huile* (f.)

Okay. *D'accord.*

old *vieux / vieil / vieille* (m./m. before a vowel or silent h/f.)

once *une fois*

one (number) *un / une* (m./f.)

one (pronoun) *on*

oneself (reflexive pronoun) *se / s'*

onion *oignon* (m.)

   onion soup *soupe* (f.) *à l'oignon*

only child *fils / fille unique* (m./f.)

open (to) *ouvrir*

   open a file (to) *ouvrir un fichier*

opera *opéra* (m.)

or *ou*

orange *orange* (f.)

organize (to) *organiser*

original *original / originale* (m./f.)

original version of a film (not dubbed into French) *version* (f.) *originale (v.o.)*
other *autre*
our *notre / nos* (m. or f./pl.)
ourselves (reflexive pronoun) *nous*
outside (preposition) *hors*
outside (noun) *extérieur* (m.)
oven *four* (m.)
over there *là-bas*
own *propre*

P

paint (to) *peindre*
painting *tableau* (m.)
pajamas *pyjama* (m.)
pants *pantalon* (m.)
Pardon (me). *Pardon.*
parent *parent* (m.)
Paris *Paris*
park *parc* (m.)
part (in a play, movie, etc.) *rôle* (m.)
part-time *à temps partiel*
party *soirée* (f.), *fête* (f.), *partie* (f.)
pass (to) *passer*
   pass (a test) (to) *réussir à (un examen)*
passport *passeport* (m.)
pastry *pâtisserie* (f.)
   pastry shop *pâtisserie* (f.)
pâté (spreadable purée of meat) *pâté* (m.)
pay (to) *payer*
peach *pêche* (f.)
   peaches with ice cream *pêche Melba*
pear *poire* (f.)
people *gens* (m. pl.)
people in general (pronoun) *on*
pepper (condiment) *poivre* (m.)
pepper (vegetable) *poivron* (m.)
perfect *parfait / parfaite* (m./f.)
perform (to) *jouer*
perfume *parfum* (m.)
person *personne* (f.)
pharmacy *pharmacie* (f.)
phone (to) *téléphoner*
photo *photo* (f.)
   Can you take our picture (photo), please? *Pourriez-vous nous prendre en photo, s'il vous plaît ?*

physical education *gymnastique* (f.)
piece *pièce* (f.)
pig *porc* (m.), *cochon* (m.)
place *place* (f.)
plant *plante* (f.)
plastic *plastique* (m.)
   made of plastic *en plastique*
plate *assiette* (f.)
play (theater) *pièce* (f.)
play (to) *jouer*
   play a sport (to) *faire du sport*
player (CDs, DVDs, etc.) *lecteur* (m.)
   CD player *lecteur de CD*
   DVD player *lecteur de DVD*
player (games, sports, etc.) *joueur / joueuse* (m./f.)
playing cards *cartes* (f. pl.) *à jouer*
pleasant *agréable*
please (infml./pl., fml.) *s'il te plaît / s'il vous plaît*
Pleased to meet you. *Enchanté. / Enchantée.* (m./f.)
pleasure *plaisir* (m.)
   With pleasure. *Avec plaisir.*
plumber *plombier* (m.)
police (adjective) *policier / policière* (m./f.)
policeman/woman *policier / femme policier* (m./f.)
pond *étang* (m.), *mare* (f.)
pool (billiards) *billard* (m.)
poor *pauvre*
pork *porc* (m.)
   pork chop *côte* (f.) *de porc*
post office *poste* (f.), *bureau* (m.) *de poste*
potato *pomme* (f.) *de terre*
powder *poudre* (f.), *talc* (m.)
practice (to) *pratiquer*
prefer (to) *préférer*
prepare (to) *préparer*
present (to) *présenter*
pretty *joli / jolie* (m./f.)
printer *imprimante* (f.)
professor *professeur / professeure* (m./f.)
professor (infml.) *prof* (m./f.)
progress *progrès* (m.)
purple *violet / violette* (m./f.)
put (to) *mettre*
   put in the mail (to) *mettre à la poste*

Q

quarter *quart* (m.)
  quarter after/past ... *... et quart*
  quarter to ... *... moins le quart*
quiche *quiche* (f.)
  type of quiche made with bacon *quiche lorraine*
quiet *calme*
quite *assez*

R

race *course* (f.)
rack (of meat) *carré* (m.)
  rack of lamb *carré d'agneau*
radish *radis* (m.)
rain *pluie* (f.)
rain (to) *pleuvoir*
  It's raining./It rains. *Il pleut.*
raw *cru / crue* (m./f.)
razor *rasoir* (m.)
reach (to) *arriver*
read (to) *lire*
ready *prêt / prête* (m./f.)
real *vrai / vraie* (m./f.)
really *en effet, bien*
recent *dernier / dernière* (m./f.)
reception desk *réception* (f.)
recess *récré(ation)* (f.)
red *rouge*
  red wine *vin* (m.) *rouge*
refrigerator *réfrigérateur* (m.)
relative *parent* (m.)
repeat (to) *répéter*
  Repeat (that), please. *Répétez, s'il vous plaît.*
reply (to) *répondre*
report card *bulletin* (m.) *scolaire*
reservation *réservation* (f.)
reserve (to) *réserver*
restaurant *restaurant* (m.)
restroom *toilettes* (f. pl.)
  Where is the restroom? *Où sont les toilettes ?*
retired *à la retraite*
retirement *retraite* (f.)
return (to) *revenir, rentrer*
reunion *réunion* (f.)
rib (meat) *côte* (f.)

rice *riz* (m.)
rich *riche*
right (opposite of left) *droite* (f.)
  be right (to) *avoir raison*
  right? *n'est-ce pas ?*
ring *bague* (f.)
rise (to) *monter*
river *rivière* (f.)
roast (of meat) *rôti* (m.)
roast(ed) *rôti / rôtie* (m./f.)
rock *rocher* (m.)
role *rôle* (m.)
romantic *romantique*
  romantic comedy *comédie* (f.) *romantique*
room *pièce* (f.), *salle* (f.), *place* (f.)
rosé wine *vin* (m.) *rosé*
run *course* (f.)
running *course à pied*
rural *rural / rurale* (m./f.)
rush (to) *se hâter*

S

Sacré Cœur (Sacred Heart) *Sacré-Cœur* (m.)
sad *triste*
sailing *voile* (f.)
salad *salade* (f.)
salary *salaire* (m.)
salesman/woman *vendeur / vendeuse* (m./f.)
salt *sel* (m.)
same *même*
sand *sable* (m.)
sardines *sardines* (f. pl.)
  sardines in tomato sauce *sardines sauce tomate*
Saturday *samedi*
sauce *sauce* (f.)
save a document (to) *sauvegarder un document*
scarf (fashion) *foulard* (m.)
scarf (winter) *écharpe* (f.)
scary *effrayant / effrayante* (m./f.)
schedule *horaire* (m.)
school *école* (f.)
screen *écran* (m.)
sculpture *sculpture* (f.)
sea *mer* (f.)
seat *place* (f.)
seated *assis / assise* (m./f.)

second *deuxième, second / seconde* (m./f.)
secondary school *collège* (m.)
secretary *secrétaire* (m./f.)
see (to) *voir*
sell (to) *vendre*
send (to) *envoyer*
  send a file (to) *envoyer un fichier*
  send an email (to) *envoyer un mail / mél /*
    email / courriel / courrier électronique
September *septembre*
server *serveur / serveuse* (m./f.)
seven *sept*
seventeen *dix-sept*
seventh *septième*
seventy *soixante-dix*
shame *honte* (f.)
  be ashamed (to) *avoir honte*
shampoo *shampooing* (m.)
shave (to) *se raser*
shaving cream *crème* (f.) *à raser*
she *elle*
shelf *étagère* (f.)
shirt *chemise* (f.)
shoe *chaussure* (f.)
  shoe store *magasin* (m.) *de chaussures*
short *petit / petite* (m./f.), *court / courte* (m./f.)
shoulder *épaule* (f.)
show (to) *montrer, présenter, donner*
shower *douche* (f.)
shower gel *gel* (m.) *douche*
shrimp *crevettes* (f. pl.)
sick *malade*
side *côté* (m.)
  next to (at the side of) *à côté de*
sidewalk *trottoir* (m.)
silk *soie* (f.)
sing (to) *chanter*
singer *chanteur / chanteuse* (m./f.)
sink *évier* (m.)
sir *monsieur*
sister *sœur* (f.)
sitting (down) *assis / assise* (m./f.)
situated (to be) *se trouver*
six *six*
sixteen *seize*
sixth *sixième*
sixty *soixante*
size *taille* (f.)

skate/skating *patin* (m.)
skiing *ski* (m.)
skin *peau* (f.)
skirt *jupe* (f.)
sky *ciel* (m.)
sleeping car/sleeper car *wagon-lit* (m.)
sleepy (to be) *avoir sommeil*
slow *lent / lente* (m./f.)
slowly *lentement*
small *petit / petite* (m./f.)
smile *sourire* (m.)
sneaker *basket* (m./f.), *chaussure* (f.) *de basket*
snow *neige* (f.)
snow (to) *neiger*
  It's snowing. *Il neige.*
so ... *alors...*
soap *savon* (m.)
soccer *foot(ball)* (m.)
  soccer player *footballeur / footballeuse* (m./f.)
  soccer stadium *stade* (m.) *de foot*
social *social / sociale* (m./f.)
sock *chaussette* (f.)
sofa *canapé* (m.)
soft *doux / douce* (m./f.)
soft drink *boisson* (f.) *gazeuse*
sole (fish) *sole* (f.)
  sole covered in flour and sautéed in
    butter *sole meunière*
some *du / de la / de l' / des* (m./f./m. or f. before a
  vowel or silent h/pl.), *en*
sometimes *parfois*
son *fils* (m.)
son-in-law *beau-fils* (m.)
song *chanson* (f.)
So-so. *Comme ci, comme ça.*
sound system *chaîne* (f.) *hi-fi*
soup *soupe* (f.)
  onion soup *soupe à l'oignon*
  consommé (clear soup made from
    stock) *consommé* (m.)
  vermicelli pasta consommé (noodle
    soup) *consommé aux vermicelles*
sour *aigre*
south *sud* (m.)
speak (to) *parler*
  Speak more slowly, please. *Parlez plus lente-*
    ment, s'il vous plaît.

I speak a little French. *Je parle un peu français.*

specialty *spécialité* (f.)

spoon *cuillère* (f.)

spring *printemps* (m.)

  in (the) spring *au printemps*

square *carré* (m.)

stadium *stade* (m.)

  soccer stadium *stade de foot*

staff *personnel* (m.)

stairs *escaliers* (m. pl.)

stamp *timbre* (m.)

standing (up) *debout*

star *étoile* (f.)

start (to) *commencer*

station *station* (f.)

  subway/metro station *station de métro*

statue *statue* (f.)

stay (to) *rester*

steady job *emploi* (m.) *régulier*

stepdaughter *belle-fille* (f.)

stepfather *beau-père* (m.)

stepmother *belle-mère* (f.)

stepson *beau-fils* (m.)

still *toujours*

stomach *estomac* (m.)

stop *arrêt* (m.)

  bus stop *arrêt de bus*

store *magasin* (m.)

storm *orage* (m.)

story *histoire* (f.)

stove *cuisinière* (f.)

straight *droit*

  straight ahead *tout droit*

street *rue* (f.)

streetlight *lampadaire* (m.)

strong *fort / forte* (m./f.)

student *étudiant / étudiante* (m./f.)

study (to) *étudier*

subject *sujet* (m.)

subtitle *sous-titre* (m.)

suburban *de banlieue*

suburbs *banlieue* (f.)

subway *métro* (m.)

  subway station *station* (f.) *de métro*

sugar *sucre* (m.)

suit *costume* (m.)

summer *été* (m.)

  in (the) summer *en été*

sun *soleil* (m.)

  It's sunny. *Il fait (du) soleil.*

Sunday *dimanche*

sunglasses *lunettes* (f. pl.) *de soleil*

Super. *Super.*

supermarket *supermarché* (m.)

sweet *doux / douce* (m./f.)

swimming *natation* (f.)

  go swimming (to) *faire de la natation*

Swiss *suisse*

synagogue *synagogue* (f.)

T

table *table* (f.)

  table for two *table pour deux*

tail *queue* (f.)

take (to) *prendre*

  take a bath (to) *prendre un bain*

  take a shower (to) *prendre une douche*

  take a tour (to) *faire un tour*

  take along (to) *emmener*

  take a picture (to) *prendre une photo*

  Can you take our picture? *Pourriez-vous nous prendre en photo, s'il vous plaît ?*

talented *talentueux / talentueuse* (m./f.)

talk (to) *parler*

tall *grand / grande* (m./f.)

taste *goût* (m.)

taxi *taxi* (m.)

  taxi driver *chauffeur* (m.) *de taxi*

tea *thé* (m.)

teach (to) *enseigner*

teacher *professeur / professeure* (m./f.), *enseignant / enseignante* (m./f.)

teacher (infml.) *prof* (m./f.)

teakettle/teapot *théière* (f.)

team *équipe* (f.)

teenager *adolescent / adolescente* (m./f.)

telephone *téléphone* (m.), *appareil* (m.)

television *télé(vision)* (f.)

  television program *émission* (f.)

temperature *température* (f.)

temple *temple* (m.)

ten *dix*

tendon *tendon* (m.)

tennis *tennis* (m.)

tennis shoe *basket* (m./f.), *chaussure* (f.) *de basket*

tenth *dixième*

test *examen* (m.)

  fail (a test) (to) *rater (un examen)*

  pass (a test) (to) *réussir à (un examen)*

textbook *livre* (m.) *scolaire*

thank you *merci*

that *ce / cet / cette* (m./m. before a vowel or silent h/f.), *ça / c', que, qui*

  That makes .../That is *Ça fait...*

  that is *c'est*

  Is that all? *C'est tout ?*

the *le / la / l' / les* (m./f./m. or f. before a vowel or silent h/pl.)

theater *théâtre* (m.)

their *leur / leurs* (m. or f./pl.)

them *eux / elles* (m./f.)

themselves (reflexive pronoun) *se / s'*

then *puis, ensuite, alors*

there *là, là-bas*

  over there *là-bas*

  there is/are *il y a, voilà*

  there it is/they are *voilà*

these *ces*

they *ils / elles* (m./f.)

thin *mince*

thing *chose* (f.)

think (to) *penser*

third *troisième*

thirst *soif* (f.)

  be thirsty (to) *avoir soif*

thirteen *treize*

thirty *trente*

this *ce / cet / cette* (m./m. before a vowel or silent h/f.), *ça / c', ci*

this is *c'est*

those *ces*

thousand *mille*

three *trois*

throw (to) *envoyer*

thunder *tonnerre* (m.)

Thursday *jeudi*

ticket *place* (f.)

tie (in a game/match) (to) *faire match nul*

time *fois* (f.), *temps* (m.)

  once (one time) *une fois*

  What time is it? *Quelle heure est-il ?*

to *à, pour, en, jusqu'à*

  to the *au / à la / à l' / aux* (m./f./m. or f. before a vowel or silent h/pl.)

  next to *à côté de*

  To your health! *À votre santé !*

today *aujourd'hui*

toe *doigt* (m.) *de pied, orteil* (m.)

together *ensemble*

toilet *toilettes* (f. pl.)

  toilet paper *papier* (m.) *hygiénique*

tomato *tomate* (f.)

tomorrow *demain*

tongue *langue* (f.)

tonight *ce soir*

too *aussi*

tooth *dent* (f.)

tour *tour* (m.)

tourist *touriste* (m./f.)

towel *serviette* (f.)

  bath towel *serviette de bain*

tower *tour* (f.)

  Eiffel Tower *Tour Eiffel*

town *ville* (f.)

traffic *circulation* (f.)

train *train* (m.)

  train station *gare* (f.)

travel (to) *voyager*

tree *arbre* (m.)

trout *truite* (f.)

  trout cooked in wine and vinegar *truite au bleu*

true *vrai / vraie* (m./f.)

T-shirt *T-shirt* (m.)

Tuesday *mardi*

turn *tour* (m.)

turn (to) *tourner*

TV *télé(vision)* (f.)

twelve *douze*

twenty *vingt*

two *deux*

U

ugly *laid / laide* (m./f.)

umbrella *parapluie* (m.)

uncle *oncle* (m.)

underpants *caleçon* (m.)

undershirt *maillot* (m.) *de corps*

understand (to) *comprendre*
  I don't understand. *Je ne comprends pas.*
underwear *sous-vêtements* (m. pl.)
unemployed *au chômage, sans emploi*
unemployment *chômage* (m.)
unfriendly *peu amical / peu amicale* (m./f.)
university *université* (f.)
until, up until, up to *jusqu'à*
urban *urbain / urbaine* (m./f.)
us *nous*

V

vacation *vacances* (f. pl.)
vain *vain / vaine* (m./f.)
vegetable *légume* (m.)
vermicelli pasta *vermicelle* (m.)
  vermicelli pasta consommé (noodle
    soup) *consommé* (m.) *aux vermicelles*
version *version* (f.)
very *très, bien*
  very good *très bien, très bon / bonne* (m./f.)
  very well *très bien*
veterinarian *vétérinaire* (m.)
video game *jeu* (m.) *vidéo*
Vietnamese *vietnamien / vietnamienne* (m./f.)
village *village* (m.)
violin *violon* (m.)
visit (a place) (to) *visiter*
vocabulary *vocabulaire* (m.)

W

wait in line (to) *faire la queue*
waiter/waitress *serveur / serveuse* (m./f.)
wall *mur* (m.)
want (to) *vouloir*
  I want ... *Je veux...*
wardrobe *armoire* (f.)
warm *chaud / chaude* (m./f.)
  It's warm./It's hot. *Il fait chaud.*
  be warm/hot (to) *avoir chaud*
wash (to) *laver*
  wash up (to), wash oneself (to) *se laver*
washing machine *machine* (f.) *à laver,*
  lave-linge (m.)
washroom *salle* (f.) *de bains*
watch *montre* (f.)

watch (to) *regarder*
water *eau* (f.)
way *direction* (f.)
  this way *par ici*
we *nous, on* (infml.)
weak *faible*
wear (to) *porter*
weather *temps* (m.)
  What is the weather today? *Quel temps fait-il aujourd'hui ?*
webpage *page* (f.) *web*
website *site* (m.) *web*
Wednesday *mercredi*
week *semaine* (f.)
weekend *week-end* (m.)
weight lifting *haltérophilie* (f.)
Welcome. *Bienvenue.*
  You're welcome. *De rien. / Je vous en prie.*
  (fml.)
well *bien*
  very well *très bien*
  It's going well. *Ça va bien.*
  Well done. *Bravo.*
well ... *alors...*
west *ouest* (m.)
what *qu'est-ce que, quel / quelle* (m./f.), *quoi, que*
  What is this/that? *Qu'est-ce que c'est ?*
  What is the weather today? *Quel temps fait-il aujourd'hui ?*
  What time is it? *Quelle heure est-il ?*
  What's your name? (pl./fml.) *Comment vous appelez-vous ?*
  What's your name? (infml.) *Comment t'appelles-tu ?*
where *où*
  Where is ... ? *Où se trouve... ? / Où est... ?*
  Where is the restroom? *Où sont les toilettes ?*
which *que, quel / quelle* (m./f.)
white *blanc / blanche* (m./f.)
  white wine *vin* (m.) *blanc*
who *qui*
  Who is it?/Who's calling? *Qui est à l'appareil ?*
whom *que*
wife *femme* (f.)
win (to) *gagner*
wind *vent* (m.)
  It's windy. *Il fait du vent. / Il y a du vent.*

window *fenêtre* (f.)
wine *vin* (m.)
   red/white/rosé wine *vin rouge / blanc / rosé*
   wine list *carte* (f.) *des vins*
winter *hiver* (m.)
   in (the) winter *en hiver*
with *avec*
   With pleasure. *Avec plaisir.*
without *sans*
woman *femme* (f.)
wood *bois* (m.)
wooden *en bois*
word *mot* (m.)
work *travail* (m.)
work (to) *travailler*
wrist *poignet* (m.)
write (to) *écrire*
writer *écrivain* (m.) *(sometimes: écrivaine,* f.*)*
wrong *faux / fausse* (m./f.), *mal*
   be wrong (to): *avoir tort*

Y

year *an* (m.), *année* (f.)
yellow *jaune*
yes *oui, si (answer to negative question)*
yesterday *hier*
you *tu* (infml.), *vous* (pl./fml.), *toi* (infml.)
   you have to/need to/must *il faut*
You're welcome. *De rien. / Je vous en prie.* (fml.)
young *jeune*
your (infml.) *ton / ta / tes* (m./f./pl.)
your (pl./fml.) *votre / vos* (m. or f./pl.)
yourself (reflexive pronoun) *te / t'* (infml.), *vous*
   (fml.)
yourselves (reflexive pronoun) *vous*
youth hostel *auberge* (f.) *de jeunesse*

Z

zero *zéro*

TRADITION AND

CREATIVITY IN

TRIBAL ART

Published under the auspices of the
Museum and Laboratories of
Ethnic Arts and Technology
University of California, Los Angeles

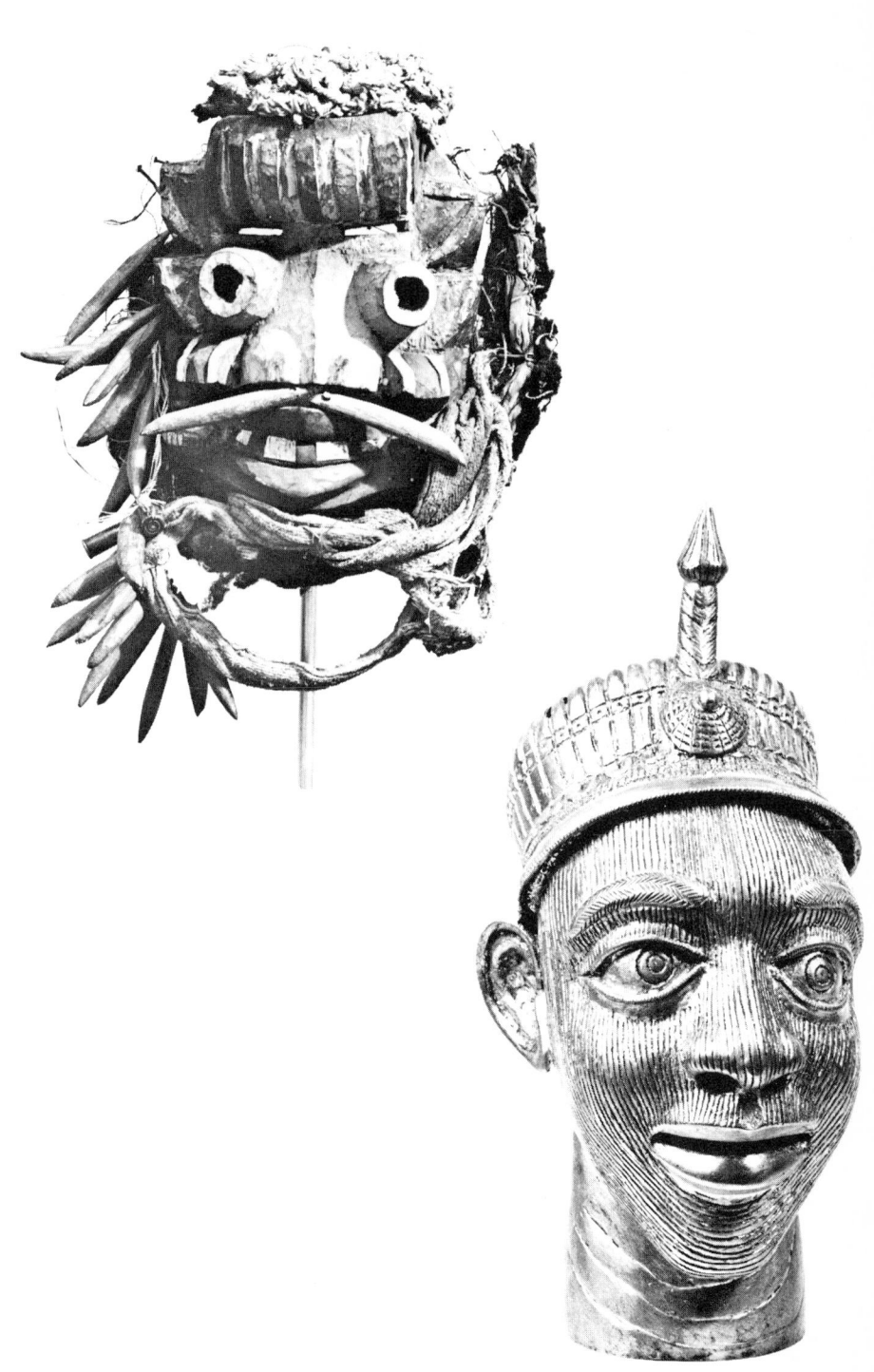

TRADITION and CREATIVITY in

TRIBAL ART

Edited and with an Introduction by **DANIEL P. BIEBUYCK**

UNIVERSITY OF CALIFORNIA PRESS

BERKELEY, LOS ANGELES, LONDON

University of California Press
Berkeley and Los Angeles, California

University of California Press, Ltd.
London, England

Preface

FROM December 6, 1965, through May 13, 1966, the Museum and Laboratories of Ethnic Arts and Technology at the University of California, Los Angeles, organized an exhibition, "Masterpieces from the Sir Henry Wellcome Collection at UCLA," in order to celebrate the gift from the Wellcome Trust in London of thousands of art objects and artifacts from all over the world. In conjunction with this exhibition, a lecture series and symposium were sponsored under the title "Individual Creativity and Tribal Norms in Non-Western Arts." An international group of distinguished authorities on the so-called primitive arts participated in these proceedings from December, 1965, to May, 1966. The formal lectures, all richly illustrated with slides and film, were presented consecutively by R. Goldwater, W. Fagg, A. Gerbrands, R. Thompson, I. Bernal, and J. Guiart. A panel composed of R. Altman, W. Bascom, E. Carpenter, R. Sieber, and D. Biebuyck discussed some of the issues and problems raised during the lecture series.

This book contains the revised lectures, together with the revised and expanded comments made by the members of the panel and the introduction written by the editor. The photographs included in the book represent a small selection of the material that originally illustrated the lectures. With the exception of the essays contributed by R. Thompson and W. Bascom, the original sequence in which both lectures and comments were presented has been respected. In the course of the revision process, R. Thompson's paper developed into the full-scale artistic biography of one Nigerian artist. This longer contribution has been placed at the end of the lecture series as an example of a thus far rare case study in the literature on the meaning and development of a single artist's oeuvre. W. Bascom's contributions to the panel discussions are presented here as a self-contained essay. The editor acknowledges the support of the Ford Foundation and the UCLA Committee on International and Comparative Studies. He is also grateful to Miss B. Jones, Mrs. V. Dawson, and Mr. R. Abbott, all at the University of Delaware, for the work contributed in the editing and final presentation of the manuscript.

D. B.

Photographic Credits

I. Bandi, Paris, plates 50 to 68
British Museum, London, plates 13, 14, 24
L. K. Carroll, Lagos, plate 20
W. Fagg, London, plates 16 to 19 and 21 to 23
Wilson Perkins Foss IV, Yale, plate 94
Institute of African Studies, University of Ghana, Legon, plate 97
Instituto Nacional de Antropología e Historia, Mexico City, plates
    33, 41, 42, 44, 46, 49
Mark Kinnaman, Yale, plate 86
W. Moore, Los Angeles, plate 25
Musée National des Arts Africains et Océaniens, Paris, plates 50
    to 68
Museo Nacional de Antropología, Mexico City, plates 38 to 40, 43,
    45, 47, 48
Museum of Primitive Art, New York, plates 1 to 12
Alex Nicoloff, Berkeley, plate 79
Nigerian Museum, Lagos, plates 15, 87

Contributors

ALTMAN, RALPH C. Late Lecturer in the Department of Art, and Director, Museum and Laboratories of Ethnic Arts and Technology, University of California, Los Angeles. Publications include "Comments on Studying Ethnological Art" in *Current Anthropology*, "North American Indian Arts" in the *Encyclopedia of World Art*, and numerous exhibition catalogues.

BASCOM, WILLIAM. Professor of Anthropology, and Director, Robert H. Lowie Museum of Anthropology, University of California, Berkeley. Field experience in Nigeria, Cuba, Caroline Islands, North America. Publications include *The Sociological Role of the Yoruba Cult-Group, Continuity and Change in Africa* (with M. J. Herskovits), *Handbook of West African Art* (with P. Gebauer), *African Arts*, and *Ifa Divination*.

BERNAL, IGNACIO. Professor of Anthropology, and Director, Museo Nacional de Antropología, Mexico City. Field experience in various sites in Mexico. Publications include *Mexico before Cortez, Teotihuacan, Descubrimientos, Reconstrucciones, Bibliografía de Arquelogía y Etnografía: Mesoamérica y Norte de Mexico, 1514–1960, Urnas de Oaxaca* (with A. Caso), and *The Mexican National Museum of Anthropology.*

BIEBUYCK, DANIEL.   H. Rodney Sharp Professor of Anthropology and Sociology, University of Delaware. Field experience among Zoba, Bembe, Lega, Nyanga, and other ethnic groups of Congo/Kinshasa. Publications include *African Agrarian Systems* (ed.), *Congo Tribes and Parties* (with M. Douglas), *The Mwindo Epic from the Banyanga* (with K. Mateene), *Anthologie de la littérature orale nyanga* (with K. Mateene), and *Lega Culture.*

CARPENTER, EDMUND.   Professor of Anthropology, Adelphi University. Field experience in Canadian Arctic, Micronesia, Siberia, Borneo. Publications include *Eskimo, Anerca: New Directions, Explorations in Communications,* and *We Wed Ourselves to the Mystery.*

FAGG, WILLIAM.   Deputy Keeper of Ethnography in the British Museum. Field experience in Nigeria, Dahomey, Ghana, Ivory Coast, Sierra Leone, Congo/Kinshasa. Publications include *The Sculpture of Africa* (with E. Elisofon), *Nigerian Images, African Art* (with M. Plass), and *Tribes and Forms in African Art.*

GERBRANDS, ADRIAN.   Professor of Cultural Anthropology, Leiden University, Holland. Former Vice-Director of the Rijksmuseum voor Volkenkunde, Leiden. Field experience in New Guinea and New Britain. Publications include *Art as an Element of Culture, Especially in Negro Africa, Wow-Ipits: Eight Asmat Wood-Carvers of New Guinea,* and *The Asmat of New Guinea: The Michael C. Rockefeller Expeditions* (ed. and introduction).

GOLDWATER, ROBERT. Professor of Fine Arts, New York University, and Chairman, Administrative Committee, Museum of Primitive Art, New York. Publications include *Primitivism in Modern Art, Modern Art in Your Life, Bambara Sculpture from the Western Sudan,* and *Senufo Sculpture from West Africa.*

GUIART, JEAN. Professor of Anthropology, University of Paris. Field experience in New Caledonia, New Hebrides, Loyalty Islands, New Guinea. Publications include *Océanie, Structure de la chefferie en Melanésie du Sud,* and *Nouvelles-Hébrides.*

SIEBER, ROY. Professor of Fine Arts, Indiana University, Bloomington. Field experience in Ghana and Nigeria. Publications include *African Sculpture, Sculpture of Northern Nigeria,* "The Visual Arts" in *The African World,* ed. R. A. Lystad (1965), and *Sculpture of Black Africa* (with A. Rubin).

THOMPSON, ROBERT. Associate Professor of Art History, Yale University. Field experience in Nigeria, Dahomey, Liberia, Cuba, and Brazil. Publications include "Yoruba Artistic Criticism," in *The Traditional Artist in African Society,* ed. W. d'Azevedo, "Yoruba Beaded and Brass Crowns" in *Art and Leadership in Africa,* ed. D. Fraser and H. Cole, "An Aesthetic of the Cool: West African Dance" in *African Forum* (1966), and *Black Gods and Kings.*

Contents

Plates

1. Introduction

DANIEL BIEBUYCK

IN THEIR many studies on morphology and distribution, students of primitive art have, more or less convincingly, established evidence to prove that there exist larger or smaller geographical areas within which, over a certain period of time, characteristic types of art objects, forms, designs, motifs, and style elements occur. They have, with varying results, tried to establish stylistic relationships among several such areas. Various descriptive concepts have been used to identify these areas of relatively uniform styles, such as stylistic area, art-culture area, style province, and tribal style. The specific terms by which these areas are labeled represent a heterogeneous set of geographical terms or tribal labels; sometimes they are borrowed from particular categories of objects, institutional complexes, or style elements. In addition, the literature abounds with dubious and imprecise ascriptions of objects that cannot be conveniently placed within the recognized stylistic areas. The methodology that underlies stylistic classifications is often lacking in consistency and rigidity. Some so-called stylistic areas, indeed, seem to be constructed merely on the readily observable occurrences of highly distinctive objects rather than on the clear-cut isolation of precisely defined style elements. In many milieus, it has become a standard practice to speak about tribal style and tribal art. Surely the labels are convenient, but the identification of such concepts as "tribal" is uncertain. The reasons for this vagueness are obvious: cross-culturally valid definitions of these concepts are absent from the anthropological literature, and even in the better monographs one is often left in doubt as to the boundaries or the degree of uniformity of the cultures studied. Regardless of these difficulties, however, there is ample evidence to show that specific categories of art objects or specific art styles are often correlated not with whole cultures but with particular institutions, such as initiation systems, cults, voluntary associations, restricted belief systems, and myths. These institutions represent only one dimension of the entire culture; sometimes they have a local rather than a pantribal distribution; sometimes they are transtribal. For example, the literature on Africa occasionally makes reference to Bembe art and attempts to define Bembe style. The Bembe form a fairly closely knit cultural entity in the eastern Congo, but it is generally meaningless to speak about Bembe style. One finds among these people, first, an art (bichrome, wooden, bell masks facing in four directions) of the *alunga* association, which has a limited distribution in the southern part of Bembeland and extends into some adjoining northern Luba groups. One encounters, second, the *butende* art (bi- or trichromatic, wooden, plank-board masks). The boys' initiations, for which they are made, are held throughout Bembeland but are organized autonomously by localized maximal lineages, thus leaving scope for local specialization (which entails, among other things, the total absence of such masks in some parts of Bembeland). Third, there is the *elanda* art (masks made from hide or cloth, and studded with bead designs). *Elanda* is a semi-secret association found only in some of the sixteen partially dispersed Bembe clans. There is the art of the *punga* association (small, wooden figurines) which is of Luba origin and was introduced into

Bembeland within the last fifty years. There is the art of the *bwami* association (small, ivory figurines; rare, wooden face masks; and wooden animal figurines) which is so similar to the well-known art of the Lega that no writing on African art ever distinguishes one from the other. In addition, there are other art objects (wooden figurines) carved in styles reminiscent of the northern Luba, which are made in Bembeland by small, partially submerged groups of other than Bembe origin.

In defining styles, the literature tends to focus on basic similarities and to ignore the significant differences that are easily discovered when one compares the various known pieces of a given class of objects found in a restricted area and within a closely knit cultural entity. Sometimes these differences and variations are just acknowledged; sometimes they are accounted for under such labels as substyles, local or village styles, schools, and much more rarely, at least for large parts of the primitive world, they are ascribed to different style periods. For our purpose, it is necessary to investigate further some of the factors underlying these differences and variations. In many areas of the world, artists of a single culture express themselves in a wide variety of material media (wood, bark, cane, fiber, rawhide, stone, clay, iron, bronze, gold, silver, ivory, bone, and others). Sometimes several of these materials may functionally be substituted for one another; in other instances, art objects made out of different materials are destined to serve the purposes of different segments of the population or of diverse art-using institutions. Sometimes artists are used to working in different materials; in many cases, they are more specialized, restricting themselves to artwork in a single medium. Different style traditions in the same society may or may not be linked with the handling of these diverse media (ivory carving against wood carving, or brass casting against wood carving) (e.g., Fagg and Plass, pp. 18, 21–25). Thus, in descriptions of style the use of different media with correlated techniques and traditions must be taken into consideration as a possible source for style differences. In many regions both two-

and three-dimensional art are produced concurrently. As Schmitz (1956, p. 113) has pointed out, these two categories of technique create different problems and possibilities and cannot be intermixed in a general characterization. Basic differences in style are linked with these two categories of activity, and recourse to such concepts as substyle or style period is often unnecessary in this respect. There are many societies where certain types of objects are always made by men, according to what one could call male style traditions, in contrast with other objects that are women's specialities. Among the American Northwest Coast Indians, the arts of weaving and basketry are practiced only by women, whereas painting and sculpture in wood and stone are done exclusively by men. Inverarity (1967, p. 45) finds that discrete style traditions are associated with this type of division of labor. Moreover, the time factor is a significant element in the assessment of stylistic difference. In any culture there is constant change going on, sometimes slow and uneven, often affecting certain spheres of activity more than others. Our documentation of the chronological distribution of artworks produced by separate cultures is, in general, very poor, and many of the collected works of art extend over only a short span of time. Yet, this factor of changing values, taste, aesthetic criteria, and needs, combined with changing influences, is necessarily a potent element in determining the gradual or consistent occurrence of variations.

Other significant factors in variation become apparent if we restrict ourselves to art objects made in a single medium by artists of the same sex, and if we assume that all products under consideration fall within a very limited period of time. Different contexts of purpose and usage may impose different kinds of demand on the artists. Objects such as a Bambara mask made for the *flankuru* society have little in common with the *komo* masks among the same people. This very fact may, in turn, affect the number of artists operating or specializing at any given time in any given society. Functional purposes, volume of demand, number of artists can, in one way or another, enhance or lessen the possibilities for variation. Thus, the needs for conventional objects may be strictly circumscribed in some cases and flexible in others. Excessive demand for specific objects may lead to mass production, copying, and the acceptance by society of many mediocre artists. Invariably, societies are divided into many kinds of subgroupings, such as local kinship units, distinct political entities, ritual communities, age groups, and voluntary associations. The various subgroupings, although participating in a basic common culture, do not necessarily form common action groups; each may represent a self-contained unit, have its own set of specialized values, preferences, and action patterns, and possess its own interpretation of the common culture. In the literature on art, unfortunately, emphasis on this aspect of variation has often gone not much further than the so-called subtribe, the village, or the loosely defined district. Without indulging in cultural-historical speculation, there is also enough evidence available for many parts of the world that so-called homogeneous societies are composed of various substrata of peoples and of many incorporated groups of diverse ethnic origin. Although participating in an overall common culture, these component entities have steadfastly maintained or developed distinctive patterns and traditions in their technology and art. Finally, the art-producing societies do not exist *in vacuo*; isolation, self-containment, and self-sufficiency are relative concepts. There are many examples of wide-sweeping reciprocal influences that different peoples have exercised on one another's art traditions. Some groups have shown more receptivity and creative originality in the process of borrowing than others that were either resilient or slavish in imitating. Whatever the case may be, in any society some component groups are more exposed to outside influences and eager to incorporate some of the extraneous art elements than others. It accounts in part for the widely observed spread across tribal boundaries of institutional complexes such as associations, initiations, cults, and their correlated art traditions.

Beyond these many factors that contribute to the variations

within culturally well-circumscribed groups, we have to consider the artists, themselves, as individuals, as members of particular "schools," as proponents of local traditions, conventions, and systems of thought. Ultimately, most works of art are created and shaped by individuals, whether or not they are helped in some phases of their work by pupils or by other artists, and even though the patinaed finish or thick coating of their work may be the product of several anonymous generations of users. Some authors speculate about the absence of the concept "artist" in most primitive societies. There is no equivalent for "art" either, yet nobody doubts that primitive societies have produced objects that are pleasing and that strike one as beautiful. Obviously, these objects are not sheer replicas of one another, but works made by gifted individuals who in Malraux's (1953, pp. 310, 416) words *create* forms and do not merely *reproduce* them. These artists then, have different personalities, different skills and proficiencies; they differ in age and maturity and are trained and steeped in local traditions. Some are highly specialized in one technique, others are versed in several crafts; some work publicly, others in secrecy; some work with models, others only with mental images and dreams. Some work in ateliers in the company of other artists with whom they can compare their works, under the direction of their patrons by whom they can be guided and of the larger public by whom they can be criticized. Other artists work privately and avoid or ignore criticism. Some work only when commissioned to make carvings; others create more freely when they feel an inclination to do so. Undoubtedly, whatever the stringencies and conventions of style, purpose and expectation, the individual element is a powerful factor in explaining differences. Artists necessarily differ in training, in skill and technical proficiency, in maturity and social position, and in personality. Society can impose upon its artists a certain objective subject matter and style but the artist himself has his own personal conception of the subject matter, a particular feeling for the style, and a certain technique in executing the form.

The feasibility of the expression of individual taste, skill, and temperament in artistic productivity is a much debated question in regard to communities that focus heavily on corporate solidarity and collective action, and doubts are raised as to whether or not it is possible to speak about creative originality and conscious innovation. Surprisingly little work has been done in depth on the many aspects of this problem. Yet, the first attempts at unraveling some of its elements date back to the twenties and thirties in studies written by Firth (1925, 1936) on the Maori carver and on New Guinea, Bunzel (1928) on the Pueblo potters, O'Neale (1932) on Yurok-Karok basket weavers, Himmelheber (1935, 1938) on West African and Eskimo artists, Herskovits (1934*b*, 1938) on Dahomey, Griaule (1938) on Dogon, Vandenhoute (1948) on Dan.[1] Some authors, like Firth, discussed the personality, the social position, the method of training of the artist, and the place of his work. An initiation ceremony was performed over the Maori artist which claimed "to render him apt to receive instruction" and "fixed the learning firmly in his mind. . . . Innovations were not permitted; mistakes were *aitua* (evil omens)" (Firth, 1925, p. 283). Others, like Bunzel, were involved with local and individual variation, its character and causes. Bunzel learned to distinguish the work of several potters in San Ildefonso, Acoma, and Hopi; the distinctions were more often a matter of mastery of technique than of style. She found more emphasis on originality and individualism in some Pueblo cultures than in others (Bunzel, 1928, pp. 62–68). Originality was apparent in two spheres: in minor, distinguishing, technical characteristics, such as texture of paste or use of color; in the highly distinctive treatment of form and of decorative elements (Bunzel, 1938, p. 566). In an unsurpassed analysis of typology, ethno-aesthetics, standards for excellence in the choice of materials, design arrangements, pattern placing, size and proportions of baskets, O'Neale (1932, *passim*) stated that within "a compact body of established

---

[1] For a brief appraisal of some of these works, see Fraser, 1966, p. 244, Fischer, 1962, pp. 161–163.

traditions" choices are possible and alternates sought for certain portions of the basketry work more than for others. The rules for learning the craft, for selecting and using materials, for form, proportion, and design were rigid, but choice-making was permitted, for example, in the tone and rearrangement of color or in the selection of material for a design element. O'Neale concluded (1932, p. 165): "Far from being deadened by a craft in which so much is reduced to conformity, the women of the two tribes have developed an appreciation of quality, design-to-space relationships, and effective color disposition, which are discriminating and genuine."

Aspects of individual style and creativity are, of course, treated in recent works. Some of the more elaborate discussions are to be found in Himmelheber (1960), Smith (1961), Fischer (1963), Fagg (1951, 1958, 1963), Gerbrands (1967), Carroll (1967), Forge (1967), d'Azevedo (1966), Goodale and Koss (1967). Many other studies have index entries for "artist," but often the so-called artist is unnamed and treated in abstract and nonspecific terms.[2] All in all, little attention has been paid to the problem, and the reasons for it are numerous. Most objects that form the subject of art studies were torn away from their social context by untrained foreigners who were barely interested in the products themselves, let alone their makers. Most anthropologists have shown an enduring disregard for detailed field studies on the aesthetic dimensions of primitive societies. Most students of primitive art have been satisfied with classification of products into so-called homogeneous styles and substyles, with the distribution of motifs, and with general stereotypes about their meaning and function. Emphasis has been placed only on select aspects of the total artistic activity or on se-

---

[2] In one of the most comprehensive accounts yet published on a single primitive art, Bodrogi (1961, pp. 149–150) has only slightly more than one page on the artist. The comments boil down to such elementary statements as "It seems that the artist in northeast New Guinea received adequate moral recognition and material compensation for his work." *A Bibliography of African Art*, compiled by Gaskin in 1965, has only twenty titles listed under "artist," and many of them have reference to the modern African artist.

lect categories of objects, leading to an unfortunate compartmentalization of otherwise closely integrated artistic activities.

In most general handbooks on primitive art the authors are concerned with the principles of individual style variation and creative freedom, accepting, sometimes with several reservations, that they do exist.

Wingert (1965, pp. 15–17) claims that the artist was not so completely restrained by his society and his patrons as to be a mere copyist; he "could endow the traditional forms with his own interpretation and insight" and "In this controlled material he created, following traditional patterns, his own renderings of the requisite forms."

Fraser (1962, p. 22) writes: "Not only does the primitive artist strive to be understood, but also every step of his selection and training forces him in a traditional direction." Buehler, Barrow, and Mountford (1962, p. 42) summarize their point of view as follows: "Each work of art is therefore the expression not merely of individual experiences, sensations, and values, but also of the influences and attitudes of the culture concerned. The message of a work thus expresses cultural as well as personal attributes."

Himmelheber (1960, p. 23) also takes a moderate stand: "Der Künstler hält sich ziemlich streng an die ihm von diesem Stammesstil vorgeschriebenen Formen." He stresses, however, the marked differences with which four Guro artists render an elephant head, and demonstrates how various Senufo artists represent in different degrees of stylization the traditional women's coiffure in the form of a bird's head and beak (Himmelheber, 1960, p. 64, figs. 52, 53).

At this stage of very limited knowledge on individual style and freedom many of our questions must await an answer because so few specific data are available. But the questions relating to the general nature of the limitations imposed upon artists by different societies can be fruitfully pursued.

It is true, as Read (1961, p. 124) points out, that a work of art is essentially individualistic in origin, and that from artist to artist there are differences in personality and temperament. It is equally true that the artist is deeply steeped in his milieu, versed in its values, eager to be in conformity with them and to be acceptable by his group. The artist is usually not a solitary person, cut off from his milieu by his own will, engaged in a full-time pursuit of the aesthetic, involved merely in a world of forms which he creates for himself. Firth's statement that "the artist-craftsman is only a part-time or leisure-time worker in this activity" generally holds true (Firth, 1951, p. 172). Moreover, the artist is himself frequently an active participant in the rites and ceremonies in which his products are used. All this implies that, as Firth remarks (*ibid.*, p. 173), the artist is not divorced from his public and that "the primitive artist and his public share essentially the same set of values." Yet, in societies where some of the art is used in the highly esoteric contexts of initiations into closed associations, the artist may not be familiar with the ultimate meaning and destination of his products. The artist has a message to convey, a concept or belief to sustain with his work of art; he must, therefore, be "readable" and understandable to his public. But again this public, of which he is himself a part, is highly skilled in reading symbolic messages; it may cultivate, as Leach notes (1954, p. 29), "a faculty for making and understanding ambiguous statements." It is my experience among the Lega of the Congo that this public is also flexible and creative in the interpretation of symbolic messages conveyed through the art forms. We may conclude that there is a close, reciprocal bond between the artist and his community, which both compels him to do certain things and allows him to do other things in his own way.

In what terms, then, can the problems of individual choice-making, creativity, and innovation be understood? Definitely the binding forces of conformity differ in nature and intensity from society to society, from activity to activity. The creative process is channeled through a great many variables, some of which are examined here.

It should be realized that, whatever rules, standards, and conventions a society may set up for its members, there is, as Kroeber

(1952, p. 138) suggests, "always a gap between values and behavior, between ideals and performance." Values, he goes on to say, "always influence the behavior . . . of men, they never control it exclusively." In the study of primitive art we have been working mostly with the finished products, with the concrete results of the performance. From these forms, scholars have constructed rules and standards. But few of us have any knowledge about the rules and criteria as they are actually formulated by the art-producing societies, and of which the finished products are incomplete projections. The conventions we construct for ourselves from the study of the finished products cannot help us in ascertaining precisely to what extent a gap exists between the norms and the performances, to what extent there is mere mechanical deviation from them or conscious creativity, to what extent are tolerated anomaly, error, reinterpretation, and conscious deviation. Art forms must not be taken at their face value. Society presents the artist with its complex ideals, values, and behavior patterns. Only certain of these demand expression in art forms; only certain symbols can find direct expression in wood or other media. Many facets of the symbolic system find their expression in oral literature, song, dance, gesture, or dramatic performance rather than in art forms. Thus, most art objects acquire their full meaning only in an appropriate context of song and drama and in their wider association with other art objects, simple artifacts, or natural objects. The artist makes these symbols into motifs. Once these motifs have come into being they belong to the realm of art; that means they can be technically modified, amplified, or reduced, regardless of their meanings or without changing their meanings.[3] The art forms belong to the artist, the meanings belong to the broader community that makes the demands, sets the patterns, and then uses what the artists are able to produce. It has been widely observed that forms almost never speak for themselves (e.g., Guiart, 1963, pp. 91–136). Those who try to explain the meanings behind these forms, without the appropriate knowledge of the cultural context

[3] For a further elaboration on this point, see Schmitz, 1956, p. 112.

in which the forms occur, generally come up with the most fantastic, simplistic, or merely poetic interpretations. Thus, some have interpreted the well-known Lega carvings of the figure with one arm and hand raised as an imploration of celestial powers, whereas the Lega themselves are not involved with sky-gods and consider the gesture not as a form of imploration but of prohibition. Lega carvings representing pregnant women with excessively distended bellies were thought to be associated with fertility cults, whereas they merely represent the Ugly Woman (symbolized in this case by the destructive effects caused by adultery during pregnancy). So, for those not instructed in reading meanings into forms, there is always a certain vagueness, nebulosity, and ambiguity involved in these artworks. Indeed, it may well be deliberately so intended, for many of these works are destined for use in the esoteric contexts of cults, initiations, and so on. The objects must be mysterious for the noninitiates, and they must retain something of their transcendent mystery even for the initiates. The interpretation of the symbols conveyed through the works of art, then, can accommodate to the unusual motif and form. When I studied the Lega, the *bami* initiates were altogether serious about the substitution of Western-made madonnas, dolls, electric light bulbs, or tree roots in suggestively distorted shapes, for some of their ivory figurines; they had no difficulty whatever in finding symbols and explanations for the substituted objects in their patrimony of traditional interpretive proverbs. Faced with an unusual carving or with one that did not correspond very well with the original demand, the Lega initiates did not reject it on the grounds that it was bad, but went through a painstaking process of justifying the interpretations that they associated with it.

Societies differ with respect to the nature of their codes of behavior and in the relative rigidity or flexibility with which rules and conventions are enhanced and sanctioned. Not all societies stimulate and validate individual effort and free initiative to the same extent. Some are highly individualistic and oriented toward self-assertion, prestige-seeking, originality. Others are creative and apt at introducing and synthesizing new elements of culture. Linton, Wingert, and d'Harnoncourt (1946, p. 105) found that as the result of constant trading in the Sepik River area some groups, like the Iatmul, practiced an easy eclecticism; others, like the Arapesh, developed a parasitic art (characterized by the large-scale import of alien elements and the systematic copying of them). Still others, like the Abelam and Kwoma, adhered to their own, very distinctive styles. Vandenhoute (1948, p. 4) observed that the Dan-Ngere-Wobe of West Africa explicitly recognized the value of an *original* mask form and were willing to attach superior social efficiency to it. Even in such societies with rigid, totemic codes as are found in Arnhemland, Elkin, Berndt, and Berndt (1950, pp. 14–15) found the conscious search for form, line, balance, rhythm, and color arrangement to be so strong that even "the expression of a myth does not override these factors." Limitations are, of course, set by the local style tradition itself. Boas (1955, pp. 156–158) attached great importance to this factor: "the style has the power of limiting the inventiveness of the productive artist. . . . The controlling power of a strong, traditional style is surprising," and "Although the artisan works without copying, his imagination never rises beyond the level of the copyist, for he merely uses familiar motives composed in customary ways." Without taking this extreme viewpoint of Boas, we can undoubtedly agree with Malraux (1953, p. 281) that "One of the reasons why the artist's way of seeing differs so greatly from that of the ordinary man is that it has been conditioned, from the start, by the paintings and statues he has seen; by the world of art." It is against this style that every great artist has to struggle (*ibid.*, p. 359). In all societies there are only a few great artists. Many of the works that we have collected and studied were probably made by mediocre artists. Fagg (1951, p. 119) has remarked that, owing to various circumstances, mediocre African works have been preserved in large quantities. Some were made by individuals whose social system or social position required them to make conventional types of objects regardless of their skill and training. No wonder, then, that many works reveal this trend toward conformity and uniformity of style which is attributable not to the stringency of the restrictions on creativity but to the carver's incapacity to produce original work.

In different societies, artists and users both focus their attention on different aspects or qualities of works of art to judge and to interpret them. Among the Lega of the Congo focus is first on the size, material, and gloss of a piece, and only then on its general form and design. Bunzel (1938, p. 570) noted that the Hopi potters always spoke of line, the Zuni potters of the number and the distribution of designs, San Ildefonso potters of the surface texture and the luster. In Polynesia the value of a drum is determined by its shape and the quality of the wood (Guiart, 1963, p. 112). It is very likely that for those features of the artwork on which the main aesthetic and functional focus rests, the rules are more stringent than for the other, secondary qualities.

There are the social position of the artist himself, the status attached to his person and to his works, the motivations behind his activity. Is the carver recruited within a limited descent group? Is he a member of an abject caste? Is he, regardless of lineage or caste, recruited because of mystic values associated with him because of the special circumstances of his birth?[4] Or, is the position of the artist, as among the Dan-Ngere-Wobe, the result of vocation, talent, and apprenticeship? (Vandenhoute, 1948, p. 4). Not only are differences in skill and workmanship, but also relative freedom from local "schools" and traditions, intimately connected with this aspect of recruitment. But even where the craft is inherited within a rigid line of descent (e.g., from father to son) it would seem that the pupil can still specialize in the sculptural form and designs that he realizes best, in which he is most successful, and for which he

[4] Schmitz (1962, p. xv), for example, points out that in the Sepik River area when a child is born with the umbilical cord wrapped around its neck, women believe that it will become a great carver.

has more taste. Moreover, as Forge (1967, p. 78) has brought out, the importance of visiting and traveling as a result of various kinship connections, with subsequent exposure of artists to diverse local traditions, must not be underestimated in assessing the degree to which an artist can free himself from locally imposed traditions and inherited conventions. In many societies, also, the artist, regardless of the patterns of recruitment, is not treated just like any other craftsman or like a laborer whose services are bought by patrons with strong demand rights in him. It should be realized that the artist often works for the members of closely knit kinship groups or of ritual communities, or for congeners who do not *pay* him for his work but reward him with food, tobacco, drink, and other presents. There are artists with wide fame, reputation, and prestige whose works are in high demand, as there are famed singers or musicians or storytellers.[5] There are many indications, too, that some artists are nonconformists, although not rebels; some are "originals" whose motivations differ from those of the rest of the population.[6]

Artists in different societies adopt different working methods. How specialized is the artist in making only one set of objects, and how familiar is he with other categories of artworks? Does he work on several items at a time? Has he models or are his images purely mental and personal? Or does he express the dreams dictated to him by shamans? How careful is his planning of designs? Does he work in an inspired spontaneous way without much preparation? How much time is he willing to devote to any one of his creations? The last differs considerably from culture to culture. Himmelheber (1935, p. 85) reported that the Kuskokwim Eskimo always finish their work in one day. Elsewhere, as in parts of New Guinea or

---

[5] In the more exhaustive studies on primitive art, explicit or implicit reference is constantly made to the existence of these outstanding and widely recognized artists.

[6] Herskovits and Herskovits (1934b, p. 128), for example, note that in Dahomey artists were admired for being gifted and respected for their art but, at the same time, were looked upon with scorn because they lacked interest in the prestige and wealth that are primary goals for the majority of Dahomeans.

Africa, the work progresses slowly over weeks and months. Willett and Picton (1967, p. 66) have shown that the north Ekiti sculptors conceive their work in four stages and that apprentices and assistants play a great role in helping to finish the product, progressing as their training develops from the final stage (cutting the details) to the earliest stage (blocking out the main form of the piece). Variability of output among Ekiti sculptors is undoubtedly linked in some way with the amount of work left to apprentices, the point in the progression of the work at which apprentices are allowed to intervene, the maturity of the apprentices, the diligence and firmness of the master himself. There are societies where the number of artists is very limited, and where the artists work in widely scattered places and have little or no contact with one another. There are others where the artists, as members of certain descent groups or castes, live together in villages of their own, thus facilitating consultation, criticism, joint work, and conformity.

Criticism is obviously known in primitive society.[7] But how it is expressed, how far it goes, and what impact it has on the artist's work are unclear. Artists who work in isolation, like the Northwest Coast totem pole carvers or the Abelam, cannot be influenced very much by such criticism. Others, like the Kuskokwim Eskimo, who work publicly in the presence of many spectators are theoretically more exposed to it. Yet Himmelheber (1935, p. 82) for example, has observed that when the Kuskokwim artist's wife would draw his attention to specific details the artist would, frequently and deliberately, retouch an entirely different feature of the work.

The ways in which art products are evaluated by their users are relevant to ascertaining the role of art criticism. When we outsiders review, for example, art objects collected from the Lega, we tend to classify them as good, mediocre, and bad carvings. But for

---

[7] Bohannan (1961, p. 94) has strongly emphasized the significance of criticism. He writes, "Problems of creation in primitive societies are interesting; but they may be overshadowed, from the standpoint of their significance in the societies concerned, by the problems of criticism."

the Lega themselves, *all* pieces commissioned by the members of the *bwami* association—who have the exclusive control over the artwork—are *good*. That means they fulfill their purposes and functions. Criticism of the physical appearance of such objects is not tolerated; or, rather, such criticism is inconceivable from their point of view. By purpose, all these objects are *isengo*, that is, sacred and dangerous. Through use and anointment with oil and perfume, all objects acquire a patina and a gloss that make them part of the "gathering of mushrooms," as the Lega call it. This stereotyped attitude of the users and the public toward art products is all the more significant since it was widely held that carvings were meaningless unless they had been consecrated, charged with forceful ingredients, and impregnated with emotion through usage. On the other hand, not all art is destined to express mythological or religious concepts, or to symbolize the power structure or the social cohesion of the society. Some art is made for enjoyment, for fun; some art is humorous and burlesque.[8] Among the Pende of the Congo, certain masks representing such characters as Tundu, the clown, Mbangu, the epileptic, or Mazumbudi, the Pygmy, are almost never carved in the classic *katundu*-mask style of the Pende.[9]

The next vital question relates to the function and meaning of the primitive work of art. Some authors continue to make largely arbitrary distinctions among religious, magical, secular or utilitarian, and ceremonial art, the implication being that greater or lesser freedom of expression may be correlated with these broad functional categories. The problem, however, should be explored further in terms of more restrictive questions that follow. Is the art object understood to be the iconic transcription of a myth? Is it a mnemotechnical device or a didactic element used in a system of teachings and initiations? Is it understood to represent some es-

[8] In general, this aspect of the artwork has been neglected in the literature. Bohannan (1964, p. 150) has correctly stressed the fact "that some 'art' may be no more than playful decoration added to the basic ideas for producing something that is 'needed.'"

[9] De Sousberghe (1958, pp. 22–23) brings this point out very clearly.

sential aspects of a dead person or of an ancestor, or is it meant to be a stereotyped rendering of a supernatural being? Is it intended to express several meanings in one or to illustrate the opposite of what the value code stands for? Is it intended for masquerades and choreographed dances, or is it to be used, rather, as an emblem, a crest, a token, or as an initiation object? Is it made for private purposes or for public display? Is it meant to be a mark of difference and autonomy? Does it symbolize the integral unity of a large group of people or express the power structure of that group? These and many other purposes obviously exercise different pressures on the artist. Some purposes require conformity with fixed patterns and rigidity in the handling of the subject matters; others invite ingenuity, specificity, and conscious originality. Since art objects are generally used for several purposes and mean many things to their users, it is normal for certain parts or features of the object to be subject to a more rigid conventionalism than others. The basic forms of the *tapa* masks of Oceania did not exhibit wide-ranging differences for the simple reason that they represented a limited number of mythical beings whose names they bore. But the colored motifs around the faces of the masks showed great variation because they were peculiar to specific lineages. Smaller masks representing totems were less esoteric in meaning than the *tapa* masks and showed more originality (Guiart, 1963, p. 132). We may therefore assume that some artistic activities are restrictive and strongly governed by prescriptions and proscriptions, and that other elements of the art product permit or require greater personal inventiveness and choice-making.

In this connection we should also examine the general nature of the demands made on the artists. This question—about which little or no evidence is found in the literature—relates to the problem of what exactly the patrons of the art ask from the artists, how and with what degree of precision they formulate their demands, and what they expect to receive in return for their requests. This point is all the more vital since we know that in most primitive societies artists create works of art only when commissioned to do so. Sieber explains elsewhere in this book that in one of the African societies he had studied, the demand was merely for a human figurine. The people were satisfied when a human figurine was carved, thus leaving all other choices and decisions to the artist. I have found among the Lega that these demands are expressed in different ways and with varying degrees of precision. The Lega artists have produced, among other things, large quantities of animal figurines which fall into two functional groups. By far the largest number of such pieces is individually owned and classified under the generic term *mugugundu*. This is neither the common name nor the drum name for a specific species of animal, but a taxonomic concept that seems to be the equivalent of *the* animal par excellence, as indicated by the contexts of usage and symbolic associations. For the high initiates of the *bwami* association, who have the exclusive right to use these pieces, *the* animal par excellence is either a pangolin, an aardvark, a bongo antelope, or a terrestrial turtle. Here the demand is only for a carving of *the* animal. Consequently, although *mugugundu* objects are always rendered in a stylized, simple, and unsophisticated form, with little or no decorative design, individual artists have been able to demonstrate their skill and ingenuity in many ways: size—height and length of the pieces; proportions—details of the head, eyes, legs, and tail; patination and quality of material. The artists were bound only by an unspecified, but large, demand for a general form category. The users focused their interpretations on general form, not on details, and particularly on the ceremonial associations and the context of song, proverb, and dramatic performance in which these forms occurred. The second group of Lega animal figurines is much rarer and is not classified under a generic term. The animal figurines of this group are larger, more realistic renderings of particular animals, such as pangolins or hunting dogs—a realism that is sometimes enhanced by the adornment of the wooden figurine with real pangolin scales or with wooden dog-bells. These objects are owned

by only a few preceptors or initiation experts; in some cases they
are part of baskets, the content of which includes other carvings
and natural objects. The baskets themselves are symbols of ritual
cohesion in large lineage groups. The forms and details of these
carvings are much more conventionalized and standardized for
they stand for the dog prototype *kafyondo* or for the pangolin prototype *kilinkumbi*. In general, the pieces are rudimentary in appearance. The demand is specific and limited. These various aspects
of stylistic diversity, then, are not linked with distinct regions or
subgroups in Legaland, but with different functions and types of
demand.

As outside observers of primitive works of art that were torn
away from their associations with music, drama, literature, and
other manufactured or natural objects, we anthropologists and art
historians have tended to overstate the importance of form and design. In this process we have been inclined to overrate the rigidity
and conventionalism of form and to underrate the multivalence
and flexibility of usages and meanings attached to them. It may be
said that forms are, to some extent, incidental, transient, illusive,
and epiphenomenal. Newton (1961, p. 33) finds that in the Gulf of
Papua area some objects are more sacred or powerful than others;
yet these differences cannot be related to the art motifs. The awe-
inspiring quality of some objects here is related to their relative
ages and to the addition to them of paint or other objects (skulls).
Elkin, Berndt, and Berndt (1950, pp. 8–9) further substantiate this
point of view by pointing out that in Arnhemland the *waninja*
ritual objects of the very same design are used in more than one
totemic ceremony. The authors contend that this sameness is purely
external. In other words, when a single *waninja* object is used in
different contexts it is no longer the same thing because of its association with different songs, myths, and types of participation.
This is very much my experience with Lega art, where single objects of specific form and design are used constantly in totally different contexts of initiation, and possess different associations of

meaning as expressed in proverbs, dance movements, and gestures. If our knowledge about the thought systems hidden behind these art objects was deeper, we would probably find that, very frequently, single forms or categories of form occur in a multiplicity of social and ritual contexts with different complementary meanings attached to them, meanings that are not directly illustrated by the forms but which adhere to them because of traditional associations. The phenomenon implies, among other things, that a gap exists between what the artists create and what the users need, that the demands are for basically functional types, and that artists automatically have much leeway in creating forms that, in a general way, fit these types.

The study of local stylistic variations, as aspects of time, place, culture, and of individual skill and conscious self-expression, must take into account a large number of variables. The configurations formed by these interrelated variables differ not only from society to society, but also within a single society from subgroup to subgroup, from time period to time period, from category of objects to category of objects, and even from one motif and style element to another. These variations are to be sought not only in the overall forms and structures of the products and in their various details, but also in the associated meanings and functions. Judgment of minute variations is particularly difficult and requires profound familiarity with basic forms. Schmitz (1962, p. xiv) has gone as far as to affirm that, within the limitations set by the basic forms, the range of possible variations is almost limitless but that the superficial observer can scarcely recognize them because his knowledge of the basic forms from which variations derive is insufficient. He observes that for Melanesia these basic forms are rarely rendered in full, and that they are either abstractively simplified or baroquely enriched. Stringent conventions often apply, not to the product as a whole, but to its component elements, and they frequently bear, not on the form as such, but on such particular aspects of the product as material (and method of obtaining it), color, height, size, place of the decorative element, and so on. In judging the significance of self-expression and of creativity one cannot apply the term "artist" indiscriminately to the makers of all the objects produced. For many art products are made not by individuals with special training or vocation or social recognition, but by persons whose social positions and social and religious aspirations compel them to make the art object. Moreover, among the latter there are beginning artists and mature ones, there is "a genius, a clever and industrious mediocrity, or a mere copyist" (Linton, 1958, pp. 9–10). Obviously, the creative capacities of these various individuals differ radically. In addition, in function of the fame and reputation of the artist, unusual and original stylistic features become more or less acceptable and socially compelling. How diverse societies really feel about this matter would have to be investigated in the concrete context of more permanent taxonomic concepts than mere statements. Among the Nyanga of the Congo, for example, the master storyteller, the master zither player, the master carver—persons who command wide recognition regardless of their village or lineage and whose products or performances are in big demand because of their outstanding quality—are all referred to by a compound noun that includes the element *shé-* that is also used in all teknonyms for males. These masters are never referred to as *miné-*, a frequently used morpheme that establishes a relationship of property, possession, and usufruct. In my opinion, the use of *shé-* (derivative of *ishé-*, his father) in reference to the highly talented person, indicates an emphasis on a Man's creative ability, rather than on the sheer mastery of conventional technique and style. Moreover, the study of individuality in primitive art must not be reduced to the identification of individual hands or to the developmental aspects of the individual style. It must be placed in the wider perspective of the social motivations and values that underlie the making of art objects. Some of the vital questions begging answers are: Why is art needed? How and for what purposes is it used in a particular society? What is needed and what is made?

How is a reconciliation made between what is needed and what is produced? How far is the pursuit of prestige, originality, fame, and excellence institutionalized? Finally, creative force must not be measured just against innovation and inventiveness per se; as Wingert (1965, p. 18) has pointed out, it is also to be determined in terms of the artist's "success in fusing tradition with invention and innovation."

2. Judgments of Primitive Art, 1905-1965

ROBERT GOLDWATER

BEFORE THE discussion by others proceeds to the role and function of the artist in the many and various non-Western societies, I wish to examine the history of European and American judgments of the so-called primitive arts. This history is intended to serve as an introduction to the papers that follow by furnishing an awareness of the past and present background against which these discussions take place. It should help to explain the aesthetic context and the sequence of partly subjective attitudes that have led to present efforts at more objective analysis of primitive art.

First of all, what of the adjective "primitive" itself, incorporated into the name of the Museum of Primitive Art, with which I am connected? Some anthropologists have considered it unfortunate, or incorrect, and have tried to find a more accurate substitute. With that search I am not concerned here; even though words are conventional counters and "primitive" has entered into current usage with a no-more-than-normally ambiguous meaning, I do not believe that fabricated replacements are especially useful, nor indeed likely to prevail. Much more important than any ideal denotation of the word "primitive" are the effective connotations it has come to have when coupled with the word "art." There is the realization that for more than fifty years, first among modern artists and then among those connected with and influenced by them (writers, critics, collectors, and public), the word "primitive" has been not merely a description, but a term of praise. The phrase is "primitive-art" or "primitive-arts," inseparably joined. It has nothing to do with lack of skill or with either technical or aesthetic crudity, but refers to a wide variety of styles and sources, connected by a vitality, intensity, and formal inventiveness which have appealed to the modern artist and have had a considerable, even though largely indirect, effect upon him. This aesthetic context and all its associations have, after all, shaped our responses to the primitive arts, as much, if not more, than any ethnological studies, and we should therefore be aware of its nature and its history.

The importance of such an awareness is borne out by the fact that the Wellcome Collection, now at the University of California, Los Angeles, will be studied in the future under double auspices, ethnological and artistic. Its first public showing thus provides an excellent occasion to tie together some of the attitudes toward the primitive arts which we in the West have had, and, more particularly, at least to suggest a resolution of the profound misunderstandings and the assorted antagonisms that have divided anthropologists from artists and from art historians in their discussions about the primitive arts.

My reasons for wishing to attempt such a reconciliation are first of all personal ones. Since my own training was in the history of art (through examining problems in the meaning and direction of modern art, I first became interested in the primitive arts), I have some sympathy for the point of view of the artist and what he has contributed to our understanding; this is an attitude not always shared by my colleagues who come from other disciplines. For illustration I go back to a time just after the opening of the Museum of Primitive Art in New York in 1957 and to a discussion with a distinguished archaeologist concerning a lecture series we were then trying to arrange. He suggested that there were two points of view that the museum might present to its public. That of the scientists, which he and his friends shared, was the inductive approach which, working from the evidence out to the theories, arrived, of course, at the correct theories. The other, taken by the artist, the art lover, and the art historian (he put them together in a single quick phrase), was the deductive approach which, starting with agreeable theories, selectively gathered evidence in support of entirely subjective points of view.

I am, unfortunately, not an artist; but neither, I believe, am I an art lover in the pejorative sense that the archaeologist intended. As an art historian, however, I am conscious that my initial attitudes and approaches toward works of art, what I stress or overlook or what I like or dislike, especially in unfamiliar works, are very much conditioned by what artists have taught me to see. Without accepting the artists' insights uncritically, I realize that I must be aware of them, for they are the measure of my aesthetic conditioning, just as I must be familiar with the scientific sources of my views in the information provided by the archaeologist and the anthropologist. Being conscious of both attitudes, I should like to be able to resolve the problem posed by these two divergent (and supposedly antagonistic) points of view.

My reasons for attempting this reconciliation are also theoretical. It has been said, the phrase is Fagg's, that in 1905 Picasso and his friends "took over." He meant that when the modern artist found or "discovered" the primitive arts, the objective investigation of those arts, which had already begun on a scientific basis, was interrupted and arrested. From that date on, for several decades, the primitive arts were perforce viewed through the eyes of artists, with all the subjectivity, mistaken emphasis, and romantic speculation that this implied. A sequence of artistic generations—expressionist, cubist, abstract, and surrealist—imposed their views on the informed and the uninformed public alike, at the expense of the objective anthropologist, while he, in turn, seemed to have lost his former interest in material culture and the arts and devoted himself largely to other aspects of primitive society. It is understandable that the anthropologist may deplore such a sequence of events, because in his view it inhibited the correct understanding and appreciation of the primitive arts. But precisely as an anthropologist he must consider that if for a period in our own society the artist did in fact take over, that if for a time in our own culture these subjective judgments replaced more objective research and evaluation, such a development could hardly have been the result of historical accident alone. There must have been some reason why for several decades a subjective, culture-bound, primarily aesthetic attitude toward the primitive arts was dominant. Perhaps it could not have been otherwise. I should like to address myself to this question.

The profound effect that primitive art exerted upon modern art is known and recognized. Although this influence is part of the evidence of the essential significance of the period of subjective understanding, I do not wish to examine it here. I would for the moment prefer to give some attention to the other side of what has been a reciprocal relationship. Granted the primitive arts have influenced the modern artist for the last fifty or sixty years—and so through him have affected our artistic understanding—it is also through the eyes of the modern artist that we have learned to see and appreciate certain qualities of the primitive arts. The artist has thus been both student and teacher, and we can evaluate our attitudes today only if we acknowledge the part he has played in their formation, and what, quite literally, we now see when we look at an African or an Oceanic sculpture.

The artist's role as teacher and as student began with his so-called discovery of the primitive arts. I am suggesting that the years since then (more than a half century, if we employ 1905 as the symbolic, if not the exact, date of that discovery) have been not only a contributory prelude, but perhaps also an inevitable prelude, to a just understanding of the primitive arts. This subjective stage had in fact to precede and to play itself out before a more objective one became possible.

A similar evolution and change have taken place more than once. Each time the West has become conscious of new non-Western art, or even of an earlier forgotten period in its own artistic history, there has been a time during which it has been seen through the eyes of the artist rather than through the eyes of the analytic historian. (I am, of course, referring not to new knowledge of individual works but to the impact made by the consciousness that there exists an unfamiliar kind of artistic imagination.) Generally it has been the acute sensibility of the artist which has made the initial discovery. After the artist has absorbed from the unfamiliar style those elements that are useful to him, transforming and adapting them to his own purposes, and the new art, now become familiar, is no longer a source of inspiration, then a more objective point of view has taken over, and external unbiased analysis has begun. Surely, in a large sense this was true for the first contact of the Renaissance with the ancient world, made by its artists, by its poets, and by its poet-philosophers in a highly selective, unhistorical, and biased fashion, ignoring all those historical distinctions between Greece and Rome, Republic and Empire, all the accurate cultural correlations and changes that later scholarship was to work out. This process repeated itself in the late eighteenth century when (despite Winckelmann) the neoclassic artist made personal contact again with the classical styles (using and abusing scholarship), and found in them something more than the Renaissance had found. Just as, somewhat earlier in the century, rococo painters had created an imaginative Chinoiserie that would have been the despair of any scholar who hoped to find in its adaptations a correct understanding of any single period of oriental art or iconography, but nevertheless revealing it to Western eyes. Similarly the churches of the Gothic revival, and even the restorations of medieval buildings carried out by revivalists, are hardly the places to look for historical precision. It was not until Gothicism was played out as an inspiration to a lingering romanticism that the Middle Ages could be seen in perspective. During the years since 1905 the sequence of artistic discovery, enthusiasm, inspiration, and gradual fading has once more been repeated, this time in relation to the primitive arts. We are therefore today at a point where the anthropologist and the art historian can come together and look at these arts with some objectivity. But to do this they must also be conscious of, examine, and evaluate all those ways of "seeing" that the artists have been teaching them throughout the indispensable interim period.

How this has come about can best be understood by examining in sequence a series of primitive works of art, each of them traditional, each of them altogether typical of the style and culture from which it comes, but each also, from the point of view of Western aesthetic consciousness, representing a new stage in a process of expanding awareness. It is a development bound up with the evolution of Western art but revealing at last the enormous variety of non-Western forms, separating them out in turn from a mass of styles until then lumped together, so that each one, becoming visible, can be examined on its own independent terms. (Again I am not talking of particular works, or even of tribal styles, but of ways of seeing.) Admittedly, this has been a process that has concentrated on form and on the reading of the expressive qualities of form and has neglected context, function, and iconography. It is not the less important for such emphasis, which has served to correct the tendency of anthropologists toward overly intellectual analysis.

At the end of the nineteenth century, during what may be called the prehistory of our subject—it anticipates the so-called discovery of primitive art by some fifteen years—the name of

Gauguin occupies a prominent place. The romantic tragedy of his life in the South Seas is part of a different (even if related) subject which there is no need to evoke here. More pertinent, because it affected his vision of his surroundings, is the indication in his paintings that he shared two conflicting traditions concerning primitive peoples: the idyllic and the malevolent. The first is the partly biblical, partly classical tradition of Rousseau, Bernardin de Saint-Pierre, Chateaubriand, and other subsequent writers who imagined that primitive peoples were inherently good and that like all people they were later corrupted by civilization. The second tradition supposed that violence and brutishness manifest themselves initially in the primitive mentality, and that those characteristics are only partly tamed by later civilization. Such a picture as the "Day of the God" (1894) combines the two conflicting attitudes, the people indolent and idyllic, the dominating figure of the deity in the background suggesting dangerous, occult forces.

Even more directly related to our history is the question of how Gauguin saw the primitive art with which he came into contact and which of its elements he was able to absorb. The praise of Maori art which is scattered through his writing comes as no surprise; in this, as in his own creation, he was ahead of the taste of his time. What is surprising is to find that his vision was not so exceptional, after all, but was instead somewhat similar to that of the contemporary anthropologists who were studying South Seas art. Painter and sculptor though he was, and it is above all in his sculpture that he borrows directly from Marquesan art, it is the flat, decorative elements that he is able to absorb into his own work, not the handling of mass and space in three dimensions for which the primitive arts later became famous. He takes a Marquesan Tiki figure (in the original a freestanding form of considerable bulk even when executed on a small scale in ivory or wood), draws it out flat, and makes a design or a frieze of it (pl. 1). Or he adapts the various parts of a Marquesan club top, with its subtly balanced, flaring, concave surface and the projecting heads placed at the eyes of the Tiki mask and transforms them into a surface decoration, a contrast of filled and empty areas so cut into the skin of a wood cylinder that it can later be transferred to black and white as a woodcut. In other words, Gauguin is seeing in terms of schematic patterns, just as did A. C. Haddon and H. Balfour when they traced the evolution of decorative motifs (pl. 2). These men had, of course, their own scientific interest in the progressive trans-formation or "degeneration" of naturalistic forms; Gauguin, on the contrary, found "mystery" in the same stylized shapes. Although both their concerns and their methods of thinking were in oppo-sition, they saw in remarkably similar fashion. They shared a preoccupation with design and a willingness to break down the design into its component parts. It is a first step in the modern real-ization of the wide variety of expressions to be found in the prim-itive arts. As the century progresses it will be replaced by other kinds of awareness seeking out other facets of expression.

Gauguin's emphasis on the qualities of the "mysterious" to be found in primitive art belongs to the antiscientific aesthetics of the end of the century, mystery being the term symbolists use for the reality beneath appearance which it is the purpose of art to evoke. A decade later, at the beginning of the twentieth century, the power of those hidden forces was even more strongly felt, and also more personalized. The German artists of the Brücke group were uninterested in refinements of surface. They regarded pattern, like naturalism, as the mark of an enervating decadence. They saw in primitive art the expression of an immediate and irrepres-sible vitality; they found in it that direct transcription of emotion they sought in their own work. As a result, they were able to view African and Melanesian sculpture in a new light, undisturbed by conventional prejudices concerning likeness, skill, control, and finish. They were the first to understand that if a mask or figure has a demonic or magical intention, such qualities are at best irrel-evant, and that rough, broad handling, so-called crudity of carving, and clash of colors can be expressively effective. In consequence, such characteristics, far from being the unwanted by-products of a more "civilized" aesthetic aim, desired but still unattainable, had best be grasped as essential parts of the artist's controlled intention. The Brücke painters found these qualities in the roughhewn, brightly colored figure sculpture of the Cameroun (available to them in the Berlin and Dresden museums) and, thus freed from the evolutionary conventions of the time, were able to appreciate not only its vigorous qualities of expression, but also the way in which such qualities were tied to the free, rhythmic handling of mass, color, and design. Undoubtedly the vision of these artists was one-sided but at least they were not subjecting Cameroun art to the canons of some other sculptural style, whether African or European. Moreover, they sensed that much African art expressed, not aspects of the visible world, but rather the invisible forces behind that world, and that this explained its strength. Their intuitive understanding was, of course, related to the aims of their own art; it in no way diminishes their pioneering role in the acceptance of this sort of expressive power as proper to the arts.

I have already mentioned Picasso's "discovery" of primitive art and the symbolic year of 1905. There is no need for us to go into the exactness of that date, or into questions of priority and credit, or of who told whom about just what masks and figures. These are problems for the detailed history of modern art, and the continuing debate about them is an indication of the important role primitive and especially African art played in that history. It is more pertinent for us to reexamine briefly the nature of the discovery.

In point of pure chronology, Vlaminck, Derain, and Matisse all preceded Picasso in their recognition and appreciation of African sculpture, even if by only several months. Yet there is little, if any, evidence of the formal influence of this sculpture on their own art. From this fact alone we might reasonably conclude that it was hardly only its compositional structure that attracted them. Such a conclusion is borne out by the written records we have; it seems clear that what they, too, admired was a certain expressive energy, communicated, to be sure, by plastic means, which they felt no need to analyze too carefully.

Picasso, on the contrary, was strongly affected by the appearance of some styles of African masks and sculpture. It seems to me, however, that underlying this influence—in fact, making it possible—was an emotional attraction that affected him as it did his colleagues. It is not generally the way the story has been told. In describing Picasso's relation to African art, stress has usually been placed upon the purely formal derivations: the adoption of lozenge shapes for eyes and facial contours, the use of surface striations as a means of differentiating areas, the simplification of outline, the reduction of rounded modeling to flat, faceted planes, and, most of all, the rhythmic interrelation of solid mass and hollow interval. There is no doubt that these African solutions of abstract problems of structure and composition played an important role in Picasso's attraction to Dan masks and to Bakota figures (pl. 3). One has only to compare the studies done in connection with "Les Demoiselles d'Avignon" of 1906–07 to see how direct this formal influence was. But what made possible the acceptance of the stylizations and formal rearrangements he found in African art was his willingness to perceive and accept their inherent power. We can see this by the way in which Picasso alters the African forms he uses in order to achieve the force, the rhythm, and the intensity that he has found there. It is clear that he cannot free himself entirely from a naturalistic derivation and that he therefore still maintains a relation to muscular tension and to physical movement. But it is clear that he has understood that the African artist creates his intensity by even more stylized means. Picasso has taken the work as it was intended—not as the representation of what is around us everyday in the physical world, but as the presentation of some power beyond or behind that world (pl. 4). In the vocabulary of a more recent artistic language, he has sensed that the African artist creates a presence, an imagined form—an imagined form, however, which has the power of its own intense existence. Picasso's own works done in 1907 and 1908 under Negro influence never match this achievement, never have that impersonal presence, but they retain an assertiveness, an individualistic bravado entirely foreign to African art. It is this, as much as their simplifications, which contributes the most to their "savagery." Insofar as this is true, Picasso's view was a romantic distortion. All the same, he saw and taught others to see qualities that had not previously been grasped; his frame of reference, subjective as it was, opened up new insights and new possibilities on the road to a larger understanding.

The aspects of primitive art stressed by Picasso and his friends in Paris and by the Brücke artists in Dresden had little to do with skill and technique. They were concerned with qualities of formal expressive imagination and so with what was created rather than how it was accomplished (pl. 5). In fact, if we are to judge from what we know of the works they collected at the time, it would appear that traditional qualities of craftsmanship would have gotten in the way of their grasp of the more intangible qualities they were the first to see. Hardly giving conscious thought to the methods by which the primitive artist arrived at his result, they thought of him as an intuitive artisan and imagined that those qualities of structure and incisiveness they admired were in large measure obtained only by neglecting the more accepted aspects of beauty, including those usually associated with the traditional *objet d'art*.

Yet for some time we art historians have said just the opposite about the primitive arts; namely, that they are not really "primitive," that the artist is in control of his material, that he knows exactly what he wants to do, and that within the cultural context that gives him his framework (a traditional but nevertheless living context) the artist is a master worker. The realization that this was so did not come all at once, of course, nor did it come entirely from the aesthetic-subjective lineage we are tracing here. The anthropological study of primitive art goes back at least as far as Boas (and in isolated instances beyond that) and his influential studies of the Northwest Coast. Boas' definition of art, or of that evolutionary point at which art emerges, includes as a fundamental precondition the achievement of consciously controlled skills by which a society is able to repeat traditionally accepted and meaningful forms.

The artist and the aesthetically oriented public also made a large contribution toward an awareness of the more conventionally accepted artistic aspects of the primitive (pl. 6). During the second and third decades of this century, notably in Paris, there were those who began to appreciate precisely those characteristics the "discoverers" of the first decade had chosen to ignore. In the postwar period the emphasis was on gentler rhythms and more subtle stylizations, on smooth surfaces and fine patina, on subdued rather than violent expressions (or at least on expressions that could be so interpreted), and on a greater naturalism. The technology and skill of the primitive artist were approached in terms of a variety of objects that, whatever their provenance and their style, lent themselves to the taste of the European collector of antiques, a taste accustomed to finely grained surfaces and polish and to forms that were composed more in graded harmonies than in sudden contrasts. For a period the primitive arts were praised in these terms. It is no accident that for some years the styles that were the most appreciated were those of the Baule, of the gentler, polished type of Dan mask, and of the Fang (pl. 7). They were all accessible as *objets d'art*, as antiquities, on these terms. They fitted with distinction into eclectic surroundings with a reserve that did not demand interpretation. One might say that they were treated as secular arts, which, indeed, the Baule works in large part actually were. Such an attitude was, once again, very partial; it ignored some works and denatured others. But it permitted the detailed and sympathetic examination of the workmanship of primitive art and an understanding of the skill, the subtlety, and the careful judgment that went into its making. More important, this viewpoint implied the acceptance of their creators as artists, that is, as men who were not simply the unconscious medium of a group expression, but reflective individuals of varying talents and, sometimes, of genius.

Here again an artist was a precursor. Only a few years after Picasso extracted force and directness of expression as the essence of African art, Modigliani carved his famous series of sculptured heads based in part upon African prototypes but executed in an altogether different spirit. By concentrating on the decorative elements of technique and material and on a brooding, mystical expression, he fused African and Asiatic sources with the traditions of his native Italy to create works that suggest a generalized and sophisticated exoticism, gently and undemandingly. This is the very opposite of the earlier, more forceful vision of the primitive, and it well characterizes the more aesthetic, cabinet quality of the collectors' taste of the following years when certain kinds of masks and figures became part of a well-arranged modern decor. Yet, biased as it was, and distant from the psychological sources and social uses of most primitive art, this very eclectic appreciation, by assimilating the techniques of the primitive artist into those of artists everywhere, added one more facet of understanding.

During these same years, while the craftsmanship of primitive art was being accepted and at length taken for granted, intuitive comprehension of its meaning was also being widened. A comparison of the work of two sculptors will perhaps make its basis clear. Epstein's "Venus" has been influenced by the proportions of African figures. Although the work refers to no specifically stylistic source, it is evident that its masklike head overhanging the long neck, its thickened, bent legs, and its summary treatment of arm and hand are reminiscent of Africa. The same can be said of Brancusi's much more simplified "Caryatid." He, too, has realized that in African sculpture the upper portion, particularly the usually large head of the figure, is balanced by the curve of shortened, heavy legs to achieve a vertical composition both stable and powerful (pl. 8). But there the similarity ends. Epstein has transposed a subject of Western mythology into formal rhythms that suggest African art; he has perhaps widened its meaning, but that meaning remains specific, and exotically literary.

Brancusi has also started with a classical reference interpreted through relations of form having their sources in African figure sculpture. He has, however, left his subject general, and by making it into a caryatid with nothing to support, he has allowed it to retain its reference and has stressed a vitality that springs from its own inner tensions. In contrast to Epstein whose work remains discursive, Brancusi has created a symbolic object that is at once allusive and self-sufficient.

One of the elements of primitive art given importance in recent analyses is the lack of specific, discrete, that is to say, discursive, reference. It is an awareness that has found its place on the labels in the exhibition of the objects in the Wellcome Collection. We have come to realize that it is not possible to say whether a given figure is, for example, a figuration of a human ancestor or of a divine ancestor or a god of some sort. Such a determination is impossible not because of lack of knowledge, but because the sculpture in question may be all of these things at once. This way of putting it is a concession to our own traditional way of thinking, which, so to speak, separates things, whereas the African figure has, instead, gathered them together. These overlapping meanings inherent in the African sculpture exist simultaneously and thereby give the sculpture its total significance. Brancusi seems to have had an intuitive grasp of this collecting of meanings, some of which can be described because they antedate the figure or the mask and are, indeed, the reason for its creation, whereas other meanings cannot be traced because they come into being with the fact of its creation. Brancusi transposed this understanding to his own work which for this reason appears to have affinities with the primitive, although, significantly, we are never able to pin down any precise formal derivation. Brancusi is a crucial figure in the history of modern sculpture. He transmitted his vision to other artists and caused the modern public, of which we are a part, to be receptive to his way of seeing. An essential characteristic of primitive art, not conceivable from the point of view of the nineteenth-century figure sculpture (a character essential even if not always present in every work), became accepted, without having been given a scientific formulation. This acceptance prepared us for the understanding we have today.

If the decade of the twenties began to acknowledge primitive craftsmanship and control, the thirties corrected what was in danger of becoming a purely aesthetic or decorative point of view. And here again the attitude of a modern art movement made a significant contribution. We are presently willing to admit to the category of "art" a wide range of works that lack the conventional disciplines of technique, from sculptural forms that are almost entirely unelaborated and without detail to objects that are conglomerations of various materials (pl. 9). Certainly this sympathetic leniency is due in some measure to our increased knowledge of the traditions of craftsmanship, which determine even such apparently haphazard fabrications, and of the functional role they play. We realize that a Ngere mask with bells, a Senufo *kafigueledio* with its stick figure inside its sacrificial coating and costume, an enormously encumbered Mundugumor flute stopper are in both senses as much works of art as objects more conventionally conceived and executed (pl. 10). But neither must we neglect the historical fact that, just as earlier artists had "discovered" certain kinds of clearly composed primitive art, artists of the thirties, with or because of another kind of bias, saw the power of such disparate and untidy objects. The Dakar-Djibouti Expedition of 1931, which first brought back the strangely simple works of the Dogon, so different in workmanship from the previously admired Baule and Dan, was, after all, carried out under joint auspices and included men who were much interested in a particular kind of contemporary art, namely surrealism (pl. 11). The surrealists, M. Griaule, M. Leiris, and others were more concerned with art's unconscious "magic" than with its conscious forms; in certain works of primitive art, they found support for their ideas. Seeking out these, so to speak, new and unorthodox kinds of primitive objects and pointing out with enthusiasm qualities until then overlooked, they brought them into our field of vision. It seems to us today that the 1931 expedition collected surprisingly few objects; this is partly because we are heirs to an attitude they first conceived, because we so freely admit that there are works of art that employ means unfamiliar to our own limited experience (deliberate simplicity or great elaboration, denuded form or extraordinary mixtures of materials) and which use them successfully to attack the imagination. The surrealists, who in the forties also collected Eskimo art, helped us to attend to such works and to realize that it does not matter so much whether or not they are "beautiful" as that they are effective (pl. 12). Thus the range of what was visible in primitive art was further broadened.

We have been reviewing a series of partial "discoveries" of the primitive arts, each one subjective, and all related to the creative needs and problems of modern artists. This relationship was the condition for the discovery; its possibilities and limitations, stemming as they did from the same kind of intuitive insight, could not be separated. In the course of reviewing these changing viewpoints, I have used as illustrations few works of modern art, concentrating instead on the types of primitive art from which they drew their inspiration. Even fewer among those modern works bear any kind of direct formal relationship to the primitive. This is, of course, not accidental and indicates only that modern artists sought and found in primitive art some more fundamental qualities which they turned to their own account.

I suggested at the start that this subjective stage, immensely fruitful and perhaps inevitable, is now completed, has, in fact, been completed for some time, and that for the modern artist, the primitive, although still respected and admired, has now become part of the neutral history of art. It is the artists themselves who first documented this new attitude for us, not by the neglect of the primitive, but by showing a new, increasingly objective point of view. Two very different examples will serve as illustration.

Paul Klee's "Picture Album" makes use of certain primitive motifs. His exact model, even the particular stylistic source (if there was only one), is difficult to determine, although the oval, lined shape would seem to indicate the Gulf of Papua region of New Guinea. One can hardly carry such determinations further, and the attempt is in any case rarely useful. What is more important is to recognize that Klee is choosing certain design motifs, extracting them from the context of the object, and then reusing them. His degree of accuracy hardly matters. What counts is his ability to isolate these forms because it indicates a distance and an objectivity on his part. Klee employs only the separate elements; he ignores the totality, and in this and in his willingness to recombine them in his own design, he suggests the attitude of Gauguin; neither is really affected by the inherent expressiveness of his model. A distance, then—and being by Paul Klee, an ironic distance—has been established, a step toward the detachment of our own contemporary vision.

Henry Moore is far from ironic. He has described in some detail how he spent many hours in the British Museum looking at its collections of primitive art, much more interested in the sculpture of Africa and pre-Columbian Mexico than in his own Western tradition. He felt strongly that these works were both more plastic, because their creators had an innate sense for three-dimensional composition, and more vital, because they were directly expressive of the forces of natural and human growth. Yet, when we come to Moore's work, what do we find? On the one hand there are some half-dozen works that derive from individual examples of primitive sculpture in a very closely reasoned, analytic fashion, and on the other there is the great bulk of his sculpture altogether without this influence, having its sources quite clearly and directly in modern Western art of the immediately preceding generation. All in all, this suggests that, as much as Moore admires the primitives, he is not very close to them and views them with analytic detachment as examples of the universal principles of true sculpture, works upon which he can draw but which have none of the attractive, almost magical power they had possessed for the older artists.

The so-called discovery of primitive art by the artist (and, because of his intervention, by the art-loving public) was, as we have seen, not a sudden and single event. It has been a drawn-out, evolving process, with different emphases at different times, finally revealing a whole gamut of styles and qualities. It has involved little direct derivation of specific forms at any time, and when such derivative art occurs it indicates that a more fundamental influence has begun to wane. I have tried to point out that in the history of this relationship the usual stress should perhaps be reversed. It is less important that the artist has made use of primitive art than that he has made it amenable to our experience. By his series of enthusiasms, by his sequence of partial views, he has in the long run helped us to become aware of its variety of methods, of materials, and of intended effects, to realize that all are valid (even if sometimes strange) and that each demands, so far as possible, a response in its own terms. In the course of half a century, the artist has embraced the whole of primitive art. He has done even more. He has intuitively understood, and made many people understand, that art is not technique and aesthetic alone (a mere illustration of function). Someone has said, "art begins where function ends"; this is a false separation. The art is part of the function, not simply its later illustration, and the function is part of the art, not simply its precondition. The aesthetic is not an overlay but an integral part of primitive culture. First understood through immediate visual confrontation, and with considerable subjective bias, this knowledge can now be put to objective use. Although the artist's role is completed, it has played an essential part in our comprehension of primitive art today.

3. The African Artist

WILLIAM FAGG

I SHOULD LIKE to begin this paper with a series of assumptions a little in the manner of the aphorisms of my favorite American author, Josh Billings, although I cannot hope to be quite so pithy as he was.

As my first assumption I take up a point made by Goldwater in the preceding paper. Doctrinaire ethnologists and archaeologists who insist on inductive and objective methods alone are "tailless foxes," seeking to impose their own incompleteness on others. Such people may make useful contributions in the consolidation of knowledge, but they cannot advance it. They appear to be unaware that science itself advances by subjective bounds and not by objective pedestrianism. How much more must this be so in the study of art, which is by its very nature subjective, even if some current manifestations of contemporary art may make us think that after going around for some time in ever decreasing circles it has at last disappeared up its own computer.

"Critics," said an American critic before the last war, "are like eunuchs; both know how it is done, but neither can do it." I also am a critic in this sense, but I believe that we ethnologists and archaeologists can discharge the most important part of our duty, which is the study of the highest manifestations of culture, only if we recognize our limitations and seek to profit by, and, if possible, learn to imitate the insight of artists. There are some artists, such as my friend the English sculptor Leon Underwood, who have the faculty of divining the history of art and of its intimate union with technology. Underwood's contributions in books on African art and in some articles are only a foretaste of his major work, which may soon be ready. If I have acquired any competence to speak about art, and about the African artist in particular, it is largely under his influence.

The second assumption that I put forward to guide us in our attitude toward the African artist is that African tribal art is a classical art, and not in any way a romantic one. It is worth considering this, for our vision is unconsciously conditioned by the art of our own time, and Western art is still wallowing, even though ever more uncertainly, in the lotus-eating autoerotism engendered by the romantic movement. That major revolution, of which the so-called modern revolution in Paris sixty years ago was a delayed specialization, was, it has always seemed to me, at least in part a guilty reaction to the industrial revolution. It is no coincidence that both these great revolutions, the industrial and the romantic, came to birth in my country within a few years of each other, the rise of the nature poets and painters following hard on the slag heaps. The vastly increased popularity of the painting of natural landscapes in Britain and later in other countries was evidence of our suddenly aggravated alienation from nature. Tribal man is, and conceives himself to be, a part of nature, subject to its vicissitudes and its bounteous opportunities; civilized man is the adversary of nature, predestined, he believes, to be its master, and to confine it in national parks for the recuperation of the alienated. Since artists have at all times been inspired by nature, it seems to follow that, whereas the classical art of the tribal artist is accepted by his society, the romantic civilized artist pursuing his private vision is generally at odds with his—unless, indeed, like some that we could name, it is art itself that he is revolting against.

There is a further important point that arises here in that we have the strange situation of an essentially classical art being widely loved and collected in our society for romantic reasons; some collect it as an adjunct of modern art, some for therapeutic reasons, some to be in the fashion, but most frankly collect what pleases them in the free exercise of private taste, which, except for the absence of creativity, is closely comparable to the attitude of the romantic artist. Now this is far removed from the true connoisseurship that formed the great art collections of the past, of which the keynote was the mastery by the collector of the artistic standards that informed the art of his choice. To be a member of the stable of a Duveen, pathetically dependent upon a dealer for the signal to buy and for authentication and documentation, would have been unthinkable for those true connoisseurs. The great art collections of the past three centuries were formed by men who, although amateurs, were the equals and sometimes the superiors of the professional experts, and this is still true of a few collectors today.

In the field of tribal art, such connoisseurship necessarily involves some knowledge of anthropology and technology and, if possible, some personal experience of the chosen field. Without such knowledge, the unfortunate collector is at the mercy of those who are making purported objects of tribal art for his taste and not for the tribe. It is certain that millions of dollars change hands every year for works that, to a true connoisseur, are not worth a single penny. Of course, the collector must exercise his personal taste, but it must be an informed taste or he will be progressively debasing both his own taste and that of others. These considerations are not at all irrelevant to my theme of the African artist. Private collectors and museum curators are, or should be, the leaders and the standard-setters of our taste in African art. Too often they unwittingly guide us not toward the African artist, but toward the African forger or even sometimes toward the European forger.

I still have one or two general points to make before addressing my main theme. One is the tribality of African art—the facts are that this greatest gift of Africa to the world is a product and a function of the tribal system so often and so indiscriminately decried by politicians, and that for artistic purposes each tribe forms a separate universe. We must qualify the rigidity of this generalization by adding that tribe is not a static concept, but a dynamic one, and that tribal styles are subject to constant change, as we should expect from the fact that they are the concretizations of an essentially dynamistic belief, that is, one based on the concept of force. We shall see later that the tribality of style in Africa does not restrict the individuality of the traditional artist.

I finish this preamble, which, as it turns out, Josh Billings would be the last to recognize, with a definition of what I mean by the African artist. I mean the traditional carver in wood, ivory, and stone, the metal-caster or the artist in pottery working in the context of the tribal system for the members of his own tribe and expressing the religious and artistic values of his community. Many such artists still exist and, though they are undoubtedly on the way out (such is the destructive force of westernization), they will not disappear completely for a long time to come.

I exclude from this definition three classes of artists, real or so-called. The first of these is the contemporary African artist and, although many are true artists, they are not truly African artists, although of African race, because they have been trained in art schools in the Western romantic tradition and conform unmistakably to the international style, whereas their patrons are almost exclusively not African.

The weaker brethren of this class tend to slide into the second class, the makers of tourist art, which, of course, is not art in any proper sense, but more or less mechanically produced *Kitsch*, or trashy souvenirs, for the less sophisticated traveler. There is too much of this about in the world to make it worthwhile for me to illustrate it.

The third class, and the most dangerous to our correct appreciation of the real African artist, is the forgers, who make and carefully age imitations and fantastications of the traditional works of their own or of neighboring tribes. Their work is addressed, and often very expertly addressed, to the international art market, and therefore is both commercially oriented and intended to deceive. Moreover, it takes the bread from the mouths of long-established, European forgers.

I must exempt from these criticisms the bona fide replicas of museum specimens made by African carvers at certain museums, such as those at Livingstone and at Abidjan, where Baule artists produce very close copies of Senufo and other works besides those of their own tribe. No excuse can be made for those Benin brasscasters and their nonhereditary imitators who forge ancient Ife heads, such as several that are based on plate 1 of Underwood's *Bronzes of West Africa* (1949).

The decks are now sufficiently clear for me to approach the African artist proper. A number of other fieldworkers besides myself have collected information about the life histories of traditional artists, their place in society, and so forth. For example, I could tell you that Arowogun of Osi, one of the master carvers whom I shall mention later, was born with curly hair on his head, this being indicated by his first name, Dada. I do not feel under any obligation to give much of this information here, however, and this is not only because I do not wish to take unfair advantage of Bernal, who will have no such help when he speaks about individual creativity in pre-Columbian Mexico. After all, what was important about Richard Wagner was not his life with Cosima von Bülow, or even his addiction to Nietzsche, and least of all Hitler's subsequent addiction to Wagner, but the music of *Die Meistersinger* and *Der Ring des Nibelungen*. So, in this paper, I try to suggest the special character of a few African artists whose works, but not necessarily their persons, are known to me. It is my contention that the artist as an artist is known by his works, and it is on the identifiability of the works of the African artist that I especially rely to illustrate their originality.

The earliest known African sculptures, those of the Nok culture of the last few centuries before Christ, are so scattered in the archaeological record of northern Nigeria that there is little hope yet of finding two by the same artist. A thousand years or so later, at Ife in central Yorubaland in western Nigeria, we can identify two or more bronze heads by each of several masters. I illustrate (pl. 13) a magnificent head by one whom I call the Master of the Aquiline Profiles, for there is no reason why we should not adapt the conventions of European art history to our use. (For two other heads that I take to be his work, see Underwood, 1949, pls. 2, 3, 12; the bronze figure illustrated in Fagg, 1965, pl. 32, may also be by him.)

At Benin too, which learned bronze sculpture from Ife, we can identify many more or less prolific masters, especially in the early period. One of their finest sculptors in the round was the sixteenth-century artist of two heads of queen mothers (pl. 14), one in the British Museum and one in the Nigerian Museum. No one who examines them closely can doubt that they are by one hand. We can make even more profitable comparisons if we consider the bronze plaques, numbering about a thousand, which were made over a period of about a hundred years in the late sixteenth and early seventeenth centuries according to our estimates of Benin chronology.

A plaque illustrated by Dark (1960, pls. 30, 31) and Underwood (1949, pl. 54) is a very fine example of the more conventional type of plaque, which accounts for perhaps well over nine hundred of the thousand known plaques. Note the stiffness of the figures of the Oba and his supporting chiefs, the general tendency to symmetry, and a somewhat pedestrian approach to the work. This plaque is intended as a kind of frame of reference for the next two or three illustrations.

Another representation of the same subject (Trowell, 1966, pl.

lxix*a*) is one of about twenty or twenty-five plaques by one master (Dark, 1960, pl. 44; Underwood, 1949, pl. 58; Fagg, 1963, pl. 20; and Fagg and Plass, 1964, p. 111), whose hand is unmistakable and whom I call the Master of the Circled Cross after the background pattern of a cross within a circle that distinguishes his works from all the other plaques known, the latter having a four-leafed or quatrefoil motif on a larger scale all over the backgrounds. Apart from this distinguishing signature, so to speak, we note that the figures are much more slender and delicate and, indeed, in some ways more lively than on the first plaque, even though in this one the figures are not free of stiffness. In fact, I think it very probable that this artist was the original maker of the plaques, and that only when he had made the first plaques for the palace of the king of Benin did a number of other artists join him to form a real guild of bronze-casters to make this vast mass of plaques to line the pillars of the palace. I suggest that, apart from two or three of these early masters, the others soon developed a kind of stolid and safe style.

The plaque reproduced in Underwood (1949, pl. 60) is by another, very original caster who might be described, from a technical point of view, as the greatest virtuoso among Benin bronze-casters from the complication of the forms that he cast by the lost-wax method. Casting the cow out in front of the figures is a very difficult feat by the methods available to them. Because he seems to have made two or three such plaques, I call him the Master of the Cow Sacrifices. The scene probably represents the sacrifice of a cow to the ancestors of the king of Benin at the annual ceremony of Making Father, as it was called in pidgin English.

The most original of all the plaque masters was the artist whom I call the Master of the Leopard Hunt, after a plaque illustrated by Fagg (1963, pl. 23). He has broken away completely from the four-square attitudes of the majority of the plaques. In this composition, different elements are seen from at least three different points of view, in what is known as "synoptic vision." First of all, the scene as a whole is viewed from above, as you can tell by the corral into which the leopards have apparently been driven, then the leopards are seen in profile, and finally five Portuguese who are hunting the leopards are seen in a kind of in-between view. The artist seems to be responsible for half a dozen or so of the finest of all the plaques. Fagg (1963, pl. 22) shows another one, which, according to some authorities, is the most beautiful of all Benin plaques; it certainly is a far cry from the stolidity of most of them.

So much for the antique cultures of Africa. Let us now come up to more recent times.

I found a wooden figure of a woman seated on a stool in a London dealer's shop; it is by a locally famous carver of the Idoma tribe in northern Nigeria (not illustrated; for a similar work probably by this carver see Pitt Rivers Museum Exhibition Catalogue, 1965, no. 105). His style was identified first, I believe, by Kenneth Murray of the Nigerian Antiquities Service, but later his work was thoroughly studied by Sieber who confirmed my identification of the piece as being by the carver Ochai of Otobi village. It is a standard type of figure-carving in that area of the Idoma country. Ochai, however, was also given to more original flights, and plate 15 is one of the most remarkable of them. It is a unique dance headdress, which he made once, more or less by whim, I think, although it was for a cult in which different masks were used and in which freedom of subject was permissible. You see with what remarkable skill he has built up the composition of separate heads sprouting from a single stem.

A figure of a kneeling woman with a bowl (Olbrechts, 1946, pl. 136) is from the Congo. It is the best-known work of one who is probably the best known of traditional Congo artists. Although nobody knows his name, he seems to have flourished at or around the village of Buli in the northern Baluba country of the eastern Congo, most probably in the last years of the nineteenth century. Another of his more impressive works (Olbrechts, 1946, pl. 121) is a chief's stool in the British Museum. There are about fifteen or eighteen known works in this style, but only about eight or ten are by this master, the others being in a different wood and in a slightly different style; they are certainly less moving in their artistic qualities and appear to be by another member of his family or by one of his pupils.

Another fine artist in this area of the Congo, a little further south, several of whose works are prized in collections in various parts of the world, is one whom I call the Master of the Cascade Coiffures (Fagg and Plass, 1964, p. 88). Nearly all his figures wear a very elaborate cascade hairdo, which was actually used in this area of the Congo among the Shankadi subtribe of the Baluba. Plate 16 shows another of his headrests, this time supported on two beautifully interlocked figures. It is in the British Museum and is, I think, one of the two finest examples of his style. We are able to identify his work even when it has no figures on it by a certain sort of "handwriting" about his treatment of the decorative work around the bases and by the line of the headrest surface at the top. I have seen one that I would guess to be by him in the Wellcome Collection at the University of California, Los Angeles.

The remainder of my paper is illustrated from one tribe, the Yoruba of western Nigeria.

Among Yoruba artists I have an old friend, whose name I do not know although I can pinpoint his address to within about 20 miles, just to the west of Lagos, but unfortunately he lived about 1900, and I have not quite tracked him down yet. I meet him in his works all over the world. Almost all collections that have more than a handful of Yoruba masks have one of his works, and I very soon christened him the Master of the Uneven Eyes, for in many of his works, as in one in the Cologne museum (pl. 17), it looks as though he has worked around the head, starting with one eye, going around the back of the head, and not looking again at the face until he had finished the other eye. Few of his works have been published (Pitt Rivers Museum Exhibition Catalogue, 1965, no. 26), for he was far from being one of the major artists of Yorubaland, and I really mention him as an exception to my rule; in truth, he is an artist distinguished by his badness rather than by his merits. I was very glad to see him again in the Wellcome Collection; he is not quite so uneven in your specimen, but it is a good example of his work.

In Abeokuta, about 60 miles north of Lagos, there lives a carver whose name is Salakatu Ayo Adugbologe. He is the son of a great carver, although he is a rather indifferent one himself. His brother Makinde and several other carvers work in a flourishing atelier built in a rock shelter under the Olumo rock. The family's style is represented at its best in this long-eared mask for the Egungun Society (Fagg and Plass, 1964, p. 90) made by Ayo's father Adugbologe, who died during World War II at a fairly advanced age and was probably the best artist of this century in the important carving center of Abeokuta. There is a fine strength about his faces which is rather debased in the works of his followers, mostly other members of his family like Salakatu Ayo. Several Egungun masks from the Adugbologe family are included in the Wellcome Collection.

Plate 18 illustrates the largest work by Adugbologe, the father, which I have seen. I identified it in a collection in Switzerland two or three years ago. The fact that he was quite a humorous carver can be seen from the way in which he has carved some of the smaller figures, such as the trumpeter in the front.

A carver by the name of Bamgboye of the village of Odo-Owa in northeastern Yorubaland, quite far up in the bush, who became famous among Europeans, is illustrated together with one of his best works now in the Nigerian Museum in *L'Art Nègre* (1951, pls. 40, 41). It is a great mask for the Epa cult, representing a nineteenth-century mounted warrior, and was carved in his prime, probably in the 1920's. Shortly thereafter he was induced by some English educationists, who admired his work, to take the post of teacher of carving in a government school. Immediately his art changed, becoming self-conscious, and he became merely a turner-out of exercises in carving. When he does attempt large works in the traditional style they no longer seem to have anything like the same feeling and intensity as his older pieces. A mechanical slickness has supervened.

Plate 19 represents, I think, one of Bamgboye's finest works: a mask whose superstructure has as its subject the excellence of having many children. It represents two sisters with several children each. The delicacy of feeling inherent in the sculptural relationship between the sisters is admirable. Before he sold this work (which was still in his possession after nearly thirty years) in 1952, Bamgboye was persuaded to carve another similar, but this was a dramatic demonstration of the replacement of art by craftsmanship.

Clarke (1939, p. 256, pl. xiii) has an example of the work Bamgboye produced in large quantities after the change in his career, in the form of coffee or cocktail tables for Europeans consisting of an Ifa divination tray supported by a caryatid. They are excellently carved but are without the instinctive feeling for design that occurred in his earlier work. They are exercise pieces in which he always repeats himself exactly. There are many examples of this subject, all the same, whereas in his earlier works one never finds two carvings alike (and this is generally the case among the Yoruba).

Five miles away from Bamgboye's village there lived the carver Arowogun of Osi, whom I have already referred to briefly. Bamgboye is still alive but Arowogun died in 1956. We see him (pl. 20) with two or three of his last carvings done in 1954. The photograph was taken for me, for I never met him, by my friend Father Kevin Carroll, who is one of the best authorities on Yoruba art. Even at the end of his life when Arowogun was about seventy-five the strength of his forms was very apparent, and his hand is readily distinguishable in many places all over northern Ekiti in northeast Yorubaland. I have pictures of about sixty or seventy of his works which I photographed in the field: large and small doors (Fagg and Plass, 1964, p. 103; Fagg, 1963, pl. 93) and house posts (*L'Art*

Nègre, 1951, pl. 45) and many other kinds of carvings. He was by far the most famous carver in that area within a radius of about forty miles.

I would like to say a word about a piece that is not a traditional work of art but is descended in a way from the carver I have been discussing, Arowogun of Osi. It is a crucifix carved by a sculptor whose name is Lamidi Fakeye and who is now working in Ibadan in western Yorubaland. He was taught carving by being apprenticed to the son of Arowogun, whose name is George Bandele. Bandele was working for Father Carroll, who was at the time heading a most valuable and important experiment in the use of African carvers in Christian liturgy. Bandele followed his father's style very closely, so that we find it difficult to tell their works apart. He then taught the style of Osi to Lamidi. Although Lamidi came from the famous Fakeye family of Ila, another important carving center, he had not yet acquired the family style, so he adopted the style of Osi. The crucifix is a somewhat perfunctory piece, but it was interesting to me that it should turn up and be available to illustrate at second remove the art of Arowogun. It has a characteristic forehead line derived from Arowogun's own style. Lamidi makes a large number of such pieces; they may even be made by apprentices and may simply be checked by him to see that they conform to his style before being sold to Europeans.

Fagg and Plass (1964, p. 93) illustrate a work of a carver who was original in a very different way. His name was Agunna of Oke Igbira near Ikole, also in Ekiti, but I identified this fine house post in the palace of the Owa of Ilesha, about 50 miles away. His work differs from that of any other Yoruba carver I have come across—and I know the works of many hundreds—in the sharpness of his features and the triangulation of most of his forms which introduces a severity into his carvings in opposition to the general character of Yoruba carvings, which tend to be rather full-faced and full-bodied with emphasis on curved forms. Plate 21, in which is seen very clearly the same sharpness of features, illustrates one of his masterpieces, one of two great house posts in the palace of the Ajero of Ijero. He had various followers who more or less imitated his style so that in and around Ikole in northern Ekiti are a number of carvings that show to some extent this sharpness of forms, although none of them quite so markedly as Agunna's own.

The fuller forms typical of most Yoruba carving are evident in the work of a master (pl. 22) from Efon-Alaye, one of the greatest centers of carving nearly in the center of Yorubaland. This great artist's name was Agbonbiofe. He was one of a famous family of carvers and makers of beaded crowns for the kings of Yorubaland, the Adeshina family. They still supply beaded crowns for kings over a very wide area. Plate 22 shows one of about twenty-five magnificent posts by him which support the roofs of the audience chamber and other courts of the palace of the Alaye of Efon-Alaye. It illustrates one of the two typical subjects in Yoruba house posts, a scene depicting a mother with one or more children, and one can easily observe the boldly cut forms of face and body. The other main subject favored by the house-post carvers (Fagg and Plass, 1964, p. 92) is the mounted warrior, or Jagunjagun as he is called in Yoruba. These carvings do not represent gods or earth mothers or anything like that; they are simply generalized representations of warriors and of mothers with children.

Agbonbiofe's work is representative of the best in the typical style of Efon carving, and I want to compare it with the work of my last carver who also, it is said, came originally from Efon but who migrated early in life to the southeast to a village called Ise in southern Ekiti. He was called Olowe. When he grew up he became an *emese* or messenger of the Arinjale, or king, of Ise, and for many years until his death in 1938, he had great fame in the area as a carver of architectural sculptures such as doors and house posts. I have an example (1963, pl. 83) of his work, which I spotted in a private collection in Düsseldorf in Germany, which serves to illustrate the fact that he is one of the most humorous of Yoruba carvers. It shows the enormously exaggerated bearers carrying a very little king, who is wearing his beaded crown with a beaded bird on the top. This is a carving that may have been made almost for fun as a gift to one of the local kings. We do not know anything about its history, and it was only because I was so familiar with some of Olowe's works that I immediately recognized this as by his hand.

One of his most important house posts (pl. 23) supports part of the roof of the palace of his chief patron and master, the Arinjale of Ise. The Arinjale himself is seen enthroned with his beaded fan while behind him his senior wife is carrying out the actual work of supporting the roof. There is a similar carving in the neighboring town of Ikere. Olowe was obviously lent by the Arinjale to the Ogoga, the local king, of Ikere, in order to execute a group of carvings (Fagg and Plass, 1964, p. 91) which he did magnificently. There is even evidence that he must have been lent to several kings in fairly widely scattered sections of eastern Yorubaland. I found one of his best doors, for example, in the palace of the Owa of Ilesha, which is about sixty miles from his home village.

Plate 24 shows the Olowe piece I came to know first. It is a very fine pair of doors in the British Museum, which we got by an elaborate process of palavering and exchange in 1925 after the Wembley exhibition, that is, the British Empire exhibition held in London in 1924. It was apparently sent from the palace of the Ogoga of Ikere to be shown at the exhibition, and I am glad to say my predecessors at the museum were so taken with it that they asked if they could buy it. The Ogoga of the time said that he certainly could not sell such a thing, but that he would be very pleased to give it to us if we would make him a throne designed to his specifications. That does not seem to me to have been a very good bargain for him, for the wooden throne is not a very distinguished piece of British craftsmanship, but I am happy to say that Olowe, being still alive, carved a fine new door to fill the gap left by ours.

Several details of this door reveal in a remarkable way the originality of Olowe's style. Almost all Yoruba palace doors—they are common in hundreds of villages and towns all over Yorubaland—

are carved with figures in low and even relief. They are often extremely lively, but the figures never stand out very much from the doors. Olowe, entirely on his own, seems to have introduced the practice of carving the figures to stand out at an angle from the door, so that the heads may project as much as six inches, whereas the feet are still firmly attached to the wood of the single block from which the whole is carved.

The main subject of this pair of doors is a British officer being carried in a litter and received by a local king, namely the Ogoga of Ikere in whose palace the door was. It commemorates an actual historical occasion in about 1895, when the first British administrator, whose name was Captain Ambrose, reached Ikere and was received by the Ogoga. There are a row of prisoners who are carrying Captain Ambrose's loads and who are shackled together. There are two rows of ladies, presumably wives of the king, all carrying children on their backs. Others of the Englishman's entourage appear on the right-hand leaf of the door. With considerable humor Olowe has carved Captain Ambrose himself as almost a suppliant of the king, who, by contrast, has a very condescending expression. Olowe appears to have used European oil paints on his carvings often, but, unlike nearly all African artists who have done so, he has used them with remarkable restraint and taste and must be regarded as a very fine colorist indeed.

Plate 25 illustrates a work by Olowe which I consider to be one of his finest and therefore one of the finest works made by the Yoruba in this century.

This masterpiece by Olowe is a bowl for the divination cult of the Yoruba, called Ifa, and it is used for holding some of the Ifa paraphernalia, especially the palm nuts that are thrown from hand to hand in the main process of divination. You see how Olowe, as distinct from most Yoruba carvers who conform to the usual African practice of carving their figures rather stiffly looking straight forward, succeeds, as on his doors, in putting a good deal of movement and life into them. The four girls on the top appear to be really dancing, and the figures below, who are not in any way stiff, are leaning out at various angles; the whole is a very lively composition. Once more we can observe the humor of Olowe, although you may think it slightly sick humor in this case. The figures around the base form a cage and inside it, but from the same piece of wood, is carved a large head that is freely movable. In fact, it is a severed head, presumably of someone who has been either executed as a punishment or sacrificed to some cult. It moves around freely inside its cage, but it cannot be taken out.

It is somewhat useless to try to express in words the beauties of sculptures, even more than of paintings, and I shall not attempt to do so. But in the fine collection of the African sculpture in the Wellcome Collection, I know that there is unlimited scope for the kind of study I have been suggesting. I myself have been studying it with profit and recognizing quite a number of old friends, that is to say, works by hands that I know. I hope that this impressive gift will lead to Los Angeles becoming an important center for research into not merely African art but also African artists.

4. The Concept of Style in Non-Western Art

ADRIAN GERBRANDS

N CULTURAL anthropology *style* is usually understood to be a constant form or a constant combination of forms by means of which one is able to establish the origin of objects made and used by man and also, to a certain degree, the relative age of such objects.[1] Until shortly before World War II, this anthropological concept of style was a research tool used by museum ethnographers, that is, by anthropologists dealing with material culture. The museum ethnographer in charge of collections of some size usually deals with objects from many parts of the world made and used by men and women who belong to a bewildering variety of human cultures. He is confronted with the problem of bringing order to what at first glance seems to be a chaotic diversity of forms and shapes. Admittedly, his problem is partly one of storage. But, of course, if it was only that, he would have to do nothing more

---

[1] Compare also Schapiro, 1953, pp. 287–312.

than put together the objects having the same or similar forms, that is, spears with spears, shields with shields, paddles with paddles, and so forth. Actually, the work of the museum ethnographer is vastly more complicated than separating apples from oranges. To elaborate somewhat on the metaphor of the apple and the orange: the museum ethnographer is not just satisfied with establishing the fact that the apple differs from the orange but also, and in particular, wants to know why they are different, why they grow under different climatic conditions, and so on. The complicating factor is, of course, that the objects the museum ethnographer is dealing with are not natural objects, but objects made, shaped, worked, and created by man.

The concept of style comprises two components: one of place and one of time. European art history has taught us that a given art form, or a given "style," is conditioned by the period in which it evolved in a certain area. That is why we are able to identify a certain painting in such terms as Italian Renaissance and another as French Impressionism, in which the words "Renaissance" and "Impressionism" are, of course, time indicators. It is clear that the notion of style is based on empirical evidence, that is, once a sufficiently large number of art objects is known to be from the same region and the same period they provide the corpus that characterizes the art style of that area and that era.

Unidentified art objects—objects without a pedigree and of unknown origin—may be compared with the corpus of a style and, if the similarities are convincingly sufficient in number, may be attributed to that style. In reality this task is not as simple as stated. To be able to attribute an unidentified art to a particular style, the art historian has to have a thorough knowledge of art styles or at least of the art styles of a certain region or period. Moreover, the object to be identified has to be analyzed in minute detail with respect to the materials from which it is made and the forms given the materials by the artist. In other words, the object has to be examined in detail in the same way that the systematic zoologist or systematic botanist analyzes and describes his precious specimens. Indeed, the techniques the art historian uses to arrive at an identification of an unknown object of art show striking resemblances to the techniques the systematic biologist uses to bring order in the animal and plant kingdoms. Basically, the approach consists of finding what one might call a "type specimen" a fully identified object with known origin and known age, and of using this type specimen as a standard for comparison.

In museum ethnography the technique is applied to establish order in the collections. The problem is the same: to find good type specimens, objects with reliable data about the place of origin—no easy task, especially when one is dealing with older collections that are usually extremely poorly documented. It is a method that museum ethnographers have been using since the 1880's and which had great impetus toward the end of the nineteenth century when scholars like A. C. Haddon and K. H. Stolpe exerted much influence in ethnographical museums and hence played an important part in the development of ethnographical theories and methods. Previous to their involvement in ethnographical theory, Haddon and Stolpe had been well-known, systematic zoologists. Being familiar with the systematic arrangement of the animal kingdom, they were well trained in searching for discrete differences that, however minute, might prove to be very significant. One is inclined to say that museum ethnography borrowed the principle of classification and its methods from systematic zoology more or less as a ready-to-use tool. The application of the principle in its purest form is undoubtedly to be found in the famous Pitt Rivers Museum in Oxford, England, where spears are shown together with spears, shields with shields, and so on.

Every ethnographical museum, however, has to use the method in one form or another. Usually the main frame of reference is a geographical area that shows a certain cultural unity, and within this framework the material culture is presented according to what one could call cultural chapters or paragraphs: warfare, religion, subsistence, music, weaving, pottery, and the like. But the main point of interest of Pitt Rivers, the founder of the Oxford Museum, was not to collect objects solely for the fun of collecting exotic objects, but to prove an evolution from "oldest" forms to "recent" ones. This sequence ranged from primitive forms to sophisticated ones, or from what Rivers considered to be their equivalents, the simple forms to the complicated ones. No doubt the work of their famous predecessor Darwin was the source that suggested to men like Haddon, Stolpe, and Pitt Rivers the evolution from the simple to the complicated. In their minds, however, "simple" was to be related to naturalistic, "complicated" or "developed" was to be related to geometric. In order to prove this hypothesis, ten or twenty people copied successive drawings of what were originally naturalistic representations of trees or birds. The end product in no way resembled the original realistic representation but was a transformation of it into something purely geometrical. Or, as it was usually expressed, the drawing had degenerated into a mathematical form. It is true that in many non-Western societies art is the result of faithful copying from generation to generation. The difference between the experiments conducted by the evolutionists and the actual process of perpetuation of ethnographical objects in the non-Western societies was that in the latter the copying was done by highly skilled artists and not by individuals chosen at random. In due course the archaeological discoveries strongly indicated that naturalistic and "geometrical" forms were equally old or "primitive" (Gerbrands, 1957).

To repeat, style is a constant or fixed form, or a fixed combination of form elements. If style is to be of any value in determining the geographical origin of an object, it must be characterized by a typical combination of form elements which identifies the objects from one area. The combination must therefore be fairly constant over a certain period of time; otherwise it would be impossible to recognize and hence to describe and define. In this respect the concept of style was greatly influenced by the results of archaeological excavations, where layer after layer of soil and pottery clearly showed how shapes and forms of pottery and of ornamentation changed so slowly over long periods of time that the shapes and forms seemed fixed. This relative permanence, in turn, could serve as a measure for age.

The interest of the archaeologist in style stemmed from the same preoccupation with evolutionary stages as that of the zoologist. His main concern was to know exactly not only where an object came from, but also, and especially, how old it was. In the event that no absolute date could be determined, as was usually the case, the archaeologist had to be satisfied with a sequence of relative ages. Interest in the origin of the archaeological findings naturally led to inquiries about the origin of art and ultimately about the origin of human culture as such. Thus the use of the archaeological concept of style as a measure of time coincided in many respects with the use of this concept by ethnographers and museum workers as a referent of geographical origins.

Since World War II there has been a remarkable increase in the application of statistical methods to the sciences of man. It seems as though the social scientists have been trying to create a "scientific image" by means of the depersonalization inherent in the use of large numbers. Man is indeed very difficult to study empirically as absolute laws cannot seem to be formulated with which to explain or predict his behavior. Time and again the social scientist is baffled by unexpected reactions of the human individual toward his environment and he is thereby unable to apply a law to his behavior. The only available solution seems to be the submergence in large numbers of the nonconforming individual, quantitative scaling, and similar statistical techniques.[2]

Statistical methods were introduced recently in the study of the arts and were combined with a refined identification technique called componental analysis. Componental analysis is the analysis

[2] To mention only one recent example of the use of statistical correlations in ethnographical research, see Sawyer and Levine (1966).

of the components of a given art form and of the interrelationships of these components. Based on a methodological article by Schmitz (1956) on the concept of style, Schefold's (1966) stylistical analysis of Middle Sepik suspension hooks is one of the first attempts to apply the statistical method to art. By the application of a very detailed componential analysis in combination with statistical factor analysis to a collection of over five hundred suspension hooks in the Basel Museum of Ethnology, Schefold has been able to refine considerably previous similar research such as that done by me on the art styles in western New Guinea (Gerbrands, 1951) and that done previously by Olbrechts (1946 and 1959) on the art styles in Central Africa. As one of the interesting results of this analysis, Schefold has been able to determine the age of objects from one area by a few specific style elements. That the relative chronology of objects can eventually be ascertained by this method justifies its further use.

A distinguished componential analyst, Olbrechts was also one of the most prominent representatives of an approach that is presently called the structural analysis of art in anthropology. Olbrechts wrote of this analysis as "the social function of a work of art," or the integration of a work of art into the social, the religious, and the economic life of the community that had produced it. Such an analysis must begin with the study of the individual artist: his training, his technique, his motivations, his sources of inspiration, his social position, and the social, religious, and economic framework within which he works.[3] A student of Boas, Olbrechts was understandably interested in art and particularly in the role of the individual artist. It was Boas who claimed, when discussing the problem of style, that

> we have to turn our attention first of all to the artist himself. . . . We may hope that knowledge of the attitude and actions of the artist will contribute to a clearer understanding of the history of art styles. Unfortunately, observations on this subject are very rare and unsatisfactory, for it requires an intimate knowledge of the people to understand the innermost thoughts

[3] Olbrechts as quoted in Gerbrands, 1957, p. 78.

and feelings of the artist. Even with thorough knowledge, the problem is exceedingly difficult, for the mental processes of artistic production do not take place in the full light of consciousness. The highest type of artistic production is there, and its creator does not know whence it comes. It would be an error to assume that this attitude is absent among tribes whose artistic productions seem to us so much bound by a hard and fast style that there is little room for the expression of individual feeling and for the freedom of the creative genius [Boas, 1955, p. 155].

Thus in 1927, Boas presented a very modern view of the role of the artist in the shaping of a given art style. Until then the different styles of the primitive arts were mainly conceived of as technological *trouvailles*, engendered by the skills of weaving, plaiting, chipping, chopping, and such. It was believed that, in the course of time, these *trouvailles* were fused together in a rigid framework of stylistic convention and tradition. Inspired by Boas, Olbrechts was the first to formulate in detail the principles of modern ethno-aesthetic research. Curiously enough very little has come from Olbrechts' viewpoint. Two of his students in 1938 went on an expedition to the Ivory Coast in West Africa to carry out research in line with Olbrechts' efforts. Unfortunately, only a small part of their results has been made accessible in print.[4]

Himmelheber has studied the African artist independently from Boas and Olbrechts. In the course of some twenty years he has made several expeditions to Africa. The results of six of these expeditions were published in his book *Negerkunst und Negerkünstler* (1960). Several artists, especially from among the Dan and the Baule, are discussed in this work. Only sporadically is an illustration of their art presented in the text, however, thus making it next to impossible to form an opinion of the personal style of an artist in relation to the style of the geographical area. Another Africanist who has much unpublished material, particularly concerning Nigerian artists, is Fagg (1963) from the British Museum. Up to the

[4] Vandenhoute, 1948. Admittedly part of Vandenhoute's investigations was published by Gerbrands, 1957, pp. 78–93. The results of the research among the Senufo by the second student of Olbrechts, A. A. L. Maesen, were used by Goldwater, 1964.

present, Fischer (1962) has been the only one to publish a personality sketch of African artists together with illustrations of their work. D'Azevedo (1966) has published a preliminary report on the artist archetype in Gola culture in Liberia, but he fails to include illustrations of their work.

One must turn to a different part of the world to obtain more information about the role of the individual artist in relation to local style. In 1950, Elkin and Mr. and Mrs. Berndt published a thorough examination of the artistic production in Arnhemland, north Australia. Bark paintings and sculptures are illustrated in their book with the name of the artist and a detailed explanation of the design. Although it does not include much information about the artists and their personalities, the analysis of the works of art is nevertheless sufficient for Elkin to conclude:

> Since Aborigines differ as individuals, we can expect to find, and we do find, variations in workmanship and interpretations according to individual talents and personalities. The general pattern and range of variation are traditional, but much depends on the skill of the artist, his treatment of the work and his selection of materials. Moreover, one artist influences others and schools of art develop, but in the case of the Aborigines, each school is functionally related to the society and culture in which it occurs. It is not aberrant, revolutionary, protestant, formless. Its primary task is to express myth and belief, as part of ritual, in forms coming from the distant past [Elkin, Berndt, and Berndt, 1950, p. 110].

Following the example set by Elkin and the Berndts, Karel Kupka also studied the art of the aborigines of Arnhemland and published the results of his research in 1962. Little reference is made in his text to the artists themselves except when explaining a myth painted on a piece of bark. Of the many objects illustrated, about forty are identified by the name of the artist and by the place of origin. Upon analyzing these objects, one realizes that within the framework of a regional style, limited or rigid as that framework may be, the individual artist is easily recognized. Once the individual artist has emerged from anonymity, he is allowed much stylistic freedom.

The range of variation within the standards set by tradition is something that particularly impressed me when I did my own research among the Asmat Papuans on the southwest coast of New Guinea. In 1960–61, I lived for eight months in the village of Amanamkai to study the cultural background of the artist and his work. I returned with about four hundred carvings which now form part of the collection of the National Museum of Ethnology in Leiden. I can directly identify the artist of most of the objects because most of them were made during my residence in Amanamkai. Living for eight months in close contact with some twenty artists and the seven hundred other inhabitants of Amanamkai, I was able to gain insight into their personalities and characters. I was at first totally unable to distinguish one man's carvings from those of his colleague. To begin with, I simply did not know who the carvers were. In the social pattern of the Asmat culture, the ownership of a carving was more important than its actual production. This fact made it even more difficult for me to determine who the carver of a particular piece of work was. As time went by, however, I was able to identify the carvers by their work almost as well as could the art connoisseurs of the village. Just as it takes time for a student of the Western arts to learn to distinguish a painting done by Degas from one done by Renoir, one needs time and patience to learn to distinguish a figure carved by Tarras from one carved by Ndojokor.

It was almost by accident that in the early days of my stay in Amanamkai, I became acquainted with the *wow-ipits*, as the woodcarvers are called in the Asmat language, *wow* meaning "carving," *ipits* meaning "man" or "men." I arranged to have four pieces of hardwood made which I intended to use as legs for a table. As there is no furniture in an Asmat house, the Asmat had no conception of what "table" meant. Moreover they had few tools other than an ax, which was usually made of iron, or a knife. The four pieces of wood which four men brought to me after a few days' work were consequently of no use as legs for a table. The four men who had made the pieces of wood were Bishur, Ompak, Sipo, and Jayen. Although they did not understand why I had turned down their carvings, the men were nevertheless upset by the fact that they had apparently not been able to work to the satisfaction of the stranger. Because I had obviously made too little allowance for the limited technological means of the Asmat wood-carver, I, too, was discontented. To correct the situation, I proposed, as a kind of experiment, that they add to the four pieces of wood the same kind of relief carving with which they decorated their bamboo horns. Apparently the proposal was successful for the four men immediately went off with their respective pieces of wood to the ceremonial house, or *yeu*, to undertake the task. That is to say, I assumed that was what they were going to do. The next morning, when I dropped in at the *yeu* to see how the task was progressing, I found to my amazement that of the four original men only Bishur was decorating his own table leg; the other legs were being done by different people whom I did not recognize. I discovered that they were *wow-ipits*, wood-carvers. Bapmes worked on Ompak's table leg, while Matjemos and Itjembi were occupied with Sipo's and Jayen's. It took them about three days of fairly continual work to finish the pieces.

The completely unexpected development that the experiment had produced later turned out to be of key importance to my research. I had been told that every village had one or more wood-carvers, but had not learned the exact natures of their functions. My interpreter had evaded my questions about the matter by telling me that each man did his own carving. His answer was not completely incorrect but lacked precision. I discovered by this experiment that each man did his own carving only when it concerned simple and undecorated objects of everyday use such as bows, paddles, digging sticks, sago-pounders, and the like. When a more difficult object was needed, such as a drum, a canoe, a figure, an ancestor pole, or a decorated bamboo horn, a specialist, someone of reputation as a wood-carver, a *wow-ipits*, was commissioned. The decoration of my four table legs was apparently something that only Bishur among the four original men had the ability to do.

For still another reason, however, the experiment was of extreme importance. I had in my possession four objects of the same kind executed under the same conditions by four different artists. This presented itself as an ideal situation in which to make comparisons of the individual style. As even a cursory examination of plates 26, 27, 28, and 29 makes abundantly clear, each of the four artists had been working in a different style. That it was indeed the personal style of the individual artist, as characteristic as anybody's handwriting, was demonstrated by Assaji some time after the completion of the decorated objects. Assaji, a clever and intelligent chief, one of the best art connoisseurs in the village, had no difficulty in identifying the carver of each of the table legs.

In the study of individual style, I found very useful a collection of approximately a hundred and fifty decorated bamboo horns which I had been able to collect during my stay in Amanamkai. As shown in plates 30, 31, 32, and 33, the differences in individual style are striking. In dealing with a hundred and fifty objects, the diversity of styles was wide, though somewhat less than anticipated. It turned out that the decorating of bamboo horns was generally considered to be a relatively easy job, one that an inferior artist might attempt. Lacking imagination and technique, however, the lesser artist often contented himself with copying the design of the master artists. A good illustration of this is the bamboo signal horn shown in plate 33, carved by the much younger and less versatile artist Itjembi who used as a model the horn shown in plate 32, carved by the famous artist Ndojokor. Ndojokor's horn is not only an excellent piece of work technically speaking, but also shows an exceedingly well-organized design. The nervous cluster of hook-shaped ornaments in the center of the horn is cleverly counterbalanced by a few broad and quietly meandering wave lines. The design carved by Itjembi on the horn of plate 33, however, is poorly organized and shows little or no rhythmic feeling. The technical execution lacks subtlety when compared with plate 32.

The design on the horns in plates 30 and 31 consists of standing human figures representing ancestors. They were made by two different artists, Matjemos and Ndojokor. The styles of these horns and of those in plates 32 and 33 differ to the degree that in attempting to identify the origin of the horns by the traditional method used in anthropological museums, one might believe that they originated in different subareas within the Asmat style province and that they therefore represented different substyles of Asmat art. Actually, they all originated in the village of Amanamkai, and, moreover, two of them (pls. 31 and 32) were created by the same artist, Ndojokor. When one realizes that these two horns are both made by Ndojokor, one recognizes the neatness, the ease, and the well-balanced design that characterize the style of this master artist. The same diversity in style is found among the ancestor figures of which four examples are given in plates 34, 35, 36, and 37. A superficial examination might lead one to think that the figures in plates 34 and 35 were done by the same carver. With further analysis, however, it can be seen that they are distinguished by details: ears, nostrils, jaws, shoulders, proportions of arms and legs, pelvis and penis, and knees and feet. Actually the figures shown in plates 34 and 35 were made respectively by Bifarji and Finerus, both equally young and equally gifted artists. The difference between the two other figures is much more pronounced. The figure in plate 36 was made by Matjemos, one of the best artists from Amanamkai; versatile, flexible, eager to try new shapes and concepts, he was a complete master of his tools and materials. The last figure (pl. 37) is a poor one, even under Asmat standards of beauty and excellence, mainly because of the clumsy way in which the legs are made. Its poor quality is easy to understand as it was made by two different men. Kamis, one of the ordinary men in the village who occasionally carved his own paddle or sago-pounder, made the body of the figure. Allured by the tobacco and axes I gave to the other *wow-ipits*, he had attempted to carve a full-sized figure. The task, however, proved to be too difficult for him; he had to ask Omsa, one of the lesser *wow-ipits* to carve the head.

Space does not allow for more examples of Asmat art and artists (but see Gerbrands, 1967) or for an analysis of the fascinating symbolism which finds its expression in the art of the Asmat (see Gerbrands, 1962).

We are slowly coming to realize that the alleged anonymity of the so-called primitive arts is a fiction. In European art history the personal style of an artist has become a well-accepted facet of the general concept of style. We are now able to understand the idea that in the non-Western arts the individual artist also plays an important role in the shaping of a style. Just how important his influence is we have not yet determined. This undoubtedly, future research will reveal.

5. Individual Artistic Creativity in Pre-Columbian Mexico

HAVE BEEN persuaded to discuss something about which I know very little. There is, of course, a very good point in my favor: no one else knows very much about the subject either. In view of these facts and without complete confidence, I undertook the task of trying to discover what Mesoamerican people thought of their own art and what the position of the artist was in that particular society and to examine many related problems.

What do we know about the individual artist in Mesoamerica? What was his position in his own society? What were his norms, his freedom to do what he pleased, or his conformity to established rules? Especially now that his society is entirely dead, how can we recover his ideas or what we might call his psychology? Or, what is still more difficult, how can we assess what the people thought of the artist and of the works that he created? Of course we have objects that have survived, but except for very minor exceptions we have no contemporary information of any sort on any of them.

Today it is much in the fashion, and I think too easy, to psychoanalyze any ancient art. If we go a little bit deeper into the question, what do we find? Are we really psychoanalyzing, or are we trying to understand the motives of a long-dead artist which pertained to a totally different mental structure and to a totally different culture than ours? Well, really no. We are only psychoanalyzing ourselves. Of course, that is great fun, but how much does it really enlighten us or how much does it help us to understand what happened in another society in an entirely different frame of reference? I doubt that this approach is of much value and so do not plan to follow this course. I have tried to find out what information there is about the artist and his problems in his own society, as meager as that information is.

Before going directly into the subject, it is important to call to mind something that is well known: in contrast with the previous lectures of this series we are not dealing with primitive art. We are dealing with the art of a civilized society. This is very basic from my point of view, not only as a general *aperçu*, but because the whole set of problems and, of course, the whole set of possibilities are different. We cannot study, for instance, the art of the Melanesians in the same way that we study the art of Mesoamerica. If we want to understand something about a dead civilization, we must think about it in different terms. We must think of it in the same frame of reference as Egypt or Mesopotamia, that is, as those cultures, also dead, which attained a higher level of art than primitive peoples. This, in a way, produces a set of interesting and complicated problems about how to deal with the situation. In academic circles we are all accustomed to thinking of an Egyptologist as representing a normal field of study. We are not accustomed to thinking of a Mesoamericanist as such. I do not know why the Egyptologist is considered to be an archaeologist and historian, whereas the Mesoamericanist, if he exists, is really thought to be an anthropologist. I am not pursuing the implications of this difference because it is beyond the scope of this paper, but I mention it to emphasize the basic premise of my study: I am dealing with the art of a dead civilization and not with a primitive art.

I have said a number of times that the civilization of Mesoamerica is a dead one. You might say that there are nevertheless strong survivals of it. We all know that a large percentage of the people living in Mexico still hold to their ancient ways and to their ancient norms. That is quite true, but what has remained is more the rural life and not the urban civilization of pre-Columbian days. I think it is important to stress this difference. On the other hand, this sets a limitation to our study and to our comprehension of the problem. Modern or nineteenth-century ethnological studies are of no great help precisely because they deal not necessarily with the earlier civilization but instead with the remains of Indian communities which have only the rural aspects of ancient life plus the Spanish legacy. In this sense the rupture between the past and present has been so complete that the information we can gather today about the position of the artist in contemporary Indian society is hardly applicable to the position of the artist in ancient Mesoamerican society. I think that the whole structure of the society is now entirely different and that therefore what occurs today does not necessarily reflect what occurred previously.

Simply for the purpose of this paper, which deals only with plastic arts, and without trying to be at all categorical, we can divide human aesthetic production into two main groups. One is what today we call folk art. Folk art was usually made by nonspecialists, nonprofessionals, people who do various things, not just by those who have a basically intuitive approach to aesthetics. I think that folk art generally has aesthetic rules but not at all the type of aesthetic rules which the other art has. A very good illustration, even if it is outside Mesoamerica, appears in Bunzel's work (1928) on the Pueblos. She mentions how a Pueblo Indian of today would say, "Now this pot is not good." Why is it not good? "It is not good," he answers, "because it has five flowers when only four should be there." This sort of rule is typical of folk art, but I do not think it is applicable to the other type of art with which I shall deal in a moment. Folk art is basically anonymous or was so before the advent of tourists. In this respect and perhaps in many more, it can easily be compared with primitive art. It is this type of art which— for reasons that escape me—was usually housed amid the frightful combination of objects in the so-called Museum of Natural History along with the plants and the animals. What primitive man would have to say about that, I do not know, but I suppose that he would not have been very happy about this association. When I find that this same type of situation occurs occasionally in dealing with other types of art—with nonprimitive arts, for instance, simply because they are outside the Western tradition—I view it as being even worse.

The second group I propose is what we might call simply art with a capital *A*. In Mesoamerica, this art has a few, very clear, social characteristics. First, it is obviously a professional art, that is, the makers are specialists. This does not mean, as also happens in many other cultures, that a man may do nothing but that, but it does mean that he does essentially that. Such specialized professional art is obvious in the few examples, chosen at random, illustrating this paper. They are taken from different places and show how impossible it is to think of the sites or objects as having been done by anybody but a professional or a group of professionals.

An excellent example is the Maya palace of the governor in Uxmal (pl. 38), an extremely sophisticated piece of architecture with its very simple lower level and very elaborate upper level reminding one of other such sophisticated masterpieces as the ducal palace in Venice.

Another example is a group of buildings: the great plaza at Monte Albán (pl. 39). Again we have something very well planned, something that must have been conceived by either a group of architects or one architectural genius whose name we do not know. It is an unbelievably beautiful Mesoamerican ruin in which the depurated simplicity of line is again extremely sophisticated.

Sculpture illustrates the same point. A Maya stela from Copán (pl. 40) cannot possibly have been performed by anybody on the folk-art level. A superb Aztec jaguar (pl. 41), a product of nearly two thousand years of great carving tradition, is a huge monolith that intentionally preserves only the simplest elements, yet does not lose any of its essence. Every necessary component is present. As another example, there is the well-known, so-called Aztec calendar (pl. 42), a votive stone to the sun, which, independent of its technical perfection—the rendering of a perfect circle, of all the inner circles, and of all the intricate lines that are beyond any possibility of execution by a nonprofessional—contains a complex of religious symbolism and the extensive, solar knowledge of these people. This is, of course, a mythological representation and not, as wrongly thought at times, a true calendar.

These few examples suffice to illustrate how the quality of specialization in the artist is obvious in many different Mesoamerican societies, and not just in such late ones as the Aztec.

A second quality is immediately apparent in the illustrations: it is an urban art, which is equivalent to saying that it is a civilized art. Unlike modern folk art, it was produced not by countryfolk, but by city folk, by people who lived in large communities and who had an urban approach to their problems.

A third trait, which seems to be in contrast with the other two, is that in one way this art *has* a characteristic of folk art: it is entirely anonymous. This problem of anonymity, which seems to us to be extraordinary, may not be so unusual when we consider certain cultural aspects. For that purpose, I examine three other basic characteristics of Mesoamerican art, from a social rather than from an aesthetic point of view. The first two characteristics have to do with the question of who creates the art, and the third one with the question of for whom the art is created. These two approaches might help to understand more of the problem of anonymity.

We do not know the name of a single artist in any Mesoamerican culture. Even among the Aztecs, about whom we have a great deal of information, not one name is ever mentioned. In the eighteenth century, Clavijero, a man who belongs to what might be called the first generation of Mexicans, was the first to show deliberate admiration of this art, yet he never mentioned the name of an artist. He certainly never found any record of a name, and no one has found any since. We find that either in actual fact or simply in the minds of people, it is always a collective art and never a personal art. Even when a work was done by only one man, it was nevertheless attributed to a group of individuals. This collective attribution to a group occurs in different ways.

First, we have what we might call the attribution of artistic production to cities, to areas, or to ethnic groups. Historical sources provide an example of the first case. It is stated that when Moctezuma I planned to build the great temple at Tenochtitlan, his capital, he did not solicit an architect but rather "the architects" from Chalco, that is, from a city, a collective symbol. Referring to areas, we recall the famous Tlailotlaques, the "returned people." They were probably Mixtecs who had gone to the Mixteca, and, having learned there the arts of the area, returned with their knowledge to the valley of Mexico, where they executed very fine works in the Mixtec style. Here again we have the same situation: objects attributed to the group, to the Tlailotlaques, not to any one, discrete person. As for large ethnic groups, we have the famous Toltecs who in later legend among the Aztecs were thought to have invented art. Again it was the achievement of a group, not of an individual, even though their god personified inventions.

Second, attributions of artworks were made to kings or to important persons who undertook to commission a large public work; obviously, they did not create the structure themselves but simply commanded the people who built it. Thus the aqueduct that brought the water into Tenochtitlan is said to have been built by Netzahualcoyotl, king of Texcoco. It is manifestly clear that Netzahualcoyotl did not build it personally. He probably simply ordered his specialists to do it, quite a different matter. Another similar situation, and a very illuminating one, is illustrated by the famous palace of Netzahualcoyotl of Texcoco. Archaeologically we have no record of it, but fortunately a descendant of the king Ixtlilxochitl wrote a description of how the palace was built and of how enormous it was. What does he imply about those whose job it had been to build it? He never mentions them. He simply refers to the king of one place or another as being responsible for it. Always the same situation. Obviously, Netzahualcoyotl had groups of fine workmen brought in from different places, and the artistic results were attributed to the rulers of those places, not to the workers.

A third instance of this sense of collective and therefore anonymous production is illustrated by the following example. According to the chronicle, when Moctezuma I was in his glory, toward the end of his reign, he said to a man called Tlacaelel, supposedly his brother and second in importance only to him: "Brother, it is only just that a memorial be set up to you and me, and I have determined that two statues be carved within the limits of the garden of Chapultepec. Let the stone workers choose the part of the living rock that most pleases them and carve our likenesses on it. It will be a reward for our endeavors and our sons and grandsons will see our images there and remember us and our great deeds, and will struggle to imitate us." Tlacaelel at once ordered the stonecutters to begin the statues at Chapultepec and to carve them upon the year *ce tochtli*, the year in which the famine had begun. The sculptors worked rapidly, and the statues were soon finished. Then Tlacaelel said to the king: "Lord, our vassals have done what you commanded them and it would be good for us to go and see what statues they have made for us." So one morning, unattended and unseen, they left the city and went to Chapultepec. They found the statues very lifelike as much in the features as in the ornamentation. The king then said: "Tlacaelel, I am well pleased with those images." The illustration of this passage in Durán's work (pl. 43) shows how the painter represented the text in pictures. The king is seated on his throne and his likeness is being copied on the rock, the living rock at Chapultepec. What else is there? Four men at work. Again it is not one artist but a group of people working. I think that the artist of this illustration quite spontaneously drew four men because he considered this to be typical of the procedure that occurred.

It is, of course, a marked contrast with what occurs in our culture. Our concepts of art and of the artist are totally different. To us, art is in a certain way both comprehensible and definable. We easily distinguish, or at least think we easily distinguish, manifestations of art from other cultural manifestations. In our fury to classify everything, we place art in its own pigeonhole. To us, the name of an artist is a necessary thing. We can think of Michelangelo, Rembrandt, or Picasso—it makes no difference who—as a genius who creates a style or founds a school which is later imitated by others. Our notion of individual genius is a fairly recent one. It seems to begin only with the Renaissance in Italy; then it spreads to other European countries. I do not discuss the validity of this point of view or the fascinating problem of whether the genius personally originates something new that the society later adopts or whether he is simply the reflection of his society and produces only those things that are already in existence in that society. I simply mention the problem to show the deep contrast between our concept of the artist and the Mesoamerican concept as we might imagine it from the little discussed so far. I actually think that owing to the anonymous production of his art a Mesoamerican probably would not have understood what we are talking about when we speak of art and beauty. He would say: What is this about art and beauty? What are they? The words themselves hardly exist in Nahuatl because, as I point out later, beauty is not a concept in itself. The classification of the aesthetic qualities seems to be an entirely foreign idea, one that was not part of their process of thought.

I quite agree that our knowledge is very scanty. We can see, however, that in no sense are we entitled to speak of a school of

Mesoamerican art, meaning a personal school of art and referring to groups of objects as made by one man or by one man and his immediate pupils or followers, as with European art. This does not mean that style is not discernible. On the contrary, style is very strongly and definitely marked. Mesoamerican style, in truth, can hardly be confused with that of any other region. Even considering the area as a whole and without considering obvious differences in themselves or in the various cultures that form the total area, the mass of those productions is easily distinguishable from any other object produced elsewhere. This proves to us how distinct and how specific the style is.

Here again we should deal with different levels of style. The first is the general Mesoamerican style, which is the basis of all the styles of Mesoamerica. It naturally underwent changes owing to passage of time and to difference in region. In spite of the variations, the total production remains fundamentally and basically similar in essence and can never be confused with any other style.

On a second level are the regional styles, which differ from, yet are also related to, one another. These differences and similarities pose another set of problems. To give an example, it is clear that the architectural style of Teotihuacan in many ways resembles that of Monte Albán: we can say that Teotihuacan influenced the valleys of Oaxaca and therefore its style to a certain degree. It might be a good explanation for the resemblances. How can we explain the differences? Only by going into far deeper problems, that is, into the different or at least nonidentical heritages of both sites. Monte Albán retains more of the old Olmec tradition and later in time mingles it with the Teotihuacan ideas. Still, this explanation does not seem to suffice, because none of the differences between the two cities can be ascribed to any previous styles existing in either one or the other or even in the neighborhood of either one or the other. There must have been something else and something more in answer to the question, but I venture only to present the problem.

On a third level of style is what we might call a regional school, that is, limited differences within an area. An example would be the colossal Olmec heads of which we know three groups: one from La Venta, one from Tres Zapotes and one from San Lorenzo (pl. 44). Obviously the total exhibits similarities: the head is always cut in a great stone according to a similar technique, probably depicting the same idea, whatever that idea was. But in each city minor differences arise which are easily distinguished. Within the general style of colossal heads, a subdivision of style is present in each of the three places. This is what I call a regional school within one area. Here again we are concerned with groups and not with individuals.

Finally, there is the group style. I have already mentioned the Tlailotlaques, the people who were supposed to have gone into the Mixtec area to observe and to learn, and then to have returned. Whatever the story was is irrelevant for the moment. The fact is that the Tlailotlaques possessed a special type of object executed in a unique way. Even when they moved from one area to another, they retained their particular technique and style. Still—and I think it is only a normal and logical result since they moved from one place to another—their style changed, if only slightly, and was no longer identical with that of the Mixteca, from which it sprang, with that of the valley of Mexico, or with that of other places of Mesoamerica. Precisely these changes are probably attributable to the traveling of the group within one large given area.

We have studied the question of who was responsible for the art. It is of considerable importance that we examine briefly for whom it was done. Apart from archaeology, we have a little information from the written sources of the later period. Thus, some information is simply archaeological inference, other information is clearly based on historical data, but all offer the same answer.

First let us consider civil architecture, buildings dedicated not to the gods but to man. Irrespective of whether or not these men were priests, the important fact is that the buildings, like the palace at Mitla or the Court of the Butterflies in Teotihuacan (pl. 45), were not places of worship. In both examples we are dealing with what are obviously the dwellings of men or at least structures to be used by men, rather than places dedicated to the worship of gods.

Another type of nonreligious art is what might be called the imperial personal style. Each section of the great stone of Tizoc (pl. 46) shows how that Aztec emperor conquered different localities. It has sometimes been considered to be a sort of Trajan column of the Aztec empire. Even though the stone shows the emperor arrayed as a god, it is not a religious monument. It is, in fact, a historical document erected for the vanity of a conqueror to perpetuate his triumphs in stone.

Another similar but more uncertain example would be some stelae at Piedras Negras (pl. 47). Tatiana Proskouriakoff thinks, and I believe quite correctly, that individuals, even though we do not know their names, are represented here. The stelae depict human rulers of the area together with the dates of their reigns. The purpose is somewhat similar to that of the Tizoc stone, that is, to perpetuate the memory of the ruler of the group, although here his victories may not be related.

It has been said that the Olmec heads (pl. 44) may be portraits of dead chiefs or of people who won ball games. The important point is that we are dealing not with gods but probably with a civil situation in which a certain category of man is represented. In a painting at Bonampak (pl. 48), an entirely warlike affair is illustrated depicting the victory over an unknown foe. Again, a military and rather imperialistic subject is represented.

I have chosen these examples of nonreligious art on purpose to prove it existed but certainly not to make it appear that they were the basic aspect of Mesoamerican art. Some objects, of which I have shown a few, were done for the high level of kings, lords, or chiefs, in other words, for actual living people and for civil, imperial, or simply vain purposes. But this is not the basic motive or the basic purpose of Mesoamerican art. The actual purpose is a religious and not a civil or political one: the only aspect that explains Mesoamerican art is its final function. Art is made for the gods. Without going into all the implications of this fact, I want simply to emphasize the sacredness of their art and that this sacredness is its essential characteristic. When we look at the position and structure of their artworks—for instance, the tombs that permit us to study the importance of the dead and of the offerings —we might have the mistaken impression that it is a civil and not a religious art. In my opinion, however, since the dead have to a considerable extent been divinized, it certainly was a religious motive that forced people to build those hundreds and probably thousands of tombs. Similarly, the act of placing the stelae or great monuments in important positions—usually in the center of plazas or on the line, always marking or helping in the planning of a site— is part of the same religious idea. Many more examples could be given of this dependence on religion even where it is least expected. Thus, we may conclude by saying that irrespective of the amount of art produced for man—usually only for chieftains, or persons highly placed in society—the function of Mesoamerican art was a religious one.

The extraordinary image of the Mother Earth (pl. 49), which has frequently been thought of, especially in recent years, as the highlight of Aztec art and perhaps as the most extraordinary sculpture ever produced in pre-Columbian Mexico, is, to us, a work of art. I do not think that it was carved for the Aztecs to admire for its beauty must have been entirely secondary. The essential point was that here stood the terrible goddess of earth, the terrible mother with all the implications of it: the serpent that is the origin of most things, and the monstrous earth that she has under her feet. This masterpiece is better explained by the various ideas that it conveys about this world and the other world, than by any discourse concerning its beauty. Ultimately, the high quality of the statue is found precisely in its sacredness and not in its aesthetic excellence.

As Redfield (1959, *passim*) mentioned so brilliantly, I think that the form or the aesthetic quality is actually only a sort of window or frame through which we see, or, rather, not we but the ancient Mesoamerican mystically saw, the spiritual values of the image. Form was secondary as a frame is secondary to a picture or a window to the panorama beyond it.

I have strived only to present, as well as I was able, a few problems that I think are relevant to the understanding of what the Mesoamerican people thought of their own art and of their own artists, and that is that they did not think highly of their own artists. The anonymity, the fact the artists are never mentioned individually anywhere (and remember I am not speaking about literature because that would be an exception), and the apparent confusion of the individual artist with the group prove to us that the artist must have been an unimportant person in his society, no matter how excellent or great a genius he may actually have been. The position of the pre-Columbian artist may be compared to that of the architect of the famous Gothic cathedrals. The great genius who planned and, to a certain extent, directed their construction, was not important in his society. This is in strong contrast with what has happened since the Renaissance. I think that a similar situation prevailed in Mesoamerican society. The obvious appreciation of the work done was not generated by the man who accomplished it and not even, at least consciously, by the beauty of the object, which was simply an added attraction. Important to appreciation was its religious function. It was an art of the sacred, done in honor of the gods.

6. The Concept of Norm in the Art of Some Oceanian Societies

JEAN GUIART

HE STUDY of primitive art ("primitive" being used as a convenient term for lack of a better one, employing the presence of rhythm and power of expression in nonclassical forms) for a long time has been despised by anthropologists and restricted to a growing area of the progressive intelligentsia. For the purpose of this study it is well to try to reconcile the aesthetically minded approach of the nonspecialist and the bewilderment of the social anthropologist when, astonished, he wonders what all these Philistines are doing?

I think the principal factor causing the difference in attitudes has been a too strict use of the functionalist doctrine. It took some years after the strong impact of Bronislaw Malinowski's thesis on anthropology before someone had the courage to point out that no society could be considered an integrated whole and that the nature of function in social structure badly needed reappraisement. Theories have tried to explain what primitive art was: magic, religion, never simply art. It was believed that primitive man with his alleged prelogical mind could not have the same aesthetic senses as modern man. It was thought that he could only be different and that the definition had to suit this pervasive belief.

These attitudes have changed. Thoughts too, I would hope. So many of our world-renowned artists have taken their inspiration from Negro art or from specific styles—for instance, the influence of New Ireland art on French cubism—that the time has come for some plain talk on the subject.

The primitive artist is restricted in his choice by the availability of material and by the techniques he has in hand: types of wood, their resistance or resilience to tools. Hardwood warrants a careful use of fire with the stone adz: the dimensions of the chips depend as much on the wood as on the quality of the stone blade. If the blade is brittle, it can remain reasonably sharp only if the artist keeps to soft wood. Other tools such as pigs' tusks, dogs' teeth, or broken flakes of stone or shell can be used only at the finishing stage. The possibilities of stone art are still less varied. Volcanic tuff is easy to work yet fragile and has been used only for works of small dimensions. Coral stone, difficult to hew, does not allow for any but rough figures. Accordingly, the best pieces are often small and done in hard stone such as serpentine or jade, which allows for the maximum effect given the inbuilt limitations of tools and materials.

In the same way, restrictions stem from the orientation of the local market. Pieces of art are born under a form of compulsion for a purpose. The artist, as in our society, is trying to answer a need, the aspects of which can vary. The Chambri Lake female potter will go in a canoe to the Middle Sepik to exchange her wares for sago. She needs the food, having little garden area in her island village in the middle of the lake and the swamps. Whoever buys from her might be attracted by a new design, or by a more subtle rendering of the usual figures, which can mean for the new owner of a piece an acquisition of some prestige. If the potter has been working for her husband's group, making a pottery finial, for instance, there is lasting prestige attached to the better piece, the mediocre one being of indifferent value. As an example, plate 50 illustrates one of the better pottery sculptures available from the Lake Chambri district. It comes from an old German collection and had remained in private hands in Australia before I had the good fortune to buy it for the French state. Up to the present, I do not know of any such piece either in German museums or in the Basel Museum. It represents a couple, the woman sitting at the top massaging the forehead of her husband.

The Huon Gulf sculptor who repeats the design of a kneeling man as the body of a betel-nut crusher is making one of a hundred pieces which will be exchanged in the area or kept by him. The design is very stereotyped, with less flexibility than in the first example. The demand is constant: these things break, get burned, or are buried with their owner. The maker will repeat the traditional shape, except, maybe, for his own use or for a higher price. Yet in an area of little variation, the best collection available, Ludwig von Biro's in the Budapest Museum of Ethnology, shows quite a wide variation of craftsmanship at an early date.

In the Admiralties, the carver is held not only by the accepted canon, but by the fact that his group, or district, has specialized over the centuries in a specific type of object. He can only make one type of object and must obtain the others by exchange from other similarly specialized groups or by impinging upon other peoples' rights of ownership, conduct that could present some danger. To escape this situation he would have to produce an entirely new shape for an object of no known use, which is much to ask of a man, even an artist.

This brings us to the subject of this paper. What is norm? On the basis of what has already been said we might offer this judgment and say that norm is inseparable from freedom, being its antithesis. What artist is really free, except to make certain choices? The amount of flexibility offered to him is restricted by decisions concerning his techniques and media of expression. Some choices are made by the environment, for instance, color. The availability of colored pigments is of supreme importance, although pigments can be supplemented by experimental research. Chalk is nonexistent in the Pacific. The discovery of lime has been a big advance, very probably achieved under the impetus of aesthetic factors; lime is evidently essential in betel-chewing, but nonbetel areas have acquired the same use of lime, through the burning of shell, for other purposes. The use of vegetable coloring is equally the result of research. In the case of red or yellow, one should add that the vegetable species needed are conscientiously planted and tended and that recourse to them implies complex techniques, such as the use of heat to expedite tincturing and of reserve coloring processes.

A progressive technique, very modern in many aspects, is the one that allows the building of fragile vegetable structures using weightless vines and pieces of light wood, sticking them together with vegetable pastes—some of which are far from simple mixtures —and obtaining structures, some quite high, which a man can don as a headdress or as a fully masked gown. We have been able to find only a limited number of these pieces, partly because of their impermanent nature, partly because they had to be destroyed after a public appearance, so that women or children would not be able to discover the secret of their construction. In a number of cases one must search in very old German journals to find testimony on such pieces. These techniques could be incredibly subtle. For instance, banana leaves, the shiny surfaces of which allowed little aid in composition, were left to partly rot until the skeleton of the leaf appeared on which pastes could take a normal hold. In the New Hebrides, the south Malekulas' protection of a certain species of spiders is typical of this attitude; the spider's web was strong and could be used as a base on which to attach small human faces made of local vegetable paste: sap mixed with sawdust and the flesh of certain fruits. We could say that our most unusual modern artistic research can always be referred to a more elaborate, so-called primitive counterpart. In both cases the fruits of a successful research, once socially accepted, can become a norm.

We now come to a more central, and more difficult, concept. What is norm in terms of shape, design, form, in two dimensions or in the round? One possible approach is circumstantial. I resort to it as a first step. Let us take two widely differing cases: Polynesia and the Sepik.

The art forms of Polynesia, widely known since the first voyages of discovery, deal mostly with what is known as the *tiki*. These round-eyed, or at least globulous-eyed, squat, human forms are very similar to one another in a given area, and they inspired only one modern artist, Gauguin; since then they have been largely forgotten, except for Easter Island figures which have benefited from the permanent romantic appeal of the island that has called itself the navel of the earth. In fact, we seem to have remained attracted only to a certain tormented aspect of such objects which is manifest in the case of some Hawaiian and Easter Island pieces.

When one looks at the Easter Island *moai Kava Kava*, it becomes evident that such pieces represent, not a corpse, but a man in a state of great hardship such as we saw coming out of concentration camps at the end of World War II. A factor, which has often been unclear in the minds of many people, is that these so-called tropical island paradises are given to long periods of drought, even in the South Pacific or in volcanic islands; during these periods the yams die out, the leaves of the coconut fold down along the trunk, and the banana stems break and fall to the ground. In these cases people would have to subsist, for very long periods, on small amounts of food. A piece from southwest New Guinea (pl. 51) represents people in such difficult circumstances. One should not forget that the weight of biological factors on life tends to prey on the mind of the primitive artist.

In our never ceasing quest for aesthetic expression, we are searching for something that has a soul. The inexpressive Marquesan pieces, stamped with tattooed designs, have few lovers today. The simplicity of form attained has changed here from norm to stereotype and has been hideously multiplied with the use of iron tools for the benefit of European passersby. Further south, in the Australs and in the Cook Islands, Reverend F. E. Williams had to save the last ancient pieces by tying them along the rigging of his ship as a proof that Jehovah had won the battle against the local gods to prevent the over-zealous Polynesian teachers from burning the whole lot of them. This is the origin of the wonderful early collection of the London Missionary Society, now in the British Museum. In New Zealand, the carver's art is taught in schools today; in the process the traditional figures, although similar in appearance, have lost the little power of expression they had and certainly also the bulging sexes, which at the very start of contact were considered objectionable. Only pieces dating to the beginning of the last century show any inventiveness and feeling, such as the piece of whalebone carved as a fork to give food to priests under taboo (pl. 52).

On the contrary, to Sepik art is certainly attributed, if only statistically, a greater amount of variability. Even today, with interested parties flying into Anggoram every week and with every crocodile-skin buyer having become a dealer in primitive art, the variations of individual creativity remain great, unless an idea sweeps over the area about what should be done for sale to the white man.

Specialists of the Sepik area have tried over the years to map the styles along the Sepik. I believed in the validity of such an attempt until I went there myself on a kind of pilgrimage and found out that geographical convenience and the logic of available transport hide behind part of our classifications. We have dealt with the styles along the banks of the river and its tributaries. The difficulty of traveling where a large canoe and outboard motor cannot be handled has allowed us to forget about the other, so-called marginal areas. In the same way the only good map of the Sepik valley remains the one drawn by the first German exploration units. Today, with the multiplication of small airfields, we have come into close contact with many new places and people and have learned more of their creativeness, at the very moment that we are introducing among them the means of losing it. An intensive and detailed survey being carried out by the Basel Museum should allow, at last, a systematic picture to be drawn. For the present, on the basis of our scant knowledge, we can raise the problem of what can be called a style in the Sepik wonderworld. I would like to give some thought to this problem. First of all, we should quickly scan the area to obtain a glimpse of some possible traits distinguishing certain styles.

We start with the highlands, with a shield from the G'Hom area, quite high in the headwaters of the Sepik (pl. 53). In my view it should be compared with another piece, coming from the Asmat area (pl. 54); there are some striking similarities in the way the human face appears. The Asmat shield illustrated, which is one of the best I know, shows the design of birds, but between each bird design is a human face, which is sometimes shown in reverse, and which is indicated only by a very few elements. A pottery sculpture from the Washkuk area (pl. 55), found quite far behind the Washkuk hills, is a rather rare piece, which was unfortunately broken. It is very striking in its technique. The impressive aspect of pieces of the Washkuk area resides in the fact that they are not shown in a well-lighted area on the open floor of the men's hut, but are displayed in low structures the walls of which extend to the ground so that the carvings receive no other light than the flicker of the flames inside the huts. The elements of the carvings are organized so as to catch any available light, thus projecting a long shade that is accounted for in the carver's vision and in his choice of strong, simple, protuberant shapes, the sum of which is a human body, in fact broken down into its constituent traits.

In the classic Middle Sepik double hook (pl. 56), the representation of the eye is very characteristic as a kind of under cup with eyes bulging in the middle. In fact this representation of the eyes is the only stable element in a relatively small area. Outside the Iatmül area, one finds other types of eyes yet a similar treatment of the rest of the body.

Executed in the classical treatment of the Lower Sepik area is a first-rate betel-nut crusher (pl. 57); the betel nut is crushed in the cup at the top; two human representations support it and there is an intricate design on the side with other, very small representations of the human figure. One can notice how the eyes are linked with the beaked nose; although wickerwork masks are found still much further inland, the comparison of this type of representation of the eye and the nose with the wickerwork masks shows how similar they are in structure.

Going back to the area known as Middle Sepik, we can try to see in greater detail what elements could allow us to determine the limits of a stylistic area. From the valley of the Korewori River, which is a tributary of the Sepik, the piece shown in plate 58 is a quite small and very old hunting charm that could be carried. The comparison between this carving and a more recent one (pl. 59) is interesting in that the recent one was probably made with a steel blade, which means that the intervals between the different elements could be made much closer resulting in a more complex treatment of the human body. Also apparent are the significant changes in the treatment of the nose and of the eye.

Plate 60 shows a double hook which was acquired recently in Aibom in the Chambri Lake region and which is interesting because the carving is very similar to the work of the Korewori area, although both regions are a wide distance apart from each other. I have seen one bearing similar traits in a private collection in Los Angeles. A much taller sculpture, also from the Korewori area, is very beautiful in its way but quite different from the classical *kamanggabi*. The treatment of the face comes closer to that of the

Maprik area. When one realizes that the road from Maprik meets the Sepik River very close to the mouth of the Korewori River, one can understand how these objects could travel.

Following another tributary of the Sepik, a piece from the Yuat area (the Yuat is the region where the celebrated Mundugumor have been living) is illustrated in pl. 61. It is a wooden top for a lime spatula, completely covered with ocher and colored sand, which gives it a very fine, old patina. Another piece, also a lime spatula from the same area, is of interest in that it is nonclassical (pl. 62). Distinctive of the Yuat area is the projection of the human head in front of and hanging over the rest of the body; but in plate 62 the body has disappeared, leaving only the human head, with the arms hanging down and resting on the knees. Another piece of the same origin shows a human thighbone on which has been fixed the pottery representation of a human being. It is very much in the normal style of the Mundugumor. The eyes are slanting and have almost disappeared from the sculpture. Not only traits but also materials can travel. Mother-of-pearl is obtained from the Wewak through the Maprik areas to the Yuat River. It is used on carvings to indicate the eyes and as a personal ornament set on the upper lip which is folded toward the top with the aid of hook-shaped bits on either side to help the man who is wearing it hold it between the tip of the upper lip and the nose; the ornament is thus held practically horizontally.

Two so-called canoe shields, acquired recently, are quite nice pieces (pl. 63–64). If we use the normal criteria of the shape of the eyes and eye sockets, we would say that one is from the Lower Sepik, and the other from Iatmül. In fact, the second was bought in a village close to the mouth of the Korewori River much before one gets to the Iatmül area, and the first was similarly acquired further up the river. Either these pieces have traveled, or the types of treatment of the eyes and eye sockets have been used much more widely than we thought.

Now we turn to artifacts that pose problems: old pieces from German settler collections at the time when the Sepik River was called the Kaiserin Augusta Fluss. The pieces are not documented, but from their general shape one can infer that they come from the Sepik area; they show such inventiveness and gracefulness that one wonders how to classify them. What I have said about the Middle Sepik region has shown that it is difficult to define a stylistic area except in very broad terms, or except in speaking of certain types of objects such as the *kamanggabi* of the Korewori or of certain traits such as the projecting head that distinguishes the Yuat pieces. As we move along the Sepik it becomes increasingly difficult to give precise definitions.

In plate 65 a lime spatula with a wooden top is represented, still evidently from the Sepik but with a body treatment different from the one usually illustrated. In each case a human face is rendered which is at the same time the face of a bird. The superimposed layers of paint have been so numerous (i.e., a new layer for each ceremonial use) that the feel of the wood has been replaced by a semimodeled finish.

Another Sepik piece, certainly one of the more interesting ones aesthetically speaking, is a squatting human being with no head but with arms finished with human heads in profile (pl. 66). The idea of the bird form is suggested only by a beak stuck between the two arms. It is a striking type of expression and cannot be ascribed to any given village within this area.

A carving, which is probably Yuat or at least from the lower reaches of the Yuat River, is shown in plate 67. It could have been illustrated as an Easter Island or as a western New Guinea piece. It is a representation of a man which comes close to a walking skeleton.

One of the more curious types of expression is the representation of a man covered with small beings that bite him in the fleshy parts and crawl all over him (pl. 68). This, too, cannot be ascribed to any given place, except that in a certain way, the techniques of the carving of the head remind one of the pottery finial of Chambri Lake illustrated in plate 50.

The few carvings discussed here, big and small, painted or

blackened, allow us to draw the conclusion that one must be very careful in asserting what a stylistic area is. If one bears in mind that when the Australian administration took over from the Germans in New Guinea, it found itself confronted with a great number of local conflicts brought about by the historical drive of inland groups that had pushed toward the Sepik or the lower reaches of its tributaries, one wonders what could have been the Middle Sepik stylistic picture before the advent of the white man. We certainly know from Margaret Mead that the Mundugumor had barely moved into the area. I would venture to say that the plastic richness of the Sepik area is the result of the role played by this vital valley as a melting pot. Convenience and lack of exhaustive documentation lead us to think that we can safely draw lines on maps. If we had the information needed, we would very probably speak in terms of art schools, establish chronologies, and analyze the influence of given artists. Some of us have already tried. It is my contention that primitive artists reacted in the same way as our own inspired ones, once account is taken of the circumstances, of the physical and material determinants, and of the subtler aspects of their place in the functioning of the local group and the society at large.

One might say, however, that this is an impressionistic view of the problem which only provides some directions and a few illustrations. I would like to insist that this is not so. Aesthetic studies show how much our spoken or written language lacks in depth concerning the analysis of artworks. And surely, if an artist could be satisfied by expressing himself in words, he might not wish to go further.

As in any other science, our first problem in primitive art is certainly that of classification. You will have noticed how much a single theme pervades a wide area: the human head (or figure) surmounted by a bird, sometimes by a crocodile. Each element may be only indicated, but it is there. This is norm versus creativity: the themes are few—man and bird, man and crocodile, man alone—but none of the better and older pieces are alike. Man-shape has thus been translated in widely differing terms.

The second problem is documentation. The Sepik is one of the highlights of art compared with any in man's centuries of history. Thousands of pieces that are in collectors' hands or in museum vaults have never been made public. I have tried to show some unknown shapes, some new faces. Let us imagine that we had a way of superimposing all known pieces in their comparable traits. We could then have a physically defined measure of the stylistic differences. Unhappily we are unable to do this. Our next best attempt is to develop a standardized language allowing recourse to computers so as to arrive at classification that would not be based solely on impressionistic description. Something of the divinity of man appears in the difficulty to organize an objective vocabulary that can take into account simultaneously man's natural form and its possible artistic translation. We are presently caught between our desire to attain a better defined knowledge and our impulse to admire quietly the works of art of others than of our own forebears. These works have already had an impact on modern European art, and since they are part of man's general heritage, this impact can only become greater.

We have visually established the fact that the definition of art styles becomes somewhat blurred when we have recourse to the older pieces or rather to the more classic ones collected over the last forty years. This could mean that when society had not yet been upset through contact, individual creativity was at its greatest. Is this a fact? The trend toward Christianity in the Middle Sepik is subsequent to World War II. When Margaret Mead, Felix Speiser, or Alfred Bühler was first in the Sepik area, the Australian administration's hold was less pronounced than had been the preceding German control. Even today, when economic development admittedly goes no further than the crocodile-skin trade, one can obtain, amid mediocre work, aesthetically quite good although recent pieces. People still will not sell some older pieces because they remain equated with the cohesion of the group or with the memory of the sculptors.

Finally, I would like to insist on a little-known aspect of such situations which is evident in many parts of Melanesia and more so in the New Hebrides, and which can give us a clue to the Sepik area situation. I am referring to the copyright system that allows an individual or a group to buy not a given piece but the right to reproduce it, in part or *in toto*. This means that stylistic elements can travel far and wide, given a minimum of peaceful, ceremonial, or trade relationships. In the same way a lineage can cling to its particular version of a widely dispersed myth when it is linked with land tenure; a group or an individual can insist that the result of the compromise between norm and creativity, in his (or their) case, asks for adequate retribution in riches or pigs before it can be used elsewhere as an inspiration or a model. In such a case, one will insist on minimal details to establish one's originality and one's claim to a higher price than one has had to give at the start. Such a system allows us to analyze an art piece into its component elements, reinterpret each, and use it to build another form. Stereotype only then becomes established if a certain form is taken over by society and integrated into a specific ritual or a trade distribution, allowing then only the variability among good, bad, or indifferent craftsmanship, or among minute details that can be understood as a kind of signature.

Here again we run into the problem of spreading our anaylsis along a certain time span. In the New Hebrides Archipelago, it is evident that certain traits have thus caught on from place to place or from island to island, through direct or circuitous routes, and that one can therefore follow them, thanks in part to John Layard and A. B. Deacon, over more than half a century. All our knowledge about the area indicates that ever since the beginning we have been dealing with fluctuating social structures, which have experienced a great deal of change both before and after our intrusion into their field of vision. The study of art forms is one of the rare means we have of trying to comprehend their universe. When these art forms occur in sufficient numbers, we can pursue our study further. But what of the numerous areas where few forms have evolved, and why? These are the questions we should next try to solve. I am still at a loss, in the Pacific, to find valid explanations. I must pause at this stage.

7. Creativity and Style in African Art[1]

WILLIAM BASCOM

HE RECOGNITION of well-defined ethnic or "tribal" styles was a major contribution to the study of African art and of the art of other nonliterate societies as well. It provides, first of all, a useful classification of the varied forms of African art. Secondly, it is a key to the understanding of African aesthetics. For any of us, or for any other outsiders, to make aesthetic judgments about African art may reveal our own aesthetic standards, but it tells us very little, if anything, about what the Africans themselves find aesthetically satisfying. Through the analysis of tribal styles, however, we can at least begin to understand the standards of worth and beauty which African artists attempt to achieve, and by which their works are judged by others in their own society.

The concept of tribal styles also has important implications for the understanding of creativity. The stylistic features that so

[1] This paper was presented as an address at the First International Congress of African Culture in Salisbury, Southern Rhodesia, in September, 1962. Because the publication of the proceedings of this congress has been delayed for various reasons and in view of the local political situation which now seems highly problematical, it has been submitted and accepted for publication in the present volume.

clearly distinguish the arts of the Bini, the Yoruba, and the Fon, for example, can be attributed only to the creativity of artists in the past. The only possible source of divergence and specialization of art styles which have derived from a common origin lies in innovations by individual artists. Even when changes in technology or in habitat and natural resources have given rise to stylistic changes, they inevitably involve the innovations of individuals. And even when changes are the result of external influences, as in the case of diffusion or acculturation, they involve innovation and often modification by individuals within the society, and they derive from the creative efforts of other individuals outside the society.

Nevertheless, creativity and change in art are exceedingly difficult to analyze in all nonliterate societies both because we lack historical records and because, of necessity, studies are so often confined to a limited period of time or even to a single time plane. We need much greater historical depth, which archaeology may be able to supply in some cases, to determine whether in specific instances these styles have been the result of (1) gradual and almost imperceptible changes that can be ascribed to minor modifications by a series of individuals, or (2) sudden, radical, major innovations that are ascribable to the inspiration and creativity of a single artist, or (3) a combination of both.

What little we know about the persistence of tribal styles through time, and particularly what we know of their consistency, in terms of individual variation within a society at any given period of time, suggest that radical innovations are the exception. This does not, of course, rule out the possibility of revolutionary change from the accepted stylistic standards of any society, although it may take time for radical changes to become accepted and established. But with the rapid disappearance of traditional art in many nonliterate societies, we may have to rely upon the archaeologists to supply answers to these questions.

What these tribal styles do tell us is that, although they have developed through the creative efforts of numerous individual artists in the past, they impose certain limitations on the creative expression of the individual artists who are producing at any given period of time. Artists work within these recognizable limits, creating pieces that their customers or teachers find acceptable and they themselves find aesthetically satisfying. These limitations derive from the accepted standards of a given style, and, in trying to produce something appropriate, correct, or beautiful, an artist is trying to achieve these standards in his own work. Whether he knows it or not, and even when he may be consciously striving for originality, he is, in fact, trying to conform to the stylistic and aesthetic standards that he accepts. There are obvious implications here for the periods and "schools" of art in Western societies, even though these may change more rapidly than did tribal styles in nonliterate societies before European contact.

That most African artists work within these limitations is demonstrated by the fact that most African art is identifiable in terms of these styles. That they do not slavishly copy the works of their predecessors, without originality or creativity, is demonstrated by the fact that these many styles—so readily distinguishable—have been developed.

When the artists of Europe first "discovered" African art in the anthropological collections of European museums, they saw in it a freedom from the narrow tradition of naturalism or realism against which they themselves were rebelling. By psychological projection they and the art critics of the period attributed to African artists a degree of creativity and freedom from conventional rules and stylistic limitations which they themselves had been attempting to achieve.[2]

---

[2] This statement obviously suffers from the distortion of oversimplification for the sake of brevity. A detailed analysis of what happened would be inappropriate here, but it should be noted that for about forty years European artists had been moving beyond the stereotyped standards of naturalism of the Academy of France, that some wished to formulate new standards of naturalism while others rejected naturalism for other modes of expression, and that they also saw in African sculpture constructive ideas for the development of their own art.

Today, with larger collections to compare and a more complete knowledge of African arts, it is evident that, while the conventions differed, African artists were creating within stylistic limitations that were comparable in scope to those of Europe. There are marked differences among the many local styles in Africa, but within each of these distinct styles there is usually considerable uniformity and obviously far less creative freedom than was originally believed.

Once this fact was recognized, however, there was a tendency to shift to the opposite extreme and to regard African artists as rigidly repeating and monotonously copying the tribal styles, without any creative expression, and to attribute the development of these local styles to the revolutionary innovations and creative abilities of unknown great artists in the past. There was no evidence for this equally erroneous view, but it was indirectly supported by a familiarity with tourist art, which emerged with the decline of traditional religious and secular art.

Tourist art, or "airport art" as it has more recently been called, has no meaning or function within traditional African cultures. It is produced for non-Africans to take home as souvenirs or curios. In some cases it represents an adaptation by traditional artists to new markets, as with the Bambara carvers of Mali. In others it represents an innovation by a new set of individuals, untrained in the traditional skills, as with the Yoruba thorn-carvers of Nigeria. It may even involve a craft that has been introduced by European entrepreneurs in a society where it had not previously been practiced, as with the Kamba wood-carvers of Kenya, whose products are exported in quantity to America.

Tourist art is of considerable interest for the study of culture change and innovations in African art, particularly where there has been continuity in styles and forms, like masks, rather than, as so often has been the case, the introduction of new styles and new forms, like bookends or letter openers. In some cases tourist art has aesthetic merit, but often it is both technically and aesthetically inferior. It has been increasingly mass produced, in advance, for sale through traders at hotels and airports, and for export abroad, whereas most traditional African art was individually commissioned by known customers. Furthermore, tourist art usually has an emphasis on realism which is out of keeping with traditional African art. If European artists denied their heritage of naturalism at the turn of the century, inspired in part by traditional African sculpture, African artists of this century have denied their own heritage in adopting naturalism, as the result of European contact.

Despite the importance of the recognition of tribal styles in African art, this concept is now in need of considerable refinement, and perhaps of a basic reevaluation for reasons I discuss under the following headings: Style Periods, Local Substyles, Multiple Subtribal Styles, Individual Styles, Regional Styles, Blurred Tribal Styles, Archaisms, Craft Styles. These eight categories, with Tribal Styles as the ninth, can assist us in approaching the problem of creativity. Many of the points have previously been recognized individually, but a reevaluation of the concept of tribal style must involve all of them, as well as other factors to be mentioned later.

1. *Style periods.*—There is every reason to expect periods of art style in nonliterate societies of the kind that are known in Western art and which have been discovered in prehistoric times through archaeology. We must assume that if the time depth were greater, and if the gap between archaeological and ethnological studies of art could be closed, we would have to recognize a series of styles for any given society, rather than a single style. Several style periods have been recognized in the bronze-castings from Benin. There is also a marked contrast between the early (*ca.* fourteenth Century) Ife bronzes (pl. 70) and those of the nineteenth century (pl. 69).

2. *Local substyles.*—While major art styles may be related to single ethnic groups, there may be a series of recognizable local substyles within them. Minor variations in details may enable an expert to identify the subgroup or locality from which individual carvings come, as for example among the Yoruba for whom Ketu, Egba, Oyo, Ijebu, Ekiti, and other substyles in wood carving can

be distinguished. What has been accepted as a tribal style may with greater knowledge break down into a number of local substyles, although the differences among them may be relatively minor. In terms of creativity, an artist works within the substyle of his particular period and locality.

3. *Multiple subtribal styles.*—In contrast, several divergent and clearly differentiated art styles may be found within a single ethnic group whose members share the same physical type, language and basic culture. A striking example of this in Africa is to be seen in Ibo wood carving, where the styles of Udi, Bende, Achi, and Afikpo, to name only four, are as distinct from one another as any one is from those of the Bini or the Yoruba. They are so different, in fact, that it is almost meaningless to speak of an Ibo style in wood carving, and almost impossible to abstract any stylistic features common even to a single form, such as a mask. A thorough knowledge of one style of Ibo masks is of little help in recognizing masks from other Ibo subgroups; they can be identified only through a familiarity with the various Ibo styles. This situation is quite different from that of the Yoruba, although both groups are roughly equal in size, each numbering well over five million. Multiple styles within a single ethnic group must have developed in the same manner as tribal styles, through individual creativity and relative isolation from neighboring subgroups.

4. *Individual styles.*—Individual styles can be identified in African art, as Fagg and others have shown. It should not be surprising that the work of individual artists can be recognized, but until recently there has been little interest in African carvers as individuals, perhaps in part because of the belief that African art was already dead, and because of the dominance of the concept of tribal style.[3] On the other hand, Dot-so-la-lee as a basket maker, Tom Burnsides as a silversmith, Nampeyo and Maria Martinez as pot-

---

[3] What may be the earliest published African piece of sculpture whose carver is recorded is a Yoruba mask in the Berlin Museum für Völkerkunde (III C2332), identified as "made by Angbologe, an Egbodo" (probably Egbado) (Frobenius, 1899, p. 24, fig. 97, pl. 9).

ters, and other distinguished American Indian artists had received earlier attention as individuals. We would know far more about creativity in African art today, if more attention had been paid to individual artists in the past.[4]

In 1945 I collected a hundred traditional Ibo masks from a small community near Udi, Nigeria, all of which were attributed by informants to a single carver, Ozooha-Aga. He obviously had not monotonously repeated a few forms handed down from past centuries, without concern for aesthetic problems or creative expression. Large and small, simple and complex, roughly carved or carefully finished, abstract or realistic, these masks represent terrifying spirits, humorous figures, and beautiful women.[5] The number of basic mask types in this collection, and the fundamental differences among them, are so great that if one did not know in advance, one would not be likely to recognize them as having been produced in a single locality, not to mention the possibility that they were done by a single carver. Certainly a wide range of creativity in the past must be postulated to account for this diversity, perhaps wider than in most societies, with the result that there are far broader limits within which creativity can be expressed in the present; but if more were known about the works of individual artists, this case might not seem so unusual. Individual styles, involving more or less individual creativity, must influence and may even dominate local styles and style periods.

5. *Regional styles.*—Some major art styles are not confined to

[4] Individual styles are also subject to change in time. Elsewhere in this volume Thompson discusses the changes in Abatan's work in pottery from her early period of the 1930's to the 1940's and 1950's, and again in the 1960's; and Fagg describes what happened to Bamgboye's work after he began to teach wood carving in a Nigerian school. Until we can trace the changes in the work of individual artists through their lifetimes, we will not really understand individual style and we will not be on firm ground in discussing individual creativity.

[5] Bascom and Gebauer (1953 and 1964, pl. 11–13) illustrate three of these masks. A large number were exhibited in Deering Library, Northwestern University, in 1948, and some have been on display at the Milwaukee Public Museum from 1953 to 1967 and at the Chicago Natural Museum from 1957 to 1966.

any single tribe, but are shared by a series of societies. This is to be seen for example, in the bead-working and painting of the Plains Indians of North America, or the geometric art of the peoples of the upper Ucayali River in Peru.[6] African examples are to be found in the "grasslands style" of the Cameroun, the "Ogowe River style" of Gabon, and the "Poro style" of Liberia, Guinea, and the Ivory Coast. Crowley (unpub. MS) has noted how an art style has been carried across ethnic lines through the spread of a circumcision school among neighboring peoples in the Congo, Angola, and Zambia.[7] These are clearly not tribal styles, but regional styles shared by many tribes. There may be stylistic differences that enable an expert to identify a particular piece as produced by a particular ethnic group, but the differences appear to be on the level of the local variations among tribal substyles, rather than those that differentiate tribal styles or even the multiple subtribal styles of the Ibo.

6. *Blurred tribal styles.*—In some areas tribal and subtribal styles are losing their distinctive features through acculturation, with artists in one society copying the work of artists in other societies. This may have happened in Africa, and at other times in other places, but it is perhaps best illustrated among the Pueblo Indians of the United States where, for example, paintings of deer in Zuni style now appear on Acoma pots by Lucy Lewis. It is becoming increasingly difficult to identify the tribal affiliation of a Pueblo potter from the design elements and other stylistic features of her pottery. Here distinctions among tribal styles seem to be disappearing, and perhaps a supratribal style will appear. For the moment, however, many traditional features of Pueblo styles are preserved, although some are no longer restricted to any given group, and a composite of the various styles is employed within a single pueblo.

7. *Archaisms.*—Style periods may also be bridged, as in the ren-

---

[6] Matteson, 1954, p. 66. Despite an abstract style involving simple geometric designs, the Piro were able to recognize the work of individual artists (personal communication from J. Rowe).

[7] See also Olbrechts, 1946, pp. 26–27.

aissance of Sikyatki style in Hopi pottery, attributed to Nampeyo, a woman who was inspired by the designs she saw on potsherds found at the prehistoric village site of Sikyatki, which was being excavated by the Peabody Museum of Harvard University in 1896. More recently, prehistoric Mimbres designs have been used by Zia potters and by Hopi silversmiths. In Africa Benin bronze-casting was revived under the auspices of the Nigerian Forestry Department.

These archaisms, as they are known in archaeology, are not confined to the period of Western contact, but occurred in prehistoric times in Peru on several occasions, in Neo-Babylonian Mesopotamia and Saite Egypt in the sixth century b.c., during the Hellenistic period in the first century b.c., and during the Ming Dynasty in China in the fifteenth century a.d. (Menzel, 1960; Lathrop, 1956).

A somewhat different case is that of the Cameroun brass-caster who attempted to copy a prehistoric bronze head from Ife, inspired by the design on a Nigerian 6-penny stamp (pl. 70). He succeeded in reproducing the general form in its more obvious characteristics, but he remained faithful to his own grasslands style in his treatment of the eyes, the mouth, and other details.[8] This case is interesting as an example of acculturation, because of its unusual inspiration from a postage stamp and because it was an individual innovation that was observed and recorded as it happened by Gebauer, to whom the artist turned for further illustrations of the Ife heads; but it is on quite a different level from what we have been discussing as style because it never became traditional, never having been repeated. Nevertheless, it is important to the study of creativity as a documented instance of an individual innovation which was never accepted by the artist's society.

8. *Craft styles.*—In some cases there are distinctive styles at the same time within the same society and village, associated with

---

[8] Compare Bascom and Gebauer, 1953 and 1964, pl. 44.

different crafts employing different media and techniques. Despite the local variations, a stylistic unity can be perceived in Yoruba wood carvings (pls. 71–73) but a completely different style is found in their sculpture in forged iron (pl. 74), while a third style characterizes their sculpture in brass-casting (pl. 75). There are still other styles in Yoruba calabash-carving (pl. 76), pottery, basketry and matting, weaving, embroidery, resist dying, leatherwork, and beadwork.[9] These distinct styles are associated with different craft groups as well as with different media and techniques, and craft membership is not overlapping except in the case of brass- and ironworkers. Yoruba carvers may work in ivory, bone, and stone as well as in wood, and stylistic similarities are to be found in work in these different media. But expertise in the style of Yoruba carving is of little help in recognizing other Yoruba crafts employing other media. However many Yoruba carvings one may have studied, he would be unable to identify these other crafts as Yoruba without prior knowledge of them. Again this is only possible through a familiarity with their distinctive styles, and it becomes meaningless to speak of a Yoruba art style.

This point may seem obvious once it has been made, but it deserves emphasis because it has so seldom been stated explicitly and because its general applicability has not been recognized. More than thirty years ago Boas wrote, "We have spoken so far of local styles as though in every case only a single style occurred in a tribal unit. This might seem plausible on account of the comparative uniformity of tribal life. Still there may be instances in which fundamentally different styles may be observed in the same community" (1927, p. 180). As examples he cited the contrasts between the realistic carvings and drawings of Eskimo men and the geometric designs in clothing and sewed leatherwork of Eskimo women, between the representational wood carvings of men and the geometric designs in women's basketry and matting on the Northwest Coast

[9] A Yoruba beaded bag from Igana in the Oyo kingdom is illustrated in *ibid.*, pl. 19.

of North America, between the decorative style on birchbark baskets and the geometrical patterns on coiled baskets in the interior of British Columbia, between the spiral decorations in Maori carving and the geometric style in their matting, and between the styles of painted and plastic decorations on Central American pottery (*ibid.*, pp. 180–182). Other instances can be found in the stylistic differences between Pueblo pottery and basketry, and between brass-castings and wood carvings among the Ashanti of Ghana and the Fon of Dahomey.

Despite these examples, which could be multiplied, Boas concluded that "Such differences in style are, however, not by any means the rule. As has been stated before, we find much more commonly that the most highly developed art is likely to impose its style upon other industries and that mat weaving and basketry have been particularly influential in developing new forms and powerful in imposing them upon other fields" (*ibid.*, p. 182).

Boas refers here to the imitation of interwoven patterns in Kuba pile cloth, wooden goblets, and carvings on buffalo horns. One may add the use of interwoven patterns in Yoruba embroidery, beadwork, and carving; and the similarity of design elements in prehistoric Peruvian pottery and textiles. Whether the techniques of weaving and basketry usually influence other crafts is not the major point at issue here, but it is not established beyond question by these examples. It is clearly reversed in the Chilkat blankets of the Indians of the Northwest Coast, where the style of men's carving is carried over into weaving by women, who copy designs from pattern boards painted for them by men, and into women's appliqué and quill embroidery which Boas says are "probably copied from painted designs." Similarly, Kachina figures appear on Pueblo pots and baskets, and designs from sand paintings have been adapted to Navaho blankets. The representational designs in Plains Indian beadwork probably derive from paintings. In Africa the style of Bini bronze-casting is carried over into some carved ivory masks; and the Cameroun grasslands style of wood carving is found in

Plate 2. Decorative tablet from ceremonial house, painted wood (41 3/8"). New Guinea, eastern Gulf of Papua, Elema. Museum of Primitive Art, New York.

Plate 1. Figure, bone (4 3/8"). Polynesia, Marquesas Islands. Museum of Primitive Art, New York.

PLATE 3. Mask, wood (8 5/8″). Africa, Liberia, Dan. Museum of Primitive Art, New York.

PLATE 4. Funerary figure, wood, brass plates, ivory (?) (16 5/8″). Africa, Gabon, Kota. Museum of Primitive Art, New York.

PLATE 5. Mask, wood, paint, cloth, metal, cartridge cases (12½''). Africa, Liberia, Ngere. Museum of Primitive Art, New York.

PLATE 6. Mask, wood (18 3/8''). Africa, Ivory Coast, Baule, Yaoure subtribe. Museum of Primitive Art, New York.

PLATE 7. Standing male and female figures, wood, glass beads, paint, ivory (*left*, 16 5/8"; *right* 18 1/2"). Africa, Ivory Coast, Baule. Museum of Primitive Art, New York.

PLATE 8. Funerary figure, wood (14"). Africa, Gabon, Fang. Museum of Primitive Art, New York.

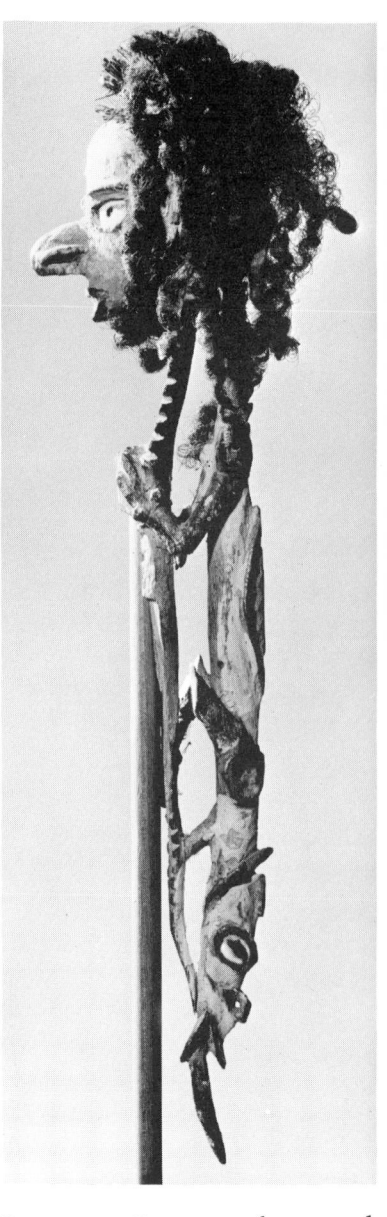

PLATE 9. Fetish figure, wood, cloth, feathers (32 1/2"). Africa, Ivory Coast, Senufo. Museum of Primitive Art, New York. Gift of Mr. and Mrs. Raymond Wielgus.

PLATE 10. Ornament for sacred flute, wood, paint, shells, feather, hair, fiber (9 5/8"). New Guinea, Southern Sepik River Course, Yuat River, Mundugumor. Museum of Primitive Art, New York.

PLATE 11. Double figure, wood, encrustation (24½″). Africa, Mali, Dogon. Museum of Primitive Art, New York.

Plate 12. Mask, wood, paint, feathers, strings (45¼″). United States, Alaska, Eskimo. Museum of Primitive Art, New York.

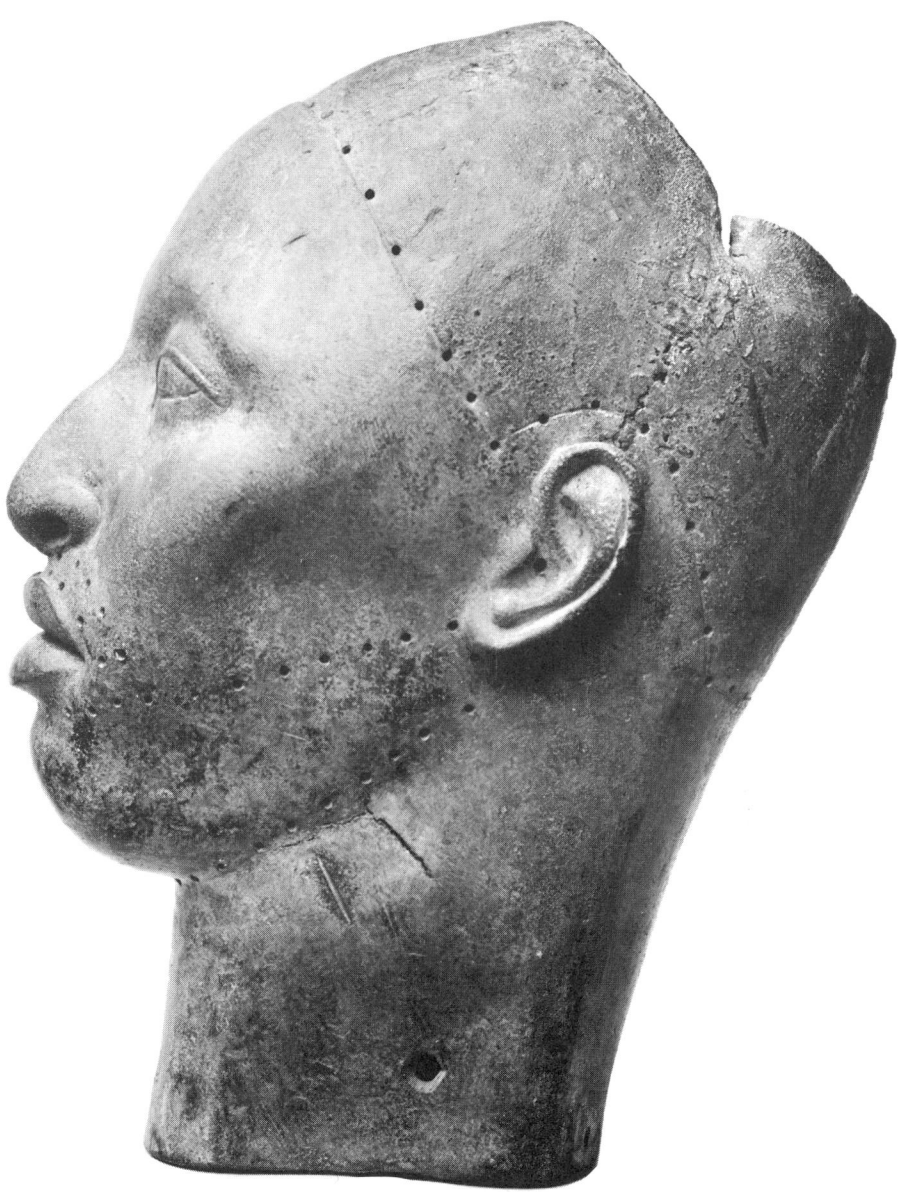

PLATE 13. Bronze head by the Master of the Aquiline Profiles, found at Wunmonije, in 1938. Africa, Nigeria, Ife. Ife Museum, Nigeria.

PLATE 14. Two bronze heads by the same hand from sixteenth-century Benin. Africa, Nigeria, Benin. British Museum, London, and Nigerian Museum, Lagos.

PLATE 15. Dance headdress by Ochai of Otobi village. Africa, Nigeria, Idoma. Nigerian Museum, Lagos.

PLATE 16. Headrest by the Master of the Cascade Coiffures. Africa, Congo/Kinshasa, Baluba, Shankadi subtribe. British Museum, London.

PLATE 17. Gelede mask by the Master of the Uneven Eyes. Africa, Nigeria, Yoruba. Rautenstrauch-Joest Museum, Cologne.

PLATE 18. Wooden group by Adugbologe of Abeokuta. Africa, Nigeria, Yoruba. Müller Collection, Solothurn, Switzerland.

PLATE 19. Epa mask by Bamgboye of Odo-Owa. Africa, Nigeria, Yoruba. British Museum, London.

PLATE 20. Arowogun of Osi with carvings. Africa, Nigeria, Yoruba.

PLATE 22. House post by Agbonbiofe in the palace at Efon-Alaiye. Africa, Nigeria, Yoruba.

PLATE 21. House post by Agunna of Oke Igbira, at Ijero. Africa, Nigeria, Yoruba.

PLATE 23. House post by Olowe in the palace at Ise-Ekiti. Africa, Nigeria, Yoruba.

PLATE 24. Door from the palace at Ikere-Ekiti. Africa, Nigeria, Yoruba. British Museum, London.

PLATE 25. Bowl for divination by Olowe. Africa, Nigeria, Yoruba.
William Moore Collection, Los Angeles.

PLATE 26   PLATE 27

PLATE 28   PLATE 29

PLATE 26. Hardwood cylinder (80cm) decorated by Bapmes. Southwest New Guinea, Asmat Papuans, As River, village Amanamkai. Rijksmuseum voor Volkenkunde, Leiden.

PLATE 27. Hardwood cylinder (80 cm) decorated by Bishur. Southwest New Guinea, Asmat Papuans, As River, village Amanamkai. Rijksmuseum voor Volkenkunde, Leiden.

PLATE 28. Hardwood cylinder (80 cm) decorated by Matjemos. Southwest New Guinea, Asmat Papuans, As River, village Amanamkai. Rijksmuseum voor Volkenkunde, Leiden.

PLATE 29. Hardwood cylinder (80 cm) decorated by Itjembi. Southwest New Guinea, Asmat Papuans, As River, village Amanamkai. Rijksmuseum voor Volkenkunde, Leiden.

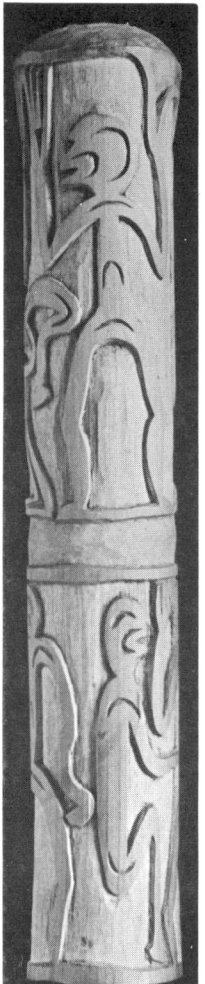

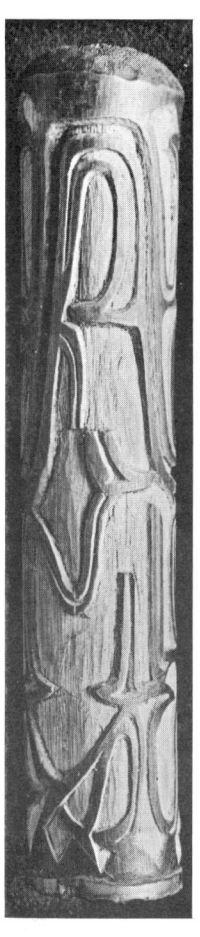

PLATE 32   PLATE 33

PLATE 30   PLATE 31

PLATE 30. Bamboo signal horn (29 cm) made by Matjemos. Southwest New Guinea, Asmat Papuans, As River, village Amanamkai. Rijksmuseum voor Volkenkunde, Leiden.

PLATE 31. Bamboo signal horn (38 cm) made by Ndojokor. Southwest New Guinea, Asmat Papuans, As River, village Amanamkai. Rijksmuseum voor Volkenkunde, Leiden.

PLATE 32. Bamboo signal horn (30 cm) made by Ndojokor. Southwest New Guinea, Asmat Papuans, As River, village Amanamkai. Rijksmuseum voor Volkenkunde, Leiden.

PLATE 33. Bamboo signal horn (28 cm) made by Itjembi. Southwest New Guinea, Asmat Papuans, As River, village Amanamkai. Rijksmuseum voor Volkenkunde, Leiden.

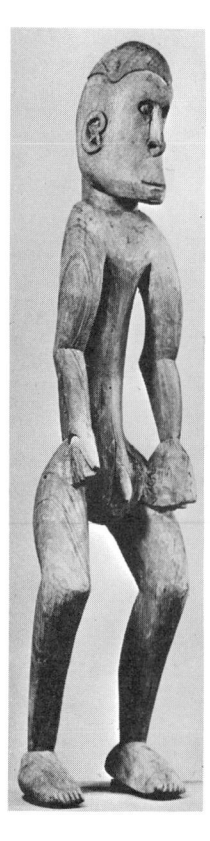

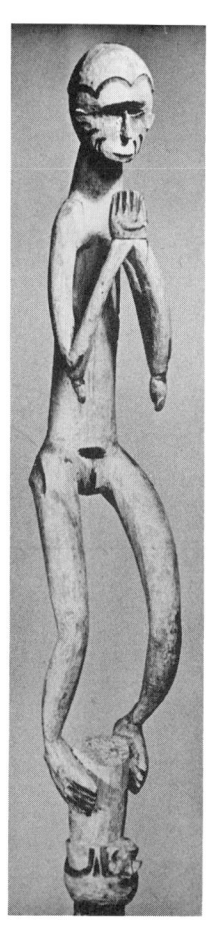

PLATE 34   PLATE 35

PLATE 34. Ancestor figure (100 cm) carved by Bifarji. Southwest New Guinea, Asmat Papuans, As River, village Amanamkai. Rijksmuseum voor Volkenkunde, Leiden.

PLATE 35. Ancestor figure (153 cm) carved by Finerus. Southwest New Guinea, Asmat Papuans, As River, village Amanamkai. Rijksmuseum voor Volkenkunde, Leiden.

PLATE 36   PLATE 37

PLATE 36. Ancestor figure (59 cm) carved by Matjemos. Southwest New Guinea, Asmat Papuans, As River, village Amanamkai. Rijksmuseum voor Volkenkunde, Leiden.

PLATE 37. Ancestor figure (100 cm); the body is carved by Kamis and the head by Omsa. Southwest New Guinea, Asmat Papuans, As River, village Amanamkai. Rijksmuseum voor Volkenkunde, Leiden.

PLATE 38. Palace of the governor at Uxmal. Mexico, Maya. Restoration drawing by Tatiana Proskouriakoff.

PLATE 39. The Central Plaza at Monte Albán, seen from the north. Mexico, Oaxaca.

PLATE 40. The hieroglyphic stairway with a Maya stela in front, at Copán, Mexico. Restoration drawing by Tatiana Proskouriakoff.

PLATE 41. A jaguar vessel of the Aztec period, Mexico. Museo Nacional de Antropología, Mexico City.

PLATE 42. The stone of the sun, usually known as the Aztec calendar, Mexico. Museo Nacional de Antropología, Mexico City.

PLATE 43. An illustration from Durán's Atlas showing Moctezuma I posing for his portrait in stone.

PLATE 44. Monument 5 from San Lorenzo, Veracruz. Museum of Jalapa, Veracruz.

PLATE 45. Partial view of the court of the Quetzal Butterflies. Mexico, Teotihuacan.

PLATE 46. The great cylindrical stone depicting the victories of the Aztec emperor Tizoc. Museo Nacional de Antropología, Mexico City.

PLATE 47. Stela at Piedras Negras, Guate-
mala.

PLATE 48. The captives scene from the murals at Bonampak, Mexico.

PLATE 49. Coatlicue or the Mother Earth, Aztec, Mexico. Museo Nacional de Antropología, Mexico City.

PLATE 50. Finial, pottery, New Guinea, Chambri Lake. Musée National des Arts Africains et Océaniens, Paris.

PLATE 51   PLATE 52

PLATE 51. Carving, West New Guinea, western
Asmat. Musée National des Arts Africains et
Océaniens, Paris.

PLATE 52. Ritual fork, whalebone, New Zealand. Musée National des Arts Africains et
Océaniens, Paris.

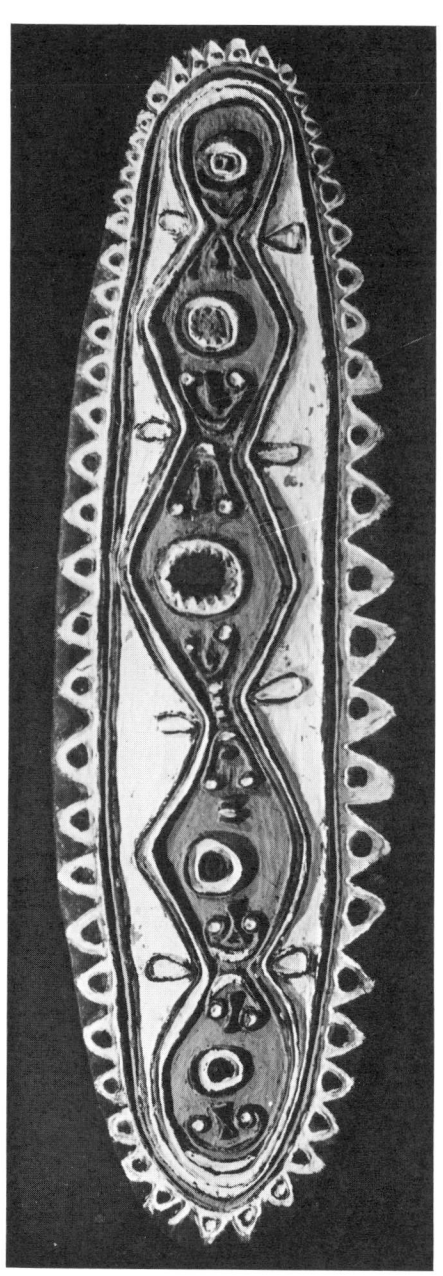

PLATE 53. Shield, carved and painted white, light ocher and green. New Guinea, Upper Sepik, G'Hom. Musée National des Arts Africains et Océaniens, Paris.

PLATE 54. Shield, carved and painted white, light ocher and white. New Guinea, Asmat. Musée National des Arts Africains et Océaniens, Paris.

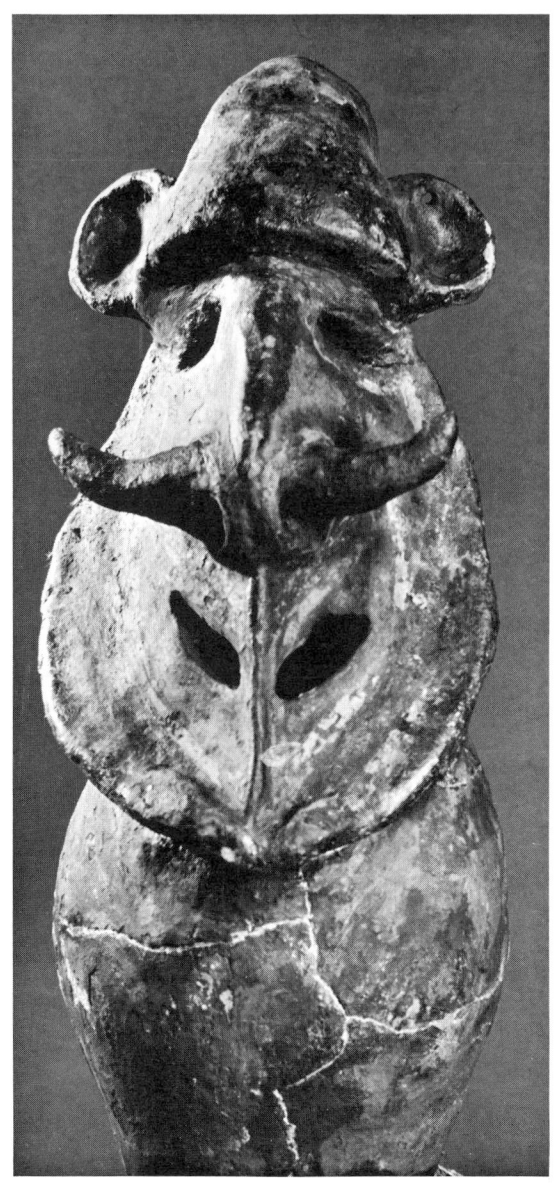

PLATE 55. Closed pottery, painted light ocher and black. New Guinea, Washkuk. Musée National des Arts Africains et Océaniens, Paris.

PLATE 56. Carved double hook, painted ocher. New Guinea, Middle Sepik, Kanganaman. Musée National des Arts Africains et Océaniens, Paris.

PLATE 57. Betel mortar, reddish black, heavy patina. New Guinea, Lower Sepik, Anggoram area. Musée National des Arts Africains et Océaniens, Paris.

PLATE 58. Hunting charm (very old work). New Guinea, Middle Sepik, Korewori River, Kamanggabi. Musée National des Arts Africains et Océaniens, Paris.

PLATE 59. Hunting charm (more recent work). New Guinea, Middle Sepik, Korewori River, Kamanggabi. Private collection.

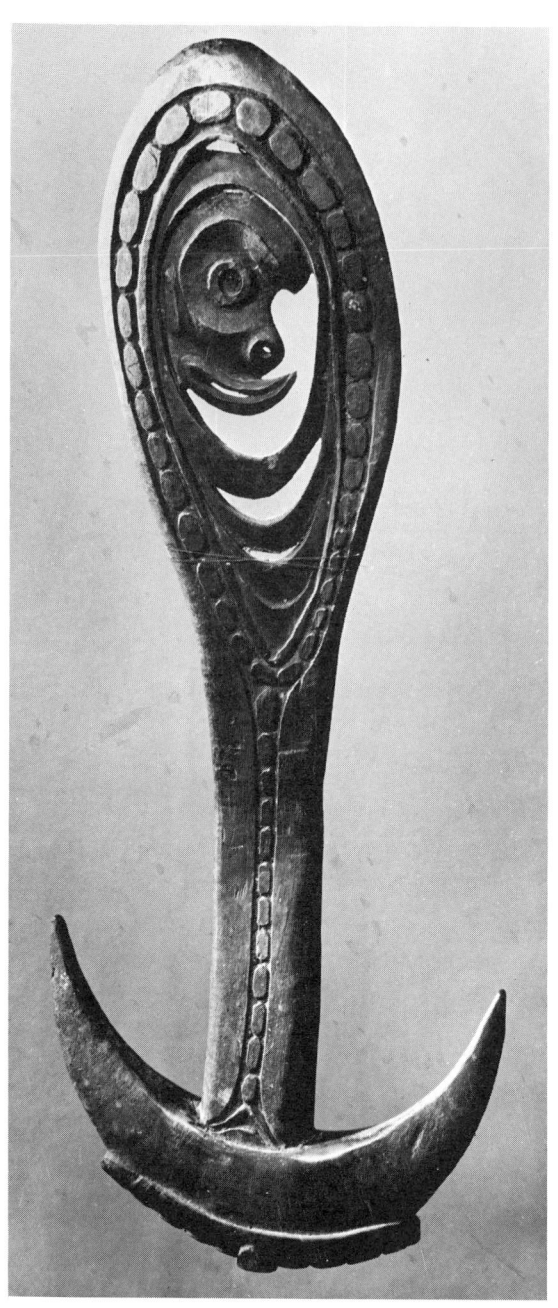

PLATE 60. Double hook with openwork carving. New Guinea, Chambri Lake, Aibom. Musée National des Arts Africains et Océaniens, Paris.

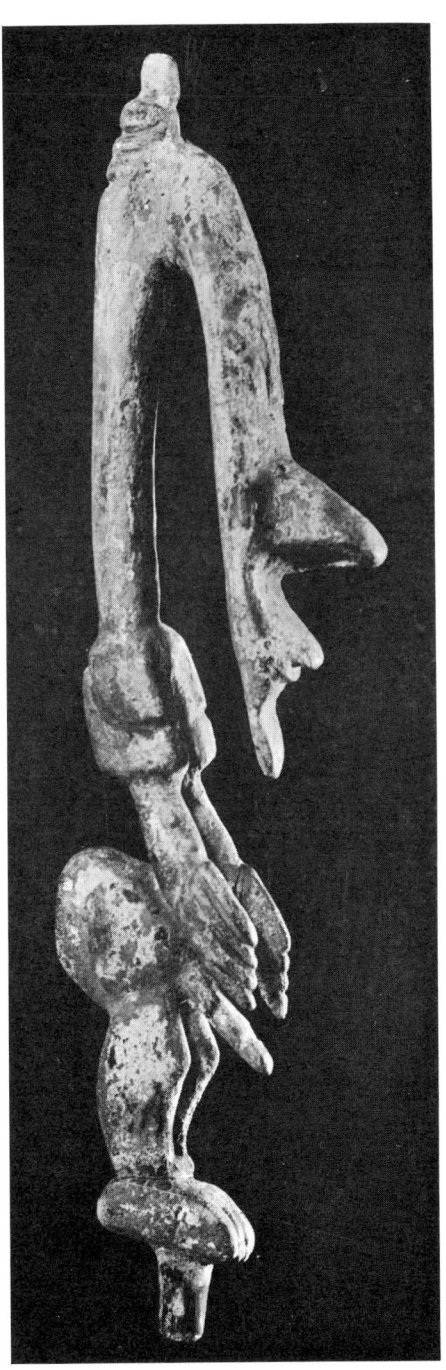

PLATE 62. Lime spatula top. New Guinea, Sepik area, Yuat River. Musée National des Arts Africains et Océaniens, Paris.

PLATE 61. Lime spatula top. New Guinea, Sepik area, Yuat River. Musée National des Arts Africains et Océaniens, Paris.

PLATE 63. Canoe shield. New Guinea, Lower Sepik, Yananambo. Musée National des Arts Africains et Océaniens, Paris.

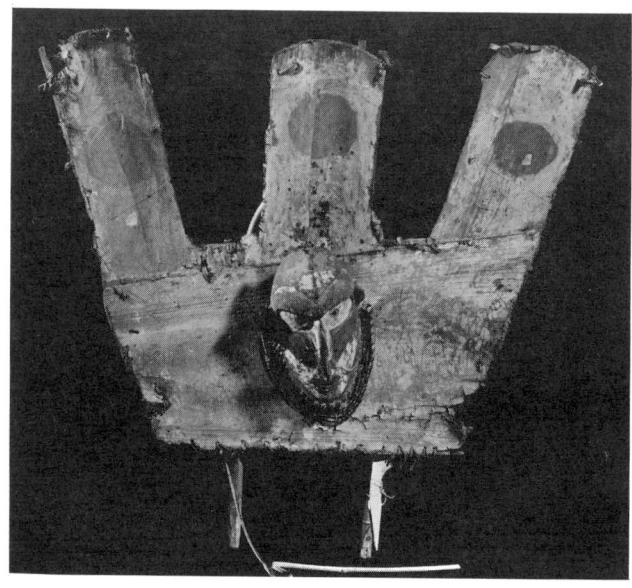

PLATE 64. Canoe shield. New Guinea, Lower Sepik, Yananambo. Musée National des Arts Africains et Océaniens, Paris.

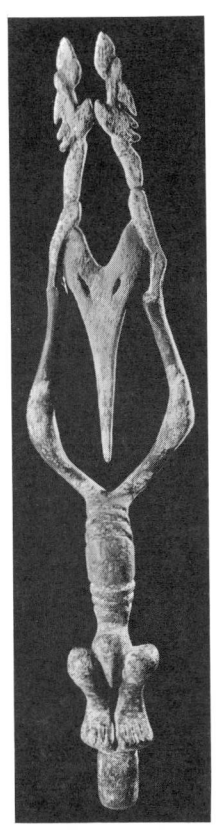
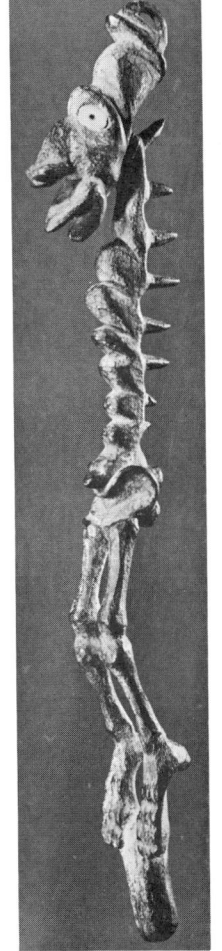

PLATE 65   PLATE 66   PLATE 67   PLATE 68

PLATE 65. Lime spatula. New Guinea, Middle Sepik or Lower Yuat (?). Musée National des Arts Africains et Océaniens, Paris.

PLATE 66. Lime spatula. New Guinea, Middle Sepik. Musée National des Arts Africains et Océaniens, Paris.

PLATE 67. Lime spatula. New Guinea, Sepik area, Lower Yuat. Musée National des Arts Africains et Océaniens, Paris.

PLATE 68. Lime spatula (?), male image covered with birdlike, crawling, small beings. New Guinea, Middle Sepik or Chambri Lake. Musée National des Arts Africains et Océaniens, Paris.

PLATE 70. Copy of an Ife (Nigeria) bronze head (9¼″), made by a brass-caster from Cameroun. Collection of Mr. and Mrs. William Bascom, Berkeley.

PLATE 69. Ife bronze head reproduced on a Nigerian stamp. Ife Museum, Nigeria.

PLATE 71. Ifa divination cup (14″) from Efon-Alaiye. Africa, Nigeria, Yoruba, Ekiti substyle. Collection of Mr. and Mrs. William Bascom, Berkeley.

PLATE 72. Ifa divination cup with hinged lid (12½″) from Deyin. Africa, Dahomey, Yoruba, Ketu substyle. Collection of Mr. and Mrs. William Bascom, Berkeley.

PLATE 73. Shango staff (20½″) by Duga of Meko. Africa, Nigeria, Yoruba, Ketu substyle. Collection of Mr. and Mrs. William Bascom, Berkeley.

PLATE 74. Iron lamp (15″) for Shango shrine from Oyo. Africa, Nigeria, Yoruba. Collection of Mr. and Mrs. William Bascom, Berkeley.

PLATE 75. Pair of brass Ifa divination bells or tappers (*left*, 17″ and 17¼″) and "messenger poker" in brass and iron (*right*, 18¼″) (nineteenth century) from Ife. Africa, Nigeria, Yoruba. Collection of Mr. and Mrs. William Bascom, Berkeley.

PLATE 76. Calabash carved with overall bird designs (10″ high; 9¼″ diam.), from Oyo. Africa, Nigeria, Yoruba. Collection of Mr. and Mrs. William Bascom, Berkeley.

PLATE 77. Pair of *ibeji* or twin figures (12″ and 11″), from Oyo. Africa, Nigeria, Yoruba, Oyo substyle. Collection of Mr. and Mrs. William Bascom, Berkeley.

PLATE 78. Four Eshu figures (4¼″), from Igana. Africa, Nigeria, Yoruba, Oyo sub-style. Collection of Mr. and Mrs. William Bascom, Berkeley.

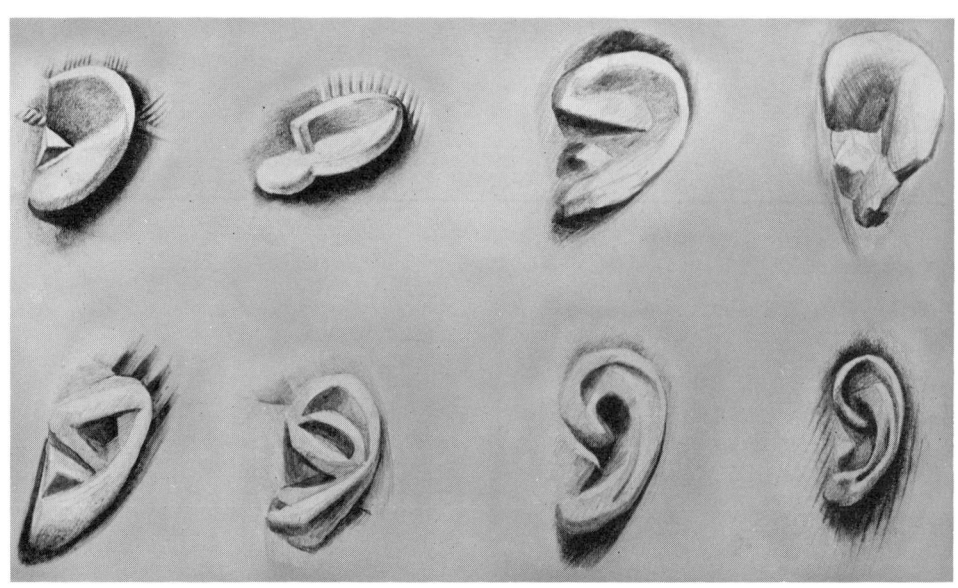

PLATE 79. Some Yoruba ear styles: *Upper row, left to right*: Ekiti (Efon-Alaiye); Egba (Abeokuta); Ketu (Meko, by Duga); Ijebu (Shagamu). *Lower row, left to right*: Oyo (Oyo); Ijebu (by Ona); Lagos (by Ona); Ife (bronze head).

PLATE 80. Abatan Odefunke Ayinke Ija of Oke-Odan, on April 24, 1966. She wears a head-tie (*gèlè*), blouse (*bùbá*), a cloth around the lower part of her body (*ìró*), and a special cloth with blue embroidered pattern over the left shoulder. A pendant ornament (*bòrósì*), made by a native gold-smith, hangs over the blouse.

PLATE 81. *Awo ota eyinle* (24″) attributed to Agbedeyi Asabi Ija of Oke-Odan. The present owner alleges the vessel was made before 1918 or 1913 but it was probably made not later than the turn of the century. Nigeria, Aworri Yoruba.

PLATE 82. Detail of plate 81, showing "child of Oten", with head turned to the left, or rear crown support. The dominant figure is marked with *keke* (*ké̩ké̩*) cicatrization, consisting of four parallel strokes running horizontally along the lower cheek, then sweeping up, at a diagonal, from the line of the jaw to the line of the hair, between the eye and the ear. These four lines accentuate the line of the jawbone. They are surmounted by three shorter vertical strokes, set under the eye. *Keke* is a very common Egbado mark.

PLATE 83. *Awo ota eyinle* (16") by Abatan. Period I. Owner alleges that the vessel was made between 1916 and 1921. The lid has been removed, revealing about 43 fluvial stones (*ota*) in fresh water collected from a stream. The figure is embellished with a gold necklace and an iron chain. The kola bowl contains Nigerian coins. The object has been set upon a mat of indigenous making. Nigeria, Aworri Yoruba.

PLATE 84. Detail of plate 83. The figure wears a form of cicatrization known as *abaja meje* ("seven abaja"), consisting of four horizontal strokes surmounted by three shorter vertical strokes, the latter group set over the half of the former which is closest to the nose.

PLATE 85. *Awo ota eyinle* by Abatan. Attributed to Period I. The figure wears a variation of the Oyo *abaja* marks known as *àbàjà méjo ibùlé*, a set of horizontal strokes closest to the nose and lips. Nigeria, Aworri Yoruba.

PLATE 86. *Awo ota eyinle* (19″) by Abatan. Attributed to Period I. The pigtail of the coiffure meets the rear crown support at a point where a fourth boss would normally stand. The meandered pattern encircling the midsection of the pot is unusual and may reflect market purchase, where a specially decorated *isaasun* pot was substituted for the traditional vessel with symbolic motifs in low relief. *Abaja meje* cicatrization. The Smithsonian Institution, Washington, D. C.

PLATE 87. *Awo ota eyinle* lid (*ca.* 12″) by Abatan. Attributed to Period II (late 1920's–early 1930's?). The single figure beneath the dominant image of a woman is unusual. The latter wears *abaja meje* cicatrization. The Nigerian Museum, Lagos (Atinga Collection).

PLATE 88. *Awo ota eyinle* (*ca.* 16″) by Abatan. Period II. Owner estimates that the vessel was made between 1926 and 1936. Figure wears gold earrings (*yerí etí*) and iron chain necklace. The kola bowl is full. *Abaja meje* cicatrization. Nigeria, Aworri Yoruba.

PLATE 89. *Awo ota eyinle* (*ca.* 16″) by Abatan. Attributed to Pediod II. The asymmetrical siting of the kola bowl is unusual. *Abaja meje* cicatrization. Aworri Yoruba.

PLATE 90. *Awo ota eyinle* (*ca.* 14″) by Abatan. Period III (Atinga replacement). Owner says that vessel was made in the year of Atinga—1951. *Abaja meje* cicatrization. Nigeria, Egbado Yoruba.

PLATE 91. *Awo ota eyinle* lid (13″) by Abatan. Late Period III. Alleged to have been made about 1957. Dominant image wears two sorts of iron chain around the neck. One flanking figure wears *kólésẹ* coiffure, the other a kind of hat; the figure on the rear crown support wears a *fìlà abétí ajá* ("the dog-ear cap"), a style of headgear still favored by the men of Egbado, Ibarapa, and central Oyo but said to be considered old-fashioned among the acculturated Yoruba of Lagos and Ibadan. Main figure wears *àbàjà méta àágberí*, a single set of three parallel, horizontal lines on each cheek. Nigeria, West Aworri Yoruba.

PLATE 92. *Awo ota eyinle* (19″) by Abatan. Period IV. The owner claims to remember exact date of making: July 21, 1962. The figure is embellished with a miniature head-tie. *Abaja meje* cicatrization. Nigeria, West Anago Yoruba.

PLATE 93. *Awo ota eyinle* (*ca.* 16") by Abatan. Attributed to Period II. Figure wears an iron chain necklace. *Abaja meje* cicatrization. Nigeria, central Egbado Yoruba.

PLATE 94. Altar for Eyinle made by Abatan for her own household about 1958. The mud figure at right is approximately 18″ high. Nigeria, southern Egbado.

PLATE 95. Dance for the Ibu Eyinle and Orisa Ogun, July, 1965. Omikunle Agbeke Asoko, master dancer of Ajilete, dances *kokan loko* in honor of the Eyinle circle. She wears a trade cloth emblazoned with the letters of the Roman alphabet. She dances before a compound whose framed windows and moldings betray distinct Portuguese influence (via the repatriation of Yoruba slaves from the northeast of Brazil). Her posture, feet flat on the ground, torso bent forward, is very common in Guinea Coast dancing. Nigeria, southern Egbado.

PLATE 96. Pottery head (2¾") fragment of full figure. This was one of the last of Azume's works available in Shendam in 1958. Africa, Nigeria, Goemai. Gift from the Long Goemai (Paramount Chief) to the author.

PLATE 97. Fertility doll *akua'ba*. Africa, Ghana, Akan. It was commissioned by the Asantehene for his daughter who had married and moved to the Kwahu area. Institute of African Studies, University of Ghana, Legon.

brass-casting and in pottery pipes (Bascom and Gebauer, 1953 and 1964, pls. 31–34, 44, 48, 50).

The list of similar styles in different media could be multiplied further without substantiating Boas' conclusion that they are much more common than instances of different styles in different media. The question clearly deserves further attention but, impressionistically at least, it seems as easy to think of crafts in the same society whose styles are distinct as those whose styles are similar.

As Boas suggests, stylistic differences between crafts are due both to the influence of their different techniques (and media) and to the fact that they are practiced by different segments of the population. The medium and the technique employed unquestionably impose limitations on an artist's work, but craft specialization and the sexual division of labor are also important. The instances cited above of similar styles in different media and Boas' conclusion about their frequency indicate that the limitations of media and techniques are not a sufficient explanation of the stylistic differences between crafts. As already noted, there are distinct styles in wood carving and brass-casting among the Ashanti, Fon, and Yoruba, but in the Cameroun grasslands work in these same media is stylistically similar.

Moreover, stylistic differences are to be found in work in the same medium in the same society, which clearly indicates that other factors, including craft specialization and the sexual division of labor, must be considered. In painting, for example, there are marked contrasts between the representational designs of men and the geometric patterns of women among the American Indians of the Plains and the Great Basin; and the same is true in bead-working. Among the Ashanti and the peoples of the Cameroun grasslands, the anthropomorphic and zoomorphic pottery pipes made by men contrast sharply with the pottery produced by women. Among the Dogon, masks and figurines are stylistically differentiated;[10] both

---

[10] Laude made this point in his paper at the 1962 Salisbury Congress.

are made of wood, but the figurines are carved by blacksmiths who specialize in wood carving, while the masks are made by male initiates for their own use. Distinct styles may develop when subtribes lose contact through isolation, or when artists in a single society are divided by sex lines or are organized into separate crafts.

This is not to suggest that there is complete compartmentalization among crafts. This is belied by the carry-over of interwoven designs into different media, already cited. A striking Ashanti female drum in the Ghana museum is decorated with low-relief designs, many of which are derived from Ashanti gold weights cast in brass.

9. *Tribal styles.*—Finally there is the concept of tribal style itself. This has proved its usefulness and cannot be discarded unless it can be demonstrated that a tribal style has never existed; but it is in need of drastic and radical revision. There is no reason for assuming, a priori, that art styles are defined in terms of ethnic or linguistic boundaries, or that they may not be associated with broader or narrower social groupings. It is clear, however, that we need both a better understanding of art styles and their distributions and a clearer definition of what we mean by ethnic groups and subgroups.

Individual styles fall within the patterns of the style that is appropriate to the artist's sex, his craft, and the medium and technique with which he works at a given period and in a given locality. The subtribal style of a particular period for a given craft and medium and technique is the sum of the individual styles of the artists concerned, as the tribal and regional style is a composite of local variants. Styles may reflect subtribal groups, tribes, or supratribal regions, periods of time, and the sexual division of labor, crafts, media, and techniques, and perhaps other factors not mentioned here.

I am inclined to believe that even these qualifications represent an oversimplification. Although neither style has been systematically described, the embroidery of the Yoruba resembles that of the Hausa of Nigeria, whereas their other crafts are clearly differentiated. Masks of the Baule resemble those of the Guro of the Ivory Coast, so much so that they are sometimes difficult to distinguish, and in brass-casting Baule gold weights resemble those of the Ashanti of Ghana; but I know of no published Guro brass-castings or Ashanti wooden masks. The boundaries of style of one particular craft may cut across those of other crafts, rather than coincide with them.

All of this reflects the fact that some artists, as individuals, may be influenced by the styles of other societies, or of other crafts, while other artists may adhere to traditional forms and styles. Contrary to what Boas said about the uniformity of tribal life—and what others have thought about the simplicity of African societies—the situation is more complex, with artists reacting as individuals and responding differently as far as art styles are concerned. Some perpetuate established styles as they have learned them, with more or less individual expression. Some produce individual styles through their own creativity, more or less different from what was known before. Some accept ideas from other societies, modifying them more or less in the process. Some take new ideas from inside or from outside their own society, adapting them so that they become accepted as part of the local style of their craft. Through such processes styles change, but usually they maintain a recognizable continuity from one period to another.

Within any of these styles there is considerable room for variation and creativity without departing from its standards, though the degree of creative freedom appears to vary with at least five factors. The amount of creative expression that is permitted or expected may differ from one society to another, from one period to another, from one craft to another, from one genre to another, and even from one part of a carving to another. The first three of these points may be self-evident, but it seems necessary to document the last two.

There are some traditional genres of African art in which creative latitude is minimized and little variation is evident. Besides such carvings as undecorated stools and *warri* boards, this is also true of some sculptured genres, such as Yoruba carvings for the deity Eshu and Yoruba twin figures (*ibeji*). Artists are commissioned to carve the twin figures (pl. 77), and these must correctly represent the sex of the twin who has died and the facial markings of his or her lineage; but otherwise they show little variation within a given locality. Despite their aesthetic appeal to us, they appear to be of little aesthetic interest to Yoruba carvers, and to offer them little challenge for creative expression. Even where forms are standardized, as in this case, no two pieces carved by the same artist are identical, if only because they are made by hand rather than by machine; and sometimes there is evidence of deliberate variation in details. For a few pennies I once bought a series of four small wooden Eshu figures (pl. 78), all obviously the work of a single carver, which had been carved in advance rather than commissioned by a customer. Though repetitively similar in their basic form, each was distinct from the others in its facial markings and the presence or absence of a beard. There is no known ritual reason for these variations, and while there is no proven explanation for this level of creativity, it may be attributable simply to the carver's desire to avoid the monotony of exact repetition.

The degree of variation may also vary from one part of a carving to another, with some parts of the body, for example, becoming standardized. In Yoruba carvings of human figures, creativity is minimized in the treatment of the ear, with the result that ear form is an important diagnostic in identifying the subtribal and individual origins of figures that may differ markedly in other respects (pl. 79).[11] Aside from local variation, ears and, to a degree, the human

[11] Recently I learned that this observation had been anticipated in the last century by Giovanni Morelli (see Frankenstein, pp. 45–46, Heil, 1967, pp. 4–12). In his *Italian Painters, Critical Studies of their Works* (1900, I, 35–59, 74–82, passim) first published in 1880, Morelli stressed the importance of details such as ears and hands in attributing paintings to individual artists. He says (1900, I, 77 n. 4), "I must here reiterate that the *typical form* (*Grundform*) of hand and ear peculiar to each of the great masters is not only to be found in all their pictures, but even in the portraits which they painted from life."

face as a whole again appear to offer Yoruba carvers little challenge for creative expression. Apparently they are content to produce standardized ear forms while making aesthetic choices among several alternative postures and forms of hairdress, and concentrating their creative efforts on the composition of groups of figures, objects held in the hand, ritual paraphernalia, and costume.

In contrast to the Eshu and twin figures, there is a wide variation in form and content in some genres of Yoruba art such as masks, carved house posts, doors, and especially divination cups. The cups used in Ifa divination may represent birds, chickens, ducks, snakes, the rainbow python, chameleons, tortoises, fish, hares, deer, men on horseback, chiefs with drummers and attendants, diviners engaged in divination, or women weaving. They may also represent seated or kneeling women holding children or ritual staffs or bowls, or offering chickens as sacrifices, or with empty hands (pls. 71, 72).[12] The choice between these and other subjects may be made by the customer, or it may be left up to the carver. Yoruba carvers probably have their greatest freedom for creative expression when commissioned to produce these genres by customers who leave the choice of form and content up to them. When ritual paraphernalia are represented in a carving they should, of course, be appropriate to the cult in which the carving is to be used, but there is no requirement that specific paraphernalia, or indeed any, be included. Again this choice may be left up to the carvers, who achieve some degree of familiarity with the ritual objects and costume appropriate to the different religious cults.

Understandably, creativity is also related to the price that the customer is willing to pay for a carving. The greater his economic return, the more time and thought the carver is willing to devote to his task. This is evident from dealing with Yoruba carvers, and it was made very clear by the prices asked for the Ibo masks collected near Udi, which ranged from small, simple carvings that

[12] A number of these forms of Ifa divination cups are illustrated in Frobenius, 1913, pp. 233, 235, 237, 239.

had been produced quickly to large and very complex ones that required considerable time and thought. Carvings that are larger, more complex, more carefully finished, and more creative are usually more expensive.

Some Yoruba carvers in Abeokuta kept small models of fairly standard types of masks which they showed to their customers for them to choose among. Yoruba carvers may also be commissioned to reproduce a piece that is already in use, as when a termite-eaten mask or figurine must be replaced and is brought in for the carver to copy. In both cases the opportunity for creativity is limited, but there is still some latitude for its expression.

In Meko in 1950, when the owner of an excellent Shango staff was unwilling to sell it, I learned that it had been carved by the town's master carver, Duga, and I commissioned him to copy it for me (pl. 73). The carving took weeks to complete because he agreed to stop at critical stages of his work and wait until I could visit him so that I could make a color movie of it, from the initial roughing out of the log to the final painting in polychrome, for which he used traditional paints made of seeds, leaves, wood, and minerals.[13]

Duga was not content with repeating exactly what he had done before; he obviously wanted to improve on his earlier work. In the first place, having been promised a good fee for his services, he carved a larger figure than the original. Second, there were minor variations in the carving, although these were largely matters of detail. Third, there were deliberate variations in the painted colors. The top portion, representing two thunderbolts that frame a ram and a dog, was painted a solid tan instead of half red and half blue. Tan was retained as the skin color of the principle figure, representing a priest of Shango, the thunder-god, but his drummer on his right was given black skin instead of red, and that of the reclining female became red instead of black. The woman represents a worshiper of Oya, Shango's wife and goddess of the River Niger, giv-

---

[13] Bascom and Gebauer, 1953 and 1964, pls. 4–6.

ing her traditional greeting to Shango's priest. The three skin colors are distinguished linguistically in Yoruba and are represented in several of Duga's carvings, but in the new carving those of the two subsidiary figures were reversed.

On several different occasions during the carving, starting when the form of the figures first began to emerge, Duga asked me what color the ram should be painted. As I wished to leave the decision up to him, I gave evasive replies such as, "As it would have been painted in the old days" or, "As you think it should be painted." For several weeks this question bothered him, and he wrestled with it like an artist trying to choose between alternatives on purely aesthetic grounds. Finally, having reached his decision, he stopped asking the question. He painted the ram's horns black as they had originally been, but instead of painting its body white, he left it the natural light color of the unpainted wood. He was obviously satisfied with his choice, for he repeated this treatment on a ram's head in another carving he made for me several months later.

Duga was appreciated as an artist by the townspeople of Meko. Informants who came to work at the house where we stayed recognized his carvings that we had purchased, stopped to look at them with admiration, and often said simply in a tone of respect, "Ah! Duga!"

Duga had an artist's dedication to his work. One could tell when he was concentrating intently on it by watching his bare feet, which became tense with his toes spread tautly apart. So that I could photograph him at work, Duga moved out into the sunlight from the shaded veranda where he normally carved, but he was oblivious to the noonday African sun. He sometimes became so absorbed in what he was doing that he remained there, intent on his carving, after I had said good-bye and driven away.

To my knowlege Duga is the only traditional artist in a nonliterate society who is known to have received a "scholarship" for his training. His father was an important member of the Gelede society, which uses large numbers of masks. This society paid the expenses of Duga's apprenticeship to a master carver in Ketu, an important art center and the capital of the kingdom to which Meko belonged. It was understood that in return he would carve masks for the society without charge, but that when he carved for worshipers of Shango or for other customers, he was entitled to charge and keep for himself whatever fees he wished.

One of Duga's memorable achievements is recorded in a letter I received after leaving Nigeria; it was from my Meko interpreter informing me of the death of his father, Chief Isiaka, on March 2, 1953.

> Duga and other wood-carvers at Meko carved many kinds of Gelede masks when we made the ceremony of Gelede for my late father. The Gelede and other dances for the sake of my father were too [very] great and interesting. People came from many towns to see the display and witness the big occasion, especially Gelede, and others came in the interest of the Onimeko [king of Meko]. The Oba [king] of Aiyetoro came, Alaketu [king of Ketu] sent his followers, and all the rest of the Obas [kings] around Meko came here and witnessed the ceremony. Duga for the ceremony carved a horse of wood and gave it four wheels to walk on, and he made it so that four people could be hid in the mat with which he covered round the horse. Two people pushed it forward and two people pushed it backward. He trained the people to push it as if it were alive, and he trained the rider to dance with it as if he were riding a live horse. It was very wonderful and interesting indeed. He carved the horse for about forty days with the other wood-carvers. Duga was given much money both by the natives of Meko and the strangers [from other towns] on the day of the ceremony. Dear Master, the people of Meko cannot forget Duga for his sense and for his many kinds of carvings.

Innovations in art cannot often be ascribed to known individual artists in nonliterate societies, both because of the limited time depth of our studies and because of the insufficient attention paid to artists as individuals. We know that Lucy Lewis introduced the fine-line decorations in Pueblo pottery, and we are aware of the contributions of Nampeyo and Maria Martinez in the same medium and of the innovations of some other important American Indian artists; but these are exceptions. And although all of them at one time or another probably produced for the tourist market, tourist art may soon provide the only point at which individual creativity and stylistic change can be studied.

Two other Yoruba carvers whose work is very different from Duga's deserve mention in this connection. Thomas Ona, a carver from Ijebu-Ode, produced a series of figurines representing familiar characters of Nigeria's colonial period. (Bascom, 1957, front cover and pp. 118–126; *Esquire*, 1957, pp. 64–65; Anonymous, 1938a, p. 138; Bascom and Gebauer, 1953 and 1964, pp. 40–43 and pls. 24–25.) He was interested in depicting the Nigerian scene as he saw it, and he carved British lawyers, missionaries, wedding couples, colonial soldiers in uniform, district officers "on tour" in canoes, and Yoruba women pounding yams, kings, court attendants, policemen, and hunters, as well as the Prince of Wales and Queen Victoria whom he knew only from photographs. These amusing figures were a form of tourist art, made for sale to British colonials who were almost the only tourists in Nigeria before World War II, but Ona's introduction of new subject matter from the world about him into an established style of carving is paralleled in more serious forms of African art. District officers, wristwatches, pith helmets, bicycles, matchboxes, and gin bottles appear on Yoruba masks, doors, and house posts; and Portuguese explorers, soldiers, and priests are represented in the famous bronzes from Benin.

As far as I could determine, Ona was the only person in Nigeria producing this genre of carving, and for some time I believed that he had originated it. Later I saw a photograph of a similar carving of Queen Victoria, identified as a Yoruba carving "made about 1890" which was exhibited in England with several carvings that were obviously Ona's work. The carving of Queen Victoria was almost identical with two others, undated, which had been published by Lips (Bradley, 1959, p. 31 and back cover; *Exhibition of Europeans Seen through Native Eyes*, 1954, nos. 18, 19–26; Lips, 1937, figs. 206, 207–208). Whether all three were carved by Ona as a young man or whether an unknown predecessor, rather than Ona himself, originated this genre of carving is still uncertain, but it is clearly the relatively recent innovation of a single individual.

Another innovation, which has since been copied by many others, was introduced by J. D. Akeredolu, who first produced miniature thorn-carvings, again for the tourist market (Bascom and Gebauer, 1953 and 1964, p. 43 and pl. 26; Anonymous, 1938, pp. 134–137; Anonymous, 1959, pp. 106–107). He not only introduced a new medium and technique and employed a very different scale, but his work is in marked contrast with traditional Yoruba carvings in the naturalism of the proportions of the human body and of details such as nails and fingernails. Although Akeredolu became familiar with European art as a craft teacher in a government school, he began carving as a young boy, and it is doubtful that his naturalism resulted from European influence.

It seems more likely that the idea of copying human body proportions from nature could be independently invented more easily than the convention of representing the human figure as consisting of three parts (head, torso, and legs) of approximately equal size, which the Yoruba share with several other African peoples. Naturalism has sometimes been regarded as the historical culmination of centuries of unsuccessful attempts; but Western artists were not content to accept it as the ultimate in the evolution of art, and the prehistoric artists who produced the European cave paintings were highly naturalistic at a very early period.

If the idea of copying from nature can be accepted as relatively obvious and apt to occur independently, then the appearance of the extremely naturalistic bronze heads in Ife is not so mystifying, and there is less reason to look to Egypt or elsewhere for their origins. The naturalism of the Ife bronzes, which characterizes the treatment of the head and facial features such as nose, lips, and ears, was a major innovation by an unknown artist in the past, but in point of fact it does not carry over into naturalistic bodily proportions. The full figures discovered in Ife in 1957 approximate the Yoruba tripartite division of the body, confirming their indigenous origin (Willett, 1959c, p. 4 and pl. K).

The arts in general, in contrast with social institutions, provide especially fruitful materials for the study of creative expression, innovation, and cultural change. In kinship and social structure, in political organization, in economics (as distinct from technology), and even in religion, the emphasis is on individual conformity, enforced by social and supernatural sanctions. On the other hand, creativity is accepted in the graphic and plastic arts, the dance, music, and in that important segment of folklore which I call verbal art. This is true of the arts in general, whether they be tourist or traditional, ethnic or Western. Certain verbal incantations must be recited verbatim if they are to be effective; some ritual songs and dance steps must be performed exactly in the prescribed manner; and some religious wood carvings require no creative expression. Nevertheless, creativity is accepted in the arts in many societies, and in some it is expected and rewarded, or even regarded as the basis for judging the worth of an artist and his works.

Acculturation and diffusion can be studied in relation to social institutions as well as to the arts, and almost anywhere in today's changing world. Although far more difficult to study, if only because they are not easily anticipated, internal innovations are far more important. They are basic to the understanding of cultural change, for even external innovations depend on the internal innovations of other societies. Every idea that is spread by diffusion or acculturation must have had its origin in an internal innovation and in the creativity of an individual. Despite their interest in cultural change, anthropologists in recent years have neglected the arts in favor of social institutions. But because creativity is generally accepted in the arts whereas conformity is expected in social and even religious institutions, the arts are a focal point for the study of cultural change, internal innovations, and individual creativity.

8. Àbátàn: A Master Potter of the Ẹ̀gbádò Yorùbá[1]

ROBERT THOMPSON

> To make of unstable clay, quick to fall to pieces or crack, a solid and watertight pottery there must have been present a scientific attitude, an alert and sustained interest in knowledge for its own sake.
> —Claude Lévi-Strauss, *The Savage Mind*
>
> King-so-cool-and-peaceful-like-the-native-herb-*Osùn* (Ọba Tí Ó Tútù Bí Ọsùn).
>
> —Praise name of Adékánbi, founder of the kingdom of Ìlóbì in western Yorubaland

ᴇᴛ ᴜꜱ examine problems of symbolism, form, and setting in the life of an African traditional artist. This essay poses three questions about the art of Abatan (Àbátàn), a potter of Oke-Odan

[1] I take pleasure in acknowledging the support of a Ford Foundation Foreign Area Training Fellowship which enabled me to pursue field study of the arts of the Yoruba-speaking peoples from September 16, 1962, until January, 1964, and for the support of the writing of my dissertation. I also heartily thank the Concilium on International Studies at Yale for a grant covering field work in Nigeria in the summer

(Òkè-Ọ̀dàn), Nigeria: (1) What is its relation to social-religious context? (2) What are its architectural and choreographic coordinates? (3) How visible within these settings is the creative sensibility of Abatan, and what is the impact of tradition upon that individuality?[2]

I hope to demonstrate that two aspects of art, tradition and innovation, normally held to be antithetical, form in her works a dynamic unity, that is, her art is embedded in culture and yet is autonomous. The problem of the expression of her individuality is perceived in time. Artistic development happens where an individual, after the mastery of the skills of his métier, surmounts this basic competence with continuous self-criticism and change. In a world of nonliterate, conservative bent, these innovations are per-

───────────

of 1965. I thank, finally, Mrs. Virginia Inness-Brown and Miss Irene Schultz for their hospitality during a trip to Senegal and to Yorubaland after participation in the Colloque of the First World Festival of Negro Arts at Dakar.

[2] I have had the friendship of three Yoruba graduate students at Yale, Akíntọ́lá Abọ́dẹrin, Modupe Odotoye, and Edwin Obayan (Ọbayàn), who checked and nuanced translations into English of the oral literature of the cult of the Yoruba riverain king, Eyinle. The merit of the translations is their accomplishment; I, alone, am responsible for any shortcomings. In Yorubaland Àjànàkú, Araba (Àràbà) of Lagos, and Ọládípọ̀ Yemitan, of the Nigerian Broadcasting Company, generously shared their rich knowledge of the traditional literature and mythology of the Yoruba peoples. Kenneth Murray, former director of the Nigerian Department of Antiquities facilitated work in the study collections of the Nigerian Museum, Lagos, and was kind enough to allow me to copy his invaluable unpublished manuscripts on Yoruba art. My field helper, Adisa Fagbemi (Àdìsá Fágbèmí), himself an Egbado Yoruba, patiently transcribed songs, praises, myths, and allegations about the god, Eyinle, and the myriad details of his worship. This work is as much Adisa's as it is my own. I owe a debt to Wilson Perkins Foss IV for lending time from a busy ethnographic calendar in order to drive me to the area of Abatan's patronage and for the use of his photograph of the altar of Eyinle in the house of Abatan (pl. 94). Warren Robbins kindly provided the photograph, by Mark Kinnaman, of one of two works by Abatan in the Smithsonian Institute at Washington, D. C. Sheldon Nodelman and Richard Henderson, both colleagues at Yale, made many helpful criticisms of a first draft of the text. The greatest thanks are extended to Daniel Biebuyck, for encouraging this work and for patiently awaiting its completion, to Abatan Odefunke Ayinke Ija for many, many courtesies, not the least of which was allowing me, on three occasions, to film her at work, against her natural instinct of craft secrecy, and, finally to my wife, Nancy Gaylord Thompson, whose idea it was that I concentrate on the art of Abatan, and to the devotees of Eyinle.

force discreet, so as not to disturb a necessary illusion of the continuity of ethical truths in their abstract purity.

To mount an investigation of this nature presupposes the existence of a province of the non-Western World where not only is there a high incidence of creativity but also the means of isolating within the milieu a single master whose corpus of works is sufficiently ranged in time to yield developmental data. At first sight, the Yoruba (Yorùbá)[3] states seem ideal. These groups, found in the southwest of northern Nigeria, most of the western portion of the same nation, along the eastern border and central zone of Dahomey, and westward into Togo, form a world where at least one million people[4] actively worship traditional gods, many of these calling for votive sculpture, hence boast one of the world's largest number of sculptors. Fagg finds: "The named carvers whose personal styles are now established by examples or photographs in the British and Nigerian Museums already number well over 100, the great majority of them Yoruba; the number of Yoruba artists alone who have flourished since 1900 and whose styles could be similarly documented certainly runs into several thousands" (1963, p. 120). Broaden this account to admit all expressive media and the magnitude of the Yoruba aesthetic universe reveals itself. A thorough census of living Yoruba dancers, musicians, brass-casters, bead-embroiderers, architects,[5] mud sculptors, painters, potters, leather-

---

[3] The orthography is standard Yoruba, somewhat modified by Abraham's (1958, p. vi) attempt to remedy a few inconsistencies in modern Yoruba spelling. I follow the conventional transcription of ṣ for sh, ẹ for a vowel sound similar to that in the English word, bet, ọ for a sound somewhat like the English word, awe. The transcription, insofar as possible, includes indication of tone. There are three main tones in Yoruba, high ('), middle (no mark), and low (`). Abraham's work is based on the dialect of Oyo, which has been chosen by modern Yoruba as their national language.

[4] This estimate, my own, is extremely conservative and does not consider those Yoruba who are only nominally Christian or Muslim. The number may actually exceed three million.

[5] The term "architect" bears further explanation. Murray and Hunt-Cooke (1938?, p. 43) point out, "In the olden days a man would invite all his friends to help with the building of a new house; he would not pay them but prepare a feast for them. Certain men were, however, recognized as professionals and were always called in,

workers, weavers, praise singers, and masters of the verbal arts might introduce more than a hundred thousand[6] individuals worthy of critical examination. We shall never know them all. But so striking is the degree and range of Yoruba creativity that one may describe their broadest goal as a quest for beauty.

If Yoruba culture is an aesthetic windfall, the individual masters within that culture are difficult to identify once information is sought beyond one generation or more because vernacular attributions are not always reliable (Willett and Picton, 1967, p. 62). Even recent artists whose works survive in sufficient depth to make viable historical analysis are few in number. The dilemma stems from the perishability and nonliterate character of the expressive means of the people. Thousands of unfilmed and unnotated Yoruba traditional dances, for example, may disappear by the end of this century. Artistic biography depends on more than a few isolated samples just as a film cannot be critically considered where but two or three frames of the print survive. Thus pottery, indifferent both to the moist climate and to the termites of tropical Africa, presents an overwhelmingly attractive opportunity.

This explains, in part, the choice of a potter. Another reason is the wide distribution of her work across the Egbado (Ègbádò), Aworri (Àwórrì), and Anago (Ànàgó) subgroups of the southwestern Yoruba, which announces the indigenous appreciation of a remarkable reputation. A third motive is the fact that, although the particular art form that Abatan makes (an earthenware vessel with figurate lid) is one of the monuments of African pottery, no study of its shape, meaning, and function exists in any language. The Reverend H. Townsend may have destroyed the figurate lid to such

---

particularly for decorative work." Their point applies to southwestern Yoruba. I have found traces of similar architectural professionalism among Ijebu and Ekiti (Èkìtì) Yoruba.

   [6] Bascom has told me that there are still some 2,500 men engaged in the art of weaving alone in the town of Iseyin (Ìséyìn), and during my own travels throughout Yoruba country, I never found a village in which there was not at least one or two dancers and singers of merit.

a vessel at Oshiele (Òshíẹ̀lẹ̀), near the Egba (Ẹ̀gbá) Yoruba metropolis of Abeokuta (Abẹ̀òkúta),[7] on September 5, 1852, and the German explorer Rohlfs may have seen a few examples for sale in the market of Iwo (Ìwó)[8] (1874, p. 269), but it was not until the report of Frobenius (1913, I, 215, 218) that a brief specific mention was published: a line drawing by Carl Arriens, a caption, and a single sentence, "The [broad-mouthed pots for the thunder-god] are holy vessels with all sorts of strange figure ornaments." It seems that Frobenius assumed all such pottery was sacred to thunder-god worship and he distinctly characterizes one type misleadingly as a sacrificial urn. Abraham (1958, p. 774) uncritically republishes the line drawing from Frobenius' text as well as most of the caption.

The second notice (Herskovits and Herskovits, 1934*b*, p. 131) illustrated, with photograph and brief caption, a mode still seen on some shrines in the Abeokuta area; the object is stylistically close to the tradition followed by Abatan, farther south in Egbado, while distinguishable from the more abstract, ornamental lid considered by Frobenius, and is still highly characteristic of some parts of northern Yorubaland. Beier (1957, pl. 3) seems to have been the first to publish a photograph of the object, which he called the "peculiar pottery piece" for the hunter-god Erinle (Erinlẹ̀), in architec-

---

[7] Abeokuta is a pottery-making center and images in clay for Eyinle are still made there. Barber (1857) reports that a convert brought to Townsend a basket "loaded with the idols of Obatalla, Oshun, the devil called Eshu . . . one of the figures was made of clay, the other of cowries." Townsend "ordered the friends who were about me to break the clay figures in pieces." Eshu and Eyinle are both darkened with indigo, the former often adorned with strings of cowries. It is possible that Townsend considered them a unit in ignorance of the nuances of Yoruba iconography. If the "clay figures" were indeed sculptures for Eyinle, they were probably figurate lids.

[8] ". . . war die Stadt Juoh (Grundemann schreibt Iwo) erreicht. Auf dem Markte standen viele Götzenbilder von Thon und von Holz, bekleidete und unbekleidete, zum Verkauf." The dressing of clay images for Eyinle is a frequent occurrence (cf. pl. 92), but I have never heard of dressed images for Eyinle for sale in markets. That figurate Eyinle pottery is sold in markets, however, has been established by field investigations—three Anago informants told me they purchased their pots not directly from the potter but at a market at Adjara in Dahomey and four Egbado bought their liturgical pots at a market in Abeokuta.

tural context upon an altar in the town of Ilobu (Ìlôbú) in eastern Oyo (Ọ̀yọ́) Yoruba country. The definition of a major form of African pottery has thus remained a matter of sometimes misleading photographic captions. The need for data is urgent. Already three works by Abatan have been published in photographic form, two in 1951 in *Nigeria* (no. 37, p. 15), the other very recently (Robbins, 1966, pl. 160), but the illustrations lack, for want of literature, argument on form, symbolism, or history.

THE EGBADO AND THEIR VISUAL TRADITION

Abatan is an Egbado. The Egbado[9] are a subgroup of the Yoruba. They are located northwest of Lagos, the capital of Nigeria, and are bounded on the north by the Oyo and Ibarapa (Ìbàràpá) Yoruba, on the east by the Egba Yoruba, on the south by the Aworri Yoruba and on the west by the Anago, the Ohori-Ije (Ọ̀họ̀rí-Ìje), the Ohori-Ketu,[10] and the Ketu (Kétu). They are primarily distinguished from their neighbors by their dialect.

An account of an Egbado form of art will hopefully add balance to our knowledge of Yoruba expressive media, thus far heavily weighted in terms of wood carving, as to media, and in terms of the art of the Oyo, Egba, Ijebu (Ìjẹ̀bu), Owo (Ọ̀wọ̀), and Ketu groups, as to artistic geography. The Egbado were importuned in 1951 by a witch-finding cult called Atinga (Àtíngà) whose impact was sometimes hysterical: "Crowds of youths, headed by supposedly entranced dancers, blowing whistles in time to their steps, would run into houses and destroy domestic shrines, drag out the images, fire volleys of magic kola into the [shrines], knock down the walls,

---

[9] The boundaries of these ethnic subgroups are only approximate. Enclaves of Ketu farmers are still found in the heart of Egbado country and in Aworri, while the "line" separating Egbado from Egba is interrupted by incursions, one of the other.

[10] The Ohori subgroup divide, according to their own definition, into Ohori-Ije, those who live in the great swamp (*ijè*) between Pobe and Ketu, and the Ohori-Ketu, those who live on dry land. A full study of their culture and its relation to the better-known Yoruba states is urgently needed.

carry off the symbols, and heap them all together" (Morton-Williams, 1956, p. 325). These heaps were earmarked for destruction.[11] The loss to the art history of Nigeria might have been serious had not the then surveyor of antiquities, Kenneth Murray, in one of the remarkable art rescues of this century, traveled through the areas disturbed by Atinga and quickly sorted out superior pieces from the heaps, regretfully leaving much behind, thus founding the Atinga Collection now in the Nigerian Museum, Lagos.[12] In the process, three works by Abatan were saved.[13]

It is important to portray briefly the artistic relationship of the Egbado, essentially Oyo-derived in culture, with the people of the ancient kingdom of Ketu in present-day Dahomey. By the turn of the nineteenth century some forty kings, allegedly, had reigned at Ketu (Parrinder, 1956) and this implies deep antiquity. On the other hand, it was perhaps not until 1775 "or shortly thereafter" that the first Egbado kingship was founded at Ijanna (Adewale, 1956, p. 252), a settlement that during the early nineteenth century appears to have been paramount among the Egbado.

[11] Morton-Williams (1956, p. 322) witnessed the handing over of an Eyinle terracotta, by a woman accused of being a witch, at Aiyetoro (Aiyétòrò), an important town between Abeokuta and Ketu. She had owned the sculpture because she had been told to become a member of the cult when she had first married and had not conceived.

[12] A full account of the rescue of art may be found in Murray, 1951a. The following excerpt suggests the value of future archaeological investigation: "The court clerk [of Ibeshe] said that there was a heap and took me to see it . . . we were directed to where it had been thrown: In a shallow borrow pit at the edge of the village where people throw away rubbish and go to latrine. There were not many things in the heap and much had been damaged, but several good carvings were found." Murray's work was later supplemented by a certain Miss Hodgson whose most interesting finding, from the point of view of Oke-Odan art history, was the fact that Atinga cultists had thrown all objects remaining after the visit of Kenneth Murray into the Yewa River. Assuming fragments of Eyinle pottery were among the pieces hurled into the water, and remembering that the denizens of the world of Eyinle are believed to swell in the depths of the Yewa, the vandalism was unwittingly poetic in its implications.

[13] These are a fragment, a female head with high-crested coiffure, 7 inches high; a lid, 12 inches high, bearing a female figure, also with high-crested coiffure, but whose kola bowl has been destroyed; a handsome two-figure lid (pl. 87) discussed at a later point in the text. These Atinga pieces are supplemented by a further example of later accession (Nigerian Museum, Lagos, 56.5.35).

The people of Ijanna came from Old Oyo (Ọ̀yọ́-Ilé), the imperial capital of the Oyo Yoruba, but they are said to have met Ketu farmers on the land. It is likely that the ancient artistic heritage of Ketu left a stabilizing mark upon Egbado sculpture, especially as the Ketu cult of Gelede (Gẹ̀lẹ̀dẹ́)[14] diffused throughout the area. By the end of the last century Samuel Johnson had written that the Yoruba of the Egbado area were said to be the best artists in the country (1922, p. 122). The wood sculpture of the Egbado, in the main, aligns with the turns of phrasing characteristic of the style range of Ketu, whereas the sculpture of Kishi (Kíshí), Igboho (Ìgbòho), and New Oyo (three settlements that received a heavy influx of refugees from Old Oyo when destroyed in the third decade of the last century),[15] although equally representational, reflects, it seems to me, a tradition of slightly (but decisively) more geometric bearing.

Oke-Odan, where Abatan lives, is one of the most important of the towns of the Egbado and is built on a plain above the Yewa River. It is thus assured of plentiful clay and water for pottery-making. The social history of the town sheds light on the nature of the "style" of Abatan. It is well known that a series of wars

[14] Many Egbado leaders of the local cult of Gelede, an extremely important witch-appeasement society, allege that the ultimate origin of their cult is Ketu. Their accounts fit the fact of the influence of Ketu sculpture upon the art of the Egbado.

[15] Cf. Johnson, 1957, p. 268: "The great metropolis was deserted, some fled to Kihisi, some to Igboho, and some even to Ilorin. As it was not a flight from an enemy in pursuit many who reached Kihisi and Igboho safely with their family returned again and again for their household goods and chattels." This picture of an orderly evacuation of possessions gives a measure of credence to the allegation that the finest antiquities at Kisi, Igboho, and, also, New Oyo were brought from the ancient capital (Nigerian Museum, Lagos, 48.9.129 and 60.6.17). The fact that three remarkable brass face masks (*ère Alákòró*), each said to have been made at Old Oyo more than three generations ago for members of the royal guard of the king of the Oyo, the Eso (Èsó), are found at Kisi, Igboho, and New Oyo is a most suggestive distribution. As to the transfer of art from Old to New Oyo via these towns, it seems that Atiba (Àtìbà) accepted the crown, after the fall of Old Oyo, "with the distinct understanding that he would lead the people home from Shaki, Gboho, Kihisi, and other places whither they had taken refuge" (*ibid.*, p. 279). In a forthcoming volume I consider the problem of the arts of Old Oyo in some detail.

disturbed all Yorubaland in the nineteenth century. Shortly after 1800, refugees from the Ketu kingdom of Ilobi (ìlóbì) resettled at Oke-Odan where they met Egbado farmers already on the land. Ilobi court historians (Ogunbiyi *et al.*, 1931) maintain, with unsubstantiated precision, that their kingdom was founded in the year 1483 by the Ketu king Adekanbi (Adékánbi), but regardless of whether or not Oke-Odan is "junior" or "senior" to Ilobi, it is very likely true that Oke-Odan did not become important until its population increased with increments of groups fleeing from villages characterized by cultural ties to Ketu or to Oyo-Ile. It is important to note, however, that the substratum at Oke-Odan was an Egbado or Oyo-derived quarter (Adewale, 1956, p. 256).

Let us compare the sculpture of Abatan the Egbado potter, with the art of Otolukan of Ilikimon, an excellent potter whose patrons mostly lived in the kingdom of Ketu. The stylistic means of Otolukan's concept of figural pottery are in sympathy with the rounding of mass, the refinement of full organic detail, and the pastel palette of the wood sculpture of Ketu. Her figures are especially curved and fleshy and the picking out of anatomic detail and dress with chalk-based colors lends to the vessels made for cults of the river especial charm. The styling of Abatan's figural pottery, on the other hand, betrays a different provenience. Her pottery by comparison seems slightly more reserved in mien and soberly presented under a monochromatic, dark-indigo patination (pl. 84). These qualities may reflect Oyo origins.

The particular class of objects that Abatan makes is, in some northern Oyo villages, entirely abstract, devoid of figural rhetoric, consisting of a pot, a lid, and a simple ornament with two intersecting arches surmounting the lid. Abraham illustrates, after Frobenius, a related object, most probably from Oyo territory, where the ornament is relieved by a glint of human presence. One of the arches bears the schematic rendering of a pigtail, thus establishing the opposite side of the object as its face (Abraham, 1958, illus.

89*a*). The art of Abatan stands somewhere between such abstraction and the full-dress mimesis of the art of Otolukan in Ketu country. The northern Oyo examples might represent, however, provincial replications of a metropolitan (Oyo-Ile) solution that *in situ* became much more elaborate.

It might be that the forced proximity of Ketu- and Oyo-influenced groups at Oke-Odan, Ilaare (Iláàré), Abeokuta, and other refugee gathering points in southwestern Yorubaland led to a process by which originally abstract forms from the north, brought by the Egbado migrations of the eighteenth century, evolved and were responsive to a new setting in which rounded representational forms were emphasized. Then, this special coexistence, Ketu roundness and Oyo angularity (to oversimplify), might have forced a more radical integration of form creating a unique pottery tradition. Or, there may have been rival modes, some figural, some abstract, and some fusions of the two, present in the imperial capital before the diaspora, then subsequently scattered and confused. It is impossible to solve this problem in our present state of knowledge but it is worth examining.

One sample of the figural pottery of metropolitan Oyo, that is, presumably finished before the 1830's, has been published (Willett, 1959*b*). It is a terra-cotta head of such execrable quality as to suggest a relic of some minor potter, jettisoned by members of a fleeing lineage. On the other hand, the Nigerian Museum, Lagos, houses a masterpiece of Yoruba pottery, allegedly made at New Oyo, whose elaboration of form bespeaks descent from a grandiose tradition.[16] An amazing frieze embellishes the sides of the vessel: human figures appear frontally, or in profile, and the depiction of one person, shown mounted, is almost wholly in the round (King, 1962, p. 20). To repeat, such expensive elaboration undoubtedly stems from a craft history of great stability, while the modeling of

[16] Carl Arriens' line drawing (in Frobenius, 1913, p. 215) illustrates a vessel with figures close, in point of style, to the Nigerian Museum terra-cotta.

the faces is in sympathy with some of the forms of northern Yoruba sculpture, for example, Oke-Iho (Òkè-Ihò) and Shaki (Shakí)
areas. These considerations imply relation to a vanished urban ceramic art and they rather suggest that the second alternative hypothesis, noted in the preceding paragraph, is correct.

THE EYINLE (EYINLÈ) CULT AND ITS TERRA-COTTA SCULPTURE

Worship of Eyinle, one of the major gods of the Oyo Yoruba,
gives rise to a wealth of regalia.[17] Devotees must wear an iron-chain
bracelet (ṣábá eyinlè) on the right wrist[18] as a mark of initiation and
as a protection against evil. It is further alleged that the chain represents, in symbolic miniature, the iron bangles worn by the hunters of Yoruba antiquity.[19] The dance emblems are the fly whisk (iju)
and the fan (abèbè).[20] The former relates to the hunt, the latter to
the goddess Oṣun (Ọṣun), "owner" of a major Yoruba river and
closely associated with the cult of Eyinle.

Altars for Eyinle are domestic. They are mud platforms, set
within one room of a compound, upon which diverse objects and
ritual paraphernalia rest (pl. 94). Seen on some altars, but apparently not essential, is a small effigy jar (ọtùn eyinlè), used when
water is spilled ceremonially during the throwing of kola nuts for
divination purposes. These effigy jars, measuring usually about 5
to 7 inches high, are not to be confused with the larger and more
elaborate form of Eyinle pottery, the awo ota eyinle (àwo ọta

[17] The description of the cult of Eyinle applies to the Oke-Odan sector.
[18] Among the Oyo Johnson (1957, p. 37) found followers of Erinle (Eyinle) distinguished by the wearing of a chain of iron or brass around the neck, in addition to
the bracelet. Such necklaces are hung around the neck of Eyinle images in southwestern Yorubaland (cf. pls. 84, 88, 91, 92, and 93).
[19] It is believed that Eyinle used to put on ṣaba; their jingle would announce his
arrival each time he returned from hunting in the forest of Ajagusi, his father.
[20] Eyinle pottery has been used as dance regalia, balanced on the heads of devotees, at Ajilete (pl. 95), at Ago-Oko (Àgọ́-Oko), Ijaiye (Ìjàìyè), and Ibara quarter,
Abeokuta, and even apparently, among the cultists of the related Yoruba hunter-god,
Oṣoosi, in Bahia.

eyinlè). Effigy jars are round, with the neck transformed into a human head. Following this analogy, the widest part of the vessel is seen as a belly, with encircling arms and projecting breasts placed above. Coffee-bean eyes (small ovals bearing a horizontal slit) and other details are clearly in the dominant mode of Abatan. The lids to effigy jars are hats or wiglike depictions of coiffure. The figure makes a gesture: one hand is placed on the belly, the other upon the breast. One finds in some Oyo villages votive wood images (*ère eleyinlè*), representing devotees or priests and priestesses.[21] The sculpture of the town of Ilobu is the richest hoard (Beier, 1957) of votive sculpture for Erinle (Eyinle), appropriate for the town near the point at which it is believed Eyinle entered the earth and became a flowing stream.

Eyinle shrines must have a wrought-iron staff for the medicine god or to honor the river-god's own considerable powers of healing. And, above all, there must be present an earthenware, lidded vessel, filled with fluvial water and stones. Of all the elements of Eyinle worship it seems that the categorically imperative items are the chain bracelet and the earthenware vessel. They form the irreducible unit of the cult paraphernalia.

[21] It may be that Eyinle is sometimes directly represented by a fish-legged human figure, an ancient symbol of divine power and kingship in Nigeria. In the study collection of the Nigerian Museum, Lagos (57.1.1), there is a carved wooden pedestal (*odó ṣàngó*) for the thunder-god, from Oyo country, bearing the depiction of a figure holding mudfish feet in each hand and "said to represent Erinle." Murray (1951*b*) discovered a similar representation, allegedly of Eyinle, in southwestern Yoruba country during the Atinga episode: it is a frontal emblem representing a human figure with raised arms that hold fish legs so that the fish feet are level with the shoulders. It is interesting that the superb pot for the thunder-god (Frobenius, 1913) bears two mudfish-legged images; this chimerical being can hardly be said to represent a human devotee, and the presence of a river serpent (for Oṣun or Erinle) makes it likely that Eyinle, whose ties to the thunder-god are extremely close, is being represented here. Outside the thunder-god cult context the motif has many meanings; the sculptor Owoeye (Owóèyè) of Efon-Alaiye told me that the mudfish-legged figure he carved on a door to the palace of the Oni of Ife stands for Oduduwa, the mythic progenitor of the Yoruba people; some Ijebu maintain the image represents the spirit of earth. In 1965, in a Columbia University symposium on "Art and Leadership in Africa," Douglas Fraser discussed this enigmatic symbol.

The vernacular name of the vessel among Egbado and neighboring peoples is *awo ota eyinle*[22] ("vessel for the stones of Eyinle"). These vessels are much larger than effigy jars, ranging from 10 to 17 inches high, in the main, in the known corpus of Abatan's works. We turn now to a detailed description of an *awo ota eyinle* made by Abatan in the early sixties.

First, all masses are dramatically curved. The primary curve sweeps up from an annular base, constricts at the neck, then flares again to form the second curve completed by the dome of the lid (pl. 81). The half-figure of a woman rises from the lid on four supports[23] (pl. 85). The side and rear supports are embellished with bosses. The front support, representing the chest with projecting breasts and connected to a small kola bowl which rests on the surface of the lid, is left plain (pl. 88). Rarely is the half-figure male.[24] The outer silhouette of the side supports, as if they were shoulders, form a third curve leading to the head, where a fourth and final curve fluently circumscribes coiffure and countenance. Below, in a gesture of positive import, the figure appears to hold, with symmetrically disposed schematic hands, a kola bowl. The arms emerge from the side supports. They form a forward curve of considerable elegance.

Within the area defined by the curves traditional detail is distributed. Small, spaced bosses encircle the pot, accenting the bottom curve. An emblem interrupts the line of the bosses, the central motif of which is the head of a ram, horns curving down to frame

---

[22] This term is often elided to *awota eyinle;* Anago Yoruba and some other groups sometimes further shorten the form, *awoteyinle.* When I used the full form for the first time in her presence, Abatan thanked me, as if I had pronounced a praise poem.

[23] To anticipate the argument on symbolism, the supports form the schematic rendering of a kind of Yoruba aristocratic headgear.

[24] Small, nubbin-like breasts, in one instance in combination with an exclusively male item of dress, the "dog-ear cap" (*filà abetí ajá*), mark the difference (cf. *Nigeria,* no. 37 [1951], 15).

coffee-bean eyes. A thunder-god dance ax and a single boss are placed on either side of the ram. This pattern is framed, in turn, by a calabash-rattle on one side, a serpent on the other (pl. 81).

Roulette impressions decorate the surface of the lid between the edge and the base of the supports. The borders of these impressions are cut with the edge of a cowrie shell into clay. The impressions vary according to the particular roller (*òyì*) used during a given period of the artist's career. The supports conceal a slight concavity at the center of the lid. The bosses that stud the supports normally number four, although three or five are not unknown, and the mother of Abatan seems to have favored seven. These bosses are framed by bands of impression in a pattern that normally repeats the embellishment of the top surface of the lid. The bands follow the curve of the arches formed by the meeting of the supports below the head and thus enhance superbly the continuity of the form (pl. 84).

The head of the woman commands the sculpture. Ears, in the form of the handles of a European cup, frame the face. Coffee-bean eyes, the nose, and small parallel lips compose a tight visual system. Equally crisp are the incisions indicating "tribal marks"; these are cut with a small, tin blade into the surface of the cheeks and forehead. The coiffure is normally done in the style called *oniidodo* (*oníìdodo*) (of which a clear actual example may be found worn by a young woman dancing to the right of the priestess who balances a pot lid on her head in pl. 95) which literally means "owner of the navel," an apparent reference to the prominent bun that is a marked characteristic of the mode. *Oniidodo* is highly favored by contemporary traditional Yoruba women. The hair is gathered in braids from the hairline toward the crown of the head, where the ends of the braid are formed into a bun. The longitudinal axes between the braids are shaved to form vertical parts. Abatan indicates the braids by means of rolled strips of clay which are applied to the crown of the head and polished after fixing with a moistened pebble. Abatan suggests the parts with roulette impressions, normally matching those on the lid, and three supports.

After firing, the potter polishes the inside and outside surfaces of the lid and the vessel with an *aṣọ wájì* (a cloth dipped in prepared indigo dye) and the decoration is alleged to be renewed every sixteen days by some devotees, imparting a magnificent ink-hued patina. The addition of gold earrings, iron or gold chains as necklaces, and miniature head ties and wrappers in sumptuous native or imported trade cloth completes a vision of consummate elegance (pl. 92).

ORAL LITERATURE AND ICONOGRAPHY

Liturgical "texts" when related to the vessel imply its sacred meaning. These texts are oral: praise poems, invocation, myth, and informal allegation. Comparison of Eyinle praise utterances with those for the cognate deities, Oshun and Yemoja, reveals concordances of imagery and nomenclature. If one proceeds "efficiently," examining only those oral literary materials directly concerned with Eyinle, it is possible to overlook the "symbol families" within which there is considerable blurring of the definition of one god into another. These groups are defined by the sharing of items of dance, regalia, praise, and art, but their presence does not mean that the gods are not distinguishable. They simply suggest that certain gods seem counterpart, as if they represented transformations, each of the other (cf. Lévi-Strauss, 1966a, pp. 75–108).

Eyinle pertains to three symbol families. Like the hunter Oṣoosi (Ọ̀ṣọ́ọ̀sì) (whom Verger implies in the Yoruba-derived cults of Bahia, Brazil, is virtually the same god), Eyinle is concerned with the use and love of iron and is closely related to the god of iron himself, Ogun (Ogún), who today is regarded as a kind of patron saint of all hunters. Oṣoosi's emblem is the miniature, iron bow and arrow, Eyinle's the miniature hunter's bangle. Eyinle also shares, in another logical grouping, the use of an iron staff surmounted by a bird or birds, as a reminder that three gods share this privileged form as a mark of common powers of herbalism, healing, and witchcraft. These gods are Ifa (Ifá), Osanyin (Òsanyìn), and Erinle, the last a northern Yoruba dialect form of the Egbado term, Eyinle.

But the most important concordance is the joint use of earthenware vessels filled with fluvial stones and water which characterizes the cults of Oshun, Yemoja, and Eyinle. Eyinle is most decidedly a spirit in the water, like the goddesses Oshun and Yemoja, and he presides over an entourage the very names of which are in some instances identical to some of the alternate names of the goddess Oshun (Verger, 1957, pp. 407–409).

The overlapping defines the god, Eyinle, as an amazing synthesis of powers of the hunt, herbalism, and water. Praise poems describe him as someone who comprehends the hunter's drum, as versed in curing the troubled head, and as water from which one takes and takes and never finishes, water that one bails and bails and yet is never dry.[25] Art rephrases this. The use of the miniature bangles speaks of the hunt, the bird staff of herbalism, and the storage vessel of the river and the sea.[26]

The Meaning of the Vessel and Its Contents

Cult singing enriches our understanding of the relationship between the deity and his element. Eyinle, as if he were a fish, lives within the water:

[25] The sources are as follows: (1) *Iru àgèrè l'ó gbọ* ("He hears the sound of the hunter's drum") was collected by Verger (1957, p. 219) at Ilobu; (2) "The confused head he will cure"—vernacular not given—is from Beier (1959); (3) *Omi abùbùtán, omi agbọ́n-ìgbẹ* ("Water from which one takes and takes and never finishes, water which we bail and bail and yet is never dry") was transcribed at an Aworri village near Badagrí in August, 1964. The word, *abùbùtan*, I think, puns on a first name of Eyinle, Abatan. The use of puns among the Yoruba was first noted, perhaps, by Bowen (1857, p. 288).

[26] These attributes do not exhaust the nature of Eyinle. Johnson (1906, p. 245) refers to Erinle as "god of eloquence" and the *Oxford Dictionary of the Yoruba Language* (p. 71) refers to him as "god of song, an elephant."

Our father, who dwells below the surface of the water,
Most important deity within the water.[27]

Myths characterize the history of the miracle. Thus an Oke-Odan
version by Àyìde Ọdúnláàmì:[28]

> Eyinle was a man. He had a maize and eree [*erèé*] bean farm. He lived on
> this farm with his children. After they had worked on the farm they came
> back to the farm hut, one day, and prepared *eree* beans and maize, drying
> the maize on the fire together with the beans. They began to eat. After they
> ate the beans and dried maize there was no drinking water and they were
> very, very thirsty. Eyinle then called his eldest son, Àìná, and told him that
> they would soon see water and that when they did they would never see
> their father again. After water appears, he commanded, worship the place
> where I enter the earth, and when you worship me bring dried beans and
> dried maize together with alligator pepper. So saying, he fell back, hands
> held high over his head and at the same time [Odunlaami at this point
> breaks into a beatific smile] water burst out of the earth. Before the sons
> of Eyinle realized that their father had entered the ground they drank the
> water. After they had drunk to their satisfaction they suddenly realized
> their father was gone but that they had been saved. This is the origin of
> water.

The foods eaten in feasts for Eyinle are those mentioned in the
myth. They are decidedly thirst provoking. This may have been intended to remind the devotee that water is a privileged blessing.
Here is another myth, told by an Aworri divination priest:[29]

[27] This song is a composite: an epithet collected at Ntetu (Ntẹ̀tù), Ipapo (Ìpàpó),
in July, 1965, has been combined with another praise from Owo in Aworriland, transcribed in August, 1964. The former is *Baba wa ṁbẹ ní ìsàlè-omi*, the latter, *Òrìṣà ṅlá
inú omi*.

[28] Cf. the theme of self-sacrifice and salvation which appears in a myth about
the origin of the river-goddess, Yewa: "It is said that the Iyewa lagoon was a woman,
one poor woman. [She had] two children and she had a hard time bringing them
up. . . . One day she and her children wandered far into the forest and got lost. They
searched in vain for the path back, and tormented by thirst, they rested under a tree.
The woman, seeing her children at the point of dying, prostrated herself on the
ground and called the gods to help her save her children. Yewa was transformed into
a lagoon from which the children drank and were saved. . . ."

[29] The distinction between the straightforward narrative of the first myth and
the richly exegetic quality of the second reflects, I suggest, considerable synthesis on

There once was a powerful herbalist named Abatan, nicknamed Erin [Elephant] because of his size. He lived and worked at Ile-Ife where his reputation as healer was considerable. The Aláààfin of Oyo-Ile called for Erin one day, inviting him to come to his capital. Erin consulted the oracle. The oracle warned him not to go. Erin made propitiatory sacrifices and departed, regardless, for Oyo-Ile. At a point halfway between the two cities his foot struck a poisonous stone. The stone immediately overcame his protective medicines (given Erin by the Ọni of Ife) and Erin died instantly. He changed into a flowing stream, later to bear his name. After the transformation his name changed from Erin to Erinle, which means Elephant-Into-Earth [Erin + ilè]. Abatan became Erinle at a point near Ilobu, and to this day his most important shrines are found there.

There are other myths. Examples have been published by Johnson (1921, p. 37) and Frobenius (1948, p. 222). The recurrent theme is transformation of a man into water. The water in the vessel suggests the primordial stream. Abatan herself says that "when we call Eyinle there, he will answer, whenever we are unable to go to the river." The vessel encloses the river. It brings the power of the river and the sea to the hearth.

Viewed as part of the river, the water in the vessel must reflect the freshness of the source. It must be changed regularly. It is taboo to collect the water from a well or from any body of stagnant water. Only water from the sea or from the river, water that is in motion *omi ti ṣon (omi tí ṣòn)*, is appropriate.

To continue the story of Eyinle after he disappeared into the swirling depths, as much as one can piece it together from shards of praise poetry, he founded an underwater kingdom at Kobaye. Details are shadowy as a function of the generic quality of many of the verses, for praise literature does not develop novelistic likenesses but consists instead of stylized, percussive fragments, often

the part of the diviner, perhaps collating various verses from different parts of Yorubaland, as from reference volumes, and arriving at an impressive synthesis. Or the crisp resolution of puzzling, cult detail may reflect the internal logic of the divination literature of the Yoruba, forever a mirror of analysis for its own sake.

recombined to the beat of drums, establishing an impressive mood and forceful atmosphere but never portraiture:[30]

[30] A version recited to me by Abatan on August 14, 1964. Her words were as follows:

> Eyinlẹ̀
> Aganna àgbò
> Aní jẹ́-nímọ̀
> Ogúnjùbí (lit., "Ogun exceeds the lineage")
> Ogúngbolu a bá èrò Òde Kobaye.
> Ọ̀yọ́ gorí ìlú (lit., "Oyo sits upon the towns")
> Oloyè ńlá,
> Arôdòdó ṣé ìgbànú esin (lit., "who puts a belt of red cloth around his horse")
>
> Gbogbo igi gbárijọ, wọn fi Ìrokò se baba nínú oko
> Gbogbo ilẹ̀ gbárijọ, wọn fi Okítì se baba nínú oko
> Gbogbo odò kékéké ti ńbẹ nínú igbó Ajagusi wọn gbárijọ,
>   won fi Àbátàn jọba nínú omi.
>
> Baba mi lọ l'òkun, òkun dákẹ́
> O nlọ l'ọ̀sà, ọ̀sà mì tìtì
> Ọ̀yọ́lọlá nlọ l'òkun, òkun mì lẹ̀gbẹlẹ̀gbẹ
> Omi ọlọ́lá.

The structure is extremely interesting. The name of the deity is called, then a first quality (Aganna of the ram), a second, a third, and so on until seven qualities have been enumerated. There follows a mirrored paradox—the silent sea, the turbulent lagoon—a technical refinement that is characteristic of the high quality of the verbal art of Abatan's lineage. A hierarchy of natural elements is suggested, with real authority, in the "stanza" beginning "all the trees assemble." The "forest of Ajagusi" seems to refer to the forest of the father of Eyinle (cf. Johnson, 1906, p. 86). When I asked Abatan to recite the same *oriki* on April 21, 1966, nearly two years later, the order of the opening litany was considerably changed, including an evidently new line about the fact that the "sea is worthy of respect because of its sheer size." She interrupted the expected flow of the "second stanza" with rhythmic repetitions of the verb, "assemble, assemble," then cited the epithet, "most important chief, who uses a crimson cloth to wrap around his horse." The interruption of the expected course of the naming was almost cinematographic, or musical in nature. Doubtless a careful study of the art of a praise singer, restricted to a particular class of praises and conducted on historical principles, would shed light on the problems of formal development and improvisation, especially as to the timing and recombining of ancient themes.

Eyinle
Aganna of the ram
Someone who eats knows what he has eaten
If you wish to rely on your lineage it is better to rely on Ogun
Ogun accepts the lord who accompanies the pilgrims to Ode (Òde Kobaye)
Oyo the highest of all towns
O most important chief,
Who uses a crimson cloth to wrap around his horse.

All the trees assemble and make Ìrokò father in the forest
All the lands assemble and make Mound father in the forest
All the small streams of the forest of Ajagusi assemble,
And make Abatan king within water.

My father is going on the sea, the sea remains silent
He is going on the lagoon, the lagoon trembles profoundly
Oyo-Is-Honor is going on the sea, the sea is in brilliant
  motion
The water of the lord who is worthy of respect.

Abatan herself greets the deity by means of these praises, rehearsing the association of the god with the powerful master of iron, Ogun, and repeating, in glittering images, how Eyinle is the suzerain of water, and how his exemplary character lifts this basic element of nature to a level of reflected virtue.

Passages of the litany shed light on the history of the vessel that stores the water from the river of Eyinle. It is extremely important to note that Ode Kobaye (the term *òde* denotes a large settlement with a central square as opposed to a farm village), the mythical underwater city of the court of Eyinle, is considered an extension of Oyo culture. Explicit Oyo imagery together with implicit allusions like the red garment, perhaps associated with the Oyo cult of the thunder-god, establish a link between Kobaye and the imperial capital. The cult of Eyinle (or Erinle) must have been part of the religious life of the metropolis since time immemorial.

An examination of the evidence on Oyo-Ile pottery reveals that the *iṣaasun* (*ìṣáàsùn*) dominated the ceramic art of the capital. The *iṣaasun* is a round-bottomed, carinated vessel with everted rim, covered with a lid with concave center (Willett, 1960, p. 76; King, 1962, p. 21). This physical description immediately recalls Eyinle pottery.

The *iṣaasun* thus provided the grain of sand around which the form of vessels for the riverain king was spun. There were many solutions to the problem of metamorphosis. The working method of Abatan hints of the probable line of development characterizing several southwestern Yoruba "styles" of Eyinle pottery. She begins by making an *iṣaasun* lid. She then adds an abstract ornament over the center of the lid, consisting of two intersecting arches in openwork. (The Oyo mode documented by Frobenius and copied by Abraham goes virtually no further than this theoretical level of development.) She adds human detail to the ornament. She makes an *iṣaasun* pot over a mold and adds low-relief symbols and a line of bosses around the midsection. The dominant ceramic form of the ancient capital of the Oyo Yoruba becomes, after an artistic evolution, an emotional experience. The achievement honors the stones that the vessel harbors.

When Abatan and the head of the male worshipers of Eyinle at Oke-Odan initiate a person into the cult of the river-god, they give him two stones together with a small amount of river sand. The stones are the sign of Eyinle. The sand is said to suggest the endlessness of his lineage, his friends, his followers. The two stones are placed upon the head of the novice: their force is believed to penetrate his character and fortune and to protect him in a fundamental way. The stones are later placed in a vessel that the devotee purchases for his own altar. The stones (and sand, if used) are covered with river water and serve as the seal of initiation, conferring upon the individual the dignity of spiritual affiliation.

The stones are believed to bear children.[31] When the annual

[31] A belief that seems to have been carried to Cuba by Yoruba slaves. Bascom (1950, p. 65) found that "the real power of the [Cuban Yoruba deities] resides in the stones, hidden behind a curtain in the lower part of the altar, without which no [Cuban Yoruba cult] shrine could exist. The stones of the saints are believed to have life. Some stones can walk and *some can even have children*" (my italics).

feast for Eyinle is celebrated, they multiply under the water. The dogma is energetically espoused: one does not place stones in the water in the vessel—the spirit increases itself. After she initiated me into the cult, Abatan revealed what in fact happens. "When we bathe in the river if we see any stones we can bring them to the vessel but before we can do this we have to have been initiated and to have received the two properly consecrated stones."

The increase of the stones thus metaphorically declares their power. It is also a precise measure of devotion; if Eyinle is loved and festivals are enacted in his honor (and the owner of the pot is living), the multiplication of the stones is assured and continuous. (A defunct cult is graphically indicated by an empty *awo ota eyinle*, filled with spider webs and dusty stones.) Old vessels in devout households are consequently filled with stones submerged in the water. The vessel of a member of a western Aworri village contains some fifty stones, including the two stones of initiation, and most of them are visible in pl. 83. (Future research will determine whether there is a mean correlation between years and stones.[32] If there is, we have a real boss tool for the dating of the pots, a science that we take the liberty of designating in advance petrochronology.)

When the lid is closed and the stones are concealed (normally to be viewed only during feasts) the presence of the stones is communicated by the bosses decorating the bulge of the pot and the supports on the lid. Abatan has stated that each boss stands for a river stone. Following this, it seems to me that the two stones that form part of the emblem at the face of the vessel suggest the sign of initiation,[33] a sign that further suggests a promise of increase fulfilled by the multitude of bosses.

[32] That there is a correlation between annual festivals for Eyinle and the increase of the stones is suggested by the following allegations: (Aworri) Ó mà pa ọmọ ní ọdọdún ("It keeps on producing children every year"); (Egbado) Ìgbàkúgbà tí a ba ti ṣé ọdún lo ma npọ̀ sí ("Whenever we celebrate the festival it multiplies"). As to the notion of increase as an element of African art, a most gifted student is Fagg (1963).

[33] Or a pair of thunder celts, as in the vessel illustrated in Frobenius 1913, p. 215. The shape of the representation of the stones on this vessel tends to confirm the exegesis of Abatan at the same time that it suggests a transformation, from celt, to fluvial stones, in the development of the motif in Oke-Odan pottery history.

The most important artistic reflection of the stones as a sign of plenty is the character of the figural sculpture. The swelling belly of the effigy jar, the exponential waist of the central figure of the altar (pl. 94), the engorged (i.e., milk-distended) breasts of the figure dominating the lid of the vessel (pl. 82), all powerfully recast the exciting notion into sculpture. One might consider the vessel a kind of womb, harboring the fertile stones, but a uterine metaphor has never been mentioned by any informant. It is true, however, that Abatan calls the stones the children of Eyinle and alleges that each rock or pebble is given a water name, such as Omikunle (Omikúnlé) or Omidiji (Omidìji).

The left-hand-on-swelling-belly motif linking various forms of the panoply of Abatan's art may be compared with Jan Van Eyck's "Wife of Giovanni Arnolfini" in which the wife, holding up her garment, places her left hand on belly in a similar way, indicating fertility and the role of woman. Figures in the Oke-Odan tradition complete, in their nudity, the suggestion by holding the right breast with the right hand, allegedly a "sign of sucking," and a final evocation of human continuity.

In sum, four meanings are attached to the stones. They are emblems of immortality, longevity, the crossing of the frontier between the sacred and the profane, and the promise of increase. Their multiplication is a beautiful restatement of the endlessness of water, the infinity of Eyinle.

THE CROWN

Eyinle is a king in the water. To express this dominant image, Abatan, as her mother before her, surmounts the lid of the vessel with the representation of a crown. It is not the conical, beaded crown with beaded fringes worn by Yoruba rulers on ceremonial occasions, the so-called clan crown. It is, rather, a special form of headgear, said to have been called *adodo*, believed to have been worn by Eyinle when he was traveling. The representation gives rise to the "peculiar pottery piece" noted by Beier in 1957: it is an openwork structure consisting of two arches that cross each other at a point above the center of the lid. Translation of the sovereign headdress into clay considerably thickens its elements and makes its recognition difficult to outsiders; to compound the enigma, as it were, the Oke-Odan potter adds a human head above the point of the intersection of the arches. So strongly does the ornament denote kingship that Abatan has referred to the structure as a crown (*adé*), virtually as a synonym for the usual term, lid.

The intersecting-arch crown prominently appears in the regalia of a few rival cults. Those who worship the thunder-god's elder sister may wear, during their annual festival, a cowrie-embroidered crown whose four supports are flat, meeting at the top to form a truncated pyramid (Beier, 1957, pl. 22). In the Ile-Ife area and in some other parts of Yorubaland the cult of the important river-goddess Oşun, also calls for a form, which I might designate the crown-lid.[34] It is virtually identical with certain nonfigurate Eyinle modes. A masterpiece of the genre may be found in the study collection of the Ife Museum in Nigeria. Elegantly formed and polished (but lacking the indigo patination of Eyinle pottery) the Ife piece is perhaps the finest nonfigurate terra-cotta crown-lid yet collected (Ife Museum, 63/9).

The potters of Old Oyo may have been inspired by ceremonial headgear, the ultimate origin of which was Afro-Islamic. One finds a distribution of related intersecting-arch crowns from the Agni of the Ivory Coast (Amon d'Aby, 1960, pl. 1), through Niger (Maquet, 1965, p. 33) and Kano in northern Nigeria (Shell Company, 1962, p. 53) to the chiefdom of Rey Bouba[35] in Northern

[34] Verger (1957, pp. 424, 426, 429) has published references to the nobility of Oşun and to the belief that she is as powerful as a king (*Oşun pe ó tóbi lí oba*) at Osogbo. At Ileşa, near Ile-Ife, the right of Oşun to wear a crown, despite her sex, is explicitly considered: *Ó jó rù gbà adé* ("She dances carrying a crown for a time"). At Ipetu the interesting phrase is sung for Oşun: *Aladé obinrin sòwón* ("A crowned woman is rare").

[35] At the exhibition, "Negro Art: Sources, Evolution, Expansion," mounted at the Musée Dynamique at Dakar, Senegal, by the Commission of the First World Festival of Negro Arts in April, 1966, two intersecting-arch crowns from Rey Bouba in northern Cameroun were exhibited (they were not listed in the catalogue).

Cameroun. The form shared by the last three examples is a round base, usually covered with crimson cloth, with a shaft rising from the center, from the top of which descend four metal ribs, forming two intersecting arches. All have at the summit a small globe or decorative device that may or may not serve as the base for feathers. These crowns are clearly cognate (although not identical) with the terra cotta crowns of Eyinle cult tradition (where the lid is the base and the central shaft is omitted). The Agni example, however, is almost identical with the *ade eyinle*.[36] These similarities suggest to me ancient contact, mediated by trade at Oyo-Ile, with the Islamic-headgear traditions of the western Sudan, a suggestion that dovetails with the probability that Islamic armor has had an impact upon the development of the clan crowns of the Yoruba and Edo peoples (Thompson, unpub., 1966). The Eyinle crown, in any event, is not an isolated phenomenon but is a branch, translated into the medium of pottery, of a distinguished history of West African regalia.

One of the most interesting manifestations of the tradition is the tomb of Chief Taiwo (Táíwò) on Broad Street in Lagos. This monumental rendering of the intersecting arches[37] of the *adodo*

[36] Cf. the statuette commemorating Amondjomo Bile of the Agni of Sanwi. I am grateful to Mr. George Preston, a graduate student at Columbia University, for bringing this reference to my attention. Brass, intersecting-arch crowns have also been found at Djerma, between Dosse and Niamey in Niger, and a fine example may be seen in the exhibition collection of African art at the Musée de l'Homme, Paris.

[37] The probability of an alternate or dual provenience must be entertained, for the impact of Western culture upon the island of Lagos has been continuous for more than one hundred years. Perhaps it would be best to refer to the tomb of Chief Taiwo as a hybrid form, given the unmistakable Brazilian baroque influences. But whereas the main structure of an obvious borrowing from British regalia, a crown of the Dágburewe of Ìdọwá in Ijebu Yoruba country (Ogúnba, 1964, p. 260) has the traditional alternation of four *fleurs-de-lys* with four *crosses-pattes*, which have traditionally heightened the circlet of the British crown since the time of Henry VIII (Davenport, 1897, pp. 23–24), the crown over the resting place of Taiwo does not. Moreover, Taiwo was deeply involved in the traditional life of his people and one of the three Gelede societies of the Lagos area is said to be administered by his descendants. A Gelede image, carved in his memory, marks a fully traditional pendant piece to the hybrid tomb.

crown, whitewashed and embellished with baroque detail, communicates to the prepared eye that a chiefly personage is buried underneath. Similarly, the crown on the lid communicates the aristocratic nature of the extraordinary power suggested by the stones within the vessel.

THE EYINLE CIRCLE

After he turned into a stone, as it is believed at Oke-Odan, Eyinle is said to have married a woman named Oten (Ọ̀tẹ̀n). She became his queen. Her face is compared in praises to the countenance of the iron god,[38] himself handsome and light-complexioned, to illustrate the quality of its beauty. Eyinle and Oten sired many children in their domain, rearing, in addition, serpents in the water as messengers.

All children born to Eyinle below the water—as opposed to children, like Aina, born before the apotheosis—take the honorific title Ibu (Ibú)[39] ("depths of the water"). The term is both an epithet of distinction and designation of divine residence: the Ibu are both the holy depths of the river and the special spirits, the descendants of Eyinle and his friends, who live within them. At Ilobu

[38] Ọ̀tẹ̀n Eleyinjú Ogún ("Oten-of-the-same-face-as-Ogun"). In western Anago country a similar praise, locally called *orúki*, is used to salute Ibu Ojutu with a different interpretation: "Owner-of-eyes-(pushing outward)-like-those-of-Ogun."

[39] Abraham (1958, p. 12) defines the term indirectly in considering the name Adelabu (Adélabú) ("Crown passed through deep water," *ibú*). Delano (1958, p. 94) says that *ibú* is: *Apá ibi tí ó jìn púpò lárin omi* ("Place in the water where it is very deep").

Ibu is also a title of Yemoja (the Yemanya of the New World Yoruba). She is known as Ibú Gbà Iyanrì ("Depth-taking-sand") and Ibú Aláró ("Depth-the-indigo-seller"). The concept of the *ibu* is also shared by the cult of Oṣun, of which an account follows: "The people of Oshogbo and the Ataoja have a pact with the River Oshun. They believe that the spirit of Oshun the goddess lives in the River Oshun and has her palace at a site in the river near Oshogbo. They believe also that all the deep places in the River Oshun, from Igede, the source of the river to the Lekki lagoon where the river empties its waters, are inhabited by the spirits of all the followers, devotees, and friends of Oshun when she was alive. They call these deep places Ibu" (Verger, 1957, p. 408).

devotees are reliably reported to believe that Ibu Àkànbí (Akanbi) or Ibu Owala are different spots on the river, or that they are the children of Erinle, or followers and priests. Actually, they may be all of these things. Their definition is appropriately blurred and hazy.

Abatan often calls the names of these riverain spirits: Ibu Ojutu (Ojútú), sometimes known as Ibu Akanbi (Àkànbí), light-complexioned, like his mother and famed for a body as hard and beautiful as polished beads;[40] Ibu Aboto (Àbòtó)[41] or Ibu Oṣekeji (Oṣékejì), responsible for collecting water for her father; Ibu Igberi (Igbẹri),[42] a woman who wears with pride a dazzling chain of brass; Ibu Ondu, tempestuous and rich, who once killed (by drowning him) a Muslim who dared to make his ablutions in the water of Eyinle without respect; Ibu Jagun, descended from warriors, but also known as Ibu Alamo (Álámó)[43] and characterized as the paddler for Eyinle; Ibu Oyan (Ọ̀yán), who presides over a river on the western boundary of the Ibarapa; Ibu Oṣo (Ọṣọ); Ibu Ofenken (Ofẹnkẹn); Ibu Ofiki (Òfìkì), master of a river at Iganna in western Oyo country; and Ibu Obaluaiye-Ore-Abatan (Ibú Ọbalúaiyé-Ọ̀rẹ́-Abatan) (Smallpox-the-comrade-of-Abatan). The name of Otin (Ọ̀tìn), a goddess who gives her name to a stream flowing through what are now Ilorin (Ìlọrin) and Oshun divisions, sometimes appears in the list. Some Egbado Ibu appear to correspond to

---

[40] Erinle himself is also compared with beads: *Ò tẹbẹ bí ìlẹ̀kẹ̀* ("He is brilliant like a bead") (*ibid.*, p. 219). Abatan says all *oriki* for Ibu come from Eyinle, "who gave birth to them all."

[41] She is believed to fetch the water from the deepest part of the water (cf. Oṣun Aboto [*ibid.*, p. 409]).

[42] I have heard Yemoja praised, at Ibara in Abeokuta, with the phrase *Ògùn Igberi Àsábá* (Igberi-Asaba-river-Ogun). A Porto-Novan fragment of praise, *Yemoja ògùn beri*, relates to the epithet.

[43] In Bahia, Brazil, Oṣun Yeye Ponda is said to be married to Oṣoosi Ibualama, a warrior who carries a sword. The characterization of Ibu Alama as a warrior would appear to confirm a historical basis for the image of Ibu Alamo as indistinguishable from Ibu Jagun ("Depth-the-warrior"). The Bahian myth is probably at least as old as the period of active slaving.

those worshiped in Oyo, as evidenced not only by their relationship with specific northern Yoruba rivers, the Oyan, the Ofiki, and the Otin, but also in terms of the names of four of the main shrines of Ilobu: Akanbi, Ibu Alamo, Apala, and Ondu. This does not mean that the details of their worship are identical in both provinces.

Frobenius (1948, p. 133) has written a very salutary warning to the effect that the images of Yoruba art rarely represent the gods and that the overwhelming majority of votive sculpture represents priests or devotees. The sole exception, in his view, was the "clearly recognizable" representation of Eshu (Èshù), the famous trickster. More recently Beier (1957) and Carroll (1967, p. 51) have repeated this point. The observation applies correctly to perishable wood sculpture, but it is not a matter of law in terms of the permanent or relatively permanent media of brass, beads, stone, or terra-cotta. Representations of earth spirits in brass are reliably reported (Morton-Williams, 1960b). The skull-like faces with bared teeth and patrilineal markings on the Yoruba beaded clan crown almost unquestionably represent ancestral spirits, especially the founder of the Yoruba kingships, Oduduwa (Odùduwà) (Thompson, unpub., 1966). And the keeper of a certain stone image at Oke Ahun, a village on a hill overlooking Efon Alaiye (Èfòn Àláìyè) in eastern Yorubaland, insists that the face represents a deity of the earth. In addition, the awesome headdresses of the Egungun (Egúngún) cult, those drenched with indigo and weighted with skulls, vials, and other heterogeneous objects, definitely represent spirit inquisitors. Both representations of the trickster and images surmounting trays worn by spirit inquisitors are darkened with indigo among the northern Oyo. And, of course, *awo ota eyinle* are also so darkened. Use of indigo seems to denote rank, as in the dyeing of indigo thread, where the darker the thread the more expensive (Bascom, 1967). The fact that vessels and altars for Eyinle are completely painted with indigo sets them above the level of the usual, just as a photograph by Bascom of the door of the palace of the king of Ila-Orangun (Ìlá-Òràngún) reveals that the figure of the king, alone among a host of images in relief, is rubbed with indigo. Where indigo darkens statuary and architecture it suggests aristocracy and the extraordinary.

I believe it is possible to accept at face value the frequent allegation that the human images on the lid of the *awo ota eyinle* and on the sides of the household altar signify members of the family and entourage of Eyinle. It would seem that the cult of the underwater king is an important exception to the "rule" that godhead is not directly adumbrated by Yoruba sculpture.[44]

The central figure of the piece (pl. 81), which I attribute to the late nineteenth century, is alleged to represent Oten with children, as is a neoclassic piece by Abatan (pl. 91). The altars of Oke-Odan without exception (I have been shown four) are said to represent Oten flanked by Eyinle and Ibu Jagun. Across the Yewa River in Ajilete (Ajílété) the shrine of the master dancer, Omikunle, has four images in mud sculpture, representing Ibu Oyan, Ibu Jagun, Abatan, and Ibu Obaluaiye (Ọbaluáiyé). The male protagonists in the Oke-Odan altars by Abatan make identical positive gestures —right hand on heart, left hand on belly—and regard the world with calm and confidence.

The character of minor embellishment strengthens the likelihood that actual deities are represented in the Eyinle tradition because the choice of detail seems directly motivated by items of

---

[44] Compare the following statements, the first by an Aworri priest, the second by Abatan, the potter, herself: (1) *Ò jẹ ìyàwó Eyinlẹ̀ atipé ẹṣọ́ rẹ̀ ni* ("It is the wife of Eyinle and his ornament"); (2) *Eleyinlẹ̀ pọdọ ni àwo ọta eyinlẹ̀ nítorí ki ó bá lè mọ̀ ohun tì ó sìn atipé èyí ni lati ti ma ṣé ètùtù tí ó bá fẹ́ bọ* ("The Eyinle devotee must have an *awo ota eyinle* so that he knows what he is worshiping. In addition, this will be the place to expiate shortcomings whenever it is necessary to make sacrifice"). To regard only the functional aspect of these and many similar comments, namely, that the image is decoration and focus of sacrifice, is to overlook crucial symbolic qualities. Note that Abatan says "to know *what* we are worshiping," not "the devotees among whom we worship." Moreover, if the fish-legged motif can, with future studies, be more precisely linked with Eyinle, the emotional qualities that saturate, for devotees, the consideration of Eyinle pottery and altars will be shown to form part of a larger "structural perspective." For a rewarding discussion of similar problems of symbolism see Turner, 1967, pp. 25–27.

praise poetry pertaining to Eyinle and the Ibu. A follower of Eyinle at Ajilete told me that the woman on the lid of her *awo ota eyinle* represented Ibu Igberi (significantly, her own list of the denizens of the deep began with this spirit), and that she had placed brass jewelry around the neck of the figure to illustrate the praise epithet,[45] "Ibu Igberi, Owner-of-the-chain-of-brass." Examination of the elements of the altars of Eyinle at Oke-Odan reveals an astonishing use of cowrie-shell mosaic, as embellishment of head-gear and coiffure, inspired by a praise poem that describes these special spirits as crowned with money (cowrie shells were the pre-colonial money of the Yoruba) (pl. 94).

THE EMBLEM

I call the decorative device on the face of the vessel (pl. 81) an "emblem" because the elements of the design have been expressly ordered—a central motif is flanked by items of thunder-god and riverain-god worship. Common counters of devotion are given un-common meaning because they have been systematically po-sitioned and more or less uniformly scaled. The ram's head at center is said to represent a sacrificial ram.[46] The thunder-god axes recall the important friendship shared by Eyinle and Shango (Shàngó), the lord of thunder. Whenever there is a storm, it is said, Eyinle will run to beg the thunder-god to calm the tempest so that the people will not die. The *sere* (*sérè*), the calabash-rattle, is another easily identifiable prerogative of the cult of the thunder-god.

[45] Similarly, the clothworkers of Abomey, in Dahomey, are motivated in their choice of decorative themes by newly adopted "strong names" of important per-sonages.

[46] It may also refer to the praise verse for Eyinle, Aganna-of-the-ram. In fact the present owner of one of the works of Abatan discussed in this study (pls. 83, 84) pointed to the ram's head and said that it signified Eyinle. It is worth pointing out, as potentially relevant, the fact that the most famous epithet for Yewa, the river that flows past Oke-Odan and whose depths are shared by spirits of Eyinle and Oṣun, is, in the Oke-Odan sector, *Àgnò Dúdú, Oníìdògò* ("Dark-colored-ram, Lord-of-Idogo"). The Yewa River runs past Idogo north of Oke-Odan.

(Eyinle worshipers, allegedly, never use this musical instrument in their own order of service.) The snake alludes to one of the three vows[47] taken by a person who becomes worshiper of Eyinle—never to eat the flesh of any serpent, for serpents, as we have already seen, are the messengers of the riverain spirits.

The Kola Bowl, Cicatrization, Coiffure

Three elements of iconography remain. They are considered as a unit because they represent, to varying degrees, an incursion of the world of the real in the world of the ideal. The small bowl held in the hand of the central figure is called the kola bowl (*àwo obì*) and is meant to contain kola nuts for sacrifice or divination. The container also shelters coins and two cowrie shells, the latter two elements used in divination. When Abatan makes an Eyinle vessel she normally includes a small separate cover for the kola bowl, but the cover is usually lost or broken within a few years of use, hence none appear in the photographs (but compare *Nigeria*, no. 15). The allusions to the emblems of worship on the face of the vessel are surmounted by a kola bowl that, despite its small scale, actually functions. It provides the lid with a focus of action and a point of rest. The near passivity of the means by which the figure holds the kola bowl is a perfect expression of divine calm.

The cicatrization on the cheeks and forehead of the figure, often cut to resemble the "marks" of the patron of the pot, relates the image to actual life. Like the portraits of donors at the base of some paintings of the crucifixion, cicatrization, albeit by means more "coded" and abstract, relates the patron to the work of art. It also enhances the notion that the gods of the depths are remote progenitors of the followers of the cult.

The highly favored coiffure, *oniidodo*, relates the sculpture to

[47] These vows are (1) never to eat snakes, (2) never to eat elephant, (3) when one has a fight, the offense must be forgotten on the day of its happening—hate must not be in your heart a second day (cf. Eph. 4:26, "Let not the sun go down upon your wrath").

its century. It also infuses the image with a quality of ephebism, further indicated by the flawless surfaces of the face and neck. Ephebism might be defined as the artistic rendering of a person of power with the full bloom of youth. Abatan associates *oniidodo* with youth—she calls it the hairstyle of the virgin (*wúndía*)—and to the extent one follows her, reading into the image the gleaming period of full bodily vigor, the concept of increase and the force of the stones are further expressed in a remarkable way.

SUMMARY OF THE ESSENTIAL SYMBOLISM

Of the panoply of Eyinle—iron chain-bracelet, fly whisk, fan, effigy jar, votive sculpture, wrought iron staff, and earthenware vessel—the position of the last element, the *awo ota eyinle* is paramount.

The very terms of the name of this element, "vessel for the stones [*ota*] of Eyinle," bracket the core element of the cult. It is the most important object because it contains the stones through which the command (*àṣẹ*) of Eyinle is made known. The vessel is composed of a lid (*ọmọrí*) and pot (*iyá*). The latter is decorated with symbols in low relief, the lid with a crown structure, roulette impressions, and indications (head, breasts, arms, hands), built upon the structure of the crown, of a woman holding a kola bowl. The *awo ota eyinle* is believed to enclose a portion of the river that Eyinle created, and within which he subsequently founded a royal city. The water, associated with the love of Eyinle for his children, is by extension an emblem of the "coolness" (concern, calm, order) without which the conditions that fulfill the spiritual dimension of life cannot be formulated. The vessel is linked to Old Oyo as to certain of its iconographic details (the dance ax and the calabash-rattle and perhaps the flanking stones allude to the virtual state religion of the Oyo, the cult of the thunder-god) and, more important, as to morphology: it is the *iṣaasun*, the paramount pottery form of Old Oyo, on a heroic scale.

The stones are counters of immortality, longevity, initiation, and increase. The last two qualities may be symbolized by the two bosses that form part of the emblem on the pot, as well as the bosses that encircle the vessel and embellish the supports on the lid. These supports are themselves defined, on the basis of the testimony of Abatan confirmed by comparison with the headgear traditions of certain Yoruba cults, as the shape of a Yoruba sovereign form of headdress which may be further compared with evidently cognate expressions in the Ivory Coast, Niger, northern Nigeria, and northern Cameroun.

The likeliest interpretation of the woman with kola bowl, and of the ensemble of human figures characteristic of Oke-Odan altars, is that voiced by the devotees: they represent members of the circle of Eyinle, sometimes the king himself, sometimes his wife, and still other times the royal couple with their helper, Jagun. The gesture of Oten, the wife, expresses increase, more dramatically manifested by the multiplication of the stones. The emblem organizes counters of worship whereas the kola bowl, cicatrization, and coiffure redress, by reference to actuality, the balance of a timeless representation.

Terra-cotta lids for Eyinle, like variations upon a musical theme, blur into discrete forms and blur again into other forms as one journeys from Oke-Odan to northern Oyo. This fact parallels the linguistic shift from the name Eyinle to Erinle and the differences between the myths and praise singing of the two areas. The recurrent theme is the crown upon the lid. The simplicity of this theme invites, and has wonderfully received, variation of great inventive wit. There are doubtless equally absorbing variations of the theme of transformation into water in Eyinle mythology but this problem is beyond the scope of this monograph.

We now turn our attention to the life and works of Abatan in order to ascertain precisely what happens when an individual accepts a traditional shape but at the same time expresses creative individuality. The definition of the phenomenon only leaps to life, however, when considered developmentally for the substance of art is historical.

A PORTRAIT OF THE POTTER

Abatan is a master of mud sculpture, pottery, and praise poetry. A group of thunder-god devotees once approached her compound during an initiation ceremony and sang of the days when she was also the finest dancer in the Yewa valley. Abatan responded, seated, with a delicate gesture of the hands. Traditional Oke-Odan relies upon the power of her memory to unfold the ancient salutes to the gods of the river.

On high occasions she wears a head tie, sometimes folded with spatial flair by one of her daughters, an embroidered cloth draped over her left shoulder (cf. Kingsley, 1901, p. 112), a crisp blouse embellished with a gold pendant, and a wrapper as expensive as the head tie (pl. 80). As the senior member of the cult of Oshun and Eyinle at Oke-Odan, Abatan lives a life of prestige, balanced just short of hauteur, in marked contrast with the alienation of many artists in the Western world.

Abatan has eleven names, here arranged as a stanza for convenience:

Abatan (Àbátàn)	I-wish-we-might-spread-far[48]
Odefunke (Odẹfúnkẹ)	Hunter-gives-us-one-to-indulge
Ayinke (Àyìnkẹ)	Child-whom-we-favor[49]

[48] The idea of prevalence or propagation attached to this name is very appropriate to the notion of the increase of the stones (cf. Abraham, 1958, p. 5). Babalola (1966, p. 72) has collected a folk etymology to the effect that "Abatan is a shortened version of Abibitan, which means 'One born in historic circumstances.'" Elsewhere in the same volume (p. 68) he gives a hunter's chant in which the word appears with the same tonal structure found in Abraham: Àbátàn (see also Abraham, 1958, p. 89).

[49] I am grateful to Oladipo Yemitan for translating this *oiriki* (see n. 54, below).

Ija   Ija
Omo-iko-bi-eni-so'gi (Ọmọ-ìkọ́-bí-ẹni-sọ'gi)
                                  Child-of-the-hook-like-
                                     someone-pecking-a-tree
Omo-r'Udofoyi (Ọmọ-r'Udofoyi)   Child-from-Udofoyi[50]
Omo-ogbogi-ṣe-dun (Ọmọ-ogbógi-ṣé-dùn)
                                  Child-of-the-ax-handle-
                                     sculptor
Omo-onila-eta-arawo (Ọmọ-onilà-ẹ́ta-àràwò)
                                  Child-of-three-facial-
                                     marks (like-the-three-
                                     prominent-stars-that-
                                     guide-the-hunter-in-
                                     the-night)[51]
Omo-Awo-de-ile-o-di-oluwa-e (Ọmọ-Awo-dé-ilé-ó-di-olúwa-è)
                                  Child-of-Awo-who-entered-
                                     the-house-to-become-its-lord
O Omo ejo wewewe abe irawe (Ọmọ̀ ejo wẹ́wẹ́wẹ́ abẹ́ ìràwẹ́)
                                  Child-of-the-small-snake-
                                     under-dead-leaves
Egberi-o-mo (Ẹ̀gbẹ̀rì-ò-mọ̀)   The-unitiate-is-unaware[52]

The elements of traditional Oyo nomenclature are discernible
here: first names, praise names, and clan-origin names.[53] The full

[50] The Araba of Lagos maintains that Udofoyi was located near Ile-Ife.

[51] It was Edwin Obayan, himself descended from hunters and familiar with the
arcana of their names, who was kind enough to supply a full form of this attributive
name. It fits the emphasis on hunting as an attribute of Eyinle.

[52] The most notable of Yoruba people are distinguished by the length of their
praise names. The complexity of Abatan's nomenclature singles her out as someone
remarkable, a scion of an accomplished lineage.

[53] Babalola (1966) very usefully points out that "the mere recognition that a
name is a personal name is not usually satisfying to a Yoruba man, for, as a rule,
Yoruba personal names have specific meanings." Biographers of Yoruba artists have
a special responsibility, not only to seek translations of each name, but also to ascertain that the full nomenclature has been recorded.

citation identifies the potter as an individual (Johnson, 1921, p. 87). Her parents believed that she came into the world through the grace of Eyinle. Accordingly, as an invocation, she received the name of the deity before his transformation, Abatan. This is a first name. Another first name is Odefunke, which communicates (in the reference to the hunt) that she was born the daughter of a follower of Eyinle, as well as the delight her parents took in her arrival. The short praise name Ayinke, is a further quintessence of familial sentiment. Emphasis on the fact that she is going to be favored is a reflection of the commonness in traditional Yoruba life of infant mortality, although it is certain she was very much wanted and was given much attention as a child. Ija is probably a clan-origin name. Like typical examples, it is short, comes after the first praise name, and does not make any sense by itself. The word was evidently inherited from her mother. Yoruba normally take the clan name of the father, but cases exist where both paternal and maternal clan names have been adopted. Iko is probably another clan-origin name for the word is so identified by Abraham (1958, p. 482).[54] Although the special phrases of her many names are sometimes enigmatic and have been inherited without explanation, their broad significance is that Abatan Odefunke Ayinke Ija was born to prestige.

Abatan is not certain of her chronological age. In the summer of 1964 she told me that she was more than ninety years old and in the summer of 1965 she said essentially the same thing, but these

---

The three elements of a Yoruba name among Oyo and Egbado are the *oruko* (*orúkọ*), the *oriki*, and *orile* (*orílè*) ("first name," "praise name," "group-origin name"). There are distinct kinds of *oruko*: (1) *orúkọ àmuǹtọ̀runwá*, birth name ("brought from heaven name"), given when a child falls within certain categories such as twins or breech delivery and so forth. (2) *oruko abiso* (*orúkọ àbísọ*), names characterizing circumstances prevailing at the time of birth. Johnson (1957) calls them "christening names." The child may have two or more *abiso*, and they often include the name of a spirit. The first two names of our potter are *abiso*. (3) *orúkọ àbíkú*, names given to a child believed to be prone to die in order to show him that his aim has been anticipated.

[54] Moreover, Johnson (*op. cit.*) gives the term as a female *orile*—a clan-origin name normally associated with women.

opinions represent more the authority of old age—a kind of reverse chivalry—and the embodiment of high position than biological fact, for her photograph (pl. 80) documents a keen eye, a firm mouth, and the alert bearing of someone not over eighty.

The potter has consistently recalled, on the other hand, that she was more than thirty when she mastered the technique of the *awo ota eyinle*. Accordingly, I provisionally date her birth to around 1885, on the ground that the first examples of her art which demonstrate full control begin to appear about the second decade of this century.

The ancestors of the father of Abatan came to Oke-Odan from northern Egbado. She cannot date the migration. Beyond Idowu Yawota (Ìdòwú Yawọta), the paternal great-grandfather, no names are recalled. The son of Idowu was Ifabiyi (Ifábíyi), who is said to have moved from northern Egbado to Oke-Odan where he fathered Oloibo (Olòìbó). Abatan does not know how long these men lived nor when they died.

The mother and maternal grandmother were both potters. The grandmother was Onipede (Onípẹ̀dé) (first name: "Consoler-has-come") Alake (Àlàkẹ́) (praise name: "One-to-be-favored-if-she-survives") Aroyewon (Aroyewọn). Abatan does not know even the approximate time of her death and the allegation that Onipede died over two hundred years ago (!) certainly underscores the fact that she was probably dead before Abatan was born around 1885. She probably flourished, artistically speaking, during the third quarter of the nineteenth century.

Agbedeyi (Agbédèyí) (first name: "That-which-is-carried-in-preparation-for-this") Aṣabi (Àṣàbí) (praise name: "One-of-high-birth") Ija (clan-origin name?) continued the work of her mother. She, in turn, provided the model for Abatan. Agbedeyi died about 1921. Six years after her mother's death, Abatan recalls that she gave birth to a daughter named Wuraola Shangobi (Wúràọlá Shàngóbí) (who in April, 1966, was about thirty-nine). A portion of the family genealogy may now be recapitulated:

▲ IDOWU YAWOTA
▲ IFABIYI   ● ONIPEDE ALAKE AROYEWON
▲ OLOIBO─────────● AGBEDEYI AṢABI IJA (d. *ca.* 1921)
　　○ ABATAN ODEFUNKE AYINKE IJA (b. *ca.* 1885)

The career of Abatan Odefunke opens about 1897 in her early adolescence. She was approximately twelve. There was no formal training, no deliberate lessons. She absorbed, very gradually (*díè-díè-díè*), technique and inspiration from constant observation of Agbédèyí at work. By 1917 her repertoire included simple clay basins used as food containers (*àwo kékèké*), soup pots (*iṣáàsùn sebè*), small pots for the preparation of a traditional food known as *àmàlà* (*ìkòkò kéké*), pots for another indigenous food (*ìkòkò èbà*), pots in which herbs are mixed with water when a child is sick (*ipo*), narrow-mouthed vessels (*àgé*) for cooling water, and broad-mouthed religious vessels, distinguished by motifs in relief under the lip, for the cult of the smallpox deity (*ìkòkò Obalúaiyé*). These specialized types, seven in number, are listed in the order Abatan suggests she learned them. It is notable that the shift from use to art comes at the very end. Abatan says that she was between thirty and forty when she accepted and successfully finished the most demanding commission of all, the *awo ota eyinle*. To fit this account, her first fully mature Eyinle vessels ought to date around the second decade of this century and this dovetails with the independent oral estimates of age by the owners of such pieces. From perhaps 1916–1921 to the present time, an artistic responsibility embracing several provinces of the Yoruba falls upon Abatan. As to artistic pottery, she is the area where the Egbado, the Aworri, and the Anago come together. Her individuality is the relevant reality and the ethnic designations merely names.

STYLE AND DEVELOPMENT

Before the art of Abatan is viewed in time perspective, it is useful to consider briefly the means of analysis and to explain the selectivity that has been applied to the choice of monuments. Kubler (1967, p. 855) has recently tested the connection between style as static situation (Schapiro, 1961) and style as dynamic situation (Kroeber, 1957) and concluded that it is probably impossible to portray the content of any formal transformation in time without invoking the idea of style as a classificatory convenience. I seek, similarly, to restore the art of Abatan to the flow of development by analyzing the morphological relationships that link certain pieces to certain other pieces.

Where a series embodies similar traits this distinguishes a unit of development that may be broadly designated as "a period." Stylistic analysis describes the common characteristics of period, whereas developmental analysis considers the traits that distinguish one period from another. Both methods are shorthand notation of a language ultimately as elusive as mind itself, the language of change and creativity. Our ciphers only dimly perceive its nature but without attempted characterizations the understanding of artistic individuality is difficult.

Works by Abatan may still remain unphotographed and undocumented in obscure villages in the field. More pieces, in fragments, probably lie in those rivers that absorbed the Atinga heaps and in village middens. Consequently, the present selection of ten works (pls. 83–93)[55] from a known corpus of thirty-seven pieces represents an interim report from a volume on artistic biography in tropical Africa which will necessitate several years for completion. Yet most of the main periods of her work are already visible and the photographs have been chosen to illustrate the salient aspects of these periods. They have also been chosen for their quality.

A Nineteenth-Century Antecedent of Abatan's Art

At the turn of the nineteenth century Oke-Odan rapidly became the Western clearinghouse of the slave trade for the territory

---

[55] The list does not include the vessel attributed to her mother (pls. 81, 82) or the vessel that appears on the altar of Abatan (pl. 94) and in the dance at Ajilete (pl. 95).

now embraced by Nigeria. This was a function of the strategic location of the town north of the port of Badagri (Bàdágrì). A dark privilege built a legacy of power. Before the destruction of Oke-Odan in 1848[56] by invading Fon forces from Dahomey, the settlement may have been one of the richest in Yorubaland. When the British governor of the newly established (1861) colony of Lagos took steps to close the slave trade—supposedly already halted but there were still markets for slavers in Cuba and Brazil—it is reported by Ellis (1935) that in 1863 he entered into negotiations with the elders of Oke-Odan. Then came another Fon invasion and Oke-Odan was again destroyed.

In their transition from slaving to legitimate trade the inhabitants of Oke-Odan displayed a speculative genius for survival. Indeed, during the thirty years from 1855 to 1885 the town attained an importance in relation to neighboring kingdoms not unlike the capital of the Egbado, Ilaaro (Ìláàró), earlier in the century[57] (Ellis, 1935, para. 4). Oke-Odan seems also to have become a flourishing art center during the latter part of the nineteenth century for the few surviving wood sculptures that have been attributed to early twentieth- and late nineteenth-century Oke Odan attest, in the sophistication of their stylistic means, a craft tradition of great moment.[58]

[56] Bowen (1857, p. 114) reported: "Ijanna was destroyed a few weeks after my arrival in the country and other and still larger towns in the same region have fallen. At one of these called Oke-Oddan, the Dahomey army killed and captured about 20,000 people, on which occasion the King presented Domingo, the Brazilian slaver, with 600 slaves." This contemporary notice implies a large settlement at Oke-Odan, and it suggests one reason why there is a concordance between the praise poetry and dance attributes of the hunter-god, Inle, at Bahia, Brazil, and Oke-Odan's own cult of Eyinle.

[57] In 1891 (Johnson, 1957, p. 606) Chief Fálọlá of Oke-Odan appeared to be the greatest of all Egbado chiefs. Thus the period of Oke-Odan's great power, 1855–1885, suggested by Ellis, probably extended to the turn of the century.

[58] The evidence consists of twin images (*ère ibéjì*) still kept in several Aworri and Egba villages. The images are clearly by the same hand and they are extremely handsome. They are dated, on genealogical grounds (i.e., by means of family histories), to the same period—roughly the last decade of the nineteenth century and the first of the present century. This conclusion is based on the agreement between the independent estimates of the owners. In each instances Oke-Odan was recalled

How tragic then, that not a single full piece of nineteenth-century pottery seems to survive *in situ*. There are doubtless fragments that archaeologists will uncover from middens and perhaps dredge up from the Yewa River but nothing seems to exist above ground from the remote past. The invasions of Dahomey occurred too early, probably, to destroy the works of Abatan's grandmother but they may have obliterated the sources of her grandmother's inspiration. The pieces that eluded the ravages of war probably did not, in the end, escape the gentler but no less final blows of careless children playing beside domestic altars, the haphazard intramural perambulations of stray goats, and other minor hazards of the Yoruba compound. The works that might have survived attrition were probably finished off by the witch-hunt of 1951.

Fortunately, one monument remains. It provides a basis for establishing the contours of a lost ceramic tradition (pls. 81, 82). I discovered the vessel in a neighboring kingdom[59] on January 4, 1963. An impressive ordering of a five-figure composition is the

---

as the point of origin of the images, although the name of the carver was not recalled. In a village near Oke-Odan I found one of the finest thunder-god axes that I have ever seen. It was alleged to be three generations old and to have been carved at Oke-Odan. It seemed a more rounded, fuller version of the mode of carving that characterized the far-flung twin images, as if the latter works were a further or parallel elaboration. No traces of either of these modes survives in present-day Oke-Odan, although the local master, Akínjọbí (who died on December 26, 1957, and in whose compound Abatan lives as widow), produced up to his death sculpture of quality, somewhat related to the earlier attributions. Given its relatively cosmopolitan ethnic composition, Oke-Odan may have once sustained two or three plastic traditions, imported by carvers from evacuated Ketu and Oyo villages. The magnificent twin-image collected at Oke-Odan by Murray during the Atinga crisis, on February 25, 1951, and now part of the Atinga Collection of the Nigerian Museum, Lagos, seems to align with the sculptural tradition of Ilaaro. In any event, a picture emerges, from the piecing together of these shards of visual evidence, of a remarkable aesthetic environment in late nineteenth-century Oke-Odan.

[59] With few exceptions I withhold the precise field location of those works of art still in ritual use in order to protect their owners from thefts such as those that occurred, at Ilobu, after Beier's (1959) famous study of the sculpture of Iloban shrines. At the World Festival of Negro Arts at Dakar (1966) I remarked that it seemed strange that, while there is concern about conserving Africa's artistic heritage, sufficient steps have not been taken to ensure the protection of those traditional Africans who are the original patrons of African art.

essential virtue of this extraordinary terra-cotta. The head of the dominant woman rises from a solid neck. Her left breast (the right has broken off) is continuously curved, uninterrupted by an indication of the nipple, and magnificently polished. The head is superbly dressed with a crisp coiffure characterized by two longitudinal ridges, two smaller braids marking their boundary, and two further braids running parallel between the twin keels from forehead to nape. This mode is remembered in some Egbado villages as having been called *okorun-meji* (*okorun-méjì*), ("hair in two principal plaits"); the dramatic opposition of two sharp accents may conceal a now forgotten allusion to duality, to the mixture of good and evil in the force of the gods.[60]

The cultivation of an almost mannerist aesthetic characterizes the work as a whole. A penchant for elongation may be considered "mannerist." The neck is long. The supports of the *adodo* crown are so exquisitely extended there is space for seven bosses in contrast with the present norm of four. Even in her early period, probably very much influenced by similar works, Abatan was never so markedly "mannerist" although many of her works of this period were about 17 inches high. But this striking vessel stands 24 inches high.

Roulette impressions are conspicuously absent. The maker incised oblique hatchings, probably with the thin blade of a piece of tin or iron, and bordered them with equally fine lines. The incisions are cut with great crispness into the hard and brilliant surfaces which resemble bronze. The siting of the hatchings predicts the future: later, in the art of Abatan, these same areas will be embellished with impression. The commanding figure personifies what I would designate aristocratic composure. Her face is an elegant mask, devoid of compromising emotion, nobly isolated from the crown by the neck, and made beautiful by the creation of a nose of slender bridge and firm sensitive nostrils. The tapering momentum of the crown as it rises is inverted by the neck which gently flares to meet the ears. The keeper of this image alleges the

[60] Edwin Obayan suggests this possibility.

major figure represents the wife of Eyinle surrounded by her children. Of the three "children" on the front of the lid, one is clearly senior. Seated, she holds the kola bowl between her legs. She is flanked[61] at left by a seated female with horned coiffure who holds her belly with her left hand while grasping the leg of the central figure with the other, at right by another figure who cups her belly with her hands, a gesture of increase. The flanking figures, both frontally positioned, give an impression of extending the crown supports to which they are lightly engaged at the head. In the area marked for special consciousness by the flanking, the eye discovers an amazing transition, from the coiffure of the central figure to the breasts of the almost certainly divine figure above her, a superb handling of two levels of hierarchy and measurement. The unprepared observer who fails to see the ingenuity behind this articulation soon discovers its depth upon attempting imitation in modeling clay.

The artist has modulated form in other ways. The eye begins at a level of abstract bas-relief, continues upward through nude figural expression, and finishes in the midst of a powerful geometry, at once human and abstract, whereas the final figure emerges from the top of the crown boldly reduced to head, neck, and breasts, at the same time that the expression upon its face freezes, and takes on the timeless gaze of divinity.

In ironic contrast with this well-weighted monumentality, a lively little figure mounts the rear support of the crown (pl. 82).[62] Rapidly modeled and informally posed, head turned to the right, following a conventional rendering of the theme of the child on the mother's back, the figure creates an impression of spontaneity.

---

[61] Cf. Fraser's (1966, p. 79) interesting observation on the "honorific character of symmetrical flanking. . . . Heraldic flanking presupposes hieratic values and the desire to represent them, because the flanking figures are subordinate and dependent, while the central one is dominant and unconditional." The fact that the figures on the Eyinle pot are not exactly symmetrical and are enlivened by certain gestural distinctions suggests a less rigid social stratification is lacking in many Pacific areas that have produced outstanding examples of flanking.

[62] Cf. the wood sculpture of Egbado, Egba, Oyo, and other groups, where the motif of the child on the mother's back, head turned to the side, sometimes appears.

That this genre-like figure is not readily visible from the front of the vessel but comes as a surprise, as the vessel is rounded, is part of the wit of its effect.

The present owner of this masterpiece of African sculpture alleged on January 4, 1963, that it was made "at least forty-five years ago." She estimated, in other words, that the vessel was made before 1918. The startling fact is that when I asked her who made the pot she said Onipede of Oke-Odan. Can this work indeed be a survival of the art of Abatan's grandmother? A return visit on April 20, 1966, elicited fairly consistent information which seemed to argue for a slightly earlier date than 1918. This time the owner said that the original owner of the piece was one Oni and that Oni had gone to Oke-Odan to have this vessel made more than fifty years ago, that is, before 1913. We are approaching the turn of the century but we are still remote from the presumed period of Onipede.

When I showed photographs of this work to Abatan she immediately commented, with the air of an American grandmother shown a specimen of art nouveau, "In the old days they used to put children on the sides and upon the back of the crown." She attributed the work to Agbedeyi. She later stated that she does not ever remember seeing the work of Onipede. When in late April, 1966, the owner of the piece was questioned anew about the maker she said that she did remember having discussed the problem with me but that in the intervening years she had forgotten the name entirely.

Faced with this conflict of oral evidence, I follow the attribution of Abatan not only on the ground of her greater familiarity with the tradition but also because of visual evidence.[63] In three known instances where Abatan was expressly commissioned to copy the

---

[63] It may be that Agbedeyi took the *abiso* name of her mother and was known by this in Aworri country. Or, the reputation of Onipede may have lingered, long after her death, as a kind of "patriotic attribution," just as several score of carvings, many by obviously different hands, are said, at Abeokuta, to be the work of Adúgbológe, in the Efon-Alaiye area, by Àgbọ́nbíofe. Recently Willett and Picton (1967, pp. 62–70) discussed the same problem.

style of her mother, she produced figural groupings in this manner. The trend of the evidence is thus a late nineteenth-century or turn-of-the-century date although I think that the former is far more likely. It is very important to note the radiant level of skill embodied in this form and the degree to which Abatan, in the course of this century, departs from the form while maintaining the skill. The work, in short, provides a precise measure against which to estimate her creativity.

ABATAN'S ART

Period I

Abatan has simplified the aesthetic of the past. She makes a single-figure composition, emergent from the lid in exquisite repose (pl. 84). Subsidiary figuration has disappeared. The play becomes soliloquy, and, if the dramatis personae have been reduced to one, the substance of the communication, the mirror of the divine patience of the spirits in the river, remains.

Very quietly Abatan has challenged traditional proportion. The neck has evaporated and the crown supports are shorter, with bosses more pointed than in the past. The luminous breasts of the figure attributed to Agbedeyi are also subtly revised. The present potter inflects the clay, pinching the end between two fingers to indicate the nipple, a slight trait that remains characteristic throughout most of her career. Transformation of coiffure may have reflected an actual shift in vogue, but the handling of the new hairdressing is organically related to the program of the new sculpture. Thus the presumed nineteenth-century design of the double keel, like the body it crowns, rises in sharp definition. The modern pattern smoothly follows the curve of the head and thus becomes a part of the whole. Indication of the parts (between the polished bands representing the braids) is done with impression,[64]

---

[64] The roulette pattern is striking: a bubbling flow of fine, embossed circles with-

an apparent innovation. The nineteenth century may have consistently incised representations of coiffure.

Elements of continuity must also be considered, lest one overstate the originality of the master. As befits a culture that esteems dignity in life and art, immobility of facial expression is maintained. The particulars of the physiognomy are remarkably similar to the presumed nineteenth-century work. Abatan also copies the relief pattern, as it appeared on the midsection of the older pot, almost element for element. But a coarser expression of these same motifs readily distinguishes a different hand.

The secret of the viability of creativity in the midst of jealous tradition is tact. As Abatan dispenses with the figural rhetoric of the past she has the wit to isolate a key element—hands holding the kola bowl—and to fuse this element to the larger image. She has merged the central act of the old composition with the solitary protagonist of the new. As she does this, the arms are curved in sympathy with the contour of the bowl. The older construction was less elegantly composed at this point. The theme of offering has been maintained, the abstract figure now plays a more human role, and gently, wonderfully, tradition is guided into change.

What visual effects are wrought by unobtrusive modulations! The haughty carriage of the dominant figure of the old vessel—"haughty" because the chin was so superbly elevated—is modified. The eyes of the old figure seemed to look down upon the world from the top of its proud neck, whereas the eyes of the new figure face the observer more directly. The figure from the past is separate from the lid and rises from it. The figure of the present integrally merges with the lid. The distinction is fundamental (pls. 81, 89).

---

in carefully incised, parallel borders. The effect is brilliant and sensitive, like sunlight reflected on fine netting. Abatan recalls that she used this pattern before the birth of her daughter, Wuraola Shangobi (i.e., before *ca.* 1921). This testimony seems corroborated by the fact that owners' independent estimates of the ages of pieces in this "style," for the most part, predate 1921.

Seven known works pertain to this first period of Abatan's work which may be provisionally placed in the latter half of the second decade of this century. Of them, two are said to have been commissioned between 1916 and 1921, and a third before the birth of one Bankole (Bánkọ́lé) Adekanbi in 1911. It is interesting that the piece said to predate 1911 is the least elegant. It is decorated, half with roulette impressions, half with incisions, in the manner of the pot attributed to Agbedeyi.

Available evidence does not permit the writing of a stylistic succession within the group, for an apparently early work might represent the natural consequence of an interval of inactivity.

Two pieces that I attribute to this period are in museum collections. On September 14, 1939, the Smithsonian Institution acquired an *awo ota eyinle* as a gift from Captain C. C. Roberts.[65] The piece had been collected in the field, apparently in the vicinity of Ilaro (pl. 86). It is distinguished from other Period I examples by lack of outline around the hairdressing, an inflected ear shape, and roulette pattern that does not run parallel to the borders but is instead disposed in diagonal strokes, as if translating into a slightly different medium the diagonally hatched incisions of Agbedeyi.

The central novelty is the coiffure. The type is *agogo* (*àgògo*), a style where the hair is divided into a series of radiating parts, from the ear toward the crown, and braided between the parts. At

[65] Smithsonian Institution 380 512, 380 514. The piece was broken by customs officials during examination and restored in the laboratory of the Smithsonian. The fact that the piece cannot be older than the late thirties dovetails in an instructive way with the dating of Period II (late twenties, early thirties?). One of the striking characteristics of this sculpture is the octagonal outline of the face, when viewed frontally. The presence of this trait leads me to suspect that the Smithsonian piece might be a transitional work linking Period I to Period II, for the octagonal facial outline is a Period II trait par excellence. There are two further pieces, in use in the field, which also appear to connect the periods. One isolated formal trait obviously does not define a period but, as in this instance, may overlap developmental phases.

The rhythmic meander (impression bordered with cursive incisions) embellishing the midsection of the pot is enigmatic. I would guess that the decoration reflects market purchase in the sense that a specially decorated *iṣaasun* was substituted for the normal cult object.

festivals extra plaits are fitted into the hair and these form a spec-
tacular crest of small, narrow, concentric braids, running from
forehead to nape and ending in a pigtail (cf., but for the pigtail,
Murray, 1950, p. 365). The mode is worn by male devotees of the
thunder-god (Abraham, 1958, p. 30), devotees of the river-goddess
Oṣun (Verger, 1957, pl. 109) and, in a special instance, by the
priest of the patron deity of the town of Okuku (Òkukù). The use
of the mode signifies that the wearer is a "wife" or servant of the
god, for in the nineteenth century it was worn by brides.

Comparison of Murray's photograph with the Smithsonian
piece sharpens the appreciation of an aspect of Abatan's inventiveness. She has omitted the horizontal concentric braids of the crest
and drawn the lines of the vertical parts from the hairline to the
peak of the crest in consonance with a taste for simplification. In
1951 a lid was rescued from the Atinga heaps in a style very close
to the Smithsonian vessel, including *agogo* coiffure. On the basis
of these details I assign the lid, now in the Nigerian Museum,
Lagos, to Period I. The traits that appear to anchor both the Smithsonian and Nigerian Museum pieces to this phase are the gently
rounded forehead, the nose, which is narrowly bridged but short
and broad at the nostrils, the narrow, horizontal projection of the
lips, the flat cheeks, and the long square chin.

Before considering the next period, we come to perhaps the
masterpiece of Abatan's early work, as we presently know it (pl.
85). The piece presides over a collection of four vessels and is regarded by the local priest as the lord (Ọ̀gá)[66] of these pots because
of its greater age. (The companion works were perhaps made in
the thirties). The right arm and hand have been lost from the
figure on the lid. Admirable are the sharpness of line, the clarity
of the incisions, the delicacy of the modeling, especially the eyes,

---

[66] Omifewà, a late devotee, owned this piece. Then another member of the lineage
was told by divination to purchase her own pot, and finally a third until the common
shrine sheltered three works by Abatan (as well as a fourth, by an unknown master
who probably flourished in the Abeokuta sector).

which taper toward their outer corners, and the shining surfaces. The quality of the luminous glasslike surfaces is very much in keeping with the presumed canon of Agbedeyi.

Period II

When change occurs we experience time. Artistic change reveals itself when one compares the art of one period with the art of another. In Period II further aspects of an inherited formality begin to dissolve although the main structure remains, of course, intact. Our introductory example is in the Atinga Collection of the Nigerian Museum, Lagos. It measures 12 inches high (pl. 87). We learn many things from this lid. It is clear, first of all, that aesthetic choice is unpredictable and that an old style may reappear without warning at any time. Abatan restores the minor figure with kola bowl but suppresses the retinue. The selectivity extends to minor details. Legs are not indicated for this figure (as they were in the past) and where the figure was once seated as a distinct entity, here it is merged with the kola bowl in an organic way that recalls the one-to-one relationship of the larger figure to the lid in the style of Abatan.

A partial revival of an old world of iconography confronts a new world of proportional relationships. Ears are smaller than they were before and the rapid modeling of nostrils and bridge is interesting. The bridge of the nose slightly projects; it did not before. The mouth is of a generous new width. It is notable that the outline of the face, as seen frontally, is now roughly octagonal. This effect must be most carefully described, as it is a key to the period.[67] Horizontal lines mark the distance between the two central braids at the hairline and the length of the chin. Diagonal lines extend from each horizontal line downward toward the top of the ear, along the forehead, and upward toward the bottom of the ear,

[67] In the sense that it becomes associated with a set of innovations. The trait by itself also seems to mark transition from Period I, where the special softness of the modeling of the most striking of Period II pieces is missing.

along the jaw. Vertical lines define the sides of the face along the length of the ear. These are the facets of the "octagon." The last points about the lid (the pot evidently lost during the Atinga episode) are: each braid in the coiffure is bisected by a parallel line, and a new pattern of roulette impression has emerged which resembles netting. It is composed of fine links of lozenge shape.

The second known example of this series rests in a small shrine in the heart of Aworri. It is adorned with gold earrings[68] and an iron chain. When photographed, its kola bowl happened to be full (pl. 88). The owner alleges that at about the time the vessel was made she gave birth to a son and that he has since grown to manhood, married, and become a father. On the basis of this evidence the owner estimated in 1966 that the pot was made thirty to forty years ago. This gives rise to a tentative chronological anchor (1926–1936) which awaits sharpening by future research. We cannot extend the series arbitrarily across the entire decade because artistic durations are usually of irregular length. I would guess, on the basis of closer resemblance to Period I, that the series overlaps the early thirties.

The piece has the power, once its date has been secured, to anchor the entire period chronologically because it repeats the plastic order of the Nigerian Museum piece in regard to the "octagonal" facial outline. The facets of the octagon come into sharper focus, although in the photograph the effect is obscured by the reflection of light on the brow and by shadow. Finally, a distinctive aspect of this piece is the lightweight roulette—concentric borders filled with a pattern of tiny squares. The flat, hanging breasts are unique.

The piece presages a lyrical moment in the history of Abatan's art (pl. 89), a climax that of itself forces a reestimation of our knowledge of African pottery. How is this amazing lyricism achieved? Suddenly, past formal habits-of-making melt away and

[68] Abatan pierces the ears of female figures with straw in the last stages of decoration before firing, unless otherwise instructed by a patron.

fuse again to form a language based upon critical new curves. First of all, the outer braids of the hair curve inward as they meet the sloping line of the temple. They appear to push toward each other. This is new. The innovation is echoed by the siting of the breasts closer to each other so that less of the breastbone is visible. The roulette impressions seem muted and do not distract from the new curvilinearity. The curve of the mouth is in affinity with the curve of the cicatrization on the cheeks. The nostrils melt fluidly into the bridge. Curve crowds on curve; the ears resemble cupped palms, and the entire face acquires a handsome delicacy of height, accented by the greater width of the base of the nose and the mouth (in comparison with Period I) which, together with the subdued chin, create a sense of enhanced facial width. Opposed lines and curves fuse in harmony.

The sum of these innovations is the creation of a softer, fleshier effect. It is less stylized and closer to the warmth of actual human expression. Nevertheless, the octagon outline of the face assumes its sharpest definition.

Period III (The Atinga Replacements of the Early Fifties)

The formal development that led to the 1950's must have been extremely absorbing, but its nature has not yet been identified. Thus Period III is not an immediate sequence to Period II but is a story resumed after a hidden portion of the thread.

When Atingaists destroyed traditional art in the spring of 1951 (with a frenzy that recalls the vandalism of the Red Guards in the People's Republic of China), the response of their victims who happened to be devotees of Eyinle was varied. Some replaced their losses almost immediately for reasons of prestige. Thus it would not do for the senior male devotee of an important Egbado settlement to be without his vessel. No sooner had the iconophobia died down than he was at the door of Abatan with an urgent request. A few did nothing at all. Others bided their time and used simple basins as receptacles for the stones, then, after a few years when they could afford it, invested in proper replacements. Some priestesses found that delay provoked dangerous divine displeasure: "Orisa (Òrìṣà) Eyinle started to trouble me because I had not got him another *awo ota eyinle*. He started to report to other Orisa like Ogun, Orisa Oluwa (Olúwa), and other Orisa and these fought with me and I became sick. Yet after I had commissioned the making of another *awo ota eyinle*, my health returned."

Transformations of shape and line define the art of Abatan in the year immediately following the Atinga incident.[69] The gentle curves of Period II have become angular. The sharp mass of the head (pl. 90), the raking angle of the back of the head, the relative straightness of the braids (in comparison with the perceptively more cursive flow of the braids in the past) are manifestations of a subtle innovation (cf. pl. 85 with pl. 90).

All features, somewhat reduced in size, are subordinate to the approximate triangle of the profile. The top of the forehead is the peak of this triangle, the neck is the base, the line of the hair and the profile the two sides. Coiffure answers this special geometry with another triangle so that the head, as a sum effect, forms a kind of lozenge above the suggestion of a neck.

New roulette impressions, creating an extremely textural herringbone pattern, are like a modulation into a new key. The new aesthetic admits, indeed, of effects textural to the point of coarseness. Incisions representing facial cicatrization seem less finished than comparable lines in the art of Abatan around 1916–1921, and they lack the precision depth and weight of the facial marks of pieces tentatively attributed to the early thirties. Moreover, all surfaces seem less smooth, especially the braids of the hair and the fleshy parts of the face. Period III pieces are angular and somewhat

---

[69] The work chosen to illustrate this period is almost identical with a companion work "bought on the very same day that the other piece was." They were purchased jointly "immediately after Atinga" (i.e., in 1951, probably in the spring). The joint sale it is not unusual; Abatan makes two pots at a time so that, in case one should crack in firing, she has a spare to sell. In cases where both original and second piece survive firing she sells both, usually to different patrons.

rough in texture, but massively and handsomely composed. Three known pieces are dated to 1951 and 1952. The piece illustrated belongs to an Egbado priest of Eyinle.

The Nineteenth-Century Revival

When ancient pots in their possession were ruined in the fifties, three devotees, treasuring the memory of the art of Agbedeyi, came to Abatan with a specific request: replace our vessels in the style of your mother. The response of Abatan varied. If the client brought the pieces of the ruined work as a model, she adjusted her own style to the older format. If Abatan was allowed, on the other hand, to revive late nineteenth-century work from memory the results were different. For example, one devotee, in Aworri country, inherited a superb vessel by Agbedeyi from her mother and when the vessel was broken in a household accident she brought the pieces (which were subsequently lost) to Abatan and put them together and "told Abatan that we wanted the kind of *awo ota eyinle* that we had brought to her, that she was to make it in conformance with the object brought before her."

The finished work is most strikingly characterized by a different sense of proportion. It is a tall vessel crowned with *agogo* coiffure and it stands a startling 31 ½ inches high. The replacement was itself smashed (in 1962) when a child stumbled against it. A reconstruction of the pieces, directed by me, showed that the most notable of the revived traits were extreme verticality and hauteur of facial composition.

In the same village a second *serviteur* said that when the vessel owned by her mother became ruined she waited until she had sufficient funds, then journeyed to Oke-Odan to commission an exact replacement. She did not take the ruined piece with her because "Abatan had previously visited my mother and she had seen the *awo ota eyinle* of my mother and when I told Abatan to remake the vessel she told me in return that she had seen the *awo ota eyinle* in the compound of my mother and she would make one for me." Abatan reproduced the figures flanking the kola bowl, but she omitted the central personage grasping the bowl. She restored the theme of the child at the mother's back (pl. 91). But the major figure wears an *oniidodo* coiffure and the subsidiary figures *kòlẹ́sẹ̀* (the hair braided from the forehead to the nape in a series of parallel lines), both contemporary modes, and the treatment of the head, with a space between the ear and the back of the head, presages Abatan's work of the middle sixties. The owner alleges that the work was finished in 1954.

A third replacement serves as our illustration of neoclassicism in the career of Abatan (pl. 91). The vessel is in use in the Aworri field. The owner has revealed the following germane scrap of genealogy: "Since the pot was finished three children have been born, the first, three years after the pot was made; the second, three years after that; the third, three years after the second." The allegation was made in 1966, hence the vessel may have been made around 1957. The piece affords us the opportunity to study carefully how Abatan copies and restructures the past. She revives again the flanking figures and child on the back, as well as the powerful double-keeled curve of the classic *okorun-meji* coiffure, eschewing roulette impression and decorating the sides of the crown with bands of incized lozenges and squares, a device not seen before. Again Abatan "censors" the central figure behind the kola bowl. Most important, the flanking figures now face each other, creating a literal confrontation. This is a vivid departure from the frontality of the vessel attributed to Agbedeyi.

Tentatively, I accept the date suggested by the owner. The elongation of the neck and the relative smallness of the head in relation to the neck are qualities reminiscent of what we take to be her mother's taste, but what tells us that the work aligns with Period III is the size of the coiffure, the thickness of the facial incisions, the length of the chin, and the forward curve of the ears, a trait distinctive of this period. Period III ears are normally thinner, forming a kind of question mark, whereas earlier ears formed a kind of fishhook.

The present shifts into the past. The relative lack of surface finish, particularly at the forehead, is an important clue. Passages of the surface of the clay are left rough with the marks of the potter's fingers.

Period IV

The study of the works of the first few years of the present decade is in progress but already promising, identifying traits may be discussed. What is new is that there is an almost globular handling of the forehead, the eyelids, and the nostrils (pl. 92). In Period I the nostrils are flattened, in II the eyelid is thinner than in IV, in III the eyelid and the nose are both thin, but in IV there is a relationship formed among the three features not seen before.

There is a general thickening of all features. The long chin, the flat cheeks, and the relatively high position of the mouth seem to have been carried over from Period III. The nose has lengthened, however; the nostrils are much thicker and the ears, too, are thicker, especially fleshy at the top. The fat ridge of the brow gives an impression of much vigor and muscularity. The example is dated to July 21, 1962, by its owner.[70]

Envoi

I end the consideration of the formal development of Abatan's art with perhaps her masterpiece, a Period III work. The oblique thrust of the coiffure is memorably softened and magnificently curved (pl. 93). The fluid curvilinearity of the braids creates a handsome aesthetic when seen from the side. The same handling shapes the line of the bridge of the nose, when viewed frontally. There is a marvelous elasticity to the bands depicting the braids,

[70] When I asked the patron, a literate Yoruba, why he remembered the exact date, he answered: "Because I was the one to spend all of the money." He paid Abatan £2 12 s. 6 d. He also told me that he first came to hear of the work of Abatan in Dahomey—a worshiper of Eyinle at Ìfọ̀nyín extolled the talents of Abatan. His testimony reveals that the reputation of Abatan is international, although the Anago of Dahomey are but an extension of the Anago that form the western "boundary" of the Egbado in Nigeria. Future research will estimate the actual extent of an alleged patronage of Abatan's sculpture in some Dahomean Yoruba villages.

swelling in and out. The expression of line is freer, perhaps, than at any other point of the artist's career.

The owner alleges the piece was made around 1960 but the conflict between style and oral testimony must be decided in favor of style[71] because the softness of the mass and the fluent curves of the details are clearly in the Period III manner. The work is a demonstration piece of an individual's reconsideration of ancient form. We recognize the voice of a creative sensibility in the contrast between the piece and the past, and between the piece and the future. We discover in this sculpture the spark of human intent that every work of art carries within itself and which subsequent artists will rediscover and heroically conserve.

ARCHITECTURAL AND CHOREOGRAPHIC SETTINGS

In general, the artistic coordinates of Yoruba sculpture are the altar and the dance. These settings create a field against which the static image is significantly opposed. They blur particularity within generic expression. By contrast, the Western world has evolved the frame, the pedestal, and the stage as artificial isolating devices that make the individuality of the work of art absolute.

The altars of Eyinle are domestic structures. They are mud platforms with a frieze of conventionalized figures and emblems of worship upon which rest cultic regalia and utensils (Murray and Hunt-Cooke, 1938 ? , p. 46). These altars are one of the main expressions of Yoruba mud sculpture. There are four known examples by the hand of Abatan, at Oke-Odan, of which her own

[71] The village in which this piece is found is one of the few that I was not able to revisit in order to compare and broaden allegations about dating. This fact by itself casts doubt on the suggested date. Repeated visits elicit details of family history (birth, adolescence, marriage, menopause, death) linked with the purchase of art objects. Abstract questions about dating do not seem appropriate in a world where people are more interested in people than they are in things. I have found that it is more useful to ask "Who was born in the year that this image was carved?" and so forth, instead of embarrassing owners with a direct request for chronological information. The revenge of their innocence, if not appreciated, may take the form of a field notebook filled with imaginary numerals. So many Yoruba art objects, whose age was baldly asked, appear to be "about sixteen years old"!

household altar serves as our example (pl. 94). Sited in the west corner of the principal room of her compound, the altar is distinguished by its remarkable frieze embellished with three human figures, almost in the round and standing approximately 18 inches high. Oten appears at center, flanked by Abatan and Ibu Jagun. The iconic quality of the pose and "mask" of the male statuary lends them a kind of generic flexibility so that one year Abatan is said to stand at the right of Oten, Ibu Jagun at left, while several years later their positions have been reversed.

To the right of Oten are positioned, from the top of the frieze, a river stone, a thunder-god calabash-rattle (the head of which has broken off), a sacrificial tortoise, and a serpent-messenger. To the far right appear a thunder-god dance ax and a smaller representation of an iron rattle (*àájà Obatálá*), with three bells on top and three bells on the bottom, for the creator-god. Virtually invisible at extreme left is a smaller mud platform for Ogun, the hot-tempered god of iron, laden with pieces of iron that support his power and receive sacrifices in his name. A stoppered Guinness Stout bottle, filled with red palm oil, leans against the frieze. Palm oil is poured into the covered cavity in the floor immediately to the right of the bottle to invoke the trickster deity, Eshu Elegba (Elégba), whenever ceremonies are performed. Two river stones,[72] the head of a ram, and a second serpent-messenger, complete the decoration in low relief; these elements are in the area above the sacrificial cavity.

The juxtaposition of elements, traditional and foreign, express a vital unity. At left, on the altar, dance wands and votive images[73] for the thunder-god have been placed in a calabash resting upon a crockery base. To the immediate right, in more crockery of Western origin, are kept emblems for Oṣun. Bottles filled with an intoxicating liquor, *otí*, to be used as sacrifice and refreshment, here

---

[72] So are they locally interpreted. Again, however, they resemble Celts, as in the Arriens drawing (Frobenius, 1913, p. 215).

[73] Wood sculpture on the altar, including dance wands for the trickster not visible in the photograph, is attributed to Akínjọbí of Oke-Odan.

flank the carved image of a dead twin (*ibéjì*). At right rests a pottery vessel for the smallpox deity, embellished with low-relief motifs almost identical with those on the frieze of the altar. The vessel was made about 1958 by Abatan, according to her own recollection. It serves as a stand for a calabash in which are placed dance clubs for the smallpox deity together with a fan and fly whisk for Eyinle.

The *awo otɑ eyinle* may be dimly discerned behind the image of the twin, a gold chain around the neck of the human figure. The iron bird of Osanyin, the lord of the primordial powers of herbalism in the religion of the Yoruba, presides over the altar, as if pirouetting on the end of its iron staff. A cloth conceals a radiating assemblage of miniature iron symbols, including an iron serpent, said to honor the iron-god as well as Osanyin; these subsidiary symbols are attached to the staff on prongs; the bird itself is a guard against witchcraft.

The figures[74] of the frieze make gestures related to the subsidiary figures of the vessel attributed to Agbedeyi, to the effigy jar (the gesture of the woman), and to the gestural rhetoric of the relief figures on the vessel for the smallpox deity. The multiple appearances of these gestures almost musically express divine calm and fecundity. The reinforcement of the art of the past, especially evident in the double-keeled coiffure at left, is striking.

Statuary and emblems are integrally interwoven, not positioned as separate registers, as in the vessel attributed to the late nineteenth century (cf. pl. 81 where statuary is separated from relief). Abatan has added a minor innovation to the iconographic program, the iron bell for the creator-god, an addition that also distinguishes

---

[74] The mud sculpture is made from a mixture of powdered shards (*erọ*), oddly resembling gunpowder in hue and consistency, and prepared clay (*amọ̀n*). The two ingredients are combined and molded into "leaves" (*ìsù amòn*). Later the leaves are moistened, wedged (kneaded to proper consistency), and the figures are built up and allowed to dry. They are then darkened thoroughly with indigo dye. The process is, of course, related to the making of Eyinle pottery, but for the firing. The surfaces of the altar and altar statuary are polished before being darkened by means of a moistened stone.

the vessel said to have been made in July, 1962 (pl. 92). Comparison of the mud sculpture of Abatan with her terra-cottas suggests the former medium is characterized by a more conservative usage because the figural rhetoric of the older style is in evidence.

The altar presents Abatan with an opportunity to recombine the traditional symbols for Eyinle in a new way. The vessel for the god of smallpox serves as a further occasion for the creative rearrangement of traditional icons. The solution suggests a wrapping of the statuary of the frieze around the sides of the broad-mouthed smallpox vessel.

The style of the altar broadly relates to the neoclassical vessel that we have tentatively dated to 1957 (pl. 91), not only as regards morphology but also as regards degree of surface finish. Of course, mud is a much coarser material so that all the modeling is considerably thickened. Abatan has stated that the altar was finished in 1958.

What does the form of the altar suggest? Media used by men to communicate with the gods (in low relief) are brought together with the gods themselves (in high relief). The figures support, quite literally, the stones in the vessel and the other tokens of divine presence. Lastly, the altar represents a kind of grand permutation: comparison of the *awo ota eyinle*, the effigy jar, the smallpox vessel, and the altar reveals that there are many ways of suggesting the power and the virtue of the gods with the same themes.[75]

The fact that the lids of *awo ota eyinle* may also be termed "crowns" hints of their occasional use in the dance. Devotees of Eyinle at Abeokuta have danced with lids on their heads from the River Ogun (Ògùn) to the center of Ibara (Ìbarà) Quarter. I have

---

[75] In T. S. Eliot's *Burnt Norton* one finds a passage that has the power to cross cultures and to illumine appropriately the peculiar beauty of this altar:

> *Erhebung* without motion, concentration
> Without elimination, both a new world
> And the old made explicit, understood
> In the completion of its partial ecstasy,
> The resolution of its partial horror.

seen a similar ceremony at Ajilete and an apparent carry-over of the practice has been photographed among the Yoruba-speaking people of Bahia in Brazil (Querino, 1938, pl. 16). Once an item of African sculpture has been identified as dance sculpture, that is, related in some way to the moving body of a dancer it becomes very important to consider the choregraphic setting as a potential extension of the symbolism of the sculpture.

Local connoisseurs of the dance consider Omikunle Agbeke Asoko (Omikúnlẹ́ Àgbékẹ́ Asoko) one of the finest dancers in the Ajilete sector, and all observations concerning the use of the lid as dance regalia apply to her alone (pl. 95). At a so-called half-year feast for the Egungun cult, she danced with the lid balanced upon a cloth on her head. She danced to seven drum pieces. The drums were *bàtá*, a choir of four double-membraned, hourglass-shaped drums especially associated with thunder-god worship. One critic remarked that Omikunle dances without smiling, or dissipating the energy of her motion with speech, or changing facial expressions. Her face is a mask. The evaluation of her dance illumines the balance struck between the composure of the face in terra-cotta and the composure of the face of the dancer.

Omikunle, as she dances, garbed in a trade cloth emblazoned with letters of the Roman alphabet, carefully maintains a more direct kind of balance, lest her head waver and the pottery lid fall to earth and smash. The extraordinary accomplishment recalls the *ajere* ceremony of thunder-god worship, where novices must carry, balanced on their heads, a pot in which a living flame is burning (Verger, 1957, p. 305). It is a dramatic metaphor of the assuagement of dangerous force and may be related to the Obinrinjuwu (Obìnrinjuwu) festival among the Ijebu Yoruba where for several hours the fate of the entire province is believed to turn upon the successful balancing of an image upon the head of a dancing priest[76]

---

[76] Cf. the Ashanti of Ghana, where, according to information shared with me by Daniel McCall, a member of the family of the deceased dances at the funeral with a basin of water on her head. If she spills the water she is suspected of having killed the deceased by witchcraft.

(Anonymous, 1948, p. 26). In the cult of Eyinle an architectural correlate to this remarkable achievement is the altar that sustains, in repose, multiple symbols of danger: death by lightning, death by smallpox, death by iron, and infant mortality.

There are normally seven dances performed for Eyinle and the river spirits. Six of these are for the special spirits of the depths of the water—dignified, impressive dances. Omikunle shuffles rhythmically, and her gestural patterns are smooth and elegant. The dance for the iron-god, however, often the seventh in the series, although its position is not fixed, is a burst of specialized motion that mingles terror with decorum. Omikunle releases energy in her body but "binds" the motion of her head—she carries her head and the lid with serene immobility over the turbulence of her shoulders, torso, hips, and feet. When the drum choir announces the dance for the iron-god, tempo accelerates. A peremptory drum salute is heard: iron-god kills, kills, kills, kills, iron-god kills, kills, kills, kills. Motion becomes explosive. Omikunle spins, hurling one arm up, the other arm down, lifting one foot and bringing it down to earth with a stamp. The quality of the motion portrays the temper of the god while at the same time placing the terra-cotta sculpture in danger of destruction. A field of violence, artfully suggested, brilliantly accents the harmonic quietude of the face of the sculpture and the dancer's face. Danger transformed into poetry edifies mankind and charms the gods, even those of harshest character, and directs their power towards the positive service of humanity (Babalola, 1966, p. 6).

Conclusion

The historical development we have traced is unique. The art of Abatan, however embedded in social happening, is a system of shifting formal relationships. The evolution of her form, the sudden reappearances of the past, are masked by architectural and choreographic settings; if these contexts dim the individuality of her work, they relate its generic significance to the main currents of Yoruba philosophy. Art and setting combine to intensify the importance of social and spiritual equilibrium.

The cult of Eyinle prescribes general outlines for a potter to follow: the creation of a vessel for water and stones and the making clear that the vessel is not a mere thing but an emblem of kingship and divinity. Various solutions to the problem were elaborated, as in the Abeokuta area where the crown of Eyinle has been boldly omitted by one potter, abstractly rendered by another. Abatan has inherited a very humanistic solution, charged with figural rhetoric, which she has gently guided into modifications of form.

The expression of her individuality is set within a world where it is believed life depends upon an illusion of social harmony and continuity. Yet art must not only honor the expression of myth and moral truth; it must embody experiments and innovation, or else lose all aliveness and emotional flavor. Study of the development of form, as opposed to cultural role and function, elicits the particularity that lifts Abatan's work above the level of a mechanical projection of the past. Her very subtle means of projecting new ideas with old materials forces itself upon our consciousness and announces the sphere of art. The problematical recombinations of form cluster in periods. Each is a new method of illusionist reference; the novelty is a matter of expression, not representation. Yet even the repertory of symbolic themes may vary, and we may be certain that the oral and choreographic arts that run parallel to the sculpture are also, subtly, remorselessly, changing.

In the motion of the dance or in the half-light of the altar the defining traits of individual expression are difficult to appreciate, as to sculpture, and the vision is generic. The perturbations of a changing sensibility are difficult to discern but this does not mean that they do not exist. Moreover, neoclassicism is possible at any time. When it occurs, the momentum of the artist's creativity is maintained and the modern taste informs the rendering of the past.

If Abatan has virtually elaborated but a single theme, the wo-

man with kola bowl, nothing holds her to an unchanging standard
of expression, as opposed to form and function, as long as she can
rephrase mass and volume in new ways and still seem to honor
tradition. Films of the artist at work show that with each commission she questions, as it were, the making of each detail. She makes
a human hand. It seems too long. She makes another. She experiments with several versions of a human head until she finds a form
that satisfies her taste. She fashions a human eye. It seems dull.
She polishes it with a moistened stone. She walks away from her
work and studies it critically then returns to rework another detail.
Problems of form thus remain forever fresh. A restless sensibility
endlessly challenges the shape of the past with departures in the
small. It is a tactful creativity, so that tradition seems set above the
flux of time by being static. A careful illusion becomes, at the end,
an exaltation.[77]

[77] Or, as Abatan once said, with a sweep of her hands that embraced her altar,
her sculpture, and her life, "glory to Eyinle!"

9. Comments

RALPH ALTMAN

OUR WRESTLING with the problem of individual creativity demonstrates how profound the gaps are in our knowledge of the arts of peoples who lived beyond or at the margins of the major oriental and occidental civilizations of the world. Precise data that might help us to relate tribal norms and creativity are scant in the literature.

What do we mean by norms? How do we define creativity? In the context of this study we might conceive of norms as referring primarily to the rules and conventions that specifically governed artistic form rather than those that shaped and reflected culture, social institutions, and behavior in general. Obviously, we can only isolate artistic norms from the total context of the culture on which they depended, a subject that has been extensively studied by anthropology. But what can be said about artistic norms, that is, norms that may regulate artistic production including style, the subject matter of representation, and sometimes also the choice of media, or tools, or even the exact sequence of steps to be observed in the manufacture of certain categories of objects and the selection of the person to be commissioned to do the work? These norms differ in kind. Some can be deduced from analysis of the objects. Others can only be abstracted from data available on the totality of the culture into which the objects had been born. Aesthetic norms elude us in nearly all instances owing to the lack of information on aesthetic criteria of the people. The paper by Thompson elsewhere in this book is one among few studies published on this subject.

Even though the recorded data on aesthetic responses and criteria are scant or inadequate and limited to a very small number of cultures, it seems to be clear that the concept of art in our civilization today has no true equivalent in any of the cultures with which we are here concerned. Our attitude toward tribal objects that we call art differs from that of their makers and users. Therefore, our discussion can make sense only if we consciously assume the right to designate objects as art subjectively regardless of the attitude their makers had toward them in this respect. In contrast, the original meaning that a given piece may have had in terms other than art, as a religious or magically potent object, for example, may have been a decisive factor for the kind of norms that may have governed its shape, and it must therefore be taken into account.

Statements relative to norms that one believes to be decisive for most forms of African, American Indian, or Oceanic arts of historic times can only apply to works made within a recent and very limited time span. The majority of the artistic production of these peoples was done in wood and in other, still more vulnerable materials that did not last in their home countries. One's knowledge is therefore confined to the work of only a few generations. The evolution, changes, innovations in the arts and norms that may have preceded the observable work remain obscure, yet they present a constant challenge to attempts at historical reconstruction. That a few regions (Easter or Marquesas islands, Nigeria, and the like) produced more durable works in stone or other time-resistant materials than others does not change the picture essentially. Many of them antedate the known corpus of wood sculpture from these countries, but the archaeological record remains incomplete, their chronology too often debatable. A different situation prevails when one focuses on the arts of ancient cultures like those of Mesoamerica, the central Andes, or the Eskimo from which a large body of artistic monuments survived. Refined analysis geared at the detection of norms or of individual style differences is lacking as well as precise information relative to the meaning and chronology of the pieces. One may be tempted to attribute a number of selected works to the hand of one anonymous master. Corroborative evidence of such an impressionistic view remains absent as a rule, and one rarely has a sufficient amount of material with which to work.

One cannot recognize norms or deviations from them without analysis of large series of comparable pieces. Few people indeed had the opportunity or inclination to do so. Few scholars concerned with the arts qua art went to study them in the field among the people who produced and used them, and only a fraction of these few lived with more than one tribal group or in more than one circumscribed area for any length of time. How then could one dare to make generalizations?

For the most part, one depends on the study of public or private collections or, worse, on illustrations in the literature based on these collections. It is understandable that few of the collections and practically no illustrated book present a series of like pieces or numbers of pieces from one limited area which are sufficiently large and documented as to provenance for abstracting norms in a quantitatively meaningful manner. Many of the slides that Guiart showed illustrated carvings from New Guinea's Sepik River area. These carvings might well have come from a different world than the mass of those represented in the literature or in exhibitions as "typical" of Sepik sculpture. I was recently shown a vast series of unpublished photographs of the arts of the high grasslands of

Cameroun. In the light of the number of completely divergent regional styles and forms they portrayed, all generalizing pronouncements on Cameroun arts in the literature impress one as being meaningless. Because of the unavailability of comparable materials, one is occasionally led to misjudge an object as a unique creation. It often seems as if one had become indoctrinated to think about styles and norms of so-called primitive arts in terms of stereotypes which never hold up in the face of the diversity of actual conditions. One must be aware of the incomplete knowledge of this diversity and of the total artistic output of one tribe or area. Too often quantitatively inadequate data have been used as evidence for premature conclusions about norms, artistic quality, or the "traditional" or "anonymous" character of primitive arts. The more one probes, the more one realizes that in a great many cases existing norms left room for individual expression. The artist is anonymous only for us, because we do not happen to know his name, while it was well known in his own society and even preserved after his death. Following the lectures of Fagg and Thompson, this point needs no further belaboring.

Fagg has no doubt been most successful and influential in creating awareness of the role that individual artists could play in "traditional arts" of some regions. He has accumulated sufficient evidence to justify his claim that if enough pertinent studies had been undertaken, it would be possible to attribute most works of Yoruba sculpture to a specific artist or at least to the school of that artist. Without specifically discussing norms he implies, whatever the norms may have been, that individual creativity always had means to come to the fore (at least among Yoruba sculpture in wood) without violation of the norms and without a conscious attempt at violating them. Thompson's fine, detailed study of one Yoruba ceramist makes one suspect that this holds true equally for artists in clay. One wonders what the result would be of an investigation of Yoruba Ogboni bronzes which are stylistically and functionally so different from Yoruba sculptures in other media and which, at first glance, are much more formalized and standardized. The situation invites comparison with the arts of medieval western Europe where the power of the then reigning norms certainly needs no argument. Yet art historians could identify many unsigned "anonymous" works of that period as the works of individual men or their schools. One may be further tempted to look at the arts of civilizations like India from this viewpoint in which the force of norms was tremendous with respect to subject matter of representation, color, iconography, and often the physical placement of images. A. K. Coomaraswamy discussed the power of these norms which was absolutely unchallenged and accepted by everybody to such a degree that a person felt no desire to rebel against it, that one was thoroughly in tune with it and could not be creative except within the framework of the sacrosanct norms. The fact that one can, without great specialized training, isolate masterpieces from the mass of stereotyped Hindu works is proof that creativity could assert itself in spite of the power of norms. Creativity, after all, is not synonymous with deliberate individualistic self-expression or radical inventiveness.

It makes little sense to think of artistic norms and individual creativity in generalizing terms, that is, as if all the cultures and their arts under discussion could be treated as one entity. We have learned to appreciate the vast differences in their institutions, configurations, and value systems; the differences in their norms, in the role of the individual, and in their art forms. But it is obvious, as Thompson too has emphasized, that a great many more monographs are needed on the arts of specific human groups, monographs that are based on investigation of the arts and the artists among the people who produced them. Further pressing are studies that would extract and synthesize a wealth of data scattered or buried in the earlier literature, be it in the records of explorers and travelers or in the works of ethnographers. There is the need for the analysis of documented museum collections; even famous collections made by men as prominent as Captains Cook or Vancouver have never been published. How great the need is for monographs of this kind is evident: if one realizes the very small number of existing publications of this nature; if one examines a specific, ill-documented object (be it a given statue from the Middle Sepik River area of New Guinea or a Northwest Coast American Indian mask) and attempts in vain to find answers in the literature pertaining to its iconography, meaning, function, and so forth (answers beyond vague generalities); or if one reads one of the classic ethnographies, McIlwraith's *The Bella Coola Indians*, for instance, and encounters many references made *passim* to the arts and artists of this Northwest Coast Indian tribe in the context of chapters dealing with all sorts of aspects of Bella Coola culture except expressly art (a word that does not appear in the index to the fourteen hundred pages of this monumental work). On the other hand the scant literature on Northwest Coast arts made little use of the significant data McIlwraith's work embodies. Some of the data are relevant to our specific set of problems.

McIlwraith stated repeatedly that some of the supernatural spirits who needed to be represented by masks had no codified iconography and that the form of the masks in which the spirits appeared was up to the initiative and inventiveness of the carver, that many kinds of masks were customarily burned after having been used in a dance once, and that the sculptors therefore had no stock of old models at their disposal which they could copy for future embodiments of these beings. The great freedom of expression a Bella Coola sculptor enjoyed in the carving of masks as well as of totem poles is emphasized repeatedly. The author cautions that conditions may well have been different in earlier times, before he studied Bella Coola culture from 1922 to 1924—a time in which Bella Coola culture was already in its death throes—in the process of disintegrating under the onslaught of the white man's civilization. There is always the possibility that the original norms became less sacrosanct or more flexible, after native cultures began to feel the impact of the West.

Many reports on the tribal arts of the Americas, Africa, or the Pacific imply the existence of individual artistic creativity. Even members of a so-called very "simple" culture as that of the Baining of New Britain have been credited with the purposeful search for new designs and experiments with new motifs. All these reports are based on observations made when native cultures had already been in contact with the Western world. Some of the most obvious manifestations of individual creativity were innovations in some American Indian arts in response to contact with the West. Among the Great Plains tribes this contact stimulated the development of painting on animal hides. Elsewhere our own demands created a new outlet for artistic expression. Well known are the unprecedented forms of sculpture and design which erupted in response to alien stimuli in the nineteenth-century slate carvings of the Haida Indian of British Columbia before they became corrupted to soulless, repetitive curios. These did not infringe on any norms. When norms were violated, as they were by the adaptation for commercial purposes of sacred sand painting motifs to Navaho woven textile designs, one is dealing with a situation that could not have arisen had Navaho culture remained intact.

Why doubt that the individual always had a chance of asserting his creativity without being a rebel, without striving for self-expression? Why doubt that there were always, in every culture, uninspired copyists and creators? Who can conceive of art without creativity? Are there noncreative artists? What else if not individual creativity could be the reason for the undisputed fact that in most cultures no two comparable objects are alike, be they masks or figures? They may conform to a very limited number of conventional types, yet they differ from one another, and certainly not only in matters of craftsmanship. They differ the more one looks, the more one attempts to study the forms in detail.

One would expect to find all shades, all degrees of expressions of individual creativity manifest in these cultures. One expects to find pronounced, unequivocal manifestations in the arts of cultures in which a positive value was attached to individualism, as for instance, among the Indians of the Northwest Coast or the Great Plains. In contrast, in the arts of societies in which ultraconservative conformity was the ideal, as in the Pueblos of our Southwest, evidence of creativity might be difficult to gather. Arts linked to a strong development of shamanism with emphasis on visions, dreams, and trance experience, as those of the Alaskan Eskimo or Huichol Indians, are apt to display individuality more strongly than arts that promulgated sacrosanct religious institutions and concepts of a complex, stratified society with organized priesthood or theocratic rulership. In these kinds of complex societies, on the other hand, one might encounter a coexistence of different styles, of more or less rigidly codified art forms with others allowing for greater freedom of expression. This would depend on differences in the function for which various categories of objects were intended and also on the subject matter of representation. Complexity of society, however, is not a prerequisite for the coexistence of different art forms. Orokolo on the Gulf of Papua, New Guinea, is a case in point where two different types of masks were used in one ceremony: one sacred, relatively uniform (*hevehe*), the other more secular, more imaginatively varied (*eharo*).

Many societies, especially among the American Indians and in Melanesia, produced art forms that were meant to serve only one single occasion, one festival of brief duration. They played a most ephemeral role after which they were either discarded or ritually destroyed. They had to be made anew for each recurring festival. Such practices ought to stimulate individual creativity and may well have done so or do so in many societies. Yet the most famous example of such ephemeral arts, Navaho Indian so-called sand paintings, seem to indicate that this was by no means necessarily the case. Sand paintings have been recorded since the early 1880's but show remarkably few variations within the time span observed. This fact proves the necessity for detailed quantitative analysis before any hypothetical correlations can be proven or disproven. I am convinced such detailed studies would be enhanced greatly if the visual arts (painting, sculpture, design, and so on) were examined in the context of all the others, including oral literature, the dance, drama, and music.

Indisputably, creativity should be judged in terms of the culture in which the arts belonged. It seems hopeless, therefore, to make generalizations about the ways in which creativity can be detected. The presence of an individual style, the invention of new forms, motifs, and themes most certainly would be evidence for creativity. But when, and where, can one still hope to gather such evidence since the paucity of comparable objects and the numerical predominance of works in perishable materials prevent significant comparisons? Can creativity be gauged by slight modifications of forms that one has become accustomed to view as standard or by the addition of some new motifs or themes to conventional groups of figures? I recall groups of figures in clay, or, better, mud, produced in honor of a deity by the Nigerian Ibo. Although these groups of figures were religiously motivated, they were desired to be original in arrangement and composition. Is originality of this kind alone a criterion of creativity? On the other hand, when one focuses on the arts in more durable material which archaeology has unearthed—be it in the Arctic, in Mesoamerica, or Africa—how can one account for observable, often radical abrupt style changes that cannot be traced to outside stimuli, without assuming that individual creativity was at work? Considering the vanished wealth of objects in perishable materials which eluded archaeology, assumptions of this kind are, of course, apt to lose ground. But then, again, comparison of the contemporaneous Maya murals at Bonampak (the "Raid" versus the others) shows striking differences one is willing to attribute to different painters, although these murals have remained unique examples of their kind only by historical accident.

How can creativity be perceived in series of objects like masks from tribes or areas like the Gulf of Papua, New Guinea, or the

Dogon of Mali which were often produced by unskilled men whose ritual duty it was to fashion them in conjunction with certain ceremonies. To our own eyes these objects are certainly art. Certainly they show wide qualitative differences, differences that do not necessarily have anything to do with craftmanship. Do we not have the right to interpret these differences in terms of creativity—regardless of what was said about them in their original milieu? Is, maybe, quality the ultimate criterion?

I concur with Bernal who said, "Who does really know anything about the subject?" I strongly disagree with him on one point. He implies that aesthetic form is but an insignificant feature, an "added attraction" to the significance of a given work. I am convinced that aesthetic form is an integral part of the work's significance. I strongly believe in the universal existence of something the ancient Greeks, in a different context, called *kalokagathia*, the inseparable unity of beauty and effective, inherent goodness or virtue. Biebuyck mentioned this concept in reference to Lega art. A Liberian carver allegedly said, " . . . a mask must be beautiful in order to be acceptable to the gods." In my mind this statement summarizes the meaning of *kalokagathia* most admirably, even if we do not know what "beauty" meant to the carver.

ROY SIEBER

EVERY AREA of scholarly concern, every discipline—as long as it remains viable—has had its growing pains. This painful existence is often hidden under polite academic terminology. Such terms as scholarly discourse, methodology, mechanisms of validation, problem structuring, and others may mask some of the most vitriolic prose in the annals of scholarship. I suspect that acrimony may be the greater when new and unexplored worlds appear: that phase of research that might be described as B.F. (before footnotes). This state very nearly applies to the study of the arts under consideration here. I am not lamenting the situation either because it is a young discipline, which is no more than historical state, or because of the controversy, for controversy I firmly believe to be the essence of scholarship. Only through the free-for-all of an open dialogue can we hope to reach a fuller understanding of man and his works. Thus it is with delight, in fact, that I note among the papers in this collection a decided lack of agreement. Each paper offers a statement and takes a stand that constitutes an end in itself if taken separately. Taken together, however, they demand that the reader make his own way among disagreements or among levels of nonagreement.

If, indeed, I have a general lament it is the tendency evident in, but certainly not limited to, these papers to oversimplify both the questions and the answers regarding "primitive" art. For example, it is misleading if not false to consider each tribe or ethnic group as a hermetically sealed unit, culturally or artistically. Both historically and ethnographically (if I may so phrase it) the interactions among groups are considerable but, to a large degree, unstudied. Bascom's paper, particularly those sections that deal with larger-than-tribal styles and blurred styles, indicates some of the problems and questions yet unexplored. Furthermore, we have a tendency to treat definitions simplistically, for our convenience, so to speak, rather than for full accuracy and precision. Undeniably, the arts (with ethics and religion) are particularly subject to value-ridden taxonomies. Hidden judgments abound in our "scientific" jargon as I indicate when discussing the term "primitive." We are too often trapped into *all-or-none* positions that fail with the appearance of a simple exception. We tend equally to establish either-or categories without adequately exploring the alternatives.

I have tried to base my study of the papers according to the points raised above on the principle that each attitude and definition is suspect, each hint of controversy healthy. This particular form of devil's advocacy is, I trust, a bit more than scholarly fun and games since the comments that follow do attempt to offer some conclusions of my own. In these I most probably fall into my own traps and pitfalls.

Some of the argumentation that appears in the papers lies below the surface. For example, a fair-sized controversy lies behind or below Bernal's use of the rather discredited term "primitive" with reference to the arts of Africa and Oceania. His point is that pre-Columbian Mexican art is *not* primitive but civilized. He not only implies but explicitly states that this means he is dealing with a higher civilization. Before arguing the bases for designating cultures on a scale from low to high, I should like to note that those of us who deal with the arts of Africa and Oceania find the term "primitive" as offensive with regard to those arts as Bernal does with regard to the prehistoric cultures of Mexico. The often hidden associations of primal, early, crude, fumbling, untrained, unsophisticated with the word "primitive" are either inaccurate or pejorative or both. Furthermore, the lumping of the arts and cultures of the pre-Columbian Americas, sub-Saharan Africa, and the Pacific Islands in one package reflects several discredited lines of thought. The first of these is the early—and I fear easy—assumption of the linear evolution of man based primarily on a tool kit which has survived archaeologically. In this view, Stone Age cultures existing today were thought to be survivals, fixed at an earlier stage, of man's evolution. Even if this were acceptable, there is no necessary correlation between man's intellectual and artistic accomplishments and his tool kit. In short, one cannot accurately determine a man's color, language, intellectual attainments, or humanistic accomplishments from his tools alone.

Parenthetically, arguing from the tool-kit base, I could insist that "my" Africans were more "advanced" (i.e., civilized) than Bernal's Mexicans because the Africans were Iron Age men when pre-Columbian Mexico was "still" in the Stone Age. I suspect that we must know or be able to infer a great deal more about man before we can attempt, with confidence, to classify him, most particularly with regard to his intellectual attainments. A second protest to the term "primitive" is also based on a historical point. The term came into use as a catchall to include all contemporary cultures that were not part of the "great civilizations," archaeological or recent, of the East or the West. Such a "definition" is based on exclusion—what I call the "all other" or "wastebasket" technique. If we ever can join these disparate and distant areas under a single term we must come to that concept and that term only after a far more careful collection and analysis of cultural evidence than yet exists.

To turn now more specifically to the subject of this panel: the interactions of individual creativity and tribal norms. The former implies freedom for the artist while the latter, the concept of tribal norms, is, in Guiart's words, "the antithesis of freedom." Stated another way we might suggest that tribal norms are the givens, the fixed points, the cultural expectancies within or around which the artist must move. Guiart notes that the artist is restricted by his tools, techniques, materials, his market, in short by the requirements imposed on him by a culture fixed in time and space. At the same time it must be emphasized that the norm is not necessarily a stereotype nor does it necessarily immobilize the artist. Indeed, it may be described as a limitation, or set of limitations, placed upon the artist's "freedom"; but this is not the antithesis of freedom.

It is wiser not to think of "individual creativity" as the antithesis of "tribal norms" functioning in an all-or-none fashion but rather to conceive of them in terms of their interactions wherein relative emphases may differ. There are instances where the constraints of a culture or ruling group predominate (medieval European art, the brasses of Benin come to mind); other instances demonstrate the "freedom" of the artist from such constraints. It is, I suspect, only in contrast with the Western artists of this century that the traditional African or Oceanic sculptor seems unfree. In the absence of a broader base and fuller documentation this "evaluation" can only be ethnocentric.

I discuss now three "proofs" of the freedom exercised by the artist within the constraints of his cultural norms: first, the visibility and identifiability of individual styles; second, the acknowledgment by his culture of the inventiveness (creativity) of the artist; and, third, the special but as yet inadequately examined role of the artist in society.

Fagg and Thompson have dealt with the works of individual Yoruba artists. Each seems to ground his observations on the assumption that it is possible to identify works of individual artists, to recognize "hands" in the terminology of art history. It is significant that Fagg's protest against "objective pedestrianism" and Goldwater's insistence on the "incompleteness" of doctrinaire ethnologists and archaeologists tend to stress insights and other subjective aspects of the study of art. They would seem to be arguing for a non- or even antiscientific approach, one of "feel" rather than of "fact." I must admit to a rather pedestrian middle path: I accept both the concept of the "intellectual leap," that flash of insight—call it what you will—which illuminates all man's accomplishments, but I also want proof where proof is possible.

The crucial point is that the tools of the art historian are not necessarily those of the archaeologist or anthropologist. Some of these, such as style studies, are considered suspect by scholars in other fields who are untrained in this method of analysis. It is odd that the scientist often questions the methodology of the humanist but does not allow counterquestions. Similarly, the scientist may use the same tools or methods under another name: much of the archaeologist's establishment of pottery typologies is, in fact, based on style analysis.[1] Nonetheless, "style" is one criterion of validation in academic terms, and stylistic analyses are a well-established part

---

[1] I have dealt with this point elsewhere (Sieber, 1967).

of art history. (See, for example, Schapiro's (1953) essay on style for the theoretical basis and the writings of Berenson for a working instance of style analysis.) As an art historian the stress placed by Goldwater and Fagg seems to me unfortunate. It quite unnecessarily weakens what is in fact a strong point of the art historian: his ability to contribute usefully and scientifically, that is, within a fixed framework open to a fixed mode of validation.

Bascom's paper on style is an admirable contribution to this problem, or set of problems, with reference to Africa. For the moment I am concerned primarily with individual style, although the other aspects raised in his paper are of at least equal importance and merit serious study.[2]

The assumption that the individual artist is worthy of study and the prior assumption that his works bear the identifiable stamp of an individual style seem seriously to be questioned by Bernal's paper. He argues that pre-Columbian Mexican art is "entirely anonymous" because it is a group art. He offers evidence that the rulers dealt with architects as a group and takes this evidence to mean that architecture was therefore a collective art. Two points are noteworthy here: first, Bernal deals primarily with large edifices which, by their nature, must be built by collective labor. Perhaps— in contrast with the size of the works of African and Oceanic art—Mexican architectural monuments are to some degree de-individualized. Second, he is dealing with a vast number of objects

[2] One of the problems facing the researcher concerned with the concepts of style larger than that of the individual artist is the assumption that style is an independent entity capable of free movement among cultures. I hope elsewhere to argue rather at length the limits of this attitude. In brief, style has linguistic and cultural links that limit its free transfer. In Western art studies, style has been treated as an entity moving freely during, for example, the medieval period. In our tendency to present the "free" movement of styles we neglect to note the context of movement: in the medieval period styles moved in the context of, first, Christianity and its iconography and, second, Latin as an official lingua franca. We have not looked closely enough at the cultural bases of the styles themselves, or at the cultural bases for their transfer. Finally, it should be noted that our tendency to freeze objects in museums almost invariably de-emphasizes the cultural context that gave rise to the objects we celebrate.

spread over a fairly broad time span. This factor again may be contrasted with the fantastic quantity, for example, of Yoruba arts all of fairly recent date, a situation that may make idiosyncratic differences more apparent.

In addition to references to architects as a collective entity and to the absence of any reference to a single artist by name, Bernal notes that the king is said to have built an aqueduct. Quite rightly he indicates that the king did not in fact build the edifice but "simply ordered his specialized people to do it. . . . " Bernal would seem not to differentiate among the specialists. Would it not be wiser to assume degrees of leadership (and ability) among the specialists? Perhaps analogous would be the instances from Egypt where the pharoah won wars in the singular, if we accept the inscriptions and reliefs. This use of the royal singular does not mean that there was no army or that the army was an undifferentiated mass of soldiers.

To take evidence of this sort literally (and Bernal obviously does not) would be similar to arguing from the instances of Egyptian reliefs or from Benin plaques that the king was physically larger than his subjects rather than as evidence for "social perspective" (to use Fagg's term). My argument, in brief, is that any document —literary or figurative—that is based on, or echoes, royal prerogative must be read cautiously as evidence of attitudes other than those directed toward royalty.

I feel that Bernal has not come to grips with an essential fact. Ultimately some one artist was at work. He may have worked with others on a single object or portion of a facade; nevertheless an individual "hand" was at work. If we omit this ultimate place for idiosyncratic[3] variation, that is, individual style, we fail ultimately to take into consideration all the factors that produce a style as well as changes in style over time. Taken at face value, the group theory would act to block the search for individual characteristics. Such a

[3] Lit., one's own mixing together; here taken to mean recognizable, individual variations or characteristics, conscious and subconscious.

search is justifiable in principle for it was not too long ago that the African artist was thought to be totally directed by his culture, totally constrained by cultural norms and traditions. In short, he was considered anonymous. It is evident from the papers of Fagg and Thompson and the work of Bascom, Sieber, and others that the concept of anonymity is not a criterion of African art but is a measure of our ignorance.

In addition to the first level of identification of individual artists through their styles (which enabled Fagg, for example, to recognize the hand of his Master of the Uneven Eyes in two pieces in the Wellcome Collection) there is also the problem of identifying the transitions in a given artist's style, changes that are evident in the working span of his life. Both these levels were identified by Thompson, first in showing the works of a grandmother, mother, and daughter and then in documenting a series of stylistic changes within the daughter's works. Obviously further research is necessary before a significant body of documentation is amassed concerning the working development of individual artists. It will be necessary to examine the works—and working patterns—of artists in many societies. In Africa there are artists, as among the Yoruba, who produce a relatively large body of works. In contrast some artists in other African cultures may produce only one or two pieces in a year or even in a lifetime. Furthermore, the effects of the audience's reactions on artist's style have not yet been examined, much less assessed. In short a great deal of field research is imperative.

It is difficult to find, much less to agree upon, a definition of creativity. Perhaps the term "inventive" can be considered a fair compromise at least to the degree that invention is a part of the larger concept. I should like to report three instances of inventiveness recognized and rewarded by the cultures in which they occurred. All three are from northern Nigeria and were observed in 1958.[4]

[4] A Foreign Area Training Program grant from the Ford Foundation made this research possible.

The first instance is from the Montol, a group that seemingly imposed few limitations or norms on the wood-carver. A generalized, but identifiable human figure, seems to have been the basic requirement.[5] Certain stylistic elements do occur with some consistency: finlike arms, keeled heads, and strongly articulated legs. But these characteristics are generally found in the area,[6] and the Montol artist seems to have been permitted a fairly large degree of flexibility. In about 1930, a young carver named Namni began working in a highly distinctive style. I have no clue what impelled him, for he had died before I arrived in 1958. His individuality was still acknowledged by the Montol and their neighbors, the Goemai. They showed his works with pride and reported that they had traveled many miles to commission works from him. Moreover, his works (or his success) had influenced other carvers.

The second example is that of a natural acrobat whose abilities had been recognized to the degree that the choreography of a masked dance had been adapted to fit his particular abilities. He had had no predecessor (or prototype) but he was training his son to succeed him.

The third instance is that of a woman potter, Azume, among the Goemai. According to the available evidence she had invented a clay figure type that met with local success (pl. 96). Although she had one pupil of indifferent ability, both were dead by 1958 and the "tradition" had ended.

These three examples document the existence of inventiveness and its recognition and reward by the peers of the artist. I like to think that examples of this sort put an end to the unfortunate myth that the African (or more generally, the "primitive" artist) was totally constrained by the demands of his society, that he was no more than the passive prisoner of a totally repetitive convention.

This conception has infected our attitude toward aesthetics as well. We have tended not to acknowledge the possibility of an

---

[5] For published examples see von Sydow, 1954, pl. 119*a, b, c,* and Sieber, 1960, *passim.*

[6] See, for example, von Sydow, *op. cit.,* pls. 118b (Jukun) and 119 (Chamba).

aesthetic attitude on the part particularly of African and Oceanic cultures. I have argued this point to some extent elsewhere (Sieber, 1959), and indeed have sustained a rebuke (Merriam, 1965, p. 271) for my suggestion of an "unvoiced aesthetic." As Merriam has pointed out (*ibid.*) the term is contradictory: by Western definition it must be "voiced" to be an aesthetic. For this, if for no other reason, the term "response" might be more useful. Indeed, the complex of responses to works of art need further research in all societies. We tend to credit critics with the only valid or meaningful responses to art. The critics tend to codify their responses, and we are encouraged to accept these as criteria of excellence or definitions of beauty. Would it not be instructive, if nothing more, to have a broader view of the responses elicited by art? To my knowledge, extensive field research of responses to works of art has been conducted only by Thompson.[7]

Not in all instances can we expect to obtain systematic data; we must at times do with less. One instance of lesser data comes to mind: in 1964 in Ghana, Kwabena Ameyaw[8] and I came upon an Ashanti figurine that had been commissioned by the Asantehene about 1874 (pl. 97). A great number of similar figurines are known. In most instances they are commissioned by a woman who wishes a child or by the priest consulted by the woman. This particular *akua'ba* is the only example of a royal commission which I have come across. As such we can consider it an aesthetic document of some importance for we may assume it records the *ne plus ultra* of fertility figurines, at least for the 1870's. It can be seen as an aesthetic ideal (as reflected in royal patronage) and used as a reference point in viewing other such carvings.

One more word about the artist. Bernal makes it clear that the

[7] "Yoruba Artistic Criticism," to be published in the results of the Lake Tahoe Conference, "The Traditional Artist in African Society," cosponsored by the American Council of Learned Societies—Social Science Research Council Joint Committee on African Studies, University of Nevada, and Indiana University.

[8] Research assistant at the Institute of African Studies, University of Ghana. Mr. Ameyaw was later able to collect the piece for the University collection. My research was made possible by a Foreign Area Grant from Indiana University.

pre-Columbian Mexicans did not think highly of their artists, that they were unimportant persons in their society. I should like to stress that from a good deal of the evidence thus far available the artist occupies a position of low status in most cultures, but his works are held in high regard. The works usually reflect and reinforce beliefs about the bases and meaning of life itself. In contrast, the leader is of high status and his acts normally are held in high regard; the criminal is low on both counts. Thus the artist occupies an unusual role well worth further investigation.[9]

In conclusion, let me stress a point that is implied but not expressly stated in several papers: art is one of the best indicators of what a culture thinks about itself, what values it places on man and his acts. It reflects beliefs and values. In the absence of other documentation—particularly the written word—it is often all we have to reconstruct the substance and not just the sequence of the past. It is not an accident that this is the case. The arts are human endeavor made as persuasive as possible. Thompson's potter is not simply making a container; she is making an object that to be fully functional must be treasured as the focus of a cult. The Aztec mother-goddess was terrible because it was aesthetically contrived to be awe inspiring. It would not be nearly as effective if it were awful in an uncontrived way. The effectiveness of the object is directly related to its effectiveness as art.

In the twentieth-century Western world we tend to ignore the ultimate persuasiveness of art; we have tried to destroy its utility and remove it from the realms of propaganda and moral discourse. It is significant that the only governments in this century that recognized the strength and—to them—the threat of art were (and are) the totalitarian governments. As a result we tend to oversimplify the role of art in other cultures. The fantastic interaction of freedom and dependence, the balance of individual creativity against the cultural norms evident in the arts of Oceania, the pre-

[9] Various papers for the conference noted above (n. 7) describe the role and status of the artist (sculptor, musician, blacksmith, and so on).

Columbian Americas, and Africa can, I think, teach us a great deal about art that we have lost or forgotten.

EDMUND CARPENTER

ᴵsʜɪ, a Yana hunter who wandered into our culture, was impressed most by roller shades and the "phoosh" of air brakes being released. San Francisco's skyline and technology held no particular interest for him. When he saw Robert Fowler begin his transcontinental flight, he asked, "White man up there?" Told, yes, he merely shrugged (Waterman, 1918). "The Kwakiutl Indian whom Boas sometimes invited to New York to serve him as an informant was indifferent to the spectacle of skyscrapers and streets lined with automobiles. He reserved all his intellectual curiosity for the dwarfs, giants, and bearded ladies that were at the time exhibited in Times Square, for automats, and for the brass balls decorating staircase banisters; all these things challenged his own culture, and it was that culture alone he was seeking to recognize in certain aspects of ours" (Lévi-Strauss, 1966 *b*, p. 121). Are we equally restricted in our approach to ethnic arts?

Art

The concept "art" is alien to most, perhaps all, preliterate peoples. But the thing itself, the artistic act, is certainly there, carefully implemented as a dimension of culture. It is not, however, always easy to recognize. Eskimo, for example, do not put art into their environment: they turn the environment itself into an art form. In literate societies, art is viewed as a storehouse of experience, a sort of blood bank. Teachers administer transfusions to the needy; critics guard against pollution. Art objects are owned, contemplated, studied. In tribal societies I know firsthand, art belongs to ordinary day-to-day experiences: the way a father addresses his son, decorates his house door, butchers a pig, dances, puts on his loincloth in the morning, or addresses his guardian spirit. When Andy Warhol recently offered to sign any object, including dinners, clothes, and what-have-you, he illustrated a point tribal peoples have never doubted: Art and Life are interchangeable. Suppose Picasso started signing Ford cars, babies, menus, old buildings, photographs? Art dealers and teachers would panic. Suddenly they would not know how to identify art.

LIFE AS ART

The distinction between art and custom is not nearly so great among tribal peoples as it is with us. Among the Naskapi, hunting is a holy occupation in which artists engage. Suppose we filmed a masked ritual, including the infinitely small human actions that make up such an event? I mean *film*, in the full sense, exploiting the bias of the medium itself. The *effect* of such a film would be quite different from the effect of the standard artbook or museum display; I suggest it could be closer to the one experienced by the original participants. All translation is imperialistic, film no less than print. But certain media lend themselves kindly, and others do not, to rendering particular experiences, and the problem is to know the media and the experiences. This involves more than simply utilizing new media. Older media have been recast in new roles. Joyce's *Finnegans Wake* and Eames's multiscreen exhibit warrant the most intensive study by anthropologists and curators.

"PRIMITIVE" ART

"Wordsworth found in stones the sermons he had hidden there" (Oscar Wilde). We have been hiding sermons in preliterate art for years. "Primitive" has been used as synonymous with "youthful," associated with beginnings. To some this meant unsophisticated efforts not worthy of comparison with Western art. To others it meant purity, simplicity, vitality. Primitive art, according to Henry Moore, "makes a straightforward statement, its primary concern is with the elemental, and its simplicity comes from direct and strong feelings. . . . The most striking quality common to all primitive art is its intense vitality. It is something made by people with a direct and immediate response to life." Picasso saw in the study of African art a return to fundamentals. Klee went further: he revived the beautiful lie of the noble savage roaming free in his native wilds, uncontaminated by the follies and vices of civilization. Kandinsky urged a return to "primary signs," derived, he believed, from direct sensory experience. But whether used in depreciation or appreciation, "primitive" meant beginnings, fundamentals.

Now it may make some sort of sense to equate, loosely, primitive and ancient economies, but it makes no sense at all to speak of any language as primitive or innocent, and it is equally nonsensical to speak of art in this way. Some tribal art is more derivative, in fact, than primary. Nineteenth-century Eskimo carvings are but crude replicas of ones made centuries earlier in the Bering Strait area, under influences from Siberian Iron Age cultures. "The discovery in Africa of the art of Ife, as refined and masterful as that of the European Renaissance, but perhaps earlier by three or four centuries and preceded in Africa itself by the art of the so-called Nok civilization, influences our conceptions of the recent arts of black Africa and the corresponding cultures. We are now tempted to see them as impoverished, rustic replicas of high art forms and high civilizations" (*ibid.*).

Those who object to "primitive" as a condescending term rarely voice concern over its Romantic associations or its use as a synonym for simple beginnings. The only term that to me makes sense in this context is "preliterate." I see literacy as the key factor

(McLuhan, 1962, 1964, and in press; also see Carpenter and Mc-
Luhan, 1960, and Carpenter, 1952–1959).

PRELITERATE, LITERATE, AND POSTLITERATE ART

Phonetic writing translated the multisensuous thing that is
spoken language into one sense only. The peculiar effect of translating the many senses of the spoken word into the visual mode of
writing was to abstract one sense from the cluster of human senses.
The phonetic alphabet and all its derivatives stressed a one-thing-
at-a-time analytic awareness in perception. This intensity of analysis was achieved at the price of forcing all else in the field of
perception into the subliminal. Literacy ushered man into the world
of divided senses. The value accorded the eye at the expense of all
other senses destroyed harmonic orchestration of the senses and
led to emphasis upon the individual experience of the individual
sense. It created a hierarchy of senses with sight highest, touch
lowest. Aristotle, in the first sentence of *Metaphysics*, says, of all the
senses trust only sight. This bias makes no senses apart from
literacy. Plato regarded touch as the lowest sense, but do lovers?
It took twenty-five hundred years, aided by Gutenberg and the
entire educational establishment, to enthrone sight. It was a much
contested ascension, but literacy won and its analytical bias per-
meated every aspect of society. Print was highly explosive; it created shrapnel. By focusing on a single, cutout factor, abstracting it,
examining it, print shattered experience into segments, fragment-
ing the field of perception and breaking movement into static bits.

What attracted Parisian and Bauhaus artists to African art was
not, contrary to their own statements, love of primitivism, but love
of sensory orchestration, what Cézanne called "plastic images."
They sought to create art based on new sensory ratios resulting
from the introduction of electronic media. These media were forcing a reorganization of the human sensorium, and the pioneers of
postliterate art needed models consistent with this new age. In

African sculpture they discovered an expression of sensory ratios close to their own goals. It served as temporary model. Their real models, however, were electronic. The telegraph, for example, when mated with the printing press, created the newspaper format with its discontinuous juxtapositions of simultaneous images. Poets and painters took the front page as art model. The electronic world soon provided its own models, and African carvings went from artist's studio to collector's cabinet. The link between preliterate art and Renoir, Gauguin, Picasso, and others, is now a past event—although one would never guess this from current literature on African art. Few of today's artists collect preliterate art and fewer still are influenced by it. They seem to accept it on its own terms, to understand it perhaps better than any of us. But they no longer use it as model.

SENSORY AWARENESS

One of the most interesting conflicts in contemporary anthropology arises from the increasing number of books by *native* authors, voices from the inside. These intruders into the visually oriented profession of anthropology are always writing about how things smell, taste, feel, sound; toes gripping roots along a slippery bank; peppery food burning the rectum; ". . . he became aware of gentle heat playing on his right cheek, and a fine smoke teasing his nostrils; while on the left he heard an odd gurgling sound. . . ." One sensory image after another. Anthropologists, most of whom are nineteenth century in outlook, do not know what to do with such data: they cannot fit them into their visual models; they do not know how to translate odors or sounds into numbers; they cannot even arrange them into sequences that lead somewhere, because these data just will not fall in line. So they put them in a new category: Native Autobiographical Reports. One cannot read these inside reports, with their descriptions of sensory awareness and involvement, without realizing how misleading the traditional, outside "observations" have been. My impression of much African art is that it should be embraced, all senses involved, not simply viewed. Putting it on display is like displaying an old, cuddly doll. Or skis.

Literate man learned to flick sight on and off. But the senses as a whole cannot be orchestrated instantly. Tribesmen begin rituals slowly, then build, as in Pentecostal services. One is reminded of slouching, tribal-faced method actors for whom all life is empty dialogue until they suddenly "get with it," erupting with startling jets of emotional power. "Getting with it" means getting involved, all senses orchestrated.

Sensory Orchestration

A child learns to separate senses when he learns, in class, to read silently. His legs twist, he bites his tongue, but by an enormous tour de force he learns to fragment his senses, to turn on one at a time and to keep the others in neutral. And so he is indoctrinated into that world where readers seek silent solitude, concert-goers close their eyes, and gallery guards warn, "Do not touch."

All this is alien to Eskimo experience. Once, with visibility zero, I traveled rapidly along a dangerous coastline, guided by an Eskimo who navigated by the feel of the wind and smell of fog, by sounds of surf and nesting birds, and particularly by the feel of the pattern of waves and current against his buttocks. With such interplay and interpenetration of senses, there can be no isolation of one sense. A hunter who relied on sight alone would return empty-handed; a traveler who ignored odors and winds and sounds would soon be lost.

Recently an experimenter, comparing paintings by blind children with those by seeing children, found the two indistinguishable until the age of six, at which point the seeing children, being members of a literate culture, moved in the direction of optical imagery.

A dreamer watches the dream in sleep, by moving his eyes. Patients who have undergone throat surgery are forbidden to read, for there is a natural tendency for a reader to evoke absent sounds, and his throat muscles work silently as he scans the page.

Nothing was more alien to medievalism than silent reading. Reading was aloud, often as song, with gestures. Physicians prescribed reading as a form of exercise. Carrels were like telephone booths, designed to keep down noise.

Interplay and interpenetration of senses offer entrance into realities that cannot be found by way of a single sense. Infants born without arms and legs cannot see in depth. Depth must first be discovered tactually before it can be recognized visually. Isolating one sense from all others calls for enormous training and self-control; it is probably never fully achieved. Test this yourself: run water into a bath while switching the light on and off: the changed visual environment appears to affect the sound of the running water, however slightly. Literate man can recite a poem and meanwhile solve simple arithmetical problems, but while he attends to the one, the other goes below some kind of threshold. Other cultures seem to differ in the way they handle this kind of multiplicity of thought. A Sanskrit nonsense word invented more than a thousand years ago as a memory aid for drummers, is also a mathematical problem and solution; it can be simultaneously recited, drummed, and depicted visually in the form of a snake swallowing its tail with the symbols as skin design.

Those who affect to appreciate such multiplicity *one element at a time* are systematically deluding themselves. The elements that constitute it are very various, and their organization is alien to analytic methods. Preoccupation with analysis and description leads critics to represent such efforts falsely and to offer delusive explanations of them. If puns were a minor feature of preliterate art, they might be dismissed as mere curiosities, but far from rare, they are often its mark and essence. Again and again the evidence indicates that the goal of the tribal artist is to create implosive patterns that require simultaneous appreciation of all elements (Carpenter, 1966, pp. 50–66). Can one simultaneously experience alternate readings of a visual pun? Wittgenstein says, No: "a shape cannot be seen apart from its interpretation." No matter how rapidly we switch from one to another, disjunctive alternate readings cannot be sustained simultaneously by anyone. Yet evidence from preliterate societies challenges this. Here artists compress knowledge into mythic forms of multiple but simultaneous determinancies. One is reminded of electronic computers. By a delightful reversal, where once preliterate art provided models that assisted us in understanding the electronic age, now the electric age provides models that assist us in understanding preliterate art.

Play

"Work" means specialism. It equals fragmented task and consequent noninvolvement of the whole person. Play equals involvement, as in hobbies or conversation. Where involvement is low, work is high. Preliterate man does not work, hence has no need for leisure, no need to recreate the whole self. His whole self is already totally involved in corporate living.

Dreams, myths, rituals are all forms of total involvement. The dreamer divests himself of private identity and unites with the corporate image of his group. Tribal Africans are reported to require far less sleep than those who become literate wage earners. The 9-to-5 African civil servant needs eight hours of sleep a night, although his physical labor is minimal. What he requires, of course, is dreaming. Rapid eye movement researchers tell us that dreaming is mandatory for human life. Tribal man requires less night dreaming because he achieves corporate identification through rituals, myths, and artistic activities generally.

Self-Expression

The title "Art" has traditionally been reserved for works of creativity and self-expression. Aestheticians and collectors, taking a belated interest in ethnic art, now accord it the dignity of this title on the grounds it meets these standards. They refuse to believe "true art" can be achieved by other means. But questions of "creativity" and "self-expression" should be asked/answered with caution. They belong to literate traditions. The labels just do not apply to preliteracy.

The image of the tribal artist as a specialist, a fragmented, roleless individual who seeks to discover himself and to reveal his private point of view, is nonsense. Tribal societies are implosive: everybody is involved with everybody, simultaneously and instantaneously, in a seamless web of human kindship and responsibility. There is no isolating individualism, no private consciousness, no private point of view. These qualities are products—and goals—of literacy. The private wits or senses of men were released from their corporate restraints by the fragmentizing power of print. Today we experience this in reverse: the explosive individual energies of literate men are being compressed and imploded by electronic circuity.

Individualism means fragmentation, self-expression, private point of view. People who fill integral roles have no private point of view; they share group awareness and wear corporate tribal masks.

Preliterate man is the conventional role-player, the faithful mask-wearer. Wearing a mask means to divest, not to express, oneself. A mask or role is not an extension of its wearer so much as putting on the collective powers of the audience. The speaker assumes the collective mask of the image he presents. He manifests a corporate attitude toward life.

Some writers say that the anonymity of preliterate art is a myth, that specialists can identify with confidence works of individual artists. But the marks of identity turn out to be details of craftsmanship or minor stylistic innovations. This is not self-expression. Carvers merely interpret traditional designs the way actors interpret parts. There is a vital difference among variations which maintain the freshness of a style and changes that upset it. The real question is: Does the artist manifest a corporate view of life or seek to develop a private point of view? Does he unite with the corporate mask of his culture or become an innovator who ignores social conventions?

"I flew by the nets," said Joyce. Did he mean *past* the nets of family, Church, and country, or *by means* of them? Literate artists fly past the nets, preliterate artists by means of them.

I am aware that there are tribesmen who use art as a means of lonely self-identity. I have known such men. In their own societies, however, they are about as common and influential as Communists in southern California. To focus attention on them, to regard them as the key to understanding ethnic arts, is to commit the error of the Kwakiutl informant who was fascinated by bearded ladies and brass balls.

HAPPENINGS

A fake art object, accepted by one generation, is often rejected by the next when art fashions change. The errors of the faker suddenly stand out when these fashions are no longer shared by the viewers. Later generations are puzzled how earlier scholars could have been misled by such an "obvious" fake.

When a scholar publishes an impressive book on the art of an alien people, his contemporaries believe this art has been "translated," that through his translation they have captured the original. Boas' students did him the compliment of believing his translation of Haida art was translucent. Not being his students, we see that Boas is more Boas than Haida.

Translation is especially imperialistic where the medium is ill-suited to the subject. Media are happenings; they create environments. A book happening or a museum happening bears little resemblance to a tribal happening. The interplay of senses is different. The *effect* is different. Print can report content, describe context, outline origins, and so on. But what is crucial in art is the relation of one sensory element to another: movement to color, sound to sound, spatial form to odor, and so on.

I doubt if print really brings us close to those happenings we loosely classify as tribal art. Film, I think, comes closer for it is capable of producing roughly similar effects, although its bias may turn out to be equally marked. Our recent awareness that print is not, as we once believed, a neutral medium for recording "reality" has made us conscious of the bias of other media as well, and of the complexity of all cross-media translation.

Today the electronic media are reprocessing all knowledge, brainwashing us of the obsolete and alien. They take the entire past as content and turn it into new, kaleidoscopic happenings. They do the same with alien cultures, with little regard for original patterns. It is pointless to protest and call such translations "inaccurate," as if they were false reports. What is important is that we understand the process at play.

Bibliography

Abraham, R. C. *Dictionary of Modern Yoruba*. London: University of London, 1958.

Adam, Leonhard. *Primitive Art*. Harmondsworth: Penguin Books, 1949.

Adewale, T. J. "The Ijanna Episode in Yoruba History." In *Proceedings of the 3rd International West African Conference*. Pp. 251–256. Lagos: Nigerian Museum, 1956.

Amon d'Aby, F. J. *Croyances religieuses et coutumes juridiques des Agni de la Côte d'Ivoire*. Paris: Editions Larose, 1960.

Anonymous. "Soft Wood Figure Carvings," *Nigeria*, no. 14 (1938a).

———. "Thorn Figure Carving," *Nigeria*, no. 14 (1938b), 134–137.

———. "Some Yoruba Customs," *Nigerian Field*, XII, no 1 (1948), 24–27.

———. "Carver in Miniature," *West Africa*, XXX, no. 377 (1959), 106–107.

Babalola, S. A. *The Content and Form of Yoruba Ijala*. London: Oxford University Press, 1966.

Barber, M. A. *Oshielle: Or Village Life in the Yoruba Country*. London: Nisbet, 1857.

Bascom, William. *The Sociological Role of the Yoruba Cult Group*. American Anthropologist Memoir, no. 63. Vol. XLVI, no. 1 (1944).

————. "The Focus of Cuban Santería," *Southwestern Journal of Anthropology*, VI, no. 1 (1950), 64–68.

————. "Modern African Figurines: Satirical or Just Stylistic," *Lore*, VII, no. 4 (1957), 118–126.

————. "Yoruba Concepts of the Soul." In *Men and Cultures*, ed. A. Wallace. Pp. 401–410. Berkeley and Los Angeles: University of California Press, 1960.

————. "Yoruba Arts." Lecture delivered at University of California Extension Program, "African Arts." Berkeley, May 6, 1967.

Bascom, William, and Paul Gebauer. *Handbook of West African Art*. Milwaukee Public Museum, Popular Science Handbook Series, no. 5. Milwaukee: Bruce, 1953. 2d ptg., Milwaukee: Napco Graphic Arts Center, 1964.

Beier, Ulli. *The Story of Sacred Wood Carvings from One Small Yoruba Town*. Lagos: Nigeria Magazine, 1957. 3d ptg., 1959.

Benedict, Ruth. *Zuni Mythology*. Columbia University Contributions to Anthropology, XXI. New York: Columbia University Press, 1935. 2 vols.

A Bibliography of African Art. Compiled by L. J. P. Gaskin. London: International African Institute, 1965.

Biebuyck, Daniel. "On the Concept of Tribe," *Civilizations*, XVI, no. 4 (1966), 500–515.

Boas, Franz. *Primitive Art*. Oslo: Aschehoug, Instituttet for Sammenlingnende Kulturforskning, 1927. Paperback. New York: Dover, 1955.

Bodrogi, Tibor. *Art in North-East New Guinea*. Budapest: Hungarian Academy of Sciences, 1961.

Bohannan, Paul. "Artist and Critic in an African Society." In *The Artist in Tribal Society*, ed. M. W. Smith. Pp. 85–94. London: Routledge and Kegan Paul, 1961.

————. *Africa and Africans*. Garden City: Natural History Press, 1964.

Bowen, Thomas J. *Central Africa: Adventures and Missionary Labours in Several Countries in the Interior of Africa from 1849–1856*. Charleston, S.C.: Southern Baptist Publishing Society, 1857.

Bradley, K. *Britain's Purpose in Africa*. London: H.M.S.O., 1959.

Buehler, Alfred, T. Barrow, and C. P. Mountford. *The Art of the South Sea Islands, Including Australia and New Zealand*. New York: Crown, 1962.

Bunzel, Ruth L. *The Pueblo Potter: A Study of Creative Imagination in Primitive Art*. New York: Columbia University Press, 1928.

————. "Art." In *General Anthropology*, ed. F. Boas. Pp. 535–588. New York: D. C. Heath, 1938.

Carpenter, Edmund. "If Wittgenstein Had Been an Eskimo," *Varsity Graduate* (University of Toronto), XII, no. 3 (1966), 50–66.

Carpenter, Edmund, ed. *Explorations*. Toronto: University of Toronto Press, 1952–1959. 9 vols.

Carpenter, Edmund, and Marshall McLuhan, eds. *Explorations in Communications*. Boston: Beacon, 1960.

Carroll, Kelvin. *Yoruba Religious Carving*. New York: Praeger, 1967.

Clarke, J. D. "Ifa Divination," *Journal of the Royal Anthropological Institute*, LXIX, Part II (1939), 235–256.

Covarrubias, Miguel. *The Eagle, the Jaguar and the Serpent: Indian Art of the Americas*. New York: Knopf, 1954.

————. "Art and Artist in Bali." In *Exploring the Ways of Mankind*, ed. W. Goldschmidt. Pp. 602–607. New York: Holt, Rinehart and Winston, 1960.

Crowley, Daniel J. "Style, Tribe, and Institution in West Central Africa." Unpublished manuscript.

Dark, Philip, W. Forman, and B. Forman. *Benin Art*. London: P. Hamlyn, 1960.

————. "The Study of Ethno-Aesthetics: The Visual Arts." In *Essays on the Verbal and Visual Arts*, ed. J. Helm. Pp. 131–148. Seattle: American Ethnological Society, 1967.

Davenport, Cyril. *The English Regalia*. London: Kegan Paul, Trench, Trübner, 1897.

D'Azevedo, Warren L. *The Artist Archetype in Gola Culture*. Desert Research Institute, preprint no. 14. Reno: University of Nevada, 1966.

Delano, Isaac. *Atumo Ede Yoruba*. London: Oxford University Press, 1958.

Dockstader, Frederick J. *Indian Art in America*. Greenwich, Conn.: New York Graphic Society, n.d.

Durán, Diego. *Historia de las Indias de Nueva España e Islas de Tierra Firme*. Mexico City: J. M. Andrade y F. Escalante, 1867–1870. 2 vols. and atlas.

Elkin, A. P., D. Berndt, and R. Berndt. *Art in Arnhem Land*. Melbourne: Cheshire, 1950.

Ellis, J. H. "A Report on the Ilobi, Oke-Odan, and Ajilete Groups of the Egbado People in the Ilaro Division, Abeokuta Province." Unpublished manuscript. Lagos, 1935.

Esquire, 47, no. 2 (1957), 64–65.

Exhibition of Europeans Seen through Native Eyes. London: Berkeley Galleries, Sept. 29–Oct. 23, 1954.

Fagg, William. "De l'art des Yoruba." In *L'Art Nègre,* Présence Africaine, nos. 10–11. Pp. 103–135. Paris: Editions du Seuil, 1951.

———. *Nigerian Images: The Splendor of African Sculpture.* New York: Praeger, 1963.

———. *Tribes and Forms in African Art.* New York: Tudor, 1965.

Fagg, William, and E. Elisofon. *The Sculpture of Africa.* London: Thames and Hudson, 1958.

Fagg, William, and Margaret Plass. *African Sculpture: An Anthology.* New York: Dutton Vista Pictureback, 1964.

Firth, Raymond. "The Maori Carver," *Journal of the Polynesian Society,* XXXIV (1925), 277–291.

———. *Art and Life in New Guinea.* London: Studio, 1936.

———. *Elements of Social Organization.* Pp. 155–182. London: Watts, 1951.

Fischer, Eberhard. "Künstler der Dan, die Bildhauer Tame, Si, Tompieme und Son, ihr Wesen und ihr Werk," *Baessler-Archiv,* n.s., X (1962), 161–263.

———. "Die Töpferei bei den Westlichen Dan," *Zeitschrift für Ethnologie,* Band 88, Heft 1 (1963), 100–115.

Forde, Daryll. *The Yoruba-Speaking Peoples of Southwestern Nigeria.* London: International African Institute, 1951.

Forge, Anthony. "The Abelam Artist." In *Social Organization: Essays Presented to Raymond Firth,* ed. M. Freedman. Pp. 65–84. Chicago: Aldine, 1967.

Frankenstein, Alfred. "Art-History's Wildest Chase," *San Francisco Sunday Examiner and Chronicle,* Feb. 12, 1967, This World, pp. 45–46.

Fraser, Douglas. *Primitive Art.* New York: Doubleday, 1962.

———. *The Many Faces of Primitive Art: A Critical Anthology.* Englewood Cliffs, N.J.: Prentice-Hall, 1966.

Frobenius, Leo. "Die Masken und Geheimbünde Afrikas," *Nova Acta: Abhandlungen der Kaiserlichen Leopoldinisch-Carolinischen Deutschen Akademie der Naturforscher,* LXXIV (1899).

———. *The Voice of Africa.* London: Hutchinson, 1913. 2 vols.

———. *Mythologie de l'Atlantide.* Paris: Payot, 1948.

Garfield, Viola E., and P. S. Wingert. *The Tsimshian Indians and Their Arts.* Seattle: University of Washington Press, 1966.

Gerbrands, Adrian A. "Kunststijlen in West Nieuw-Guinea," *Indonesië,* IV (1951), 251–283.

———. *Art as an Element of Culture, Especially in Negro-Africa.* Mededelingen van het Rijksmuseum voor Volkenkunde, XII. Leiden, 1957.

———. *Symbolism in the Art of Amanamkai, Asmat, South New Guinea.* Mededelingen van het Rijksmuseum voor Volkenkunde, XV. Leiden, 1962.

———. *Wow-ipits: Eight Asmat Wood-Carvers of New Guinea.* The Hague and Paris: Mouton, 1967.

Goldwater, Robert. *Bambara Sculpture from the Western Sudan.* New York: Museum of Primitive Art, 1960.

———. *Senufo Sculpture from West Africa.* New York: Museum of Primitive Art, 1964.

Goodale, Jane, and Joan Koss. "The Cultural Context of Creativity Among Tiwi." In *Essays on the Verbal and Visual Arts,* ed. J. Helm. Pp. 175–191. Seattle: American Ethnological Society, 1967.

Goodman, Mary E. *The Individual and Culture.* Homewood, Ill.: Dorsey, 1967.

Griaule, Marcel. *Masques Dogon.* Travaux et Memoires de l'Institut d'Ethnologie, XXXIII. Paris: Institut d'Ethnologie, 1938.

———. *Arts de l'Afrique Noire.* Paris: Les Editions du Chêne, 1947.

Guiart, Jean. *The Arts of the South Pacific.* New York: Golden, 1963.

Harrison, Tom. "The Hebridean as Artist." In *Primitive Heritage: An Anthropological Anthology,* ed. M. Mead and N. Calas. Pp. 275–279. London: V. Gollancz, 1954.

Haselberger, Herta. "Method of Studying Ethnological Art," *Current Anthropology,* II, no. 4 (1961), 341–384.

Heil, Walter. "A Rediscovered Marble Portrait of Cosimo I de Medici by Cellini," *Burlington Magazine,* 109 (Jan., 1967), 4–12.

Helm, June, ed. *Essays on the Verbal and Visual Arts.* Seattle: American Ethnological Society, 1967.

Herskovits, Melville, J. *Dahomey: An Ancient West African Kingdom.* New York: J. J. Augustin, 1938. 2 vols.

Herskovits, Melville J., and F. S. Herskovits. "The Art of Dahomey. I. Brass Casting and Appliqué Cloths," *American Magazine of Art,* XXVII (1934a), 67–76.

———. "The Art of Dahomey. II. Wood Carving," *American Magazine of Art,* XXVII (1934b), 124–131.

Himmelheber, Hans. *Negerkünstler.* Stuttgart: Strecker und Schröder, 1935.

———. *Eskimokünstler.* Eisenach: E. Röth, 1938. 2d ptg., 1953.

———. *Negerkunst und Negerkünstler.* Braunschweig: Klinkhardt und Biermann, 1960.

———. "Personality and Technique of African Sculptors." In *Technique and*

Personality, ed. M. Mead, J. B. Bird, and H. Himmelheber. Pp. 80–110. New York: Museum of Primitive Art, 1963.

Hoebel, Adamson E. "The Nature of Culture." In *Man, Culture and Society*, ed. Harry L. Shapiro. Pp. 168–181. New York: Oxford University Press, 1960.

Inverarity, Robert B. *Art of the Northwest Coast Indians*. Berkeley and Los Angeles: University of California Press, 1950. 3d ptg., 1967.

Jacobs, Melville. *Pattern in Cultural Anthropology*. Chaps. 12, 16. New York: Dorsey Press, 1964.

Johnson, J. *Yoruba Heathenism*. Extracts appear in R. E. Dennett, *At the Back of the Black Man's Mind*. Pp. 243–271. London: Macmillan, 1906.

Johnson, Samuel. *The History of the Yorubas*. Lagos: C.M.S. Bookshops, 1921. 2d ptg., 1957.

King, J. B. "Contemporary Nigerian Pottery," *Nigeria*, XXX, no. 74 (1962), 16–24.

Kingsley, M. *West African Studies*. 1901. 3d ed., New York: Barnes and Noble, 1964.

Kroeber, Alfred. "Values as a Subject of Natural Science Inquiry." In A. L. Kroeber, *The Nature of Culture*. Pp. 136–138. Chicago: University of Chicago Press, 1952.

———. *Style and Civilizations*. Ithaca: Cornell University Press, 1957.

Kubler, George. *The Shape of Time: Remarks on the History of Things*. New Haven: Yale University Press, 1962.

———. "Style and the Representation of Historical Time." In *Interdisciplinary Perspectives of Time. Annals of the New York Academy of Science*, 138 (1967), 849–855.

Kupka, Karl. *Un Art a l'État Brut*. Lausanne: La Guilde du Livre et Éditions Clairefontaine, 1962.

L'Art Nègre. Special issue of Présence Africaine, nos. 10–11. Paris: Éditions du Seuil, 1951.

Lathrop, D. W., ed. "An Archaeological Classification of Culture Contact Situations." In *Seminars in Archaeology, 1955*. Memoir II, Society for American Archaeology, American Antiquity, XXII, no. 2, pt. 2 (1956), 24–26.

Laude, Jean. *Les Arts de l'Afrique Noire*. Paris: Le Livre de Poche, 1966.

Leach, E. R. "Aesthetics." In *The Institutions of Primitive Society*, ed. E. E. Evans-Pritchard. Pp. 25–38. Oxford: Basil Blackwell, 1954.

Lecoq, Raymond. *Les Bamiléké*. Paris: Présence Africaine, 1953.

Leuzinger, Elsy. *The Art of Africa: The Art of the Negro Peoples*. New York: Crown, 1960.

Lévi-Strauss, Claude. *The Savage Mind*. London: Weidenfeld and Nicholson, 1966a.

———. "The Scope of Anthropology," *Current Anthropology*, VII, no. 2 (1966b), 112–123.

Linton, Ralph. "Primitive Art." In E. Elisofon and W. Fagg, *The Sculpture of Africa*. Pp. 9–16. London: Thames and Hudson, 1958.

Linton, Ralph, P. S. Wingert, and R. d'Harnoncourt. *Arts of the South Seas*. New York: Museum of Modern Art, 1946.

Lips, Julius. *The Savage Hits Back*. New Haven: Yale University Press, 1937.

McIlwraith, Thomas. *The Bella Coola Indians*. Toronto: University of Toronto Press, 1948. 2 vols.

McLuhan, Marshall. *The Gutenberg Galaxy*. Toronto: University of Toronto Press, 1962.

———. *Understanding Media*. New York: McGraw-Hill, 1964.

———. *Counterblast*. In press.

Malraux, André. *The Voices of Silence*. New York: Doubleday, 1953.

Maquet, Jacques J. *Afrique: Les Civilisations Noires*. Paris: Horizons de France, 1965.

Matteson, E. "The Piro of Urubamba," *Kroeber Anthropological Society Papers*, no. 10 (1954).

Menzel, D. "Archaism and Revival on the South Coast of Peru." In *Men and Cultures: Selected Papers of the Fifth International Congress of Anthropological and Ethnological Science*, ed. A. F. Wallace. Pp. 596–600. Philadelphia: University of Pennsylvania Press, 1960.

Merriam, Alan P. *The Anthropology of Music*. Evanston, Ill.: Northwestern University Press, 1964.

Morelli, Giovanni. *Italian Painters, Critical Studies of Their Works*. London: John Murray, 1900.

Morton-Williams, Peter. "The Atinga Cult among the South-Western Yoruba: A Sociological Analysis of a Witch-finding Movement," *Bulletin de l'Institut français de l'Afrique noire*, XVIII, B, nos. 3–4 (1956), 315–334.

———. "Yoruba Responses to the Fear of Death," *Africa*, XXX, no. 1 (1960a), 34–40.

———. "The Yoruba Ogboni Cult," *Africa*, XXX, no. 4 (1960b), 34–40.

Mountford, Charles. "The Artist and His Art in an Australian Aboriginal Society." In *The Artist in Tribal Society*, ed. M. W. Smith. Pp. 1–13. London: Routledge and Kegan Paul, 1961.

Murray, Kenneth. "Oloku," *Nigeria*, no. 35 (1950), 364–365.

———. "The Atinga Collection." Unpublished manuscript. Lagos, 1951a.

———. "The Atinga Catalogue." Unpublished manuscript. Lagos, 1951*b*.

Murray, Kenneth, and A. Hunt-Cooke. "Native Minor Industries in Abeokuta and Oyo Provinces." Unpublished manuscript. Lagos, [1938?].

Newcomb, Franc J., S. Fishler, and M. C. Wheelwright. *A Study of Navajo Symbolism*. Papers of the Peabody Museum of Archaeology and Ethnology, XXXII, no. 3. Cambridge: Peabody Museum, 1956.

Newton, Douglas. *Art Styles of the Papuan Gulf*. New York: Museum of Primitive Art, 1961.

Nigeria, no. 37 (1951), p. 15, illustration.

Nigeria in Costume. 2d ed. Lagos: The Shell Company, 1962.

Ogúnba, Oyin. "Crowns and Okute at Idowa," *Nigeria*, no. 83 (1964), 249–261.

Ogunbiyi, A., *et al*. *Petition from the Ilobi Tribes*. Lagos: Samadu Press, 1931.

Olbrechts, Frans M. "Centre pour l'étude de l'art africain a l'Université de Gand," *Bulletin de l'Institut Royal Colonial Belge*, XII (1941), 257–259.

———. *Plastiek van Kongo*. Antwerp: Standaard, 1946. Also published in French: *Les Arts Plastiques du Congo Belge*. Bruxelles: Standaard, 1959.

O'Neale, Lila M. *Yurok-Karok Basket Weavers*. University of California Publications in American Archaeology and Ethnology, XXXII, no. 1 Berkeley: University of California Press, 1932.

Parrinder, E. Geoffrey. *The Story of Ketu: An Ancient Yoruba Kingdom*. Ibadan: Ibadan University Press, 1956.

Pitt Rivers Museum Exhibition Catalogue: Art from the Guinea Coast. London: Oxford University Press, 1965.

Querino, M. *Costumos Africanos no Brasil*. Bibliotheca de Divulgaçáo Scientifica, XV. Rio: Civilizaçáo Brasileira, 1938.

Raum, O. F. "Artist, Art Patron and Art Critic in Changing Africa," *Fort Hare Papers*, III, no. 5 (1966), 3–13.

Read, Herbert. "A Personal Point of View: Summary of Proceedings." In *The Artist in Tribal Society*, ed. M. W. Smith. Pp. 124–127. London: Routledge and Kegan Paul, 1961.

Redfield, Robert. "Art and Icon." In *Aspects of Primitive Art*. Pp. 12–40. New York: Museum of Primitive Art, 1959.

Robbins, Warren. *African Art in American Collections*. New York: Praeger, 1966.

Rohlfs, G. *Quer Durch Afrika*. Leipzig: F. A. Brockhaus, 1874.

Sawyer, Jack, and Robert A. Levine. "Cultural Dimensions: A Factor Analysis of the World Ethnographic Sample," *American Anthropologist*, LXVIII, no. 3 (1966), 708–731.

Schapiro, Meyer. "Style." In *Anthropology Today*, ed. A. L. Kroeber. Pp. 287–312. Chicago: University of Chicago Press, 1953.

———. "Style." In *Aesthetics Today*, ed. M. Philipson. Cleveland and New York: World, 1961.

Schefold, R. "Versuch einer Stilanalyse der Aufhängehaken vom Mittleren Sepik in Neu-Guinea," *Basler Beiträge zur Ethnologie*, Band 4 (1966).

Schmitz, Carl. "Style Provinces and Style Elements: A Study in Method," *Mankind*, V, no. 3 (1956), 107–116.

———. *Ozeanische Kunst. Skulpturen Aus Melanesien*. München: F. Bruckmann, 1962.

Shell Company. *Nigeria in Costume*. 2d ed. Lagos, 1962.

Sieber, Roy. "The Esthetic of African Art." In *7 Metals of Africa*. Philadelphia: University Museum, 1959.

———. *Sculpture of Northern Nigeria*. New York: Museum of Primitive Art, 1960.

———. "Art as an Aspect of the Reconstruction of Culture-History." In *Reconstructing African Cultural History*, ed. C. Gabel and N. Bennett. Boston: Boston University Press, 1967.

Smith, Marian W., ed. *The Artist in Tribal Society: Proceedings of a Symposium Held at the Royal Anthropological Institute*. London: Routledge and Kegan Paul, 1961.

Sousberghe, Leon de. *L'Art Pende*. Beaux-Arts IX, no. 2. Brussels: Académie Royale de Belgique, 1958.

Sydow, Eckart von. *Afrikanische Plastik*. Berlin: Gebrüder Mann, 1954.

Taylor, Donna. "Anthropologists on Art." In *Readings in Anthropology*. Vol. II, *Cultural Anthropology*, ed. M. H. Fried. Pp. 478–490. New York: Crowell, 1963.

Thompson, Robert F. "Yoruba Artistic Criticism." In *Lake Tahoe Conference on the Traditional Artist in African Society*. Unpublished manuscript, 1965.

———. "The Sign of the Divine King." In *Art and Leadership in Africa*, ed. D. Fraser and H. Cole. Pp. 227–260. Madison: The University of Wisconsin Press, 1972.

Trowell, Margaret. *Classical African Sculpture*. London: Faber and Faber, 1954.

———. *African Design*. London: Faber and Faber, 1960.

Turner, Victor. *The Forest of Symbols: Aspects of Ndembu Ritual*. Ithaca: Cornell University Press, 1967.

Underwood, Leon. *Bronzes of West Africa*. London: Tiranti, 1949.

Vandenhoute, P. Jan. *Classification Stylistique du Masque Dan et Guéré de la Côte d'Ivoire Occidentale* (Afrique Occidentale Française). Mededelingen van het Rijksmuseum voor Volkenkunde, IV. Leiden, 1948.

Verger, Pierre. *Notes sur le Culte des Orişa et Vodun.* Mémoires de l'Institut français de l'Afrique noire, no. 51. Dakar, 1957.

Waterman, T. T. *The Yana Indians.* Berkeley: University of California Press, 1918.

Willett, Frank. "Recent Excavations at Old Oyo and Ife, Nigeria," *Man,* LIX, no. 135 (1959a), 99–100.

———. "A Terracotta Head from Old Oyo, Western Nigeria," *Man,* LIX, no. 286 (1959b), 180–181.

———. "Bronze Figures from Ita Yemoo, Ife, Nigeria," *Man,* LIX, no. 308 (1959c).

———. "Investigations at Old Oyo, 1956–1957: An Interim Report," *Journal of the Historical Society of Nigeria,* II, no. 1 (1960), 59–77.

Willett, Frank, and J. Picton. "On the Identification of Individual Carvers: A Study of Ancestor Shrine Carvings from Owo, Nigeria," *Man. Journal of the Royal Anthropological Institute,* II, no. 1 (1967), 62–70.

Williams, Denis. "The Iconology of the Yoruba Edan Ogboni," *Africa,* XXXIV, no. 2 (1964), 139–165.

Wingert, Paul S. *Primitive Art: Its Traditions and Styles.* New York: World, 1965.

Index